HARCOURT BRACE JOVANOVICH COLLEGE OUTLINE SERIES

PRINCIPLES OF MARKETING

Robin T. Peterson

Department of Marketing and General Business
College of Business Administration and Economics
New Mexico State University
Las Cruces, New Mexico

Books for Professionals
Harcourt Brace Jovanovich, Publishers
San Diego   New York   London

Requests for permission to make copies of any part of the work should be mailed to:
Copyrights and Permissions Department,
Harcourt Brace & Company,
6277 Sea Harbor Drive,
Orlando, Florida, 32887-6777

Library of Congress Cataloging-in-Publication Data

Peterson, Robin
 Principles of Marketing/Robin T. Peterson.
    p. cm.--(Harcourt Brace : College Outline Series)
  Includes index.
  ISBN 0-15-601641-9
  1. Marketing.   I. Title.   II. Series
HF5415.P4424   1989
658.8--dc 19

Printed in the United States of America

  9 0 1 2 3 4 5 6 0 7 4 9 8 7 6 5 4 3 2

PREFACE

The purpose of this book is to present a coverage of marketing in the clear, concise format of an outline. This outline is specifically designed to be used as a supplement to college courses and textbooks on the subject. Notice, for example, the Textbook Correlation Table that begins on the inside of the front cover. The table shows how the pages of this outline correspond by topic to the pages of six leading textbooks on marketing currently in use at major colleges and universities. So, should the sequence of topics in this outline differ from the sequence of topics in your textbook, you can easily locate the material you want by consulting the table.

Regular features at the end of each chapter are also specifically designed to supplement your textbook and course work in marketing.

RAISE YOUR GRADES This feature consists of a checkmarked list of open-ended thought questions to help you assimilate the material you have just studied. By inviting you to compare concepts, interpret ideas, and examine the whys and wherefores of chapter material, these questions help you to prepare for class discussions, quizzes, and tests.

SUMMARY This feature consists of a brief restatement of the main ideas in each chapter, including definitions of key terms. Because it is presented in the efficient form of a numbered list, you can use it to refresh your memory quickly before an exam.

RAPID REVIEW Like the summary, this feature is designed to provide you with a quick review of the principles presented in the body of each chapter. Consisting of multiple-choice or short-answer questions, it will allow you to test your retention and reinforce your learning at the same time. Should you have trouble answering any of these questions, you can locate the topics you need to review by using the section cross-references provided.

SOLVED PROBLEMS Each chapter of this outline concludes with a set of practical problems and their step-by-step solutions. Undoubtedly the most valuable feature of the outline, these problems allow you to apply your knowledge of the marketing field to numerous real-life situations. Along with the sample midterm and final examinations, they also give you ample exposure to the kinds of problems that you are likely to encounter on a typical college exam. To make the most of these problems, try writing your own solutions first. Then compare your answers to the detailed solutions offered in the book.

Of course, there are other features of this outline that you will find very helpful too. One is the format itself, which serves both as a clear guide to important ideas and as a convenient structure upon which to organize your knowledge. A second is the coverage of marketing theory and practice applications by actual companies. This provides an understanding of how managers use marketing in today's business world. Yet a third is an examination of major trends in marketing and how these affect both large and small firms in business and nonbusiness organizations.

Marketing is a field that is becoming increasingly recognized as important by managers. The format of this outline is designed to make the practical applications clear. Understanding marketing principles will be an invaluable aid to you throughout your career with a business or other kind of organization.

New Mexico State University   ROBIN T. PETERSON

CONTENTS

PART I
THE NATURE AND
PRACTICE OF
MARKETING

1 MARKETING CONCEPTS AND THE NATURE OF MARKETING

THIS CHAPTER IS ABOUT

☑ **The Traditional Definition of Marketing**
☑ **The Modern Definition of Marketing**
☑ **The Importance of Marketing**
☑ **The Marketing Concept *vs*. Other Business Philosophies**
☑ **Major Marketing Activities: The Marketing Mix**

1-1. The Traditional Definition of Marketing

General Motors, Parker Brothers, IBM, General Foods, Coca Cola, Brooklyn General Hospital, and the Red Cross have something in common. They are each involved in *marketing*—a vital activity for both business and nonbusiness organizations.

• The **traditional definition of marketing** is the performance of *business activities* that direct the flow of *goods and services* from *producer to consumer*.

In order to fully understand this traditional definition of marketing, we should examine each of its major parts.

A. Business activities are any activities that organizations carry out in order to earn profits.

EXAMPLE 1-1: Mars, Inc., runs television commercials promoting its candy bars on Saturday morning; Clairol, Inc., increases the prices of its hair rinse; Chrysler increases the size of the Plymouth Horizon, and Shell Oil Company moves refined gasoline from points of storage to service stations. These are all business activities. In addition, they are marketing activities, not production, finance, or some other kind of business activity.

B. Marketers direct the flow of goods and services from producers to consumers.
Marketers attempt to bring both the producers and the consumers together.

- **Producers** are organizations, such as Maytag, that create goods and services.
- **Consumers** are those who buy and/or use goods and services for personal satisfaction.
- **Industrial buyers** are those who buy goods and services for business, rather than for personal use.

EXAMPLE 1-2: There are many kinds of activities that marketers engage in when directing goods and services to consumers. In the case of IBM, which sells personal computers (PC's), for instance, these activities involve:

- Deciding on the physical characteristics of the PC's.
- Deciding on the best prices.
- Arranging for advertising.

- Transporting the PC's to retail locations (such as Computerland).
- Designing showroom displays.
- Selling the product through sales representatives.
- Servicing the PC's after they have been purchased.
- Other activities related to those mentioned above.

If these activities are performed properly, IBM will have a successful marketing program. Weak performance on any one activity, however, or failure to coordinate the various activities can lead to lost sales and profits.

C. Marketing activities are designed to provide *utility* or satisfaction for consumers and buyers.
- **Time utility** exists when customers receive goods or services when they desire them.
- **Place utility** exists when goods or services are situated or offered in locations where they are available to customers.
- **Possession utility** exists when customers are able to acquire legal title and physical control of the items they desire.

Marketing produces all of these forms of utility. It does not provide the last type, **form utility**, which involves the manufacture of goods and services.

1-2. The Modern Definition of Marketing

The field of marketing has grown to the extent that the traditional definition of marketing is somewhat outmoded. A more up-to-date definition of marketing is needed.

- The **modern definition of marketing** is the process of planning and executing the conception, pricing, promotion, and distribution of ideas, goods, and services to create exchanges that satisfy individual and organizational objectives.

This more up-to-date definition has been formally adopted by the American Marketing Association. Note that this definition covers both planning and execution (carrying out plans) activities. It also suggests that marketers conceive ideas, goods, and services, and also make pricing, promotion, and distribution decisions.

The modern definition of marketing differs from the traditional definition in several ways.

A. Nonprofit marketing

Recall that the traditional definition of marketing defined business activities as having the objective of earning profits. You may have noticed, however, that many organizations that have objectives other than profit use marketing today. These include hospitals, churches, museums, charities, and government agencies. Large numbers of organizations have found that they cannot achieve their objectives without well designed marketing programs.

EXAMPLE 1-3: The Historical Museum of Niagara-on-the-Lake, Ontario, Canada, uses marketing to serve consumers. Its managers have designed a product (a series of displays) that interests guests. Management has set a price ($1.00), which is high enough to cover most of the museum's costs, yet low enough not to discourage the public from visiting. Brochures placed in hotels and restaurants as well as newspaper advertisements promote this nonprofit organization. The site is convenient for visitors—only a block and a half from the main street in town—and has ample parking.

Note that the marketing activities of the museum involve conceiving and delivering ideas, services, and products; setting prices; and running promotions to satisfy organizational objectives (provide revenues and attract visitors) and individual objectives (provide entertainment and educational inputs to visitors). This organization seems to be deeply involved in marketing.

B. Exchange

Recall that the traditional definition of marketing emphasized that producers serve consumers or industrial buyers. However, marketers must also work closely with other parties besides consumers. These other parties include the public at large, suppliers of goods and services, stockholders, government agencies, wholesalers, advertising agencies, transportation companies, and suppliers.

An important element of marketing is the exchange of things of value; these exchanges are called **transactions**. Consumers give up things of value (money) in exchange for other things of value (ideas, goods, or services). Likewise, marketers make exchanges with government agencies (for example, they comply with the law in exchange for not being prosecuted). Similar exchanges take place with other parties. In short, marketing takes place whenever transactions occur.

The contrast between the modern and the traditional views of marketing indicates that this discipline has expanded. It has spread to nonprofit organizations and to exchanges involving producers and other parties besides consumers. Figure 1-1 summarizes the traditional and modern definitions of marketing.

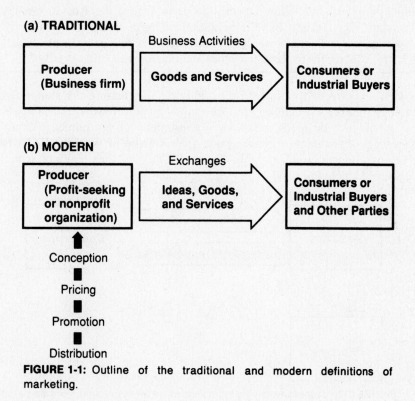

FIGURE 1-1: Outline of the traditional and modern definitions of marketing.

1-3. The Importance of Marketing

Marketing is important both to society at large and to individual organizations that practice it. The study of marketing as a participant in the overall society is called **macro-marketing.** On the other hand, the study of marketing in fulfilling the objectives of an organization is called **micro-marketing.**

A. Importance of marketing to society at large

Marketing provides many benefits to society. Marketing—

    (1) *Provides desired goods and services.* Marketing contributes to the overall standard of living by providing desired goods and services to consumers. Consumers register their preferences in the marketplace by purchasing items that fit their needs.

EXAMPLE 1-4: Managers of Chrysler Corporation design automobiles to meet the desires of potential customers and set prices that they believe will yield satisfactory sales. They also arrange for distribution from Detroit to auto dealerships, and they attempt to persuade consumers to purchase the automobiles. These activities, which are all marketing activities, are necessary so that consumers can obtain goods and services at reasonable prices.

(2) *Provides new and improved products.* Marketers contribute to the standard of living by bringing out a continuous flow of new products, such as improved home appliances and lawn care products and foods with more nutritious ingredients.

(3) *Cuts costs and prices.* Marketers discover ways of cutting costs and prices to consumers, for example, by buying and selling goods in volume and distributing through specialized and efficient wholesalers.

EXAMPLE 1-5: Prior to the 1980's, bicycle riders had to be content with products designed for children or for racing enthusiasts. Most bicycles, for example, required that the rider lean forward to reduce wind resistance. This was fine for supple children and racers, but not for commuters, leisure riders, and adults with back problems. During the early 1980's, the Ross Company and others introduced "mountain bikes." These bicycles permitted riding in an upright position, had tires that cushioned bumps, and generally made riding comfortable. This new product produced considerable consumer satisfaction and profits to Ross and other manufacturers.

(4) *Provides employment for workers.* In addition to increasing the standard of living for consumers, marketing actions produce employment for workers. If marketers do not satisfactorily provide goods and services, consumers will not purchase them, producing a decline in profits and, as a consequence, the dismissal of workers. Conversely, effective marketing produces profits and jobs. Figure 1-2 outlines these flows of money, goods and services, and employment.

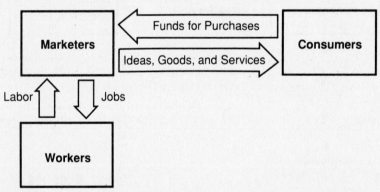

FIGURE 1-2: Successful marketing provides benefits to consumers and leads to jobs for workers.

EXAMPLE 1-6: In 1984, Sturm Ruger (a manufacturer of firearms) suffered declining sales and swollen inventories. The company was forced to lay off workers for the first time in its history. The firm's marketing department had failed to bring in adequate sales to support the workers and maintain inventories.

(5) *Promotes ideals and values of society.* Few would argue that marketing does not have an impact on the ideals and values of society. Advertisements, for instance, may be instrumental in convincing some consumers of the benefits of losing weight, staying healthy, investing money profitably, and conserving energy. (Of course, some critics believe that marketing emphasizes the wrong values, such as greed and self-centeredness.)

B. Importance of marketing to the organization that practices it

Organizations must have effective marketing in order to achieve their objectives. Marketing generates sales and public support for an organization. Failure in this area will result in inadequate sales for profit-seeking organizations or insufficient public support for nonprofit organizations. Approximately one-half of the typical firm's expenses are used to cover marketing costs, so management must use this function efficiently.

But marketing has other functions as well.

(1) *Marketing represents the organization to the public.* Marketing personnel are the main points of contact with various parties outside the organization, such as consumers, government agencies, and the press. These parties may be well acquainted with marketing personnel, but not even aware of the existence of accounting, finance, production, or other personnel. This means that *marketing is the major formulator of the organization's image.*

(2) *Marketing keeps top management informed.* In many organizations, marketers are top management's major source of information about what is happening outside the firm. Many companies have marketing research departments to acquire information from outside parties, such as consumers. Some sales representatives and other personnel also acquire information.

1-4. The Marketing Concept *vs.* Other Business Philosophies

There are three major philosophies of doing business. These are the *production concept*, the *sales concept*, and the *marketing concept*.

A. The production concept

Managers who pursue the **production concept** believe that an organization should emphasize efficiency in producing and distributing goods and services. These managers stress *low production costs* as the key to success, believing that customers mainly want high-quality goods and low prices. They feel that marketing is essentially a matter of transporting goods to markets and selling them there. In short, these managers focus more on the needs of the organization than on the needs of customers. This philosophy was widespread in the United States prior to 1930, and still prevails among some firms.

B. The sales concept

Managers who pursue the **sales concept** believe that their major objective is to persuade potential buyers to make purchases, whether they need the product or not. This objective calls for strong advertising and personal selling programs. Like the production concept, the sales concept stresses satisfying the needs of the organization, rather than the needs of the customer. Beginning in the 1950's, this philosophy proved to be inadequate, but there are still many managers who think in this way, especially in the ranks of small and newly formed businesses.

C. The marketing concept

Managers who pursue the **marketing concept** believe that an organization's major goal is to serve customer needs at a profit. These managers stress the idea that all departments in the organization must strive to produce customer satisfaction. This means that not just marketing, but production, finance, and other departments make an effort to produce customer satisfaction. The major emphasis of this approach is on solving the problems of consumers, not the problems of the organization. Management finds out what potential buyers want, then creates it. This approach is in contrast to the production and sales concepts, in which an organization produces the goods it wants to produce and then tries to sell them.

EXAMPLE 1-7: Procter and Gamble is a manufacturer that pursues the marketing concept. It introduced High Yield Folgers coffee at a time when coffee crop failures in Brazil were pushing retail prices of this product up. High Yield requires a smaller amount of grounds to produce the same amount of brewed coffee as a can of ordinary coffee does; and High Yield's price is $1 less. The company has issued coupons and sponsored advertising telling how to use this offering.

• The marketing concept is the most potentially effective of the three philosophies.

The marketing concept recognizes that the key to an organization's existence is the customer. Dedication to satisfying customer needs at a profit is likely to guide management into decisions that are in the best interest of all.

Some firms have extended the marketing concept into what is called a **societal orientation**. This concept holds that the organization should attempt to provide satisfaction to all of the important parties that it has exchanges with (including, but not restricted to, customers), at a profit.

1-5. Major Marketing Activities: The Marketing Mix

There are four major groupings of marketing activities, classified under the designations of (1) *Product*, (2) *Price*, (3) *Place*, and (4) *Promotion*. These are easily remembered as the **four P's**. Taken together, they make up what is called the **marketing mix** of a firm.

A. Product

Marketing decisions in the *product* area involve determining what products or services the organization will create and sell. This includes deciding on the characteristics of the products or services. Some company managers, for example, determine that it is in their best interest to offer a variety of items, while others choose to sell only one or a few. Some company managers choose to provide very high quality "premium" offerings, while others feature more basic items. Product decisions also include selecting a brand name to place on items and determining the nature of their packages.

EXAMPLE 1-8: The Traveling Light Company offers lightweight nylon luggage to customers, including airline carry-ons, duffel bags, and garment bags. The company also provides various travel accessories, such as compasses, flashlights, rain gear, and portable hair dryers and irons. The managers of this company have chosen to offer a variety of products logically tied together, because they appeal to travelers.

B. Price

Management must determine how much money to charge to customers and to middlemen (wholesalers and retailers). Many organizations set a **basic price** that is adjusted to the situation of the buyer. Some buyers, for instance, receive discounts from the basic price if they buy items in volume. Others pay more than the basic price because they must cover transportation charges.

Generally, marketers base prices on their costs, demand for the product or service, and competition. The price should be high enough to cover costs and leave a margin for profit. However, a price should not be so high that it discourages purchases, and it should have some logical relationship to prices of competitors.

EXAMPLE 1-9: Budget Rent-A-Car charged $39.95 per day in 1986 for a Lincoln Town Car. This was a special low price calculated to take business away from other firms, such as Avis and Hertz. Budget has a long history of placing its prices below those of major competitors in order to attract customers.

C. Place

Place activities involve moving products and services in a timely manner to locations desired by potential customers.

There are two dimensions to place activities.

(1) **Physical distribution** deals with the physical movement of goods. Marketers must make such decisions as whether to transport by truck or rail, what inventory levels to maintain, and where warehouses should be located.

(2) **Channels of distribution** are the paths of ownership that items take in moving toward potential customers. Marketers determine if wholesalers should be used (wholesalers sell to other businesses or to nonprofit organizations) or if retailers should be used (retailers sell directly to consumers). The organization must also determine how many and what specific wholesalers and retailers (if any) to employ.

EXAMPLE 1-10: The Mayo Clinic is heavily involved in place activities. Its managers found that it had to expand to meet the desires of consumers. This private medical center merged with two hospitals (St. Mary's and Rochester Methodist), giving it access to 830 physicians and the ability to serve 1,000 patients a day. The clinic set up branches in Jacksonville, Florida, and Scottsdale, Arizona, located in convenient-to-reach sites.

D. Promotion

Promotion activities involve developing communications used to convince potential customers to buy the product or to take other actions that the organization believes to be desirable. The major promotion components are *advertising, personal selling, public relations*, and *sales promotion*.

(1) **Advertising** is mass communication aimed at large groups. Examples are ads placed in national magazines or commercials on television.
(2) **Personal selling** is one-on-one and is aimed at individual customers in a personalized setting, such as when a sales representative calls on a buyer at the buyer's place of business.
(3) **Public relations** involves attempting to satisfy members of the public other than customers— such as citizens at large, employees, unions, suppliers, and government agencies. For example, a company might match employees' donations to designated charities or sponsor important civic events.
(4) **Sales promotion** consists of selling activities that supplement advertising and personal selling. Examples are contests, displays in stores, trading stamps, cents-off sales, and premiums. Firms are increasingly using sales promotion as a selling tool.

EXAMPLE 1-11: Schick once engaged in an advertising campaign to gain the patronage of young males (ages 16 to 34). The idea was to get young men to form favorable impressions of Schick disposable razors, an idea they would continue to hold as they grew older. Television commercials showed a traditional-looking college student who suddenly develops a large and ugly beard. The commercial used animation and rock lyrics and carried the message that Schick razors would provide good shaves.

RAISE YOUR GRADES
Can you explain . . . ?

☑ why the traditional definition of marketing is outmoded and why it has been replaced by the more modern definition
☑ why business firms are industrial buyers, rather than consumers
☑ why marketing is important to an individual organization
☑ why an organization would follow the marketing concept rather than the production or sales concepts
☑ what activities are included in the marketing mix of an organization

SUMMARY

1. The traditional definition of marketing is the performance of business activities that direct the flow of goods and services from producer to consumer.
2. The modern definition of marketing is the process of planning and executing the conception, pricing, promotion, and distribution of ideas, goods, and services to create exchanges that satisfy individual and organizational objectives.
3. Marketing benefits society by contributing to the standard of living. It provides desired goods and services, provides new and improved products, cuts costs and prices, provides employment for workers, and promotes the ideals and values of society.
4. Marketing benefits firms by helping to achieve sales, representing the company to the public, and acquiring information about what is happening outside the firm.
5. The marketing concept is based on the idea that the company's major goal is to serve customer needs at a profit.
6. The major marketing activities can be classified into the categories of product, price, promotion, and place.
7. Product activities involve determining what products and services the organization will create and sell.
8. Price activities involve determining how much to charge to customers and to middlemen.
9. Place activities involve moving products and services in a timely manner to locations desired by potential customers. These activities include deciding on the physical distribution of goods and the channels of distribution.
10. Promotion activities involve developing communications used to convince potential customers to buy the product or to take other actions that the organization believes to be desirable. The major promotion activities are advertising, personal selling, public relations, and sales promotion.

RAPID REVIEW   Answers

Multiple Choice

1. The traditional definition of marketing is the performance of business activities that direct the flow of goods and services from producer to (a) industrial buyer, (b) business, (c) consumer, (d) worker. [See Section 1-1.]   *c*

2. Those who buy goods for a business rather than for personal use are called (a) buyers, (b) industrial buyers, (c) consumers, (d) managers. [See Section 1-1.]   *b*

3. Which of the following is an important part of the modern definition of marketing? (a) an exchange, as when a married couple buys a house, (b) a strike, as when the union members stop working, (c) a termination, as when an employee is fired, (d) an inspection, as when a dishwasher is examined for defects. [See Section 1-2.]   *a*

4. The study of marketing in fulfilling the objectives of an organization is called (a) micro-marketing, (b) organizational marketing, (c) macro-marketing, (d) business marketing. [See Section 1-3.]   *a*

5. You could logically argue that marketing is important to society at large for all of the following reasons *except* (a) it provides desired goods and services to consumers, (b) its actions provide jobs for workers, (c) it enables companies to keep their training costs down, (d) it produces ways of cutting costs and prices to consumers. [See Section 1-3.]   *c*

6. A major reason why marketing is important to an organization is that it (a) represents the company to the public, (b) raises the costs of producing goods, (c) guarantees that sales will increase each year, (d) lowers the price that investors must pay for company stock. [See Section 1-3.]   *a*

7. A manager believes that the company should emphasize efficiency in producing and distributing goods and services. This manager is a follower   *c*

of the (**a**) marketing concept, (**b**) sales concept, (**c**) production concept, (**d**) efficiency concept. [See Section 1-4.]

8. A sales representative for the Quicksale used-car dealership has reported that, "The major objective of our company is to persuade people to buy cars, whether they need them or not." This sales representative is pursuing the (**a**) marketing concept, (**b**) sales concept, (**c**) production concept, (**d**) efficiency concept. [See Section 1-4.]   *b*

9. The General Electric Company is well known for its belief in the marketing concept, which states that the company's major goal is to (**a**) earn high levels of sales, (**b**) keep production costs at low levels, (**c**) serve customer needs at a profit, (**d**) provide numerous jobs in the communities where the company operates. [See Section 1-4.]   *c*

10. Which of the following is *not* one of the major activities in which marketers are involved? (**a**) deciding what diet foods Slim n' Trim, Inc., should produce, (**b**) setting the price of Avon skin conditioner at $9.99, (**c**) deciding to sell 20,000 shares of CBS stock, (**d**) running a Gaines Burger commercial on television. [See Section 1-5.]   *c*

11. When companies make product decisions, they also determine (**a**) what brand names to place on the product, (**b**) what price to charge for the product, (**c**) where to sell the product, (**d**) all of the above. [See Section 1-5.]   *d*

12. Many companies set a basic price that is adjusted to the situation of (**a**) the competition, (**b**) the buyer, (**c**) the company, (**d**) the supplier. [See Section 1-5.]   *b*

13. Assume that you are in charge of setting prices for the J.C. Penney Company. The major factors that you would consider include (**a**) demand for company products, (**b**) the size of the J.C. Penney work force, (**c**) the number of stores which this chain owns, (**d**) stock market prices for company stock. [See Section 1-5.]   *a*

14. Prices for a company's goods and services should be high enough to cover costs and leave a margin for (**a**) advertising expenses, (**b**) transportation costs, (**c**) employees' salaries, (**d**) profit. [See Section 1-5.]   *d*

15. Communications that an organization uses to convince potential customers to buy the product or to take other desirable actions are called (**a**) propaganda, (**b**) form utility, (**c**) promotions, (**d**) coupons. [See Section 1-5.]   *c*

16. Advertising is a form of (**a**) mass communication, (**b**) personal communication, (**c**) nonbusiness communication, (**d**) small group communication. [See Section 1-5.]   *a*

17. A Steelcase Office Equipment Company employee is employed in personal selling. The employee's efforts are aimed at (**a**) large groups of customers, (**b**) small groups of customers, (**c**) noncustomers, (**d**) individual customers. [See Section 1-5.]   *d*

18. The public relations department of a company attempts to satisfy (**a**) customers, (**b**) employees, (**c**) members of the public other than customers, (**d**) suppliers. [See Section 1-5.]   *c*

19. Place activities are designed to move products and services to (**a**) locations desired by potential customers, (**b**) times convenient to customers, (**c**) promotion areas, (**d**) other businesses. [See Section 1-5.]   *a*

20. The paths of ownership that items take in moving toward potential customers are called the (**a**) place utility, (**b**) channels of distribution, (**c**) physical distribution, (**d**) possession utility. [See Section 1-5.]   *b*

SOLVED PROBLEMS

PROBLEM 1-1 A friend has mentioned to you that marketing is used in distributing consumer goods, such as Dial soap and Kentucky Fried Chicken, but not in distributing industrial goods, such as large IBM computers and furnaces for steel mills. How would you respond to the friend's opinion?

Answer: Your friend is wrong. Some members of the public equate marketing only with consumer goods distribution, perhaps because most advertising and other promotional materials seen by the general public are for consumer goods and services. Marketers serve industrial buyers as well, however. Products must be conceived of, priced, promoted, and placed, regardless of who the end customer is— consumer or industrial buyer. [See Section 1-1.]

PROBLEM 1-2 Some lawyers contend that professions, such as the practice of law, do not use marketing. Do you agree? Support your answer.

Answer: Lawyers and others in the professions are involved in marketing. They create and sell "products" (legal services), determine prices for the services, and locate their offices in convenient and/or prestigious locations. Moreover, many promote their services through advertising [See Section 1-1].

PROBLEM 1-3 A ten-year-old textbook states that marketing consists of distributing goods and services to consumers. Your professor has stated that marketing services other individuals and groups, in addition to consumers. Which of the two is to be believed?

Answer: The professor is correct. In addition to consumers, marketers deal with numerous groups and individuals with whom they have transactions, or exchanges of things of value. The "others" include government agencies, labor unions, and the public at large. For example, marketers sell goods and services to the government, as when the Boeing Corporation sells aircraft to the U.S. Air Force. Marketers even provide useful communications to the public at large, such as safety information programs, in exchange for public goodwill. [See Section 1-2.]

PROBLEM 1-4 An article attacking marketing appears in a newspaper. It maintains that the field does not make a contribution to society at large. What arguments could you raise against this position?

Answer: Marketing contributes to the standard of living in several ways. It provides desired goods and services to consumers, as when microwave ovens help two-income families make food preparation faster and easier. It is also involved in bringing out a continuous flow of new and improved products, such as laundry pouches that contain a conveniently mixed blend of detergent, fabric softener, and antistatic compound. Marketing also helps find ways of cutting costs and prices to consumers, as when stores are located in low-rent areas, allowing retailers to pass on rent savings in the form of low prices. Also, marketing helps create jobs for workers, as when successful Chrysler Corporation ads sell more Chrysler automobiles which allows the company to hire more workers. Finally, marketing can even help promote the ideals and values of society, as when liquor producers sponsor advertisements advising consumers not to drink excessive amounts of alcohol. [See Section 1-3.]

PROBLEM 1-5 Companies such as Martin Mutual Life Insurance are well aware that marketing personnel represent their companies to the public. What is the importance of this?

Answer: Marketing personnel are often the main points of contact with various parties outside the organization, such as consumers, government, and the press. For example, Martin Mutual agents must call upon many members of the public as potential consumers. If they conduct themselves professionally and ethically, they can create a good image of the firm. If, however, they act unethically, as by trying to sell excessive amounts of insurance to young people, they can create a bad image. Having the most contact with outside parties means that marketing is often the main formulator of a company's public image. [See Section 1-3.]

PROBLEM 1-6   How can companies gain information about what is happening outside the firm through marketing departments?

Answer: Marketers are one of the major sources of information about what is happening outside of the firm. Marketing research departments acquire information from outside parties, such as consumers. They conduct telephone, mail, and personal interview surveys to discover such things as why customers make purchases, where they buy, and what items they really prefer. Some sales representatives and other personnel also acquire information. Sales representatives are in close contact with customers and get to know them well, so they are in a good position to inform management on such things as how well customers like products and what new products customers would like to see. [See Section 1-3.]

PROBLEM 1-7   The manager of an electronics firm states, "We produce the best products that we can at the lowest possible cost. That is the key to doing business." What major philosophy of doing business does the manager believe in? Support your answer.

Answer: The manager believes in the production concept, that the organization should emphasize efficiency in producing and distributing goods and services. The idea is that customers mainly want high-quality goods and low prices. The focus is more on the needs of the organization than on the needs of customers. This electronics firm manager is probably doing his company a disservice with his philosophy. It is unlikely that customer needs will be fulfilled, and this will result in lost sales. He should be more in tune with customer needs. [See Section 1-4.]

PROBLEM 1-8   A restaurant manager spends as little as possible on food, staff, and decor, but invests large sums of money on advertising, believing that, "The key to business is promotion. Tell people what they want to hear, and they will buy your goods." What major philosophy of doing business does this manager follow? Support your answer.

Answer: This manager believes in the sales concept, which is based on the idea that the major objective of management is to persuade potential buyers to make purchases, whether they need the product or not. For the restaurant, this requires strong advertising programs, probably through radio and newspaper. The approach is likely to produce dissatisfied restaurant customers. Rather than attending to their needs for such things as tasty meals, efficient service, and a comfortable atmosphere, the manager is attempting to "sell" the restaurant through persuasion. This can bring on reduced revenues. [See Section 1-4.]

PROBLEM 1-9   Executives at Union Corporation often state that they are in business to help solve their customers' problems. What major philosophy of doing business do they believe in? Support your answer.

Answer: Union Corporation executives believe in the marketing concept, which is based on the idea that the company's major goal is to serve customer needs at a profit. Stress is on solving customer needs, not problems of the organization. Management finds out what potential buyers want and then creates it. [See Section 1-4.]

PROBLEM 1-10   Under the marketing concept, what departments in the organization are involved in producing consumer satisfaction?

Answer: Under the marketing concept, *all* departments in the organization strive to produce customer satisfaction. If even one fails, customer satisfaction may not take place. If a production worker fails to make a solid weld on a wheelbarrow, for example, the product may fail. If a financial clerk is unfriendly to customers, sales may be lost. To avoid such problems, marketing personnel should coordinate their efforts with other departments to bring customers what they want. [See Section 1-4.]

PROBLEM 1-11   Some firms have taken a societal orientation as an overall guide to doing business. What is meant by such an orientation?

Answer: A societal orientation holds that the organization should strive to provide satisfaction to all of the important parties with which it has exchanges. These parties include consumers, the public at large, stockholders, the government, and employees. For example, Exxon is a corporation which follows this orientation. It makes a special effort to avoid air and water pollution. It also runs many public education advertisements, designed to keep the public informed on key issues, such as the need for improvements in public schools. [See Section 1-4.]

PROBLEM 1-12   Assume that you have been placed in charge of product decisions at Compton Computer Corp. What kinds of decisions would you be required to make?

Answer: You would be deciding what computers, computer software, and other services the organization would provide. In addition, you would determine the characteristics of the products and services. For example, if a new personal computer was to be introduced, it would be necessary to arrive at decisions on such factors as the size of the computer's memory, the design of the keyboard, and the kind of disk drive system to use. [See Section 1-5.]

PROBLEM 1-13   What major factors should executives of the Thompson Tea Company consider when setting prices for instant tea?

Answer: The three factors are demand for tea, cost of producing it, and competition from other beverage makers. The price should be high enough to cover raw material, production, and distribution costs and still leave a margin for profit. However, it should not be so high that many tea drinkers cannot afford it. Also, it should be reasonably priced, in comparison to other teas, coffee, and soft drinks. [See Section 1-5.]

PROBLEM 1-14   What is a "basic price" that a company charges for its product?

Answer: A basic price is one that is adjusted to the situation of the buyer. It is the starting point for the determination of the price that a customer finally pays. For example, some buyers may receive discounts from the basic price if they purchase items in volume. Others may pay more than the basic price because they must cover high transportation charges. Managers first set basic prices, which are average charges to customers. Then they alter the basic price to each customer in such a way that it fits in with marketing strategy. [See Section 1-5.]

PROBLEM 1-15   The Robertson Cash Register Company promotes its computer systems extensively. What promotion components is this firm most likely to use?

Answer: The firm is likely to use personal selling substantially, because interpersonal communication is needed for selling these expensive items. Potential customers want to talk to sales representatives before buying a cash register. These representatives can provide extensive information on the capabilities of company products and how these compare with the competition. The representatives can respond to questions and illustrate solutions to common problems. Also, Robertson Cash Register is likely to use advertising to build awareness of and interest in its cash register. The ads can reach many more prospects than can salespeople and help pave the way for sales presentations. [See Section 1-5.]

PROBLEM 1-16   What promotion component is the national Wally's Fast-Burger fast food chain most likely to emphasize in enticing consumers into its restaurants? Why?

Answer: This company is most likely to use advertising because it is mass communication—aimed at large groups, to which Wally's must appeal for selling fast food. Numerous consumers can be contacted through advertising at a low cost per consumer reached. Television can produce high impact with a large and diverse group of customers. If Wally's wanted to appeal to a more specific group (such as senior citizens) it might use magazines (such as *Modern Maturity* magazine). [See Section 1-5.]

PROBLEM 1-17   Physical distribution is important for Ollie's frozen concentrated orange juice. Why is this the case?

Answer: The product is grown in specific locations (orange groves) and must be transported to juice-processing centers. After the oranges have been processed, the juice is subjected to refrigerated storage and then must be transported to warehouses and to wholesalers and retailers. All of this is expensive and must be timely and not damaging to the product. [See Section 1-5.]

PROBLEM 1-18   Lawyers do not make channels of distribution decisions. Why is this the case?

Answer: Channels of distribution are necessarily direct from producer (the lawyer) to consumer. The "product", a service in this case, cannot be stored or transported. The only possible channel of distribution, then, is from the lawyer to the client. [See Section 1-5.]

2 MARKETING DECISION MAKING: FORMULATING STRATEGY AND TACTICS

THIS CHAPTER IS ABOUT

☑ **Formulating Marketing Strategy**
☑ **Formulating Marketing Tactics**
☑ **Coordinating Strategy and Tactics**

You may be surprised to learn that, like the military, marketers bring *strategies* and *tactics* into play in their operations. These two activities explain such things as why Dial soap is aimed at people who want a fresh fragrance, why Trident Sugarless Gum is promoted as a means of reducing cavities, and even why Pizza Hut specializes in pizzas.

2-1. Formulating Marketing Strategy

Every company has a **marketing strategy**—an overall plan to achieve company goals. This overall plan includes

- the kind of customer the firm seeks out,
- the customer needs that the company attempts to satisfy,
- the combination of marketing activities (product, price, promotion, and place) that management uses to satisfy customers.

Figure 2-1 outlines a marketing strategy, including the major factors that managers should consider in developing one. It indicates that companies aim marketing mixes at target customers with specific characteristics and needs. Management uses judgment and marketing research information and considers company strengths and weaknesses in constructing strategies. Management also considers the marketing environment (competition, technology, suppliers, the economy, social factors, and government), which affects the company and the marketing mix that it employs. Each of these factors is discussed in detail below.

EXAMPLE 2-1: Sabreliner has a comprehensive marketing strategy for its turboprop airplanes. This strategy is aimed at companies that want their own planes to fly executives to places where they are needed (target customers). This aircraft producer satisfies the desire for quick and convenient transportation in comfortable surroundings (customer needs). The company produces a very reliable product that is noted for its luxurious facilities (product). Its price is lower than that of most major competitors (price). The firm promotes Sabreliners through advertising in business magazines, exhibitions at air shows, and through sales representatives who call on potential customers (promotion). The planes are made readily available for convenient inspection, trial flights, and purchases (place).

A. The target customer

The first step in formulating marketing strategy is to aim marketing efforts at *particular potential customers*, called **target customers** or **target markets**. If a company devotes all of its marketing efforts to fulfilling the needs of a specific target, it is likely to win the business of many in that group. On the other hand, if it tries to please everyone, the company will compromise so much that it ends up satisfying no one.

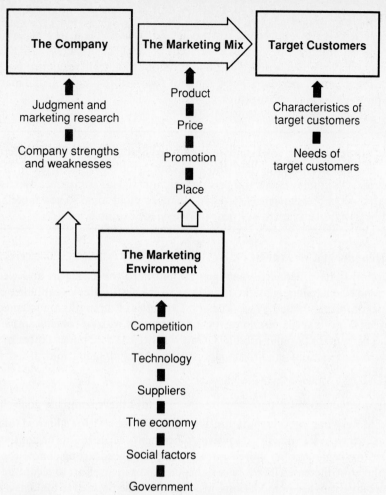

FIGURE 2-1: A marketing strategy and the major factors that should be considered in formulating marketing strategy.

EXAMPLE 2-2: McDonald's makes a major effort to target families with young children. It offers a variety of products, from McD.L.T.'s for adults to small hamburgers for children. Prices are at a level that most families can afford. Advertisements and store interiors carry the image of a "fun" place for children. The restaurants are located in places that are convenient for families, off freeways on major streets, and near schools. Ample parking is provided. This strategy has worked very well for McDonald's—it is the largest of the fast-food chains.

B. Target customer needs

The second step in formulating marketing strategy is to determine what **customer needs** to satisfy. This requires finding out what benefits the target customer wants from the product or service. Some managers rely on their past experience and judgment, others on marketing research and their sales representatives to acquire this information. Often, it is useful to attempt to discover needs that are not being satisfied or problems that are being experienced by target customers.

EXAMPLE 2-3: The Literary Guild book club provides a number of benefits to its target customers, who are mainly women in middle-income families. The Guild offers a large number of books that are of particular interest to this group, such as the *Microwave Cookbook* and *The Good Mother*. Prices are lower than those of most bookstores. An important benefit is the convenience of receiving books without shopping. Management has discovered through experience that this combination of benefits results in need fulfillment of many women in the target customer grouping.

C. The marketing mix

The third step in formulating marketing strategy is to determine the **marketing mix**, that combination of functions a company uses to satisfy the needs of target customers. Management designs an integrated program of product, price, place, and promotion that will result in a package of benefits intended to be unique and superior to the offerings of rivals. Both judgment and marketing research are useful in putting this package together.

EXAMPLE 2-4: The first budget motel chain in the United States was Motel 6. It offers basic rooms at a low price to business and pleasure travelers who want comfortable rooms but are willing to do without many "extras," such as swimming pools and private telephones. This company advertises on radio and television. It has over 400 motel units in 39 states and plans to build some 30 new motels a year. Most of these are located near major traffic flows—near freeways, for example.

D. Company strengths and weaknesses

As you may already have deduced, managers should keep the strengths and weaknesses of the company in mind when designing marketing strategy. The best strategies capitalize on strengths and avoid potential problems created by weaknesses. Examples of strengths are talented managers and other employees, large financial resources, a good reputation with customers, ample supplies of raw materials, and patents for popular products. On the other hand, some instances of weaknesses are limited funds and sources of credit, managers with poor judgment, and a bad reputation with potential buyers.

EXAMPLE 2-5: Motel 6 has a good reputation as a basic place to stay for a limited price. Its managers have extensive experience in the industry. However, when many of its rooms began to show the results of age and competitors began to offer more "extras," the chain faced strong competition and declining sales. This chain therefore increased its advertising expenditures in an effort to recapture customers who had shifted to more luxurious accommodations. Management also decided to build new motels to match the expansion plans of rivals.

E. The marketing environment

Marketers must pay considerable attention to their surroundings in formulating effective strategies. Failure to do this may result in very ineffective decision making. The **marketing environment** consists of those forces outside the company that have an important effect on the success of marketing strategy. Included in the more important environmental elements are competition, technology, suppliers, the economy, social factors, and government. Many successful companies devote special effort to **scanning** or carefully monitoring the behavior of the environmental elements.

1. Competition

Managers must keep their competitors uppermost in mind during every phase of strategy formulation. Important factors to consider are the number of competitors, their strengths and weaknesses, and the strategies that they use. Many companies seek **differential advantage** over their rivals. This involves creating a marketing mix that target customers find to be superior to those of competitors in one or more significant ways. Differential advantage can arise from superior product performance, low prices, persuasive promotions, rapid delivery to customers, and related performances. The idea is to conduct activities in such a way that the marketer stands out in the minds of customers.

EXAMPLE 2-6: Searle Laboratories brought out NutraSweet as a sugar substitute that tastes very much like the real thing but contains fewer calories. The product was not linked to cancer, as other sugar substitutes were. The company promoted the product as one made from "natural" ingredients, not "chemicals." These points of differential advantage permitted the firm to sell the brand at premium prices—higher than those of other sugar substitutes.

---

2. *Technology*

You probably have noticed the effect of many technological changes on marketing. These changes have affected the ways in which products are produced and distributed. They also have led to the development of new products. The pace of technology is accelerating at an increasing rate, leading to a wide variety of innovations. Some companies develop their own innovations as a result of internal research and development. Others are able to benefit by applying technological advances developed by universities, foundations, other firms, and individual inventors.

EXAMPLE 2-7: There are many examples of technology's impact on marketing. Innovations in computers have affected every marketing activity, even for smaller firms, which can use microcomputers and personal computers. Laser technology has been applied to many production processes, including medicine and printing. Industrial robots are commonplace in many manufacturing facilities. Bio-engineering and space satellite technology have produced numerous new offerings, ranging from antibiotics to cookware.

3. *Suppliers*

Suppliers are those companies that provide the marketer with goods and services. A firm such as Procter and Gamble, for instance, buys many supplies, including electricity, fuel, raw materials, semifinished goods, finished goods, cleaning supplies, office equipment, and industrial lubricants. For retailers and wholesalers, the major supply component is the finished goods that they sell to their customers.

A marketer with good sources of supply can enjoy differential advantage over rivals. A good marketer may be able to attain lower costs, faster delivery, superior handling of goods, valuable warehousing activities, liberal credit terms, or financial assistance in advertising. Some large marketers can acquire these forms of differential advantage simply because they are powerful and suppliers want their business. All companies, including small ones, can benefit from developing good relations with suppliers by dealing with them fairly and honestly and by granting them favors, if possible.

EXAMPLE 2-8: Sears, Roebuck and Co. has a very favorable position with its suppliers. Many strongly desire to stock their goods with this giant retailer. They are willing to furnish discounts for large-quantity purchases and provide valuable services for Sears, such as warehousing and advertising. In return, Sears offers the possibility of large-volume sales in its many stores. In addition, this company has a track record of dealing fairly with those who provide it with goods and services.

4. *The economy*

The state of the national (and world) economy has a profound effect on marketing. This environmental factor consists of the behavior of production, income, employment, and prices. Periods of economic growth are favorable for marketers in general; sales rise as production and consumer incomes increase. During such times, marketers spend freely for activities such as advertising and new product development. They may also expand or improve their physical facilities. During periods of economic decline, they reverse these actions. Unfortunately, the behavior of the economy is difficult to predict, even by "experts" employed by the government, universities, and large firms. Still, marketers are often able to obtain forecasts that allow them to plan ahead in an effective manner.

EXAMPLE 2-9: Harley-Davidson, a producer of large and heavy motorcycles, suffered severe losses during the recession years of the 1970's. Beginning in 1981, as the economy of the United States improved, H-D began to earn profits. The firm increased its sales to dealers and its share of the total market. The funds it earned through additional profits made it possible for H-D to expand and make both manufacturing and marketing facilities more efficient.

5. *Social factors*

Social influences on marketing arise from the actions and ideas of groups. An important and very large group is the **culture**. There are overall *national cultures* (that of the United States, for instance) and *subcultures* within the overall (such as the subcultures of the South, of blacks, of juveniles, and of blue-collar workers). Each culture and subculture has certain values, beliefs, customs, and morals that its members share. Since consumers are members of cultures, marketers should stay abreast of current attitudes and adjust their marketing mixes when changes in these attitudes occur.

EXAMPLE 2-10: Today's culture in the United States incorporates many attitudes that are of importance to marketers. For example an attitude that emphasizes physical fitness has benefited producers of running shoes, home exercise equipment, and aerobic dance videotapes; whereas a trend that frowns on drinking while driving has posed problems for marketers of hard liquors while opening up opportunities for marketers of soft drinks and low-alcohol–content drinks, such as light beer. Other important social attitudes include ideas about working women, the ideal size of the family, birth control, racial equality, and government spending.

In addition to cultures, there are smaller groups that affect consumer behavior. These include **social classes**, such as the upper and middle classes, and **special-interest groups**, such as those dedicated to working women, consumers, labor unions, and business lobbyists. Each of these has an impact on the behavior of its members. Also, special-interest groups can have a direct effect on the success of particular marketers.

EXAMPLE 2-11: The National Rifle Association is a special-interest group made up of those who enjoy hunting, target shooting, and related activities. Traditionally, its members have allied with manufacturers of firearms to oppose gun control and related legislation. This stance has benefited those manufacturers by helping to prevent restrictive legislation that might have cut into their sales and profits.

6. *Government*

The government is a major environmental force. It includes *federal*, *state*, and *local* units. Sometimes the government is a source of marketing opportunities, as when public agencies buy goods and services. Also, laws can open up opportunities. The federal government, for instance, deregulated certain industries, such as banking, trucking, and the airlines, in the 1980's. This paved the way for new firms to enter these industries, from which they were once prohibited.

The government has also passed various laws that prevent marketers from engaging in certain activities. These laws exist at the federal, state, and local levels, and can be very restrictive. If a firm is involved in international business, it must be aware of laws in foreign nations and how these apply to management's activities.

EXAMPLE 2-12: Some of the actions that existing laws prohibit are:

- Offering products that may endanger the health and safety of consumers.
- Misleading consumers through advertising or other forms of promotion.
- Making agreements with competitors on prices to charge customers.
- Monopolizing an industry—taking steps that give an organization control of a market.
- Engaging in "unfair competition," such as deliberately setting prices below costs to drive competitors out of business.
- Charging retailers, wholesalers, or industrial buyers different prices for the same goods, thereby restricting competition.

- Charging interest rates that exceed certain limits imposed by law.
- Selling products door-to-door (in certain cities) without a license or permit.

Failure to obey the laws can result in fines, damages to injured parties, orders to stop certain activities, and even imprisonment. Further, guilty verdicts can create bad publicity for companies. Managers should become familiar with the legislation that affects their companies and consult attorneys when technical legal questions arise.

Closely related to the government environment is the **political environment**. This consists of various special-interest groups, such as the National Organization for Women (NOW), the National Association for the Advancement of Colored People (NAACP), the American Association of Retired Persons (AARP), and various political parties. These groups exert many influences on marketers as a result of lobbying, requesting that businesses change their policies, and related actions.

2-2. Formulating Marketing Tactics

While marketing strategies are *overall* plans for reaching company goals, **marketing tactics** are specific and detailed activities that companies employ to carry out strategies. Tactics are short-run in nature, subject to change, and spell out exactly what actions a company is expected to take. Each marketer has product, price, promotion, and place tactics. These should be designed to help management make strategies work. Companies should consider the same major factors (outlined in Figure 2-1) to develop tactics as they do to develop strategies.

EXAMPLE 2-13: An example of a marketing tactic is Sabreliner's decision to run advertisements for Sabreliner business jets in *Business Week* magazine. These advertisements, which emphasize that the planes provide turboprop luxury at a low price and that using Sabreliner business jets involves much less inconvenience than traveling by commercial airlines, specifically implement this company's marketing strategy.

2-3. Coordinating Strategy and Tactics

To be effective, marketing strategies should be *coordinated* with one another. For example, if IBM computer advertisements are designed to appeal to high-income professionals, then company sales representatives should call on these individuals and the hardware and software should be designed to fulfill their needs. Lack of coordination among strategies can result in wasted effort and hostile or confused customers. Informed managers take steps, then, to ensure that a company's strategies are compatible with one another.

Similarly, tactics should be coordinated with strategies and with other tactics. The Sabreliner jet ads mentioned earlier, for example, would not be appropriate if the firm could not deliver on its promise for "luxury" or if its prices were above those of major competitors.

RAISE YOUR GRADES
Can you explain . . . ?

☑ what is meant by a marketing strategy (to a manager of a business firm)
☑ why companies choose target customers, rather than selling to everyone
☑ what is meant by a marketing mix
☑ how the marketing environment affects strategy making for a company or nonprofit organization
☑ the difference between strategy and tactics
☑ why strategies and tactics should be coordinated

SUMMARY

1. Every company has a marketing strategy—an overall plan to achieve company goals. It specifies the target customer, target customer needs to be satisfied, and the marketing mix.
2. The first step in formulating marketing strategy is to determine particular potential customers, known as target customers. Target customers are made up of groups of individuals or companies that the marketer attempts to satisfy.
3. The second step in formulating marketing strategy is to determine what customer needs to satisfy.
4. The third step in formulating marketing strategy is to determine the marketing mix that will be used to satisfy the needs of target customers. The marketing mix is that combination of product, price, promotion, and place that a company directs to target customers.
5. Management should carefully consider company strengths and weaknesses when formulating marketing strategy.
6. The marketing environment—including competition, technology, suppliers, the economy, social factors, and government—should be carefully studied when formulating marketing strategy.
7. Marketing tactics are specific detailed activities that companies employ to carry out strategies.
8. Strategies and tactics should be carefully coordinated as a means of producing effective marketing decisions.

RAPID REVIEW   Answers

Multiple Choice

1. A marketing strategy consists of (a) product, price, promotion, and place, (b) target customers, (c) an overall plan to achieve company goals, (d) a marketing mix. [See Section 2-1.]   *c*

2. Which of the following would Nabisco Brands executives *not* include in their marketing strategy for shredded wheat cereal? (a) the target customer, (b) employee needs, (c) target customer needs, (d) the marketing mix. [See Section 2-1.]   *b*

3. The marketing mix includes (a) production, (b) personnel training, (c) promotion, (d) plans. [See Section 2-1.]   *c*

4. Those forces outside of a company that have an important effect on the success of marketing strategy are known as the (a) marketing environment, (b) political environment, (c) national culture, (d) social atmosphere. [See Section 2-1.]   *a*

5. Important characteristics of competitors that marketing managers must consider when developing marketing strategy for a brand do *not* include (a) the number of competitors, (b) competitor strengths and weaknesses, (c) competitor strategies, (d) competitor depreciation schedules. [See Section 2-1.]   *d*

6. When a company seeks to produce a marketing mix that target customers find to be superior to those of competitors in one or more significant ways, it is trying to attain (a) increased sales, (b) loyal target customers, (c) a differential advantage over its rivals, (d) public support. [See Section 2-1.]   *c*

7. The pace of technology is accelerating at a(n) (a) increasing, (b) decreasing, (c) constant, (d) zero rate. [See Section 2-1.]   *a*

8. Suppliers consist of those companies that provide marketers, with (a) finished products, (b) raw materials, (c) special favors, (d) goods and services. [See Section 2-1.]   *d*

9. For retailers and wholesalers, the major supply component is (a) raw materials, (b) cleaning supplies, (c) finished goods, (d) office supplies. [See Section 2-1.]   *c*

10. Large marketers such as K-Mart can acquire differential advantage as a result of favorable treatment from suppliers because the large retailers are   *b*

(a) paying more to suppliers, (b) powerful, (c) willing to sell anything, (d) buyers of finished products. [See Section 2-1.]

11. Which of the following is *not* an important ingredient in the economy? (a) culture, (b) income, (c) employment, (d) prices. [See Section 2-1.]   *a*

12. Assume that your job is to develop marketing strategy for Radio Shack stores. During periods of economic growth, when national production is rising, you would expect Radio Shack sales to (a) increase, (b) decrease, (c) stay the same, (d) decrease at a decreasing rate. [See Section 2-1.]   *a*

13. Social influences on marketing arise from the actions of (a) government, (b) the political climate, (c) target customers, (d) groups. [See Section 2-1.]   *d*

14. Subdivisions of a national culture, such as that made up of juveniles, are called (a) special interest groups, (b) customer subgroups, (c) subcultures, (d) ethnic groups. [See Section 2-1.]   *c*

15. Members of the same culture, such as citizens of the United States, tend to share the same (a) physical appearance, (b) ethnic backgrounds, (c) values, (d) religious preferences. [See Section 2-1.]   *c*

16. Government agencies are a source of opportunity for many firms because they (a) regulate competitors, (b) purchase goods and services, (c) establish guidelines for doing business, (d) allow a free marketplace. [See Section 2-1.]   *b*

17. Marketing tactics are more (a) detailed than marketing strategies, (b) long-run than marketing strategies, (c) far-reaching than marketing strategies, (d) permanent than marketing strategies. [See Section 2-2.]   *a*

18. Each marketer has (a) finance tactics, (b) price tactics, (c) engineering tactics, (d) data-processing tactics. [See Section 2-2.]   *b*

19. When the Chrysler Corporation offers cash rebates to the purchasers of Dodge Horizons, this is an example of (a) strategies, (b) tactics, (c) product policies, (d) place policies. [See Section 2-2.]   *b*

20. To be effective, marketing strategies should be coordinated with (a) tactics, (b) management decisions, (c) customer needs, (d) tactics and one another. [See Section 2-3.]   *d*

SOLVED PROBLEMS

PROBLEM 2-1   A friend who owns and operates a small business has told you that, "The only real marketing strategy is to make money." How would you answer this statement?

Answer: The friend's response is very shortsighted. Marketing strategy involves a great deal more than this. The strategy is an overall plan to achieve company goals. It includes specifying the target market, determining the characteristics and needs of the target market, and developing a marketing mix. Some small business owners, especially if they are not experienced, take the uninformed view that marketing strategy is a simplistic process. This is one of the reasons why many small businesses fail. [See Section 2-1.]

PROBLEM 2-2   In 1986, the Kellogg Company spent $7 million to introduce All-Bran Fruit & Almonds cereal. The firm targeted this product to consumers over age 35. Why would it *not* have been better for Kellogg's to aim at consumers of all ages, not just those who are older?

Answer: It probably would have been a mistake to aim at consumers of all ages. Cereal marketers, like others, have found that the best strategy is to orient their marketing mixes to specific potential customers, rather than to attempt to satisfy every cereal consumer. This results in more satisfaction for those in the target group and more sales for the marketer. If a cereal company tries to please everyone, the result will probably be a compromise that satisfies no one. The All-Bran Fruit & Almonds marketing mix that appealed to adults probably would not satisfy teenagers and young children. [See Section 2-1.]

PROBLEM 2-3 A newly appointed manager of a restaurant that specializes in steaks is concerned about what target consumer needs the restaurant should attempt to satisfy. Should it emphasize low prices, fast service, friendly personnel, high-quality food, many food selections, or something else? How would you advise this manager?

Answer: Traditionally, managers rely on their past experience and judgment, marketing research, and sales representatives to determine target customer needs. This manager may have experience with other restaurants that can be brought into play for this decision. Certainly, personal judgment can be used. If the restaurant can afford it, marketing research may be a good choice—a survey could be utilized to ask customers and noncustomers what benefits they want. Finally, a visit with other restaurant employees to find out what they know about customer desires could be helpful. [See Section 2-1.]

PROBLEM 2-4 A friend has come across the term "marketing mix" in a magazine article and wonders what it means. Knowing that you are taking an introductory marketing class, your friend asks you to explain the term. How would you answer the question?

Answer: You should inform your friend that the marketing mix is that combination of marketing activities that a company uses to satisfy the needs of target customers. Management designs an integrated program of product, price, promotion, and place that will result in a package of benefits that it intends to be unique and superior to the offerings of competitors. [See Section 2-1.]

PROBLEM 2-5 Company strengths and weaknesses are important factors to consider when formulating marketing strategy. What are three possible strengths and three possible weaknesses that Ajax Life Insurance marketing managers should be alert for?

Answer: In the insurance industry, possible strengths are talented managers, large financial resources, and a good reputation with customers. The major weaknesses are limited funds, managers with poor judgment, and a bad reputation with potential buyers. These factors spell the difference between success and failure in this very competitive industry. [See Section 2-1.]

PROBLEM 2-6 Assume that you are in charge of developing marketing strategy for India Tea Company. What elements of the marketing environment would you consider in your work?

Answer: The elements of the marketing environment that should be considered in developing marketing strategy for India tea are competition (new products, promotions, and pricing strategies of other tea companies); technology (such as new ways of processing tea products); suppliers (their inventories and pricing tactics); the economy (tea consumption may fall as the economy declines); social factors (tea may become a more popular drink as cultural values change); and government (tariffs on tea can raise prices and restrict supply). Each of these elements should be carefully researched to determine its impact, if any, on the company and its marketing strategy. [See Section 2-1.]

PROBLEM 2-7 To what extent do you think Diet Pepsi is subject to the pressures of competition as it develops its marketing strategy?

Answer: Diet Pepsi is subject to considerable competition. It faces rivalry from major firms such as Coca Cola (Diet Coke) and, in lesser degree, rivalry from smaller firms, including regional and local bottlers. To some extent, it also competes with producers of other beverages, such as Kool-Aid, coffee, tea, and milk. [See Section 2-1.]

PROBLEM 2-8 If you were in charge of marketing strategy at a computer company, how would you expect technology to affect your decisions?

Answer: Technology affects the kinds of products that a computer firm and its competitors bring out. Technological change has been very rapid in the computer industry, as products are continually improved upon or replaced by new ones. A computer company would not only do everything to keep abreast of new technology, but would likely engage in internal research and development projects to remain in the forefront in its field. Also, advances in technology could provide new ways of producing and distributing products. [See Section 2-1.]

PROBLEM 2-9   Assume that you are a buyer for a large, national cereal company. What would you do through suppliers in order to obtain differential advantage over your rivals?

Answer: A large cereal company can obtain differential advantage over rivals through good working relationships with suppliers, such as the large companies that sell grain. This requires dealing with the suppliers honestly and fairly, and granting them favors (such as liberal credit), if possible. Such a big company may even be able to use its substantial buying power to acquire concessions, such as low prices and rapid delivery, from suppliers. [See Section 2-1.]

PROBLEM 2-10   An executive who is employed by Consolidated Candy Corp. is pondering the question, "What forms of differential advantage might my suppliers give me if our company has good relations with them? Will they grant us special favors?" How would you answer this executive?

Answer: If the Candy Corp. buyer has good relations with suppliers, he or she may receive numerous benefits. These include paying lower prices than do competitors for raw materials (items such as sugar, chocolate, and dairy products), faster and more reliable delivery, superior handling of goods, less wasteful warehousing activities, liberal credit terms, and financial assistance in placing advertisements. All of these could be of great importance to a candy company. [See Section 2-1.]

PROBLEM 2-11   What variables in the economy should Telephone Communication Corp. executives consider in developing a marketing strategy for long-distance telephone service?

Answer: There are a number of important variables that Telephone Communications Corp. executives should consider. Probably the most important areas are production (as industrial production rises, more long-distance business calls are made), income (individuals and businesses make more calls when incomes advance), employment (which also rises and falls with telephone calls), and prices (during periods of inflation, individuals and businesses have less money available for long-distance calls). [See Section 2-1.]

PROBLEM 2-12   In 1985 and early 1986, the United States economy enjoyed periods of prosperity. What are the implications of such periods for firms such as a national hotel chain?

Answer: Such periods are favorable for marketers. Sales rise as production and consumer incomes increase. Marketers, such as those with a national hotel chain, would spend more freely for activities such as advertising. They may also expand or improve their physical facilities, such as hotel units and hotel rooms. [See Section 2-1.]

PROBLEM 2-13   Would you recommend that McDonalds use the same marketing strategy in every country in which it does business?

Answer: No. Each country has its own culture and set of subcultures. Each one has certain values, beliefs, customs, and morals that are shared by its members. A marketing strategy that is very successful in the United States could be a disaster in West Germany. For example, McDonalds outlets sell beer in West Germany and wine in France. Also, their ads in various countries are very different, reflecting cultural differences. [See Section 2-1.]

PROBLEM 2-14   What would you say are the current cultural values in the United States that would be important to food-processing companies such as Del Monte?

Answer: The current culture of the United States places considerable value on physical fitness, weight control, and health. These values should suggest to Del Monte that processed food products should contain fewer ingredients that may be perceived as harmful to health, such as salt, fats, and sugar. Ingredients that may promote health, such as fiber, may be preferable. [See Section 2-1.]

PROBLEM 2-15   A fellow student has asked for your opinion as to the effect of government deregulation on an industry. What answer would you provide?

Answer: You might inform the fellow student that, based on past experience in the trucking, banking, airline, and other industries, deregulation creates new opportunities for new companies to enter these industries. It also allows existing companies, such as United Airlines and Southwestern Savings and Loan Association, to change prices, products and services offered, and methods of operation more freely than in the past. Of course, deregulation can increase competition. For some companies this has caused problems. Some banks, for instance, faced with increased competition from Savings and Loan Associations, have gone out of business. [See Section 2-1.]

PROBLEM 2-16   A skeptical politician who is seeking re-election wants to pass legislation that will restrict the messages that advertisements carry. According to this politician, "Companies, especially big ones, are free to say whatever they want in their advertisements. The government cannot regulate what appears in these messages, under current laws on the books." Do you agree with this opinion?

Answer: This opinion is not accurate. There are laws that regulate the content of advertisements. Companies cannot promote and sell products that may endanger the health and safety of consumers. Companies are also prohibited from running misleading promotions. Further, they cannot use advertising if it results in prohibited monopoly positions in an industry. [See Section 2-1.]

PROBLEM 2-17   In the classroom, a professor has asked you to explain the difference between strategy and tactics for a manufacturer such as Star-Kist (marketer of canned tuna). How would you explain this difference?

Answer: The marketing strategy for Star-Kist canned tuna is an overall plan for achieving company goals, dealing with general ideas, such as how Star-Kist will be differentiated from competing brands. Tactics for this firm are specific, detailed activities that the firm uses to carry out strategies, such as the composition of the label on the can and the messages that Star-Kist ads will convey. The firm's tactics are more short-run in nature, more subject to change, and spell out more exactly what actions the company is expected to take. [See Section 2-2.]

PROBLEM 2-18   For what marketing activities should companies, such as a life insurance company, develop marketing tactics?

Answer: A life insurance company should develop tactics for product, price, promotion, and place. As for product, management should determine the details on the provisions that company insurance policies contain. Regarding price, the firm decides on specific premium levels and discounts for special policyholders, such as nonsmokers. As for promotion, management must design the messages and choose the media that will be used to communicate with potential policyholders and other important publics. Regarding place, the company determines where sales representatives will be located and exactly how they will call on policyholders to serve them. [See Section 2-2.]

PROBLEM 2-19   Why should firms coordinate marketing strategies with other strategies and with tactics?

Answer: Coordination is necessary for marketing success and an orderly marketing effort. Lack of coordination can result in wasted effort and hostile or confused customers. Strategies and tactics that are not coordinated are simply not compatible with one another. If physical distribution functions are not coordinated with promotion, for example, goods will not be available where and when consumers and retailers want them. Coordination is necessary between pricing and product decisions so that the quality that buyers receive is in balance with price levels. The channels of distribution must be coordinated with product decisions in such a way that channel members are motivated to aggressively promote company products. [See Section 2-3.]

PART II
ANALYZING MARKETS AND MARKET BEHAVIOR

3 MARKET SEGMENTATION PRACTICES

THIS CHAPTER IS ABOUT

☑ **The Meaning of Market Segmentation**
☑ **Advantages and Disadvantages of Segmentation**
☑ **Steps Involved in Segmentation**
☑ **Various Kinds of Segmentation**

3-1. The Meaning of Market Segmentation

Every company, whether it be giant Kraft, Inc., or tiny Joe's Cheese 'n Milk (a small dairy), has an overall approach for reaching target markets. A company may use one marketing mix for all its customers if all its customers' needs are very similar; or management may decide that various classes of customers are so different (*heterogeneous*) that separate marketing mixes should be employed for each class. Often separate marketing mixes are employed, as different buyers in both consumer and industrial markets have divergent characteristics and needs.

- **Market segmentation** consists of developing and carrying out marketing programs that are aimed at subgroups (or segments) of the total market.

A company may strive to serve only one subgroup (such as senior citizens) with one program. Or it may have multiple programs, each one oriented to a different segement (such as one for senior citizens, one for families with children, and one for singles). By carefully studying needs and then presenting a customized marketing mix to each segment, the marketer is able to satisfy customers more fully.

EXAMPLE 3-1: Frozen desserts (e.g., ice cream, sherbet, frozen yogurt, and frozen fruit bars) are widely sold to consumers of all types throughout the world. The Winmore Products Company, however, markets a dessert that is designed specifically for health-conscious young adults. Its offering, Fruit Fraze, is a cholesterol-free and fat-free blend of fruit and concentrated fruit juices. It is sold in frozen yogurt shops, which draw many persons from the segment to which Winmore appeals. Radio, newspaper, and billboard ads are used to stress the product's all-natural ingredients.

A. Identifying homogeneous groups

Marketers who practice segmentation seek out subgroups of target customers whose needs are similar to those of others within that subgroup, but are different from those in other subgroups.

Consider Figure 3-1A, where each dot represents a hypothetical consumer in terms of his or her desire for butterfat and sugar in frozen dessert. The circles identify those who tend to fall into specific subgroups. One of these subgroups consists of individuals preferring relatively high butterfat and high sugar. Another is made up of persons wanting low butterfat and low sugar levels. A third segment is made up of consumers desiring low butterfat and high sugar. It is evident that a few customers do not fall clearly into any segment. These have rather unusual preferences and are not large in number. A segmenter probably would ignore them. A frozen dessert producer who discovered the consumer preference patterns shown in Figure 3-1A might create three marketing mixes—one for each of the segments.

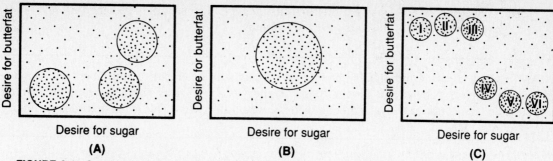

FIGURE 3-1: Consumer desire for butterfat and sugar in frozen dessert. (Dots represent individual consumers; circles represent subgroups.)

On the other hand, assume that the consumer preferences fall into a pattern like that shown in Figure 3-1B. You can see that most consumers desire a frozen dessert that has intermediate levels of butterfat and sugar. This is a **mass market**—where most target customer preferences are the same. There would be no point in appealing to different segments in this situation. For most products and services, however, this condition is rare.

Finally, consider Figure 3-1C. Here the number of segments is large and each segment consists of just a few consumers. Management could attempt to create a unique marketing mix for each segment, but there may be too few consumers in each one to justify the cost. Under these circumstances, the firm might attempt to produce marketing mixes that appealed to a *combination of subgroups*. For instance, subgroups I, II, and III are somewhat similar, and perhaps these can be assigned to a single segment. The same applies for subgroups IV, V, and VI.

EXAMPLE 3-2: Marketers sometimes find ingenious ways to segment the market. The producer of Cycle dog food, for instance, segments the market in a manner that is based on the age of dogs. Cycle 1 is for very young animals, Cycle 2 for dogs that are fully grown, Cycle 3 for mature dogs, and Cycle 4 for dogs that are very old.

B. Appealing to groups the company can serve

Firms should attempt to satisfy only those segments that they are capable of serving, rather than blindly trying to appeal to all. A company with a reputation for low-calorie frozen desserts, such as Winmore Products, may be well-advised to stick to segments preferring low butterfat and sugar. To do otherwise might confuse weight- and health-conscious consumers. Likewise, certain resources, such as engineering talent, money, technology, raw materials, and skilled employees, are necessary for serving some segments. If the company lacks these, it should not attempt to serve the segment in question.

EXAMPLE 3-3: Mars, Inc., appeals to children with its peanut and plain chocolate M & M's. The company has aimed at this segment with various candy products for years. It has built up considerable knowledge on how to appeal to children in advertisements, how to design products that they like, and how to develop packages that attract their attention and interest. It is logical that the firm appeals to this group with M & M's.

3-2. Advantages and Disadvantages of Segmentation

Segmentation is not for every company. Before following this strategy, management should consider its advantages and disadvantages and determine which set outweighs the other.

A. Advantages of segmentation

When a company segments the market, it designs a marketing mix that is attuned to the specific needs and desires of each targeted subgroup. The result may be considerable customer satisfaction.

Further, customers who buy an offering that fits their specific needs may become very loyal to it. They may be reluctant to shift to competitors' brands.

EXAMPLE 3-4: Procter and Gamble orients its Tide laundry detergent to consumers who want a heavy-duty cleanser, one that will handle "tough" laundry problems. It has been successful in building considerable satisfaction and loyalty among such individuals for years. Tide is the best-selling laundry detergent in the United States.

B. Disadvantages of segmentation

A misdirected segmentation strategy can actually result in fewer sales than a strategy of serving all potential customers, since it requires that some customers not be sought out. In addition, there is the danger that management will choose the *wrong* segments—segments that are not large enough or wealthy enough to buy sufficient amounts of the offering. Also, segmentation can be costly. If a company serves three market segments, it must create three separate marketing mixes. This is more expensive than employing only one marketing mix to serve a mass market.

EXAMPLE 3-5: Automobile manufacturers produce a wide variety of cars with different sizes, styles, colors and performance characteristics. These manufacturers have created a number of different goods for specific segments. The costs of producing and marketing all of these individualized products are more than if just one basic automobile were sold to all customers.

3-3. Steps Involved in Segmentation

Managers make two major classes of decisions with regard to segmentation. These are, "*Should the firm segment the market?*" and "*If segmentation is to be carried out, how should the firm accomplish this process?*" Usually, both decisions are made by analyzing four requirements that a company should meet if segmentation is to be successful. Figure 3-2 illustrates these requirements.

A. Subgroups of similar target customers

The first step in segmentation is to find out if there are subgroups of potential customers who can be expected to react similarly to marketing programs, but whose reaction can be expected to differ from those of other subgroups. In this case, the marketer is seeking *homogeneous* subgroups. If homogeneous subgroups do not exist, segmentation will not be successful.

EXAMPLE 3-6: Marketers of frames for eyeglasses often segment the market. The Royal Optical Company, for instance, aims at middle-income consumers and makes its products available in shopping malls and other convenient locations at relatively low prices. Logo Paul's, on the other hand, sells its individually styled frames at $100–$180. It is orienting its marketing mix to upper-income and fashion-conscious consumers.

B. Reaching target customers

For segmentation to work, the marketer must be able to reach target customers through channels of distribution, such as through retailers, or through promotion. Manufacturers of clothing, for example, can reach small women through "petite" clothing stores. Marketers of honeymoon resorts can reach prospective customers through *Modern Bride* magazine. Assume, however, that a marketer wanted to reach a segment defined as "red-haired consumers." This would be difficult, as there are no retailers or promotion media that specifically serve this subgroup.

C. Information identifying subgroups of target customers

If a company is to segment the market, it must be able to determine to which subgroup a target customer belongs; that is, the company must have information about target customers available to

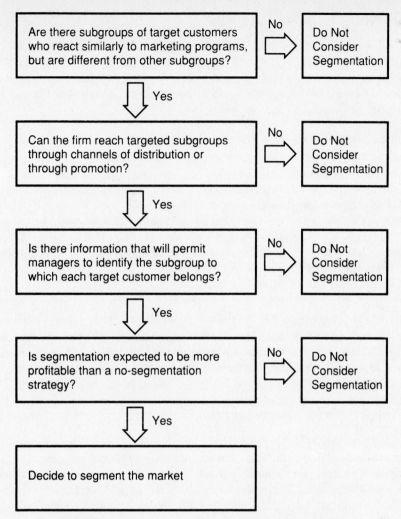

FIGURE 3-2: Requirements for segmenting the market.

it. This is not difficult if the subgroups are clearly identified—for instance, when one segment consists of the 11 western states, another of the 7 midwestern states, etc. It is difficult, however, if the division into subgroups is based on psychological characteristics—for instance, when one segment consists of consumers who are fashion-conscious and another of those who are not fashion-conscious. In this case, the only way to identify subgroups may be through costly surveys.

D. Segmentation profitability

A company should segment the market *only* if a segmentation strategy will produce higher profits than a no-segmentation strategy. This requirement indicates that management should compare the expected sales and costs of the firm under both strategies. Often, segmentation produces more sales than a no-segmentation strategy, but it also frequently leads to higher costs. The major question is whether or not sales advances will offset cost increases.

EXAMPLE 3-7: The Crispy Cracker Company (a hypothetical firm) does not segment the market for its saltine crackers. The product's sales for the next five years are expected to be $6 million and its costs $4.5 million, producing a profit of $1.5 million. The company conducts a marketing research project and estimates that if it segmented the market, sales would rise to $10.2 million and costs to $8.1 million, yielding a profit of $2.1 million. In this case, the company would benefit from segmenting the market.

3-4. Various Kinds of Segmentation

The last decision that managers make after they have elected to segment the market is, "*What characteristics of target customers should we base our marketing strategy on?*" There are six categories of characteristics that are widely used. These are *demographic, geographic, lifestyle, volume, marketing attribute,* and *benefit* variables. A company should choose the kind of segmentation that best fulfills the segmentation requirements listed in Section 3-3.

A. Demographic characteristics

Demographics consist of statistical facts on human populations—i.e., target customers. *Consumer demographics* consist of statistics on such characteristics as age, family size, education, occupation, and income. On the other hand, *industrial-buyer demographics* are statistics on such characteristics as company industry and company size.

A considerable amount of demographic data is available from government agencies, trade associations, universities, and others. Also, companies usually possess demographic information that they have collected themselves. Because of this considerable availability of information, demographic segmentation is widely used.

EXAMPLE 3-8: Many companies use demographic segmentation. Most home builders specialize in a demographically defined field, such as luxury homes for the well-to-do or basic homes for middle- and lower-income families. The Neiman-Marcus department store catalog features very expensive items for upper-income consumers. Most brewers aim their marketing efforts at males aged 19–34. Bowling alleys appeal primarily to those in blue-collar occupations. Most bookstores orient their strategies to individuals from families with college educations.

B. Geographic segmentation

Numerous marketers subdivide the total market into *geographic regions*, such as individual states or sections of the country, and aim their marketing mixes at specific regions where targets are located, while ignoring others. They may concentrate their efforts in areas where sales are expected to be high and costs low. If more than one region is to be served, the company may create a unique marketing mix for each. Geographic segmentation makes sense for products that draw different target customers in specific areas. Individuals in certain areas may be especially good targets because of their environment (such as the climate and weather), culture, or racial mix.

EXAMPLE 3-9: *Time* magazine constructs different editions for different sections of the country, such as the Pacific Coast region, and for various foreign countries. Each edition contains stories that are of specific interest to persons living in that area. The Pacific Coast edition of *Time*, for example, features stories on politics in California and the aerospace industry in Seattle.

C. Lifestyle segmentation

Lifestyle segmentation involves identifying subgroups based on the psychological characteristics of target customers. Examples of psychological characteristics are consumer attitudes, interests, opinions, and activities. Marketers often find that those with particular lifestyle characteristics are heavy users of a product or service, whereas other subgroups are nonusers. This method can be superior to demographic and geographic segmentation, since demographic or geographic characteristics may not produce subgroups with similar reactions to marketing programs.

EXAMPLE 3-10: The Longines 1000 is a jeweled quartz Swiss watch that sells for over $600. The marketing strategy for this product is oriented to men who wish to present an image of good taste and luxurious living. On the other hand, the strategy for the Swiss Swatch watch is oriented to those who want a "reverse status symbol"—who want to present an image of *not* caring for status. Each of these two marketing efforts is successful, even though each appeals to a different lifestyle group.

D. Volume segmentation

In the case of *volume segmentation*, marketers group target customers according to the extent to which each subgroup uses a product or service. A frequently used classification system for volume segmentation consists of heavy users, average users, light users, and nonusers. After grouping potential customers according to extent of use, the marketer determines which of the user groups to target. Often, these are the heavy or average users.

EXAMPLE 3-11: The Carnation Company conducted a study of nondairy coffee creamer users in Britain. It found a large group of average users of the product. There were very few consumers in the heavy-user category, probably not enough to provide much of a market for the product. The light users and nonusers were essentially not coffee drinkers. The firm decided to aim its Coffee Mate brand at the average users. This turned out to be a profitable strategy.

E. Marketing attribute segmentation

Marketing attribute segmentation focuses on subgroups made up of target customers who are attracted to the same elements of the marketing mix. Some subgroups are attracted by very high-quality products and services. Others seek low prices. Some make purchases because they respond favorably to advertisements or sales representatives. Still others buy because of "place" variables— for example, they may look for fast delivery or convenient retail locations.

EXAMPLE 3-12: The Charles Schwab discount brokerage firm buys and sells stocks, bonds, and mutual funds for investors at a much lower commission than do most other brokers. This firm appeals to those who do not require much advice from a broker (they do not look for a high degree of service) but do want low prices. This is one of the more successful and faster growing large brokerage houses in the United States.

F. Benefit segmentation

You have probably observed that different people look for different benefits from a product or service. This is the rationale for *benefit segmentation*, which classifies target customers into subgroups who seek particular benefits from the product or service. An advantage of benefit segmentation is that it is based on the reasons that individuals buy—i.e., the benefits. This is not necessarily the case for geographic and demographic methods. This being the case, numerous firms are attracted to benefit segmentation.

EXAMPLE 3-13: Different consumers look for different benefits in personal computers. Some want ease of operation, that which results from user-friendly machines. Others seek out advanced memory and speed of operation. Still others desire machines that are compatible with widely used software. Apple MacIntosh computers, for example, are aimed at those who want a user-friendly machine.

RAISE YOUR GRADES

Can you explain . . . ?

☑ why a marketer of goods to the mass market might not segment
☑ why a company decides to segment the market
☑ why the disadvantages of segmentation might outweigh the advantages
☑ why a company might choose particular segments as targets
☑ why a company chooses a particular kind of segmentation

SUMMARY

1. Market segmentation consists of developing and carrying out marketing programs that are aimed at subgroups (or segment) of the total market.
2. Marketers who practice segmentation seek out subgroups of target customers whose needs are similar to those of others within that subgroup, but different from those in other subgroups.
3. Companies that do not practice segmentation focus their marketing programs on the mass market.
4. Firms should attempt to satisfy only those segments that they are capable of serving, rather than blindly trying to appeal to all.
5. The advantages of segmentation are that it can lead to substantial satisfaction of target customer needs and strong customer loyalty.
6. The disadvantages of segmentation are that it can cut back the size of the market and increase company costs; there is also the danger that the wrong segments will be chosen.
7. There are four requirements for successful segmentation: the subgroups must be internally homogeneous but different from each other; they must be reachable through channels of distribution or through promotion; there must be information allowing identification of subgroup members; and the segmentation strategy should be more profitable than not segmenting.
8. Demographic segmentation involves identifying subgroups based on statistical facts about target customers.
9. Geographic segmentation involves identifying subgroups based on particular areas where target customers are located.
10. Lifestyle segmentation involves identifying subgroups based on psychological characteristics of target customers.
11. Volume segmentation involves identifying subgroups based on the extent to which they use the product or service.
12. Marketing attribute segmentation involves identifying subgroups made up of target customers who are attracted by the same elements of the marketing mix.
13. Benefit segmentation involves identifying subgroups of target customers who seek particular benefits from the product or service.

RAPID REVIEW   Answers

Short Answer

1. A company that practices segmentation has a _____ _____ for each subgroup that is a target. [See Section 3-1.]   *marketing mix*
2. By segmenting the market, a company is able to satisfy target customer _____ more fully. [See Section 3-1.]   *needs*
3. Marketers who practice segmentation seek out subgroups of target customers whose needs are _____ to those of other members of the same subgroup. [See Section 3-1.]   *similar*
4. A producer that does *not* segment produces goods for the _____ _____. [See Section 3-1.]   *mass market*
5. If there are too many subgroups to serve economically, a marketer may logically decide to combine subgroups into _____ ones. [See Section 3-1.]   *larger*
6. A firm should attempt to satisfy only those segments that it is _____ of serving. [See Section 3-1.]   *capable*
7. An advantage of segmentation to a company is that it may enjoy considerable customer _____. [See Section 3-2.]   *loyalty*
8. A possible disadvantage of segmentation is that some potential customers are not _____ _____. [See Section 3-2.]   *sought out*
9. A possible disadvantage of segmentation is that management may choose the wrong _____. [See Section 3-2.]   *segments*
10. Generally, segmentation is more _____ than not segmenting. [See Section 3-2.]   *costly*

11. A requirement of segmentation is that there must be subgroups of target customers who will _____ _____ to marketing programs. [See Section 3-3.]   *react similarly*

12. In order for segmentation to take place, the firm must be able to reach target subgroups through channels of distribution or _____. [See Section 3-3.]   *promotion*

13. A requirement for segmentation is that there be information available that will permit managers to _____ the subgroup to which each target customer belongs. [See Section 3-3.]   *identify*

14. The last requirement for segmentation is that it should be more _____ than a no-segmentation strategy. [See Section 3-3.]   *profitable*

15. A company should choose that kind of segmentation that best fulfills the segmentation _____. [See Section 3-4.]   *requirements*

16. Demographics consist of _____ facts about target customers. [See Section 3-4.]   *statistical*

17. The Polaris Company concentrates its snowmobile marketing effort on markets in the northern United States. This is an example of _____ segmentation. [See Section 3-4.]   *geographic*

18. Lifestyle segmentation requires creating subgroups based on _____ characteristics. [See Section 3-4.]   *psychological*

19. Volume segmentation is based on the extent to which target customers _____ the product or service. [See Section 3-4.]   *use*

20. Of the following, _____ is *not* a variable that management would consider if it were to select marketing attribute segmentation: price, place, promotion, production. [See Section 3-4.]   *production*

SOLVED PROBLEMS

PROBLEM 3-1 The owner of a newly constructed condominium complex is thinking about segmenting the market by setting aside some of the units for senior citizens. The owner wonders, however, if segmentation involves serving only one subgroup, or if two or more subgroups can be involved. How would you advise the owner?

Answer: Segmentation may involve serving only one subgroup with one program. Or it may have multiple programs, each one oriented to a different segment. The owner could market all of the units to senior citizens. This would minimize costs and would probably appeal to many seniors, who would feel that the entire complex was dedicated to their needs. Or a section of the units might be targeted to senior citizens and another section to some other subgroup, such as young couples with children. This strategy would allow the condominium management to appeal to a broader base of target customers, which could produce large sales. [See Section 3-1.]

PROBLEM 3-2 The manager of a pizza parlor has heard that market segmentation is a strategy that firms in the restaurant industry should consider. The manager knows that such a strategy requires aiming marketing programs at particular subgroups, but does not know what the characteristics of the subgroups should be. Can you help?

Answer: The subgroups of potential pizza customers should be homogeneous. This means that the target customers in each subgroup should have needs that are similar within that subgroup. Also these needs should differ from those of other subgroups. For example, the manager might aim at teenagers, who tend to be relatively homogeneous and different from other subgroups. Many of these consumers buy takeout pizzas and want many toppings. When eating in a restaurant, they prefer an atmosphere that is informal. Teenagers, then, can be a good target for segmentation in this industry. [See Section 3-1.]

PROBLEM 3-3 The same manager that was mentioned in Problem 3-2 has heard co-managers refer to a "mass market" strategy, but is unfamiliar with this term. How would you explain it?

Answer: A mass market strategy is aimed at the total market, rather than at a particular segment, such as teenagers. It is appropriate if most potential customers have similar needs and there are not homogeneous subgroups with differing needs from other subgroups. If all of the members of the population had about the same needs for pizza, it would be useful. Since this is not the case, mass market strategies are not common in this industry. [See Section 3-1.]

PROBLEM 3-4 Two marketing executives who are employed by a food processing company are involved in an argument. They have reviewed the results of a marketing research study which shows that the total market is made up of a large number of small subgroups, each of which is too small to justify the costs of creating a unique marketing mix for it. One executive argues that market segmentation would therefore be foolish. The second executive has responded that segmentation might be a useful course of action. How can the second executive justify this position?

Answer: The company executive could point out that two or more of the separate subgroups could be combined into segments that have reasonably similar needs. These resulting segments might be large enough to justify the costs of segmenting the food processing market. The firm's marketing research department might discover, for example, that both young adults and middle-aged consumers prefer frozen french fries that are low in saturated fats. Such a french fry could be produced and aimed at both subgroups, producing a large potential market. [See Section 3-1.]

PROBLEM 3-5 Assume that executives of the Le Cheapeau car rental company, which emphasizes low rental rates, have decided to aim a marketing program at high-income consumers who desire prestigious automobiles when they rent. What is the danger in such a strategy?

Answer: A firm should attempt to satisfy only those segments that it is capable of serving, rather than blindly trying to appeal to all. A car rental firm with a reputation for low prices, such as Le Cheapeau may be well-advised to stick to segments preferring low prices. To do otherwise might confuse members of the subgroup wanting competitive rates, and result in the loss of business of many in this segment.. [See Section 3-1.]

PROBLEM 3-6 Crispy Crackers saltines are aimed at the subgroup that desires few calories and low levels of saturated fat in crackers. (Many saltines contain lard—Crispy's crackers include unsaturated vegetable oil instead). Why might it be advantageous for the producer to appeal to this subgroup, rather than to the total market?

Answer: The company has designed a marketing mix that is attuned to the specific needs and desires of a specific subgroup. The probable result is considerable consumer satisfaction. Further, many Crispy Crackers consumers would be reluctant to shift to other brands—they are too brand-loyal. [See Section 3-2.]

PROBLEM 3-7 The owner of a plumbing and heating wholesale outlet is enthusiastic about segmenting the market as a means of increasing company revenues. The owner has heard, however, that segmentation can actually lead to smaller sales than a no-segmentation strategy, and has asked you to explain how this can happen. How would you respond?

Answer: It is true that segmentation, if misdirected, can result in fewer sales for the plumbing and heating market than a strategy of serving all potential customers. This market is made up of many different kinds of buyers, so the danger is genuine. Segmentation requires *not* seeking out some potential customers, so these individuals are not included in the target market. This decreases the total number of potential customers in the market. Also, segmentation can have a dampening effect on sales if the company selects the wrong segments. If the wholesaler focuses on fast-food restaurants, for example, and this segment does not grow, it can suffer decreased profits. [See Section 3-2.]

PROBLEM 3-8 Automobile manufacturers have discovered that segmenting the market, especially if the firm attempts to serve numerous segments, can be very costly. Why is this the case?

Answer: Segmentation often increases the costs of auto marketers. The strategy requires that management design a unique marketing mix for each target subgroup. This may require different styling, performance characteristics, options, advertising programs, pricing policies, and means of transport for the various segments. This is often much more expensive than developing only one marketing mix for the total market, although it may produce more sales and profits. [See Section 3-2.]

PROBLEM 3-9   The first step in segmentation is to find out if there are subgroups of potential customers who can be expected to react similarly to marketing programs and whose reaction can be expected to differ from those of other subgroups. A classmate has asked you to explain why this is the first step? Is it really that important? How would you answer?

Answer: The classmate should be informed that this is an extremely important step—one that should be taken before any others. If the subgroups do not meet the characteristics spelled out in this step, there is no point in even considering segmentation. Its main purpose is to carve out homogeneous groups from the total market and direct individualized marketing mixes to these groups. [See Section 3-3.]

PROBLEM 3-10   The marketing manager for a property and liability insurance company has decided to segment the market. The manager selects "insecure consumers" as the target subgroup because she believes that they are likely to be heavy purchasers of insurance. Do you think this is a good choice?

Answer: This segment is probably not a good choice. For segmentation to work, the company must be able to reach target property and liability insurance buyers through channels of distribution or through promotion. There are no insurance agencies or company offices that strictly serve the insecure insurance buyer. Similarly, there are no promotion media that specialize in this subgroup. As a result, the segment will be very difficult to reach. [See Section 3-3.]

PROBLEM 3-11   A manufacturer of household insecticides and repellents has decided to segment the market. Management has discovered that (1) there are several large subgroups with unique needs, (2) it is possible to reach these subgroups through promotion, and (3) members of the target subgroups can be identified. What remains before this manager should commit the firm to segmentation?

Answer: Before committing to segmentation, the manager should estimate if segmentation of the household insecticide market will result in higher profits than a no-segmentation strategy. Higher profits are really the acid test in making such decisions. The household insecticide market tends to differ considerably from one section of the country to another, so geographic segmentation may be profitable. Management may discover that mosquito repellent sells well in states such as Minnesota and South Carolina, roach killer sells well in Missouri, and that other major differences in product need by geographic area are in existence. [See Section 3-3.]

PROBLEM 3-12   A company that produces high-quality precision parts for machine tools is considering the possibilities of segmenting the market. A marketing research study reveals that the firm should be able to achieve $8 million in sales and incur $6 million in costs if it does not segment. On the other hand, sales are expected to be $12 million and costs $10 million if segmentation is pursued. Should the firm segment the market?

Answer: The precision parts manufacturer should not attempt a segmentation strategy. Such a strategy should be undertaken only if it will produce higher profits than a no-segmentation strategy. In this case, the company would only break even. It is possible, of course, that the precision parts market can be segmented in some way that is different from what management already has in mind. The resulting new segmentation plan may be profitable. [See Section 3-3.]

PROBLEM 3-13   Assume that you are the marketing manager of a newly formed company. The major product of the firm is to be "Starship" brand yachts, which are designed as very luxurious and prestigious products. What kind of segmentation are you likely to use?

Answer: Demographic segmentation is likely in this case. Specifically, the firm should aim at high-income consumers or those in occupations with high incomes and demands for status. Since yachts are expensive, only those in relatively high-income groupings are likely to be good customers. Likewise, high-income consumers are likely to have considerable desires for status symbols. [See Section 3-4.]

PROBLEM 3-14 Assume that you are a member of a management team charged with the responsibility of setting up a chain of high-fashion clothing stores for women. What kind of segmentation might you choose?

Answer: Geographic segmentation would be a good choice. The east and west coasts of the United States tend to be the areas in which sales of high-fashion items are most concentrated. Large cities in particular, such as New York and Los Angeles, are particularly good targets. In turn, each individual city has certain areas where high-fashion items sell well. [See Section 3-4.]

PROBLEM 3-15 The Classic Motor Carriages Company produces 'replicar' assemblies. Essentially, replicars are bodies of classic antique cars that can be mounted by the consumer onto existing auto frames to produce a vehicle that looks like a genuine classic. What kind of segmentation might be useful for this firm?

Answer: Lifestyle segmentation could be of value for this company. This type of segmentation identifies subgroups based on characteristics such as consumer attitudes, interests, opinions, and activities. The Classic Motor Carriages Company would probably appeal to affluent do-it-yourself consumers. [See Section 3-4.]

PROBLEM 3-16 In your opinion, would volume segmentation be useful in selling over-the-counter pain reliever?

Answer: It could be very useful. Some consumers, particularly those who have arthritis or suffer frequent headaches, are very heavy users. Others, such as those who use pain relievers to relieve muscle aches or infrequent headaches, are more moderate users. Still others are very light users or nonusers. These various groups would probably meet the four requirements of segmentation. [See Section 3-4.]

PROBLEM 3-17 Prince Matchabelli produces a "skin renewal" fluid. This company claims that, when placed on the skin, its product promotes cell renewal, encourages fresh cells to move to the skin surface, protects the skin, and postpones signs of aging. How might marketing attribute segmentation be used for this brand?

Answer: In this case, the firm might appeal to those who want a high-quality product. Those who seek a skin renewal fluid that will help provide a youthful appearance probably are not looking for the lowest priced product. Also, they are not likely to be induced to buy the product by sheer promotion effort or convenient location in retail outlets. It is the product itself that these individuals are concerned with, so marketing attribute segmentation emphasizing product quality may be the best alternative. [See Section 3-4.]

PROBLEM 3-18 Some supermarkets are described as "box" stores. They display products on racks and in cartons, are somewhat crowded with merchandise, and may require customers to price-mark and sack their own groceries. In what respect are these supermarkets pursuing marketing attribute segmentation?

Answer: These stores are appealing to consumers who desire low prices and are willing to forgo benefits from other marketing mix elements in order to obtain low prices. Their customers will accept few services, little in-store sales help, and inconvenient locations, in order to receive moderate prices. [See Section 3-4.]

PROBLEM 3-19 A classmate has read about benefit segmentation in a marketing journal article, but does not fully understand what it is. Can you help?

Answer: Benefit segmentation classifies target customers into subgroups that seek particular benefits from the product or service. It is interesting that the same offering can mean different things to different people. To some, toothpaste is a means of preventing cavities. To others, it is a way of avoiding bad breath. To still others, it is a way of preventing gum disease. Marketers of toothpastes and many other products have found this phenomenon to be a profitable means of segmentation. [See Section 3-4.]

4 CONSUMER DEMOGRAPHICS

THIS CHAPTER IS ABOUT

☑ **The Definition of a Market: Consumer and Industrial**
☑ **Population Demographics in the United States**
☑ **Income Demographics in the United States**
☑ **Consumer Expenditure Patterns in the United States**

4-1. The Definition of a Market: Consumer and Industrial

A. **A *market* is made up of individuals or organizations who have the ability and the desire to purchase a product or service.**

In order to fully understand this definition, we must look carefully at its parts.

1. Individuals or organizations

You would probably agree that the main component of a market is people. It is people who purchase and use the products and services that a firm produces and sells. Whether companies focus their efforts on *individual consumers* or on *organizations* (such as other companies and government agencies), they are always aiming at people. A market cannot be profitable if it doesn't have enough potential customers. The presence of large numbers of people in the New York metropolitan area partly explains why there are more (and bigger) markets for goods and services in New York City than there are in the state of Nevada. We can also explain why many marketers eagerly seek out consumers born in the post–World-War-II "baby boom," rather than those born in earlier years—there are more of them.

2. Ability to purchase

The mere existence of people as individuals or in organizations is not sufficient to make up a market. People must have the ability to purchase. This means that they must have sufficient incomes, savings, or borrowing ability to finance purchases. Some geographic areas are much better markets than others because of this factor.

EXAMPLE 4-1: Most of the major developers of enclosed malls have chosen locations in the suburbs of cities, rather than in downtown, inner-city areas. Middle- and upper-income consumers generally have moved to the suburbs, so the malls have followed. While inner-city areas have large numbers of residents, they do not have many medium- and high-income families. This being the case, they do not provide markets for many retailers.

---

3. Desire to purchase

Markets must contain individuals or organizations that have a desire to obtain and use the product or service. For example, automobile dealers would not profit by attempting to sell used cars to the wealthy; nor would consumers in south Florida make up a good market for snowmobiles. On the other hand, teen-agers are excellent markets for movies and blemish removers, and Minnesota is a good market for mosquito repellents.

Sometimes marketers can create desires for goods and services through advertising and other forms of promotion. In most cases, however, it is more effective to identify and locate consumers who already have a desire for the product or service and to create benefits that will satisfy this desire.

B. Markets are either *consumer* or *industrial* in nature.

1. Consumer market

Consumer markets are made up of those who buy goods and services for personal use and the satisfaction of personal desires. The markets for headache remedies, garden furniture, microwave dinners, catcher's mitts, household cleansers, and recreation vehicles are examples of the consumer variety. These items are purchased for their own sake, and not for a business-related use.

2. Industrial market

Industrial markets are made up of those who buy to satisfy the requirements of an organization, rather than for personal use. When industrial goods markets consist of nonbusiness organizations, they are sometimes called **institutional markets**. The markets for large computer systems, over-the-road truck tractors and trailors, uranium, office supplies, and management consulting services are industrial or institutional in nature.

note: In a few cases, goods and services have both consumer and industrial markets. For example, personal computers are purchased by many businesses as well as by consumers, as are automobiles, building materials, and the services of attorneys.

4-2. Population Demographics in the United States

A. Marketers use population demographics to seek out the first component of a consumer market—*individuals*.

Since the first component of a consumer market is individuals, businesses that are searching for consumer markets often begin by looking at population figures. These figures do more than just measure the number of individuals who live in a particular place at a given time. They indicate patterns and trends that are useful to marketers, such as overall population patterns, geographic patterns, urban/rural makeup, and age distribution.

B. Increases in total population result in advances in the consumption of goods and services.

Figure 4-1 presents United States population figures from 1900 to 1985. As you can see, the overall pattern is one of growth. However, the rate of increase has declined since 1960, as people are marrying at later ages and having smaller numbers of children. Still, the overall level is expected to reach nearly 270 million by the year 2000.

Changes in population have a considerable impact on marketers. Patterns of leveling off may be reflected by slower growth in the consumption of many goods—especially staples such as bread, because most consumers use staples. With the decline in the size of the average family, the demand for products such as large homes and station wagons drops. But slower growth rates and declines in population may not necessarily lead to lower consumption. Smaller families mean more income per family member, which may increase the demand for high-quality, expensive items. Further, as many young people delay marriage, they have more income left after expenses to buy luxury items.

EXAMPLE 4-2: The Bishop Construction Company of St. Louis, Missouri, was heavily involved in producing large three- and four-bedroom homes in the 1960's. In the 1970's and 1980's, however, smaller families increased the demand for one- and two-bedroom homes and condominiums. Bishop moved into this market and now specializes in smaller homes, condominiums, and duplexes.

C. Geographic patterns of population present differing opportunities for marketers.

Different areas of the country vary considerably in their population levels. Table 4-1 shows the rank order of the major regions in the United States in 1980. Within the regions there are large population

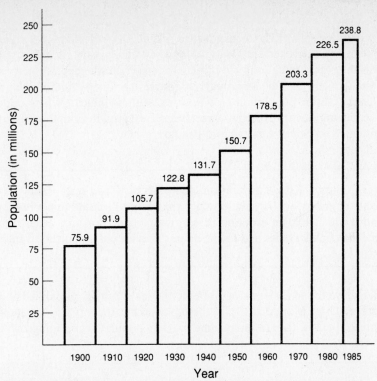

FIGURE 4-1: Total population of the United States, 1900–1985. (Source: U.S. Bureau of the Census, *Census of Population*, 1970, Vol. 1; and *Census of Population*, 1980, Vol. 1, chapter A.)

TABLE 4-1: Rank Order of the Major Regions of the United States in 1980

Region	States Included in Region	Population
East-North-Central	Ohio, Indiana, Illinois, Michigan, Wisconsin	41,682,000
South Atlantic	Delaware, Maryland, Washington, D.C., Virginia, West Virginia, North Carolina, South Carolina, Georgia, Florida	36,959,000
Mid-Atlantic	New York, New Jersey, Pennsylvania	36,787,000
Pacific	Washington, Oregon, California, Alaska, Hawaii	31,800,000
West-South-Central	Arkansas, Louisiana, Oklahoma, Texas	23,747,000
West-North-Central	Minnesota, Iowa, Missouri, North Dakota, South Dakota, Nebraska, Kansas	17,183,000
East-South-Central	Kentucky, Tennessee, Alabama, Mississippi	14,666,000
New England	Maine, New Hampshire, Vermont, Massachusetts, Rhode Island, Connecticut	12,348,000
Mountain	Montana, Idaho, Wyoming, Colorado, New Mexico, Arizona, Utah, Nevada	11,373,000

Source: U.S. Bureau of the Census, *Current Population Reports* (Vol. 12, No. 4; April 1984), p. 49.

variations. Some states, such as California, New York, and Pennsylvania, have large proportions of the total population. Others, such as Delaware and Wyoming, have a small proportion.

Regions with large populations are targets for many marketers. Numerous manufacturers, wholesalers, and retailers aim for these areas. Of course, marketers should look not only at current but also at *expected* future population growth rates, as these indicate where opportunities will be tomorrow. The regions that are expected to see the greatest growth from the present to the year 2000 are the Mountain, West-South-Central, and Pacific regions.

EXAMPLE 4-3: The Burger King Corporation locates its fast-food restaurants only in cities whose population is 50,000 or more—or in smaller cities that bring in large numbers of visitors (such as Durango, Colorado, which has an economy based mainly on tourism). This company has found through experience that smaller cities and towns do not provide enough profit to fulfill management's goals.

Some marketers have found that seeking out only the more heavily populated and fastest growing areas is a mistake. There is opportunity in these places, but there is also substantial competition. Marketing potential exists, then, even in some sparsely populated and nongrowth areas.

EXAMPLE 4-4: Days Inn motels are concentrated primarily in the southeastern sections of the United States, many of which are not heavily populated. This chain has found the competition to be less severe in these areas and profits to be substantial. This is one of the fastest growing motel chains in the country.

D. The major consumer markets have shifted to the cities as the population of the United States has become increasingly urban.

There has been a strong movement of population from rural to urban areas in the United States. Figure 4-2 illustrates this change. The percentage of the population residing in cities has advanced to the point where nearly three-fourths of the total is in this category. Thus, the main target for marketers is definitely in the cities. This makes it easier for marketers to reach consumers through retailers and promotion. For example, retailers such as K-Mart and Wal-Mart, who have large facilities available to serve consumers benefit from locating in urban areas.

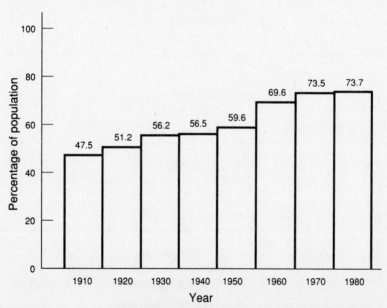

FIGURE 4-2: Percentage of the U.S. population residing in urban areas, 1910–1980. (Source: U.S. Bureau of the Census, *Census of Population*, 1970, Vol. 1; and *Census of Population*, 1980, Vol. 1.)

EXAMPLE 4-5: Limon, Nebraska, was once a financially healthy small town that included several dozen retailers. These retailers were dependent on the surrounding farm community, which provided most of their customers. Beginning in the 1960's, however, the farm population declined, as numerous families moved to cities. Today, Limon has only a few retailers and the town is economically depressed.

E. The age distribution of the population has shown a change in the age makeup of the consumer market.

Each age grouping in the population tends to purchase certain goods and services and to behave distinctively in other ways. So the proportion of the population in various age groups is important to marketers, especially those who segment markets on the basis of age.

Current population trends will have an impact on many marketers. For example, the percentage of children in the population has declined, reducing markets for items such as disposable diapers and baby food. At the other end of the scale, the number of persons aged 65 and older is growing rapidly, increasing markets for products such as gardening equipment and certain medical products. The *baby boom generation* (persons born shortly after World War II) is very large and is now in the 35–45 age grouping, providing a strong market for offerings such as homes and family restaurants.

EXAMPLE 4-6: Clairol is the producer of "Loving Care" mousse. Its purpose is to color and mousse gray hair. The company targets women aged 45 and older with its marketing effort. This segment is growing rapidly, providing Clairol with good growth opportunities.

4-3. Income Demographics in the United States

A. Marketers use income demographics to determine the second component of a consumer market—the ability to purchase.

Since the second component of a consumer market is income, businesses that are searching for consumer markets look at income figures. Individuals earn income in the form of wages, salaries, profits from business, interest, dividends, rents, Social Security, pension benefits, and charitable receipts.

B. Increases in income present opportunities for marketers, while declines present problems.

During times when incomes are low, as in the recession years of the late 1970's and early 1980's, consumers reduce their expenditures, especially for luxury goods and services. The opposite occurs when incomes increase.

EXAMPLE 4-7: During the recession years of the late 1970's, the Ford Motor Company saw its sales and profits decline to dangerously low levels. Large automobiles and optional equipment for all sizes of automobiles were particularly hard to sell, as many consumers postponed buying new cars until their incomes increased. A large percentage of those who purchased automobiles acquired inexpensive imports or used models.

C. Some regions have higher total and per capita personal incomes than others, making them more attractive markets.

Table 4-2 presents total and per capita personal income figures for 1973 and 1983, and estimates for 1990 and 2000. The data are in constant dollars; that is, they have been adjusted so that they do not show the effects of inflation.

Personal income consists of the earnings of individuals before taxes. The total personal income historical figures and estimates show a steady pattern of increase over the time periods covered. Certain regions are associated with larger total personal income levels than others. These are the

TABLE 4-2: Total Personal Income and Per Capita Personal Income of the United States and Major Regions, 1973 and 1983, and Estimates for 1990 and 2000

Regions	Total Personal Income (in billions)				Per Capita Personal Income			
	1973	1983	1990	2000	1973	1983	1990	2000
United States, Total	$1,001.8	$1,280.2	$1,603.3	$1,970.9	$4740	$5470	$6434	$7369
New England	60.7	76.2	95.5	119.0	4998	6099	7108	8073
Mid-Atlantic	193.4	220.4	263.9	310.4	5168	5956	6898	7847
East-North-Central	203.7	224.1	272.3	317.5	4975	5403	6462	7402
West-North-Central	81.3	92.3	114.7	138.4	4888	5303	6322	7262
South Atlantic	147.0	202.1	259.0	326.7	4437	5203	6102	7010
East-South-Central	49.5	64.2	80.2	98.4	3681	4299	5202	6143
West-South-Central	83.0	134.1	172.2	217.3	4038	5185	6160	7108
Mountain	41.4	63.0	85.6	115.6	4441	5100	6045	6971
Pacific	141.8	203.8	259.9	327.7	5100	6057	6978	7906

Source: Bureau of Economic Analysis, *Survey of Current Business*, May 1986.

East-North-Central, Mid-Atlantic, South Atlantic, and Pacific regions. The regions with the fastest rate of growth in total personal income are the West-South-Central, Mountain, and South Atlantic regions. These are targets for marketing opportunity.

EXAMPLE 4-8: Taco Bell (owned by Pepsico) once confined its fast-food restaurants to the southwestern portion of the United States. Beginning in the mid-1980's, however, the chain began moving into numerous other fast-growing sections of the country, including the Mid-Atlantic and South Atlantic regions. This expansion turned out to be profitable, as the sales per store were larger in the new regions than in the Southwest.

Table 4-2 also shows *per capita* (per person) *personal income* figures for 1973 and 1983, and estimates for 1990 and 2000. Steady increases are evident over the years. Certain regions have higher per capita incomes than others. These regions are the Pacific and the Mid-Atlantic, which are therefore especially attractive to marketers of high-priced goods such as swimming pools and expensive jewelry.

4-4. Consumer Expenditure Patterns in the United States

A. Marketers use consumer expenditures to determine the third component of a consumer market—the desire to purchase.

A useful indicator of the desire to purchase is the *expenditures* by consumers for various goods and services. These expenditures indicate spending patterns that are important to marketers. Table 4-3 sets forth total yearly expenditures of United States consumers in current and constant dollars, from 1970 to 1984 (constant dollars have been adjusted to show the effects of inflation). The table provides a wealth of information on consumer spending patterns.

B. Consumer expenditures on services have increased over the years.

Notice in Table 4-3 that expenditures are broken down into *durable goods*, (those that are long lasting), *nondurable goods*, and *services*. The third category has grown very rapidly and is expected to rise still further as consumers spend more on travel, medical care, home repair, entertainment, legal advice, personal grooming, physical fitness, library service, investment counseling, and other services.

TABLE 4-3: Personal Consumption Expenditures, in Current and Constant (1972) Dollars by Major Type of Product: 1970 to 1984

In billions of dollars. Represents market value of goods and services purchased by individuals and nonprofit institutions, and value of food, clothing, housing, and financial services received by them as income in kind.

Type of product	1970	1975	1977	1978	1979	1980	1981	1982	1983	1984
Total, current dollars	621.7	976.4	1,204.4	1,346.5	1,507.2	1,668.1	1,849.1	1,964.9	2,155.9	2,341.8
Durable goods[1]	85.2	132.2	176.2	200.2	213.4	214.7	235.4	245.1	279.8	318.8
Motor vehicles and parts	36.2	55.8	84.8	95.7	96.6	90.7	101.9	108.7	129.3	149.8
Furniture and household equipment	36.2	53.5	65.7	72.8	81.8	86.3	92.3	94.4	104.1	117.0
Nondurable goods[1] ...	265.7	407.3	478.8	526.2	600.0	668.8	730.7	757.5	801.7	856.9
Food, beverages,[2] tobacco	149.7	228.5	266.4	293.9	330.8	365.8	396.9	417.8	444.8	474.4
Food, excl alcoholic beverages	119.6	185.2	217.4	240.9	272.2	301.2	326.4	343.5	365.1	390.2
Alcoholic beverages	19.2	28.4	32.5	34.9	39.3	43.9	47.4	49.3	51.4	53.4
Tobacco products ..	10.8	14.8	16.6	18.0	19.3	20.6	23.0	25.0	28.3	30.8
Clothing, accessories, jewelry[1]	55.8	81.6	96.8	108.2	116.3	124.2	135.5	140.3	150.0	165.5
Clothing, accessories (except footwear)	39.0	58.8	69.5	77.6	82.7	87.1	95.8	99.3	106.4	118.0
Women's and children's	25.2	38.2	45.2	50.7	54.1	56.9	62.8	65.4	70.6	78.8
Men's and boys' ...	13.8	20.6	24.3	26.9	28.7	30.1	33.0	33.9	35.9	39.2
Shoes and other footwear	7.6	10.7	13.1	14.7	16.3	17.4	18.4	19.4	20.5	22.1
Jewelry and watches	3.9	6.4	7.8	8.8	9.5	11.1	12.2	12.0	12.8	14.2
Cleaning, storage, and repair of shoes and clothes	4.2	4.3	4.7	5.2	5.6	6.1	6.5	6.8	7.3	8.0
Gasoline and oil.......	22.4	40.4	48.1	51.2	66.6	84.8	94.6	90.4	90.0	91.4
Services[1]	270.8	437.0	547.4	618.0	693.7	784.5	883.0	962.2	1,074.4	1,166.2
Housing	93.9	149.8	185.9	209.6	236.1	266.2	302.0	333.8	363.3	397.9
Household operation................	37.7	63.3	61.1	90.1	99.3	113.0	127.5	143.4	153.6	164.0
Transportation........	22.0	33.2	46.4	51.2	56.3	61.1	65.0	68.2	72.5	78.3
Total, constant (1972) dollars........	672.1	778.4	964.3	803.2	927.6	931.8	950.5	983.3	1,009.2	1,062.4
Durable goods[1]	89.1	112.7	138.0	146.6	147.2	137.5	140.9	140.5	157.5	178.1
Motor vehicles and parts........................	38.2	47.5	63.5	66.9	62.6	54.4	56.3	57.0	66.6	75.8
Furniture and household equipment	36.1	45.9	52.9	56.5	60.4	60.2	61.1	60.3	65.9	74.8
Nondurable goods	283.7	307.5	333.4	344.4	353.1	355.6	360.8	363.1	376.3	393.6
Gasoline and oil........	22.9	25.6	27.7	28.3	27.4	25.1	25.1	25.3	26.1	26.1
Services[1]	299.3	359.3	393.0	412.0	427.3	438.8	448.8	459.8	475.4	490.8
Housing	102.0	128.3	141.3	148.5	154.8	159.8	164.8	167.5	171.3	177.7
Household operation................	42.3	49.9	55.1	57.8	60.1	62.3	62.7	63.5	64.1	64.8
Transportation........	25.2	29.6	32.7	34.0	35.0	33.2	32.0	31.6	31.7	32.7

Source: U.S. Bureau of Economic Analysis, *The National Income and Product Accounts of the United States 1929-79*; and *Survey of Current Business*, July Issue.

EXAMPLE 4-9: Physical fitness centers have blossomed in the 1980's. These centers range from small, locally owned gyms to large chains such as Nautilus. Some have even set up operations in airport terminals for travelers wanting a break from the tedium of waiting for flights. These centers emphasize weight training, stationary exercise, aerobic dancing, swimming, racquetball, and related activities. The future of these centers appears to be bright, as increasing numbers of consumers seek higher levels of fitness.

C. Consumer expenditures on specific major categories of goods and services provide guidelines for marketers as to which products to sell.

Table 4-3 provides a breakdown of consumer expenditures on various major categories of goods and services. These assist marketers in identifying product classes that might be considered as company offerings. Also, information on changes in expenditures over time point out product classes that should receive more or less marketing emphasis.

As you can see from the table, the largest expenditure classes are for foods, beverages, and tobacco; housing; household operations; and motor vehicles and parts. These account for approximately two-thirds of the total. Some major trends are apparent. The categories of clothing and accessories, motor vehicles and parts, furniture and household equipment, and household operation have grown faster than other categories. On the other hand, food and alcoholic beverages and cleaning, storage, and repair of shoes and clothes have not risen as rapidly as the other categories. Marketers who currently rely on such slow-growing sectors for important shares of their profits may wish to shift their efforts to other product classes.

D. Companies should look for changes in consumer expenditures in the particular market segments that they serve.

This necessitates obtaining data on consumer expenditures that are classified by variables such as income, area of residence, age, and occupation. The data are available in such sources as publications of the U.S. Bureau of the Census. However, many marketers require more refined data than these sources provide, and therefore turn to marketing research studies.

EXAMPLE 4-10: Marketing research conducted in 1986 showed that cigar sales to the younger generation (ages 18 to 34) segment were increasing over time. Also, sales of cigars to those over age 65 were large and growing. Conversely, expenditures by individuals aged 35–64 had stabilized, and even gone down slightly. To the producers of Swisher Sweets and Dutch Treats, this signaled a need to focus their efforts on the younger and the older generations, and to de-emphasize their efforts aimed at the middle-aged group.

Many companies study market segment expenditures that are broken down by the stages in the family life cycle. This is a useful method for locating potentially profitable markets. The stages in the life cycle are based on age, marital status, and number of children. The stages are

- Young single adult
- Young single parent
- Young married adult
- Young married parent
- Mature single adult
- Mature single parent
- Mature married adult
- Mature married parent
- Older single adult
- Older married adult
- Other

The importance of family life cycle stages is that each stage indicates particular expenditure patterns. For example, young single adults spend considerable funds on such products and services as movies, audio tapes, and clothing. Mature married parents, on the other hand, are heavy spenders on such items as college tuition for children, furniture for the home, and dining out. Older married adults spend considerable amounts on medicine, travel, and reading materials. A careful study of the family life cycle can point out numerous opportunities for marketers who seek profitable consumer targets.

RAISE YOUR GRADES

Can you explain . . . ?

☑ why a certain group of people makes up the market for credit cards

☑ why buyers of airplanes make up a mostly industrial, rather than consumer market

☑ why the producers of bread are interested in population growth trends in the United States

☑ why many retailers are attracted to the more populated regions of the United States

☑ why many companies change the makeup of their product offerings because of changes in the environment

☑ why the profits of many producers fell during the late 1970's and early 1980's

☑ why major companies often produce a wide variety of products, rather than limiting their offerings to those consumers who might fall into one restricted group

SUMMARY

1. A market is made up of individuals or organizations who have the ability and the desire to purchase a product or service.
2. Consumer markets are made up of those who buy goods and services for personal use and the satisfaction of personal desires. Industrial markets are made up of those who buy to satisfy the requirements of an organization.
3. Increases in total population result in advances in the consumption of goods and services. The overall pattern in the United States has been one of growth, but the rate of increase has slowed recently.
4. There are nine major population regions in the United States, ranging from the large East-North-Central to the less populated Mountain area. These vary considerably in their population levels, presenting differing opportunities for marketers.
5. The population of the United States has become increasingly urban in the years since 1910. The major market for most marketers is definitely in the cities.
6. The age distribution of the population has changed. Markets for babies and young children have declined, while those for persons in the early-middle and senior-citizen age groups have advanced.
7. Increases in income present opportunities for marketers, while declines present problems. Some regions have higher total and per capita personal incomes than others, making them more attractive markets.
8. Consumer desires can be measured by consumer expenditure patterns. In recent years consumers have spent increasing amounts for services, and their preferences for various classes of goods has shifted, providing guidelines to marketers as to which products to sell.

RAPID REVIEW   Answers

Multiple Choice

1. Which of the following is *not* a component of a market? (**a**) individuals or organizations, (**b**) ability to purchase, (**c**) desire to purchase, (**d**) occupation of the purchaser. [See Section 4-1.]   *d*

2. Those who buy goods and services for personal use and the satisfaction of personal desires make up a(n) (**a**) target market, (**b**) consumer market, (**c**) buyer market, (**d**) industrial market. [See Section 4-1.]   *b*

3. Those who buy to satisfy the requirements of an organization, rather than for personal use, make up a(n) (**a**) target market, (**b**) consumer market, (**c**) buyer market, (**d**) industrial market. [See Section 4-1.]   *d*

4. Population figures refer to the number of individuals who _____   *d*
   in a particular place at a given time. (**a**) work, (**b**) purchase, (**c**) vote, (**d**) live.
   [See Section 4-2.]

5. The rate of increase in the population of the United States has   *b*
   _____ since 1960. (**a**) gone up, (**b**) gone down, (**c**) stayed the
   same, (**d**) changed into a rate of decrease. [See Section 4-2.]

6. When population levels off, there may be less growth in the consumption of   *a*
   many goods, especially (**a**) staples, such as bread, (**b**) buying items, such as
   fur coats, (**c**) expensive items, such as boats, (**d**) moderately priced items,
   such as books. [See Section 4-2.]

7. Smaller family sizes in the United States may increase the demand for   *c*
   (**a**) Ford station wagons, (**b**) large homes, (**c**) expensive items such as satellite disks for T.V. reception, (**d**) childrens' toys. [See Section 4-2.]

8. Those regions within the United States that are expected to see the greatest   *b*
   growth in population from the present to the year 2000 include the (**a**) New
   England region, (**b**) Mountain region, (**c**) Mid-Atlantic region, (**d**) South-
   Atlantic region. [See Section 4-2.]

9. Some companies locate in areas that do not have large and fast-growing   *a*
   populations because (**a**) competition is not strong in these regions, (**b**) business is steady, though not growing, (**c**) they can acquire a lot of local support,
   (**d**) they cannot afford the cost of operating in fast-growing areas. [See
   Section 4-2.]

10. Approximately _____ of the United States population lives in   *d*
    urban areas. (**a**) one-third, (**b**) one-half, (**c**) two-thirds, (**d**) three-fourths. [See
    Section 4-2.]

11. Based on current population trends in age groups, one would expect to find   *d*
    increased demand for (**a**) Gerber's baby food, (**b**) Schwin bicycles, (**c**) Schlitz
    beer, (**d**) Polident denture cleaner. [See Section 4-2.]

12. During times when incomes are low, consumers reduce their expenditures,   *a*
    especially for (**a**) expensive goods, such as Tiffany's fur coats, (**b**) staples,
    such as bread, (**c**) small economy cars, (**d**) housing. [See Section 4-3.]

13. Income data that are given in constant dollars do *not* show the effects of   *a*
    (**a**) inflation, (**b**) productivity, (**c**) earnings, (**d**) changes in production levels.
    [See Section 4-3.]

14. One of the regions with the highest per capita income figures is the   *b*
    (**a**) East-South-Central, (**b**) Pacific, (**c**) Mountain, (**d**) West-South-Central.
    [See Section 4-3.]

15. Expenditures by consumers are a useful indicator of (**a**) how much income   *c*
    people have, (**b**) the ability to purchase, (**c**) the desire to purchase,
    (**d**) per capita income. [See Section 4-4.]

16. The category of expenditures that has grown more rapidly than the others   *d*
    is (**a**) durable goods, (**b**) semi-durable goods, (**c**) nondurable goods, (**d**) ser-
    vices. [See Section 4-4.]

17. Consumer expenditures on major categories of goods and services assist   *c*
    marketers in locating _____ that might be considered for
    company offerings. (**a**) market segments, (**b**) new consumers, (**c**) product
    classes, (**d**) durable goods. [See Section 4-4.]

18. Consumers in the United States spend the largest proportion of their in-   *a*
    comes on (**a**) food, beverages, and tobacco, (**b**) clothing, (**c**) transportation,
    (**d**) furniture and household equipment. [See Section 4-4.]

19. The category of expenditures that has grown faster than other categories   *c*
    in the United States is (**a**) food and alcoholic beverages, (**b**) cleaning,
    storage, and repair of shoes and clothes, (**c**) clothing and accessories,
    (**d**) jewelry and watches. [See Section 4-4.]

20. Marketers who cannot find published studies on consumer expenditures in   *d*
    the segments they seek may need to make use of (**a**) government figures,
    (**b**) experience, (**c**) knowledgeable guesses, (**d**) marketing research. [See Sec-
    tion 4-4.]

SOLVED PROBLEMS

PROBLEM 4-1   A classmate has defined a market as a place where people go to buy goods, such as a Safeway supermarket. Would you accept this as a full definition?

Answer: The classmate's definition falls short. A market is made up of individuals or organizations who have the ability and the desire to purchase a product or service. Thus, there is a market for IBM computers, made up of households, businesses, and nonbusiness organizations, both in the United States and overseas. In marketing terms, a market is not just a place, such as a supermarket. [See Section 4-1.]

PROBLEM 4-2   You probably would classify the market for Maytag washers as consumer, not industrial, in nature. Why is this the case?

Answer: Maytag washers have a market made up of those who buy goods and services for personal use and the satisfaction of personal desires—households that need washers to clean their clothing. The markets for industrial goods, however, consist of those who wish to satisfy the requirements of an organization. This means that there is a second market—an industrial market—for these goods, made up of laundromat owners. This being the case, the product is a consumer good for most buyers, but an industrial good for a smaller number. [See Section 4-1.]

PROBLEM 4-3   Assume that you are the marketing manager for a company that makes chewing gum. The company president realizes that population growth is beneficial to sales of your brand, but wonders what levels of increase or decrease can be expected from now to the year 2000. How would you advise the president?

Answer: Based on current population figures, the population can be expected to increase from the present to the year 2000. The rate of increase probably will decline over past levels, however, leading to smaller percentages of increases in chewing gum sales. Based on this analysis, the company would be well-advised to take steps, such as product improvement and increased advertising, to induce individual consumers to chew more gum. [See Section 4-2.]

PROBLEM 4-4   A magazine article raises the point that declines in population rates have hurt luxury goods marketers, such as Rolls Royce automobiles, more than staples, such as Morton's salt. How would you respond to this point?

Answer: The magazine article is wrong. Declines in population rates have their greatest impact on marketers of staples, such as Morton's Salt, Wonder Bread, and Carnation Evaporated Milk. Most consumers use staples, so the demand for staples depends heavily on population. Only a small number of consumers buy luxury goods, and many of these consumers have relatively high incomes. Producers such as Rolls Royce study the numbers of high-income consumers, not total population. [See Section 4-2.]

PROBLEM 4-5   The average size of the family is declining. How might this affect the demand for various kinds of automobiles?

Answer: Demand for vehicles with a large carrying capacity, such as station wagons and large sedans, probably will go down as consumers have less need for space to carry numerous individuals and their goods. Smaller families, however, mean more income per family member, and this may increase the demand for high-quality expensive cars, such as sports cars. It also may mean that consumers will buy more high-priced options, such as power windows and air conditioning. [See Section 4-2.]

PROBLEM 4-6   Assume that you and several partners are setting up a convenience store chain. You have decided to locate the stores in regions with high population levels, as these are expected to produce the greatest revenues. What three regions would you select for store sites?

Answer: Based on geographic patterns of population, the three prime locations would be in the East-North-Central, South Atlantic, and Mid-Atlantic regions. The convenience store chain would be in a position to serve very large numbers of individuals from locations in these areas. The managers should be on the alert for changes in population levels, however. If large numbers of consumers move from these three regions to others, sales of the chain could be hurt. [See Section 4-2.]

PROBLEM 4-7   A major grocery chain has numerous stores in regions of the United States where the population is the greatest. Based on current population trends, would you encourage this chain to locate stores in other regions?

Answer: The chain may want to consider some alternative fast-growing locations. The regions that are growing the most rapidly are the Mountain, West-South-Central, and the Pacific regions, though none of these is at the top of the list of major populated regions. Rates of growth in the fast-growing areas, such as the Mountain area, have slowed in recent years because fewer new jobs are opening up there. The grocery chain's managers should carefully study such trends. [See Section 4-2.]

PROBLEM 4-8   A classmate has asked you if the major trend in population is from urban to rural areas. "After all, most people are tired of the city, traffic congestion, crime, and air pollution, and many are moving to the country." How would you respond?

Answer: The classmate is incorrect. The trend is definitely from rural to urban areas. Since 1910, when the percentage of the population living in urban areas was less than 50 percent, the rural-to-urban pattern has continued to the point where three-fourths of the population now lives in urban areas. This means that marketers' major targets—individuals and organizations—are mainly concentrated in certain restricted areas, and that they are easier to reach through promotion and distribution. [See Section 4-3.]

PROBLEM 4-9   Based on current population trends, what is the potential market for travel agency tours of U.S. and foreign historic sites for senior citizens?

Answer: The market is very good. Currently, there are high numbers of individuals in the senior-citizen age group. Further, this segment of the market is growing rapidly, as citizens of the United States enjoy longer lives. [See Section 4-2.]

PROBLEM 4-10   Some economists predict continued growth in the total income of the United States over the next two decades. What would be the implication of such growth for Domino's pizza?

Answer: Growth in income would be very favorable to Domino's pizza. All companies benefit under such conditions. However, the producers of products that are not necessities, such as Domino's pizza, benefit even more than producers of necessity goods. When consumers' incomes rise, they are willing to buy more and pay more for goods and services that they do not absolutely need. [See Section 4-3.]

PROBLEM 4-11   Assume that you are thinking of opening a chain of high-fashion clothing stores that would appeal primarily to upper-income consumers. A friend has cautioned you, however, warning that income levels are declining as more and more families drift into poverty. How would you react to your friend's warning?

Answer: Essentially your friend is wrong. Total and per capita personal income levels in the United States have been increasing at a good rate. Further, the estimates for the future suggest that this pattern will continue. The number of high-income consumers should continue to grow at a fast rate, producing opportunities for the high-fashion clothing stores. [See Section 4-3.]

PROBLEM 4-12   A hot tub manufacturer is interested in setting up sales offices in various regions of the country to sell hot tubs to consumers. Management has completed a research study which shows that the company's products sell best in areas where family incomes are high. What regions in the United States would you recommend for sales office sites?

Answer: The best regions in the United States, based upon level of family income, are the New England, Pacific, Mid-Atlantic, and East-North-Central regions. These have the highest per capita income figures. The hot tub producer should carefully study past sales in these areas, however, to make sure that the product actually sells in greater volume there than in areas where family income is less. [See Section 4-3.]

PROBLEM 4-13 According to an article in the *Wall Street Journal*, the United States has become a "service economy" with the passage of time. In what respect is this the case?

Answer: To a large extent the United States *has* become a service economy. Consumer expenditures for services are growing much faster than those for durable and nondurable goods, as individuals spend more for insurance, home repairs, doctors and dentists, financial advising, personal grooming, air transportation, and other services. This is a strong trend and should continue into the future. [See Section 4-4.]

PROBLEM 4-14 Assume that you are employed by a national operator of vending machines—one with machines in all of the individual states. How would you use data on expenditures by consumers in determining marketing strategy?

Answer: Current data on consumer expenditures indicate which items are in demand and which ones are not selling well. This would suggest to your vending machine firm what items to stock and sell in the machines. For example, based on current expenditure data, you might stock fewer tobacco items and more health-food items (such as fruit and vegetable juices) in the vending machines. These patterns might vary by geographic region of course—tobacco products sell more in the South Atlantic than in the Pacific region. [See Section 4-4.]

PROBLEM 4-15 What are the implications of the expenditure data presented in Table 4-2 for operators of dry-cleaning establishments?

Answer: The implications are negative. Expenditures for the cleaning, storage, and repair of shoes and clothing are down. This is logical, as consumers are purchasing permanent press clothing and other fabrics that do not require dry cleaning. This change has been a factor in many dry cleaners' decisions to shift part of their operations from the cleaning of clothing to the cleaning of carpets, rugs, and drapes. It also has forced some dry cleaners to go out of business. [See Section 4-4.]

5 ANALYZING CONSUMER BEHAVIOR

THIS CHAPTER IS ABOUT

- ☑ **The Importance of Understanding Consumer Behavior**
- ☑ **Theories of Consumer Behavior**
- ☑ **Major Trends in Consumer Behavior**

5-1. The Importance of Understanding Consumer Behavior

- **Consumer behavior** consists of the process by which individuals decide whether, what, when, how, where, and from whom to buy goods and services.

Recall the importance of the marketing concept—the satisfaction of potential customer needs and desires at a profit. To achieve this goal—that is, to develop an effective marketing mix—sellers of consumer goods must learn to understand consumer needs, attitudes, habits, and motives.

EXAMPLE 5-1: Foster Grant has gathered considerable information about the marketing of sunglasses. Most individuals buy this product either for protection from the sun or to improve their physical appearance. Foster Grant appeals mainly to the latter market, and places heavy emphasis on style. The firm conducts little advertising, believing that those who want sunglasses for appearance's sake will 'impulse-buy' these items after seeing themselves in store display mirrors.

Successful marketers must not only be knowledgeable about what target consumers want, they must also be able to predict changes in these wants over time. Consumer behavior changes constantly, and companies that do not adjust to these ever-altering desires can easily lose their competitive advantage.

EXAMPLE 5-2: In the 1970's, many producers of recreation vehicles (RV's) oriented their marketing mixes to blue-collar union members who earned high wages. In the 1980's, this was no longer an effective strategy, as individuals in this segment stopped buying RV's. Winnebago managers were aware of the changes in the market and shifted their focus to persons aged 35–54 who had been exposed to the outdoors and were family-oriented. The firm introduced its LeSharo and Itasca Phasar lines, which got up to 22 miles per gallon and sold for $23,000 (the industry average price was $48,800). The new lines were very profitable.

- Most consumers follow a more or less logical problem-solving process when making purchase decisions.

First, consumers recognize a problem of some kind, such as "I'm hungry" or "the car is not running well." If the problem is not great or if they have been faced with this decision many times in the past, they may simply act *habitually* and purchase the same item that they've always purchased. For example, most consumers choose to buy the same candy bar that has given them satisfaction in the past. But if a purchase is a major or nonroutine one, consumers may engage in an *information search*; e.g., they may read ads, ask questions of friends, and/or talk with salespeople. After acquiring information, they make a decision to purchase or not. And, if they do buy an item, they *evaluate* it after the purchase to determine if it was a good decision. Figure 5-1 illustrates this basic decision-making process.

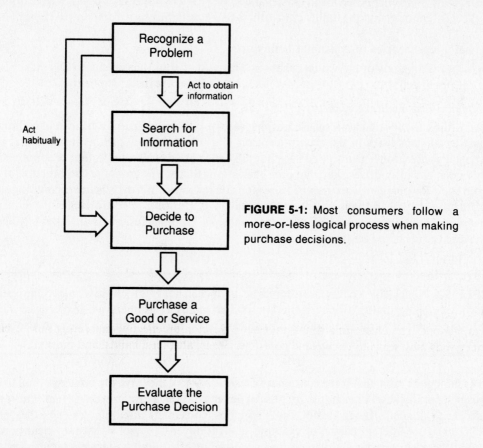

FIGURE 5-1: Most consumers follow a more-or-less logical process when making purchase decisions.

5-2. Theories of Consumer Behavior

Various theories of consumer behavior assist marketers in understanding the consumer. There are many different theories, each of which helps explain certain aspects of consumer behavior. This section will look at the economic, psychological, sociological, and anthropological theories of consumer behavior.

A. The economic theory of consumer behavior

The **economic theory** assumes that consumers are logical, fully aware of their needs and wants, and able to find the best way of satisfying these needs and wants. According to this theory, consumers will buy items having the most **utility**—i.e., capacity to satisfy needs—in relation to their costs and the consumers' financial situation. The economic theory, then, posits rational and efficient consumers who try to get the most for their money.

EXAMPLE 5-3: Recently, Terry Kuhn purchased an IBM personal computer. Before making a choice, however, Terry carefully compared the features of numerous computers in several retail stores. He tried out each computer and asked the sales force numerous questions about storage, access, software, durability, price, and so on. Further, he read many ads, numerous brochures, and several articles in computer magazines. His final purchase was based on considerable information and hours of hard thinking.

The economic theory has some limitations that force us to consider other theories to extend our understanding. In brief, this theory is not accurate in assuming that consumers are always completely aware of their needs and desires. The problem is that many of these needs are *subconscious*, so consumers are not even aware of their existence. Therefore, it is difficult for consumers to judge the satisfaction that various brands will furnish. Also, consumers usually do not have complete knowledge of the various ways to satisfy their needs. They simply do not have the time, patience, and energy needed to fully evaluate every good or service. Finally, the theory ignores the effect of emotion and the influence of others (such as family members) on purchases.

B. Psychological theories of consumer behavior

Psychology is the study of individual behavior. This field of study has produced several key insights into consumer behavior. Four of the psychological theories are discussed below.

1. Stimulus-response learning theory

According to the **stimulus-response learning theory**, consumers *learn* to behave in certain ways, just as students learn in the classroom. Consumers have *drives*, such as hunger, that require satisfaction; and they perceive *cues* (or stimuli), such as advertisements, that produce responses intended to satisfy drives. *Responses* are the actions that spring from the combination of drives and cues. *Reinforcement* occurs when a response is rewarded. When consumers come to associate specific cues with responses, learning has taken place. And if reinforcement is sufficient, a response may be repeated so that it becomes habitual. Habitual responses are especially likely if a reward is strong and frequent.

EXAMPLE 5-4: Chick-Fil-A offers free samples of its chicken nuggets to those who pass the restaurant locations in shopping malls. Management knows that many consumers will experience sufficient reinforcement to return to the restaurants in the future when they are hungry. The firm also provides reinforcement by describing the nuggets as delicious and tangy in company ads.

Psychologists know that some consumers *generalize*—i.e., they give the same response to two or more separate cues. For example, because of generalization, a loyal buyer of Heinz mustard may decide to purchase Heinz catsup. In other cases, consumers *discriminate*—i.e., they respond differently to different cues. For example, a loyal buyer of Lysol household cleaner will not purchase other brands regardless of the cues given by other brands. This is a secure position for Lysol.

2. Gestalt theory

The **gestalt theory** looks at how consumers perceive their environments. According to this theory, many consumers see things as "*wholes*," rather than as parts of wholes. To them the whole is greater than the sum of the parts.

EXAMPLE 5-5: Consumers who walk into a supermarket do not see just the merchandise or just the facilities or just the employees. Rather, they mentally organize the supermarket into a whole. If prices are advertised as low, but the store appears to be dirty, they may not shop there. The cost savings are not enough to offset the poor cleanliness image of the store.

According to gestalt psychologists, individuals see what they want to see and hear what they want to hear. Often, individuals actually resist inflows of information that run contrary to their beliefs and values. For example, a confirmed Chevrolet owner may not see, hear, pay attention to, or remember Ford ads to which he or she has been exposed. This phenomenon makes it difficult for new companies and those with few past customers to gain *market share*, that is, a significant portion of the market for their product.

Gestalt psychology maintains that individuals like order or balance. They want their beliefs, attitudes, and perceptions to be in *harmony*. If a person has just purchased a new car, he or she does not want to experience post-purchase regret—called *cognitive dissonance*—as this would be an unbalanced state. Marketers can often minimize cognitive dissonance through advertising or personal selling to recent purchasers.

EXAMPLE 5-6: One Century 21 sales representative is an expert at dealing with cognitive dissonance. Shortly after a family has purchased a home, she calls on them to answer questions and to reassure them about their purchase. Several days after the personal visit, she sends them a card congratulating them on their wise purchase. This kind of follow-through has helped make her one of the top real estate sales representatives in the city where she works.

3. Psychoanalytic theory

According to **psychoanalytic theory**, the minds of all humans are made up of three conflicting elements. The *id* is the part of the mind that seeks pleasure and avoids pain. The *superego* is the conscience or the part of the mind that holds the id in check. Finally, the *ego* is the rational or thinking part of the mind: it is responsible for logical thinking and attempts to keep balance between the id and the superego. Consumer behavior is therefore the result of the conflict among these three parts.

EXAMPLE 5-7: Mr. Tuan Tran is driving past a Cadillac dealer's showroom when he spots a new Seville in the window. He stops, talks to a sales representative, and takes the car for a test drive. He is instantly attracted to the features of the car—his id is in action. After a while, however, his superego engages. He remembers the money he needs for his children's education and the new wing he wants to add to his house. It is up to his ego to resolve the conflict. If the family budget will allow for the new car *and* for the fulfillment of his other needs, Tuan Tran may buy the car, especially if he has logical reasons to do so. The dealer sales representative can help resolve the conflict in favor of the car by pointing out those logical reasons, such as high trade-in value and low maintenance costs.

4. Self-concept theory

According to the **self-concept theory**, all persons have *self-concepts*. These are: (1) the kind of persons that they believe themselves to be, and (2) the kind of persons that they believe others think them to be. Most individuals purchase and use goods and services that are compatible with their self-concepts. Marketers, then, should attempt to determine the self-concepts of target consumers and to provide marketing mixes that are compatible with these self-concepts.

EXAMPLE 5-8: Some consumers have a self-concept of staying physically fit. Such consumers are likely to purchase health foods, exercise equipment, and other fitness supplies. Other consumers see themselves—and believe others see them—as "dating singles." These consumers purchase sports cars, rent attractive apartments, and wear stylish clothing. Other self-concepts might include the idea that one is a good mother, a religious person, an environmentalist, or an intellectual.

There are two aspects of the self-concept theory that marketers can use to help determine consumer behavior.

(a) **Consumer lifestyles.** Lifestyles reflect a person's self-concept. Lifestyles consist of the activities, interests, and opinions that may be related to consumer behavior. Examples of activities are hobbies, dress styles, and occupations. Interests include the home, the family, and friends. Examples of opinions are feelings about saving money and about using credit cards. Psychological research has shown that individuals with similar lifestyles often behave in roughly the same way as consumers, making the study of lifestyles very useful to marketers.

(b) **Consumer motivation.** Motivation, or the reasons why individuals behave as they do, is a useful variable for marketers to study. Included in a person's self-concept is the desire to establish priorities for and fulfill certain needs. According to **Maslow's theory of motivation**, people attempt to satisfy their needs in the following order:

- *Physiological needs*—survival needs for items such as food and shelter.
- *Safety needs*—to protect oneself from harm and the loss of valued items.

- *Social needs*—needs for affiliation and love from others.
- *Esteem needs*—needs for respect and prestige.
- *Self-actualization needs*—the need to achieve important aspirations and personal goals.

Figure 5-2 illustrates the order of needs in the Maslow theory of motivation. As each step is reasonably attained, consumers move up to the next step, and on to the next when that step is realized.

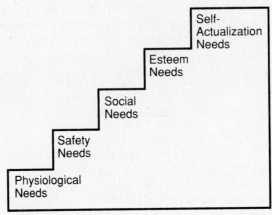

FIGURE 5-2: The order of needs in the Maslow theory of motivation.

note: The Maslow theory does not hold exactly for every consumer, but it does provide guidelines to marketers as to what might be motivating target consumers.

C. Sociological theories of consumer behavior

Sociologists study the behavior of groups. Since every consumer belongs to a number of groups, this field is useful in explaining consumer behavior. If we know to what groups consumers belong, we can use this knowledge to help us in understanding what they do.

1. Reference groups

Reference groups are those groups from which consumers seek guidance for proper behavior. Reference groups include the family, church, work groups, and clubs. An individual may not even belong to some groups, but may imitate their behavior. For example, some teen-agers imitate the clothing styles of rock groups. Each reference group has *norms*, or standards of behavior. Those who follow the norms are rewarded and those who do not are punished, sometimes in subtle ways, by ridicule, and sometimes in more straightforward ways, by ejection from the group.

EXAMPLE 5-9: College students on a particular campus quickly learn the norms of the student body and of smaller groups, such as a fraternity, dormitory, or club. Certain forms of clothing are expected. Some restaurants are the "in thing." Various types of entertainment are preferred over others. These norms may change in a relatively short time, but they are followed all the same.

Every reference group has one or more *opinion leaders*. These are individuals to whom others look for advice. If marketers can create a marketing mix that will attract opinion leaders, others will follow the leader—so the strategy may be very successful. For example, if a golf pro can be induced to try out a new golf club, others who play are likely to follow suit.

An important reference group for most consumers is the family. Children learn many consumer behavior patterns in their family settings. Each family has certain *roles*, so that some members specialize in certain activities (such as buying food items) while other members specialize in different tasks. Each family, like other reference groups, has norms that members refer to in making decisions.

2. *Diffusion of innovation*

Diffusion of innovation refers to the spread of new products, brands, and services through a group. Figure 5-3 shows the subgroups that are involved in the diffusion of innovation.

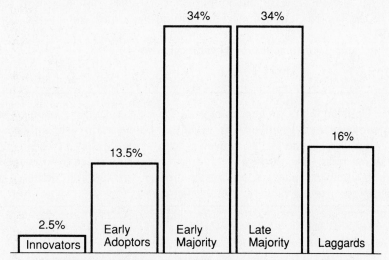

FIGURE 5-3: Diffusion of innovations through various groups.

The members of the first group—the **innovators**—are important because they are the first to try a new offering. If the innovation is useful, they will pass it on to the early adopters. Often, innovators are young and have relatively high levels of income and education.

EXAMPLE 5-10: Teen-agers are the innovators for many clothing and personal-grooming innovations. For instance, they were the first to adopt blue jeans as dress clothing, long hair, rock music, and Swatch watches.

Early adoptors tend to be opinion leaders. They adopt or accept some of the articles used by innovators for personal use. In turn, the **early majority** grouping tends to adopt the innovations accepted by the early adopters. Members of the **late majority** are slower to use an innovation, preferring to wait until it becomes popular. The **laggards** accept an innovation only when the other four groups have adopted it.

EXAMPLE 5-11: Innovators for personal computers were mainly young people who were highly skilled in computer technology. Early adopters were essentially Yuppies—persons who had money and were seeking an active lifestyle. Older professionals and business people made up the early majority. The late majority was made up of blue-collar workers and others who had little use for computers. Most of the laggards were older and uneducated persons.

Individuals go through various stages in the diffusion of innovation. First, they *become aware* of the existence of a new offering, perhaps after noticing that it is mentioned in an advertisement. Next, they *gain information* about the item, perhaps by talking with sales representatives and friends. Then, they *evaluate* the offering by noting its strengths and weaknesses. If the evaluation is positive, it may be followed by *trial*, in which consumers actually try out a new item. The last stage is *adoption*, in which consumers decide to make the product part of their regularly scheduled expenditure patterns.

D. Anthropological theories of consumer behavior

Anthropologists study large groups, such as cultures, subcultures, and social classes. This field is different from sociology, which focuses on smaller groups.

1. Culture

A **culture** consists of a large group of persons who share similar values and lifestyles. Over a period of time, individuals learn and adopt the ideas, values, and patterns of behavior of their cultures. In the United States, important cultural values are hard work, competition, and individualism.

With the passage of time, however, values change.

EXAMPLE 5-12: Until the 1950's, an important value for most American consumers was thrift. Most believed that they should work diligently, pay for what they purchased in cash, and save what remained of their income. Beginning in the 1950's, however, many U.S. consumers began purchasing large quantities of goods on credit, often through credit cards or credit extended from retailers. Today, large quantities of cars, household appliances, services, and other offerings are purchased in this manner. Thrift is no longer as important a value as it once was.

---

2. Subcultures

Each culture consists of a number of **subcultures**, which are groups within a culture whose members share certain values and ways of life. In the U.S. culture, for example, there are Southern-California, Black, teen-age, and senior-citizen subcultures. Marketers should orient their strategies to the cultures and the subcultures in which they operate. This is especially important when selling in foreign countries, where consumer values may differ significantly from those in the United States.

EXAMPLE 5-13: In the United States, many toothpaste producers promote the tooth-whitening capabilities of their products. However, some South African and Asian cultures do not value white teeth. Consumers in these areas will not buy brands of toothpaste for their whitening capabilities because consumers there value stained teeth.

---

3. Social class

Every culture contains a hierarchy of **social classes**, which are groupings of people with similar occupations, sources of income, types of homes, locations of homes, etc. The members of each social class tend to have similar values, attitudes, and patterns of behavior.

Since social class members share values, some marketers segment the market by social class. One class may value status symbols and monetary success. Another may stress "getting your kicks while you can." Still others may place emphasis on being respectable and a "good citizen."

EXAMPLE 5-14: The Loew's Anatole Hotel (located in Dallas) appeals to upper-class people. The hotel has luxurious lobbies, large guest rooms, fine restaurants, grand ballrooms, and gift shops stocked with expensive imported merchandise. Upper-class people find an atmosphere that fits in with their style of living in this hotel.

Table 5-1 sets forth a brief description of social classes in the United States. Each community of any size has a structure that resembles this pattern. Marketers may decide to appeal to one or more of these with customized marketing mixes.

TABLE 5-1: Social Classes in the United States

Social Class	% of population	Characteristics
Upper-upper	.5%	Second- or third-generation wealth, locally prominent, gracious living, sense of community responsibility. Financiers, merchants, and high-status professionals.
Lower-upper	1.5%	New wealth, not accepted by upper class. Executives; elite, successful doctors and lawyers. Gracious living.
Upper-middle	10.0%	Moderately successful professionals. Junior executives educated in better colleges. Status, child, and home orientation.
Lower-middle	33%	Nonmanagerial office workers, small business owners, higher paid white collar workers. Desire respectability and upward mobility.
Upper-lower	40%	Ordinary working class. Semiskilled workers. Not concerned with respectability. Enjoy day-to-day life rather than long-term plans for future.
Lower-lower	15%	Unskilled workers and unassimilated ethnics. Apathetic and fatalistic.

5-3. Major Trends in Consumer Behavior

Consumer behavior is subject to constant change over time. Marketers should stay abreast of trends in consumer behavior, as these trends can have a significant impact on the success of their future strategies. There are some major trends currently apparent that can have strong implications for marketers. These include:

- Increasing desire for convenience in shopping and buying.
- Demand for higher-quality merchandise.
- Demand for products and services that meet the specific needs of particular consumers.
- Less tendency to pay attention to advertisements and other promotion pieces.
- Increased fickleness (lack of brand and store loyalty).
- More emphasis on getting offerings at a discount.
- A self-concept that is based more on what one does off the job than on one's occupation.
- More informed buying.

RAISE YOUR GRADES

Can you explain . . . ?

☑ why marketers should attempt to understand consumer behavior
☑ how the economic theory of consumer behavior could be of value in explaining the purchase of goods or services
☑ how psychological theories can help explain why consumers choose one item over another
☑ how sociological theories might explain why consumers buy items that are similar to those owned by friends
☑ how anthropological theories might be useful in indicating what groups in the population are likely to purchase certain goods
☑ how culture influences consumers to buy specific brands

SUMMARY

1. Consumer behavior consists of the process by which consumers decide whether, what, when, how, where, and from whom to buy goods and services. Marketers should be knowledgeable about theories of consumer behavior if they are to carry out the marketing concept effectively.

2. The economic theory of consumer behavior assumes that consumers are logical, fully aware of their needs and wants, and able to find the best way of satisfying them.

3. Psychological theories of consumer behavior consider the conduct of individuals. These theories include

   • the stimulus-response learning theory, which states that consumers learn to behave in certain ways;

   • the gestalt theory, which states that consumers behave in response to their environment;

   • the psychoanalytic theory, which states that consumer behavior results from three conflicting elements of the mind—the id, the ego, and the superego; and

   • the self-concept theory, which states that consumers behave in a manner that is compatible with how they see themselves and how they wish others to see them.

4. Sociological theories of consumer behavior look at the behavior of groups. These theories include those dealing with

   • reference groups, which are those groups from which consumers seek guidance for proper behavior; and the

   • diffusion of innovation, which refers to the spread of new products, brands, and services through a group.

5. Anthropological theories of consumer behavior focus on cultures, subcultures and social classes. Social classes are particularly important to marketers, as their members tend to have similar values, attitudes, and patterns of behavior.

6. There are a number of trends in consumer behavior that marketers should be aware of in order to adjust their future marketing mixes.

RAPID REVIEW   Answers

Multiple Choice

1. Marketing managers should have knowledge about consumer behavior if they are to follow the (a) sales concept, (b) consumer awareness concept, (c) marketing concept, (d) marketing mix concept. [See Section 5-1.]   *c*

2. Consumer behavior does *not* include the process by which individuals decide (a) whether, (b) what, (c) how, (d) why to buy goods and services. [See Section 5-1.]   *d*

3. Consumer behavior changes (a) infrequently, (b) constantly, (c) occasionally, (d) almost never. [See Section 5-1.]   *b*

4. Each theory of consumer behavior explains certain _____ of consumer behavior. (a) aspects, (b) trends, (c) habits, (d) styles. [See Section 5-2.]   *a*

5. The economic theory of consumer behavior assumes that buyers are (a) logical, (b) not logical, (c) not aware of their needs, (d) influenced by family and friends. [See Section 5-2A.]   *a*

6. If Libby's Vienna Sausage has _____ it has the ability to satisfy needs. (a) no preservatives, (b) good packaging, (c) utility, (d) lots of promotion. [See Section 5-2A.]   *c*

7. A limitation of the economic theory of consumer behavior is that it ignores _____ needs and desires. (a) subconscious, (b) conscious, (c) most, (d) rational. [See Section 5-2A.]   *a*

8. Psychological theories of consumer behavior would help explain the behavior of _____. (**a**) groups, (**b**) cultures, (**c**) individuals, (**d**) social classes. [See Section 5-2B.] *c*

9. According to the stimulus-response learning theory, a buyer of Armour hot dogs has _____ that require satisfaction. (**a**) cues, (**b**) drives, (**c**) stimuli, (**d**) needs. [See Section 5-2B.] *b*

10. When consumers _____, they give the same response to Pepsi Cola as they do to Coca Cola. (**a**) vacillate, (**b**) discriminate, (**c**) fluctuate, (**d**) generalize. [See Section 5-2B.] *d*

11. According to gestalt theory, consumers see things as (**a**) self-concepts, (**b**) wholes, (**c**) parts, (**d**) reinforcement. [See Section 5-2B.] *b*

12. Gestalt psychologists would predict that an Alfa Romeo car buyer seeks _____ after purchasing the brand. (**a**) utility, (**b**) balance, (**c**) drives, (**d**) generalization. [See Section 5-2B.] *b*

13. Those who use psychoanalytic theory would say that a Domino's pizza buyer's _____ is in operation when he is hungry and orders a pizza. (**a**) id, (**b**) ego, (**c**) superego, (**d**) self-concept. [See Section 5-2B.] *a*

14. The kind of person a loyal Walgreen's patron believes she is makes up her _____. (**a**) target market, (**b**) personality, (**c**) self-concept, (**d**) ego. [See Section 5-2B.] *c*

15. Reference groups provide consumers with behavioral (**a**) guidelines, (**b**) desires, (**c**) responses, (**d**) cognitive dissonance. [See Section 5-2C.] *a*

16. _____ are the first to try an innovation, such as a miniature T.V. set. (**a**) Early adoptors, (**b**) Innovators, (**c**) Teen-agers, (**d**) Yuppies. [See Section 5-2C.] *b*

17. A culture consists of a _____ group of persons with similar values and lifestyles. (**a**) large, (**b**) small, (**c**) related, (**d**) temporary. [See Section 5-2D.] *a*

18. The upper-upper social class consists of (**a**) nonmanagerial office workers, (**b**) small business owners, (**c**) newly wealthy individuals, (**d**) second- or third-generation wealth. [See Section 5-2D.] *d*

19. The largest social class is the (**a**) upper-upper, (**b**) lower-upper, (**c**) upper-lower, (**d**) lower-lower. [See Section 5-2D.] *c*

20. Which of the following is *not* a major trend in consumer behavior in the United States today: (**a**) desire for convenience, (**b**) more fickle consumers, (**c**) more informed consumers, (**d**) consumers who are willing to pay more attention to advertisements than they did in the past. [See Section 5-3.] *d*

SOLVED PROBLEMS

PROBLEM 5-1 A hardware store owner says to you, "Who needs to study consumer behavior? After all, it's just an ivory tower field." How would you respond to this statement?

Answer: The hardware store owner has a shortsighted view. Marketers of hardware need to understand consumer behavior if they are to apply the marketing concept correctly and if they are to carry out successful marketing mixes. The study of consumer behavior can assist in answering such questions as, "What items do consumers want to buy in hardware stores?", "Where do consumers purchase particular goods?", and "What store interior layouts are likely to be most effective in bringing sales to the hardware store?" [See Section 5-1.]

PROBLEM 5-2 A fellow student has asked you why there are a number of useful theories of consumer behavior, rather than just one. Can you explain this situation?

Answer: Each theory of consumer behavior explains certain aspects of behavior, but not all. The psychological theory, for example, explains how consumers react to stimuli such as advertisements, but does not explain how culture influences purchase decisions. The economic theory helps explain what people buy, but neglects why they buy. It is necessary to be aware of multiple theories in order to explain and understand this complex field. [See Section 5-2.]

PROBLEM 5-3   How would a follower of the economic theory of consumer behavior probably predict that a husband and wife would conduct a search for a new home?

Answer: A follower of the economic theory of consumer behavior probably would predict that the couple would act logically. They would be aware of their needs and wants for a home (such things as size, location, building material, and landscaping.) They would use many devices to compare those which are available, such as consulting with multiple realtors, looking at homes, reading ads, reading magazine articles about homes, and talking with friends. Then they would choose the home that produced the most total utility (satisfaction) relative to its price and their incomes. [See Section 5-2A.]

PROBLEM 5-4   An economist who works for the federal government has stated that the economic theory of consumer behavior should be the basis for all new laws protecting the consumer from deception by business. What is your reaction?

Answer: This economist is obviously biased. The economic theory has limitations, which suggests that other theories should also be considered when developing laws. For instance, consumers are not aware of all of their needs and desires—some lie in the subconscious—but the economic theory deals only with the conscious needs. Also, consumers do not have complete knowledge of the various ways to satisfy their needs, which runs counter to economic theory. Finally, the economic theory of consumer behavior ignores the influence of others and the effect of emotions on purchasing. [See Section 5-2A.]

PROBLEM 5-5   Explain how the stimulus-response learning theory might help in understanding consumer behavior when purchasing a cola.

Answer: According to the stimulus-response learning theory, potential buyers of cola have drives, such as thirst, that need satisfaction. Individuals perceive cues, such as advertisements or cans on display on store shelves. They may respond to the drives and cues by purchasing and using the beverage. If the resulting reinforcement is adequate (i.e., they like it), they may continue to purchase in the future. [See Section 5-2B.]

PROBLEM 5-6   A marketing executive for Nike fears that those who buy running shoes might generalize on brands. Is there grounds for this fear?

Answer: There may be grounds for this fear. Some consumers may confuse various brands of running shoes (such as Nike and Adidas) and buy competing brands even after seeing Nike advertisements. There are many brands of running shoes in the market, and many of the producers spend heavily on advertising. As a result, runners are bombarded with appeals for many different brands, and confusion may result. In this case, consumers are giving the same response to two or more different sets of cues. [See Section 5-2B.]

PROBLEM 5-7   The head of the home-furnishings department in a major department store has asked you for advice on how to arrange the department displays and facilities. How could gestalt psychology assist you in this task?

Answer: Gestalt psychology states that consumers see things as wholes rather than as parts of wholes; that is, the whole is greater than the sum of the parts. This means that you would want to take an overall perspective in designing the department store's physical facilities. Nothing should be overlooked. Neglect of any one section or facility in the store might create a bad image for the whole. [See Section 5-2B.]

PROBLEM 5-8   An ex-classmate has launched a ladies' clothing fashion boutique in a mall located near an upper-income neighborhood. She has four large competitors in the same mall, each of which has been there for over ten years. What would gestalt psychology predict about obstacles to her success in advertising?

Answer: According to gestalt psychology, consumers see what they want to see and hear what they want to hear. Often, consumers are loyal to clothing stores they have patronized in the past. They resist new ideas and changes in purchase behavior when this is the case. Many loyal customers of the competitors may not see, hear, pay attention to, or remember your friend's promotional activities, unless they are designed in a very creative and interest-capturing manner. [See Section 5-2B.]

PROBLEM 5-9 A neighbor has just purchased a new recreational vehicle for $60,000. Is cognitive dissonance likely?

Answer: Yes, cognitive dissonance is likely. According to the gestalt theory of consumer behavior, the new purchaser of the recreational vehicle may experience post-purchase regret, especially since this is an expensive purchase. The seller of the vehicle should try to take steps to reduce cognitive dissonance in the customer by contacting the customer even after the sale has taken place. Reassurance of a wise purchase, plus fortright handling of any doubt or problems could help reduce the possibility. [See Section 5-2B.]

PROBLEM 5-10 A newspaper ad for a Cadillac Eldorado says that buyers can obtain 4.9% annual interest rate financing from the dealer. How might psychoanalytic theory explain that this is a good appeal to include in the ad?

Answer: According to psychoanalytic theory, the ids of many consumers would be activated by the thought of owning a Cadillac, which is widely regarded as a high-status and high-quality automobile. However, their superegos may not permit a purchase of this luxury car—they cannot come up with an excuse for spending so much momey. By bringing in a rational grounds for purchase, such as a low interest rate, the dealer may overcome the objections of the superegos and appeal to the egos of potential buyers and obtain purchases. [See Section 5-2B.]

PROBLEM 5-11 An owner of a clothing store has asked you how the self-concept theory might explain why particular consumers buy certain kinds of clothing. How would you respond?

Answer: All individuals have self-concepts; these are the kinds of persons that they believe they are and that they believe others think they are. Possible self-concepts are "jet setter," "super-mom," "yuppie," "pillar of the community," and "a good Christian." Consumers purchase clothing to reflect their self-concepts. For example, a business executive might buy a Brooks Brothers suit, a teenager might acquire clam digger shorts, and a bodybuilder might purchase tight-fitting short-sleeved shirts. [See Section 5-2B.]

PROBLEM 5-12 In many junior high and high schools, most of the students dress like their friends. How does reference group theory explain this?

Answer: Students belong to many of the same reference groups as their friends. These reference groups may be athletic teams, the band, clubs, or informal groups of students who have common interests. These groups provide guidance for expected behavior in dress. They have standards of behavior or norms. Those who follow the norms are rewarded, and those who do not are punished, as by ridicule or refusal by group members to socialize with the nonconformer. Members of the group may even imitate admired outsiders, such as rock groups, in their dress codes. [See Section 5-2C.]

PROBLEM 5-13 Many employees on the production floor of the Butler Company assembly plant in Dearborn, Michigan, use the same pike fishing lures as does Tom Wallace, a popular older employee. How might the sociological theory of consumer behavior explain this?

Answer: Wallace appears to be an opinion leader. Other workers probably look to him for advice on matters pertaining to fishing, probably because he has been very successful in catching pike. Fishing lure manufacturers are well-advised to appeal to individuals such as Tom in their marketing strategies. If they can convince opinion leaders to use their offerings, the followers of the leaders may also buy them. [See Section 5-2C.]

PROBLEM 5-14 A food processing company brings out new dietary frozen food dinners from time to time. What is the significance of the diffusion of innovation to this company?

Answer: The company should direct its new dinners at innovators in cooking and serving meals. These consumers are the first to try a new frozen dinner. If they are pleased with the brand, they will pass this information on to the early adopters, who tend to be opinion leaders. Many other consumers will imitate the purchasing behavior of these leaders. If the company directed its marketing mix to followers rather than leaders, the results would most likely be inefficient. [See Section 5-2C.]

PROBLEM 5-15   An executive with a leading maker of clothes washers and dryers has stated that the firm should be able to successfully use the same marketing strategy in selling clothes dryers in West Germany as it does in the United States? Do you agree with this opinion?

Answer: The opinion of the company executive is probably faulty. The cultures of West German and U.S. consumers differ. They have different values, lifestyles, and patterns of behavior. What works in the United States may be very ineffective in other cultures. Many West Germans believe that hard work is a virtue that should be pursued by everyone. They may be indifferent or hostile to ads which state that clothes dryers save effort and make the life of the homemaker less tedious. [See Section 5-2D.]

PROBLEM 5-16   Explain why consumers in the northwestern United States may have different color preferences for articles such as automobiles, clothing, furniture, and homes than consumers in the southwestern United States.

Answer: Both sets of consumers are part of the U.S. culture, so they have somewhat similar color preferences. However, each constitutes a separate subculture. Individuals within subcultures share certain values and ways of life that differ from those in other subcultures. Some of these differences relate to color preferences. Generally, subdued or muted colors are more popular in the northwestern United States, while bright colors are preferred in the Southwest. [See Section 5-2D.]

PROBLEM 5-17   The marketing officer of a medium-sized bank has informed you that he does not attempt to satisfy members of the upper-lower social class when he segments the market for savings accounts. Rather, he focuses on the upper-middle and lower-middle social classes. Is this a good strategy, in your opinion?

Answer: Yes, it is a good strategy for this bank. Members of the upper-lower social class do not have large sums of money to place in financial institutions. Rather, they spend a sizeable portion of their earnings. Also, they enjoy life from day to day rather than being concerned with the future. Banks, however, must emphasize future benefits in attracting money for savings accounts. Members of this social class would not be prime prospects for the bank's savings accounts. [See Section 5-2D.]

PROBLEM 5-18   The head of the United Fund in a large city has told you that appeals for funds are heavily directed toward members of the upper-upper social class. Is this a good strategy?

Answer: It may be a good strategy. Members of this social class are few in number, relative to other social classes; however, they tend to have high incomes, much of which is saved, invested, or donated to charities, rather than spent on goods and services. Further, many upper-uppers have a strong sense of community responsibility and a dedication to causes that they believe to be worthy. They are socially prominent in the community and may want to be active contributors in order to help fulfill their self-images. [See Section 5-2D.]

PROBLEM 5-19   In light of the trends in consumer behavior that were mentioned in this chapter, why have convenience stores prospered during the past ten years?

Answer: One of the major current trends in consumer behavior is the desire for convenience—to conserve on time and effort. Consumers want to be able to acquire goods at times and in places that fit in with their particular patterns and habits—with a minimum expenditure of time and effort. Convenience stores provide these benefits through locations near homes and major streets, ample parking, 24-hour service, and quick check-outs. [See Section 5-3.]

PROBLEM 5-20   A used-car dealer has reported to you that, "Consumers today will buy almost anything, provided that you are good at advertising and selling. I can unload any car, even a real lemon, and make a nice profit on the bargain." Based on the trends in consumer behavior that this chapter mentioned, is this a good strategy?

Answer: It is not a good strategy. Consumers are becoming increasingly informed, as they read literature and consult with friends and sales representatives before purchasing goods and services. They are less likely to be duped by an unscrupulous operator such as this one. Further, they are demanding higher standards of product quality, and the car dealer does not seem to be attuned to this trend. In addition, consumers are becoming less passive than they were in the past. When goods or services are unsatisfactory, many will demand a refund or exchange from retail stores, file complaints with government agencies, or even bring lawsuits against businesses. [See Section 5-3.]

6 ANALYZING INDUSTRIAL BUYER BEHAVIOR

THIS CHAPTER IS ABOUT

☑ **The Nature of Industrial Buyers**
☑ **Characteristics of the Industrial Market**
☑ **Types of Industrial Buyers: Classification**
☑ **A Total Theory of Industrial Buyer Behavior**

6-1. The Nature of Industrial Buyers

There are a number of potential customers that are not consumers. Examples of such customers are Exxon, Mesa Petroleum Corporation, the College of William and Mary, the Rochester Clinic, the city of Cincinnati, the United States Army, and the Arizona State Highway Department. All of these potential customers are *industrial buyers*.

- **Industrial buyers** differ from consumers in that they acquire **industrial goods**, which are defined as goods and services purchased to satisfy the needs of the organization, rather than personal desires.

Industrial buyers acquire industrial goods because their jobs require it—not because they are satisfying their individual needs.

EXAMPLE 6-1: Altos Computer Systems is a buyer of memory chips, which go into company microcomputers—the major product sold to Altos customers. The main suppliers of these chips include N.E.C. Corporation, Hitachi, and Oki Electric (the latter two are Japanese firms). Buyers for Altos acquire the chips that best meet the firm's microcomputer specifications and that are offered at a competitive price. The buyers' objective is to help turn out microcomputers that can bring in adequate revenues.

- Industrial buyers include both business and nonbusiness organizations.

Business organizations, such as Dupont and the Ford Motor Company, are important industrial buyers, but the list also includes government agencies (which are among the largest purchasers), hospitals, schools, and charitable organizations. Even churches are important buyers for some goods and services.

6-2. Characteristics of the Industrial Market

Industrial markets differ in some ways from consumer markets. This section covers some of the major differences.

A. Industrial buyers are *few* in number and their purchases are *large* in size.

Size refers to the *amounts* of goods and services that industrial buyers purchase from suppliers. In the case of many industrial goods, a small number of large customers provide most of the marketer's sales. This means that individual customers are very important. Marketers may expend considerable money on promotion to gain the business of one buyer. Also, the importance of the buyers may prompt marketers to sell directly to the buying organization, instead of delegating this work to wholesalers.

EXAMPLE 6-2: Harris Graphics is the nation's largest maker of big, high-speed printing presses for magazines and newspapers. Since each printing press sold results in substantial sales, the firm devotes considerable attention to individual customers. A sales representative may justifiably call on a customer a dozen times or more, in order to get an order.

B. Industrial buyers make many of their purchases *less frequently* than do consumers.

Industrial buyers purchase such products as buildings, metal casting equipment, forges, large computers, and large motors; which are not bought often. Industrial buyers also purchase such items as office supplies and raw materials on long-term, bulk contracts, which are also made infrequently.

The infrequent purchase rate means that individual sales are very important to the industrial goods marketer. It also means that marketers must continually promote their offerings. Continual promotion helps ensure that buyers will be aware of the offerings when a purchase decision date approaches. A steady stream of ads and calls by sales representatives is required.

EXAMPLE 6-3: Corporations purchase office computer networks very infrequently. Once bought, a network should be used for a long period of time. Marketing executives at Honeywell, which sells these networks, know this. In order to keep the Honeywell name before buyers, the firm advertises frequently in trade magazines and in specialized publications such as *Business Week*. Its sales people stay in close touch with potential buyers, so that representatives can be available when buyers are considering replacing existing networks.

C. Industrial buyers tend to be *better informed* than consumers.

Industrial buyers have to know what they want and where to get it; they have expertise in purchasing because of their training and experience. Before acquiring goods and services, they may devote hundreds of man-hours to studying their needs and evaluating potential suppliers and their offerings. In contrast, consumers often make purchases with a minimum of factual knowledge.

D. The demand for industrial goods is *derived* from the demand for consumer goods.

Since buyers use industrial goods to produce consumer goods, changes in demand at the consumer level will lead to changes in demand at the industrial level.

EXAMPLE 6-4: The demand for steel varies with the demand for refrigerators, automobiles, washers and dryers, and other items made with steel. The demand for steel also changes with variations in the demand for products such as food and clothing, since steel is required in the production of many of these items. So we can see that the demand for industrial goods is derived directly from the demand for consumer goods.

Because of derived demand, industrial marketers may be unable to increase their sales through such tactics as price reductions and increased promotion effort. If sales in an industry are down, buyers may be reluctant to acquire additional supplies—even if they can be acquired more cheaply or have been heavily promoted.

E. *Direct marketing* is common for industrial goods.

Marketers usually serve industrial customers through their own personnel, rather than through wholesalers. Direct marketing is most common when—

(1) Customers want many services from sales representatives;
(2) The size of individual orders is high; and
(3) Customers are few.

Direct marketing enables the producer to maintain close control and to be aggressive in promotion efforts.

EXAMPLE 6-5: Sanders Associates is a manufacturer of military electronics equipment. The firm's sales representatives and advertising efforts target army, navy, and air force personnel who are in charge of buying. Sanders employees have considerable knowledge about company products and policies and have close contacts with military buyers. Much of the organization's success is due to its marketing expertise in the military market.

F. In most industries the demand for goods is *inelastic*.

When we say that "the demand for goods is inelastic," it means that changes in prices do not bring about relatively large changes in revenue; that is, buyers do not purchase substantially more when prices fall, or substantially less when prices rise. Industry demand is inelastic largely because it is derived from consumer demand, regardless of the level of prices. Also, most consumer goods contain multiple industrial-good components, so a price change in one industrial good is not likely to substantially change the price, and hence the demand, for the consumer goods.

Even though total industry demand for industrial goods is often inelastic, company demand is frequently elastic. This is because one company may be able to attract customers away from its competitors through price decreases.

G. In some industries, *reciprocity* is a determinant of what goods and services are purchased.

If Firm A will purchase from Firm B only if B purchases from A, we say that these firms have a *reciprocity agreement*. Many buyers and marketers consider reciprocity to be unethical. Also, it may lead to ineffective marketing and buying because firms are purchasing and selling not because of the merits of their programs, but because of the reciprocity agreement.

H. Some industrial goods are *leased*, rather than purchased.

Leasing some industrial goods (like trucks and warehousing equipment) gives the acquiring company a major advantage because leasing does not tie up funds in assets that are purchased. In addition, the lease agreement may stipulate that the marketer, rather than the acquiring company will be responsible for the maintenance—and even the operation—of the goods. On the other hand, leasing may be more expensive than buying, especially since it provides fewer tax deductions.

6-3. Types of Industrial Buyers: Classification

A useful method for classifying buyers is to use the **Standard Industrial Classification (SIC) system**, which The U.S. Bureau of the Census has created. Table 6-1 sets forth the overall classification and the code numbers that have been assigned to each category.

TABLE 6-1: Major Standard Industrial Classification (SIC) System Categories

Code Number	Industry
01–09	Agriculture, Forestry, and Fishing
10–14	Mining
15–18	Contract Construction
19–39	Manufacturing
40–49	Transportation and Other Public Utilities
50–59	Wholesale and Retail Trade
60–69	Finance, Insurance, and Real Estate
70–89	Services
90–98	Government
99	Others

Two-digit code numbers identify the major industry of each buyer—the industry from which the bulk of its revenues originate. Other digits further refine the classification. The code for "Food and Kindred Products Manufacturing," for example, is 20. Further classification allocates the number 201 to producers of meat products, and the code 2011 to meat-packing plants.

Marketers use the SIC system extensively to study industrial markets. The U.S. Bureau of the Census and other government and nongovernment agencies collect a wealth of data and break these data down by SIC categories. Marketers can obtain information on such variables as what volumes of various kinds of goods and services industries in specific SIC categories purchase. This information is very useful in choosing market segments and in making other important marketing decisions.

6-4. A Total Theory of Industrial Buyer Behavior

How do industrial buyers go about acquiring goods and services? Answers to this question are critical to industrial marketers because they can use such information to guide the entire marketing effort. Figure 6-1 presents the major elements of an overall theory of industrial buyer behavior. This section discusses each component of the figure.

A. The *buying center* is made up of persons who are involved in a purchasing decision.

The first element in Figure 6-1 is the **buying center**. It is made up of those persons who are involved in a purchasing decision. However, its membership changes from one purchasing occasion to another. When a company buys machinery, production and engineering executives are likely to be members of the buying center, along with the **purchasing agent**, who has formal authority to buy. When the company buys a computer, the head of the computer center is likely to be a member of the buying center, along with executives from finance and marketing, and maybe even some computer programmers.

The members of the buying center may take on various roles; they can act as—

(1) **Users**—Those who use the goods and services that are purchased.
(2) **Buyers**—Those (usually purchasing agents) with formal authority for contracting with suppliers.
(3) **Influencers**—Those who influence decisions by providing information and criteria for evaluating goods and services.
(4) **Deciders**—Those with the authority to choose particular goods and services. For expensive goods and services, these may be senior executives. For less expensive offerings, they may be purchasing agents.
(5) **Gatekeepers**—Those who control the flow of information into the buying center.

Often one person will serve in more than one of these roles.

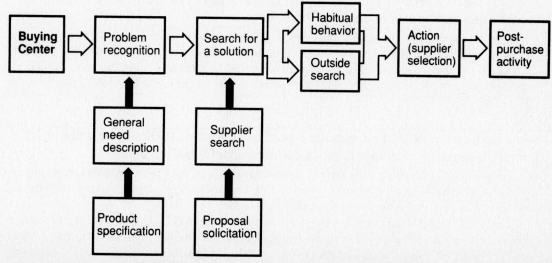

FIGURE 6-1: An overall model of industrial buyer behavior.

EXAMPLE 6-6: At Flying Tiger Airlines (which transports freight, not passengers) the president, Mr. Stephen M. Wolf, is an important member of the buying center when the company purchases airplanes. Mr. Wolf acts as an influencer, a decider; and as a gatekeeper. When the company purchases office supplies, he is not a member of the buying center. Because airplanes are very expensive and their purchase vitally affects the success of the company, he belongs to the airplane buying center; but because office supplies are routine purchases, he is not a member of the buying center for office supplies.

B. *Problem recognition* **occurs when someone in the company detects a significant difference between a** *desired condition* **and an** *actual condition* **that can be resolved through buying.**

Industrial buying begins with *problem recognition*. Problem recognition may occur, for example, when a Montgomery Ward store manager discovers that the janitorial firm which cleans the store is not doing the job well. Or it may take place when an Oldsmobile production manager finds that the paint the purchasing agent buys does not leave Oldsmobiles with a satisfactorily shiny finish. Or it may take place when a financial manager for the Bulova watch company discovers that the company is paying too much for gold that goes into company watches. There are two steps that enter into problem recognition.

   (1) General need description. Here, someone in the company describes, usually in writing, the nature of the goods or services that are needed. Sometimes this is specified in a *purchase requisition*, which requests that the purchasing department acquire a particular item.

   (2) Product specification. This follows general need description. One or more members of the buying center decide exactly what the features of the desired purchase should be. These features are often spelled out in detailed blueprints and specifications.

C. **The** *search for a solution* **to a problem begins with the buyers' deciding what criteria to use in evaluating suppliers.**

After recognizing a problem, members of the buying center begin the *search for a solution*. They decide what criteria to use as a starting point in evaluating suppliers. Possible criteria include low price, fast delivery, reliable delivery, good quality of services provided, high product quality, and satisfactory product consistency. There are two methods that may be used to find and evaluate suppliers.

   (1) Supplier search. After developing criteria, the buying center seeks out various suppliers who may be able to fulfill the criteria. This is known as supplier search.

   (2) Proposal solicitation. The buying center may seek out proposals for goods to be sold from some of these suppliers.

D. *Habitual behavior* **occurs when the company routinely places an order with a supplier that has been used successfully in the past.**

When the buying decision is routine and recurring, *habitual behavior* may occur. In this case, the company (usually through a purchasing agent) routinely places an order with a supplier, probably one that has been used successfully in the past. Inexpensive items and those that do not have an important effect on the profitability of the company, such as office supplies, are often purchased in this manner.

E. **When the members of the buying center cannot find a solution to the buying problem through habitual behavior, they begin an outside search for information.**

Members of the buying center may read advertisements, talk to sales representatives, read professional journal articles, talk with employees of other companies who have purchased the goods and services in question, and look to other information sources.

There are three general conditions that the buying center may face. One is **straight rebuy**, in which case a product bought previously is satisfactory and the firm will continue to purchase it. In the case of **modified rebuy**, the buying center is not satisfied with a current supplier, so management decides to re-evaluate this firm and its products to see if it should still be used. With **new task buying**, the buying center has no experience in buying a particular kind of product and is not familiar with appropriate suppliers or their products. This third case requires more information search than do the other two.

F. Action takes place when the buying center decides to make a purchase from a particular supplier.

After evaluating suppliers and conducting any information search necessary, members of the buying center make a decision to purchase from a particular supplier. The decision is based on their judgment as to whether or not buying from a given supplier will solve the problem they are facing. Sometimes a buying center will decide that the best action is no action.

EXAMPLE 6-7: The Flying Tiger buying center decided not to purchase any airplanes in 1986. Rather, they decided that the existing stock was adequate to handle their current and expected future work load. Further, the company was experiencing financial difficulties during that year owing to strong competition from rivals, so the action decided upon was that efforts should be made to conserve funds, rather than spend them.

G. *Post-purchase activities* **take place after buying and are important determinants of customer satisfaction.**

Post-purchase activities include product delivery, installation of equipment, training of buyer employees, inspection of the product after a period of trial use, repair service, and financing. Marketers should not neglect post-purchase activities, as they have a strong impact on customer satisfaction. The arrow leading from post-purchase activities back to the buying center in Figure 6-1 suggests that these activities influence future purchases. For example, if Flying Tiger has extensive maintenance expenses with Boeing 747's, it may not purchase those planes in the future. Performance reviews can be instrumental to the success of an industrial marketer.

EXAMPLE 6-8: The Xerox Company provides considerable service to buyers of the company machines. Xerox employees make sure that an order has been filled properly and that it has been delivered on time. They assist with installations of copiers and train buyer employees in copier use. When problems occur, Xerox employees help in finding the cause and correcting the problem.

RAISE YOUR GRADES
Can you explain . . . ?

☑ why some items are classified as industrial goods and other items are classified as consumer goods.

☑ why the SIC system is valuable to a number of manufacturers

☑ what parties might be in the buying center of a typical manufacturer when it purchases operating supplies

☑ how industrial buyers attempt to solve problems when the buying decision is routine and recurring

☑ why many industrial marketers serve their customers through company sales forces, instead of using wholesalers

☑ why many industrial marketers spend thousands of dollars to train individual sales representatives

☑ why a number of industrial marketers do not raise their advertising expenditures during times when their sales have fallen

SUMMARY

1. Industrial buyers purchase goods to satisfy the needs of an organization, rather than personal desires. Industrial buyers include both business and nonbusiness organizations.
2. The industrial market differs from the consumer market in many ways. It is characterized by a small number of large-volume buyers, low purchase frequency, informed buying, derived demand, direct marketing, inelastic demand for goods, reciprocity, and leasing.
3. Useful statistics on industrial buyers are organized by the Standard Industrial Classification (SIC) system, which categorizes firms by industry. Marketers use the SIC system to study industrial markets.
4. The buying center is made up of persons who are involved in a purchasing decision.
5. Problem recognition occurs when someone in the company detects significant differences between desired and actual conditions that can be resolved through buying.
6. Buyers search for solutions to problems by deciding what criteria to use in evaluating suppliers.
7. Habitual behavior occurs when the company routinely places an order with a supplier that has been used successfully in the past.
8. An outside search for information occurs when the members of the buying center cannot find a solution to the buying problem through habitual behavior.
9. Action takes place when buyers decide to make a purchase from a particular supplier.
10. Post-purchase activities take place after buying and are important determinants of customer satisfaction.

RAPID REVIEW   Answers

Multiple Choice

1. Buyers of industrial goods purchase in order to satisfy the needs of (a) individuals, (b) an organization, (c) themselves, (d) the industry. [See Section 6-1.]   *b*
2. Industrial buyers include those who acquire goods for (a) households, (b) the satisfaction of personal desires, (c) nonbusiness organizations such as the Heart Fund, (d) individual families. [See Section 6-1.]   *c*
3. Compared to consumers, buyers of industrial goods and services are (a) few in number, (b) large in number, (c) lacking in funds, (d) unable to secure credit. [See Section 6-2.]   *a*
4. Because of the relative number and size of the customers for a firm such as the Boeing Company, individual customers are (a) very important, (b) not important, (c) just a small portion of a large group, (d) becoming less important. [See Section 6-2.]   *a*
5. Industrial buyers make many of their purchase decisions (a) without engaging in problem solving, (b) infrequently, (c) from outside the buying center, (d) without habitual behaviour or outside search. [See Section 6-2.]   *b*
6. Because purchases are not made often, companies such as Reed Tool (a manufacturer of oil well drilling equipment) continually _____ their products. (a) try to sell, (b) update, (c) promote, (d) change. [See Section 6-2.]   *c*
7. Which of the following is *not* a reason why companies find individual customers to be very important? (a) the number of customers is small, (b) customers are large in size, (c) customers purchase infrequently, (d) customers are involved in post-purchase activities. [See Section 6-2.]   *d*
8. In comparison to consumers, industrial buyers tend to be (a) more informed, (b) less informed, (c) large in number, (d) smaller in size. [See Section 6-2.]   *a*
9. The demand for industrial goods is _____ the demand for consumer goods. (a) not related to, (b) derived from, (c) higher than, (d) lower than. [See Section 6-2.]   *b*

10. When industrial goods marketers serve their customers through their own employees, rather than through wholesalers, this is called (a) promotion, (b) advertising, (c) post-purchase activity, (d) direct marketing. [See Section 6-2.]   *d*

11. The SIC system refers to (a) Standard Industrial Classification, (b) Statistical Industry Compilation, (c) Special Information Codes, (d) Security Information Communications. [See Section 6-3.]   *a*

12. Companies are assigned to SIC categories based on the _____ they are in. (a) state, (b) financial classification, (c) industry, (d) region of the country. [See Section 6-3.]   *c*

13. The membership of the buying center (a) stays the same from one purchase decision to another, (b) changes from one purchase decision to another, (c) consists of only one executive, (d) does not include executives. [See Section 6-4.]   *b*

14. In the buying center, those who have the authority to choose particular goods and services are called (a) influencers, (b) gatekeepers, (c) deciders, (d) users. [See Section 6-4.]   *c*

15. Industrial buyers recognize a problem when they see a significant difference between a(n) _____ and an actual condition. (a) desired condition, (b) authorized condition, (c) supplier's product, (d) straight rebuy condition. [See Section 6-4.]   *a*

16. After recognizing a problem, members of the buying center search for a (a) supplier, (b) general need description, (c) product specification, (d) solution. [See Section 6-4.]   *d*

17. When the buying decision is routine and recurring, _____ behavior may occur. (a) outside search, (b) problem recognition, (c) stimulus-response, (d) habitual. [See Section 6-4.]   *d*

18. When industrial buyers engage in outside search, they may (a) seek proposals from suppliers, (b) talk to sales representatives, (c) think about past purchases, (d) engage in habitual behavior. [See Section 6-4.]   *b*

19. In the _____ phase of industrial buyer behavior, buyers make a decision to purchase from a particular supplier. (a) problem recognition, (b) post-purchase, (c) action, (d) supplier search. (See Section 6-4.)   *c*

20. Post-purchase activities for a company do *not* include (a) installation of equipment, (b) training of buyer employees, (c) information search, (d) repair service. [See Section 6-4.]   *c*

SOLVED PROBLEMS

PROBLEM 6-1   When the Pitney Bowes Corporation sells a postage meter to the Salvation Army, this transaction is classified as industrial goods marketing. Why is it not consumer goods marketing?

Answer: The postage meter is used by the Salvation Army employees to satisfy the needs of the organization, rather than individual needs. The employees' jobs require purchasing behavior. If these individuals used the postage meters to satisfy personal needs and desires, as by posting letters to friends, the meters would be classified as consumer goods. [See Section 6-1.]

PROBLEM 6-2   Potential buyers of American-made submarines are few in number and large in size, consisting mainly of the military in the United States and its allies. What are the implications of this situation to the firm that makes submarines?

Answer: Because its customers are small in number and large in size, individual customers must be very important to the company. A single order can amount to tens of millions of dollars, so considerable effort must be devoted to establishing good relationships with potential customers. The firm should spend considerable money on promotion, especially on personal selling, to gain the business of individual buyers. Also, the firm should sell directly to buyers rather than through wholesalers. This is the case because customer relations is too important a function to entrust to outside parties. [See Section 6-2.]

PROBLEM 6-3 The Rolm Company, a leading maker of computerized telephone switchboards, sells its products only infrequently to individual buyers. What are the marketing implications?

Answer: There are two major implications. One is that individual sales are very important to the firm—they must be large enough to bring in adequate revenues. The other is that Rolm must continually promote its products. This helps ensure that buyers will be aware of the products when a purchase decision date comes up. A steady stream of advertisements and calls by sales representatives is required. [See Section 6-2.]

PROBLEM 6-4 A fellow student has read that buyers for the National Aeronautics and Space Administration (NASA) are very well-informed, but wonders just what is meant by "well-informed." Can you explain this to him?

Answer: NASA, like other industrial buyers, tends to be well-informed as to what they want and where to get it. NASA's buyers have expertise in purchasing because of their training and experience. Before buying goods and services, they may devote hundreds of hours to studying their needs and evaluating potential suppliers and their offerings. This behavior differs from that of many consumers, who often make purchases with a minimum of factual knowledge. [See Section 6-2.]

PROBLEM 6-5 One of your professors has stated that demand for the Phillips Can Company's products is "derived." What does this mean to you?

Answer: The demand for Phillips Can Company cans is derived from the consumer demand for products that are packaged in cans. As consumers buy more canned beverages, soups, vegetables, juices, meat products, and other items, industrial buyers, such as Coca Cola, Campbell Soup and Del Monte, purchase more cans, thereby providing more demand for Phillips Can offerings. This demand takes place even when can producers raise their prices. [See Section 6-2.]

PROBLEM 6-6 A marketing executive at a chemical company has informed you that, despite decreasing costs for petroleum products, the company does *not* plan to reduce its prices on several grades of plastics sold to industry this year because of the current derived demand for plastics. Do you agree with this statement?

Answer: Yes, you should. The demand for industrial plastics is in fact derived from the demand for consumer goods that use plastics, such as telephones, toys, and dishes. Companies that produce such items will not necessarily buy more plastic because the prices fall. Rather, they will wait for increases in consumer demand before buying more. If, for example, Mattell sells more plastic toys, it will buy more of this raw material; otherwise, it will not. [See Section 6-2.]

PROBLEM 6-7 Triangle Industries, a producer of juke boxes and vending machines, serves customers through its own personnel, rather than through wholesalers. Why doesn't it use wholesalers?

Answer: The firm's direct marketing plan probably enables it to maintain close control over marketing efforts and to be aggressive in promotion. Wholesalers might not be willing to carry out company strategies and tactics in the manner that Triangle executives want. Also, wholesalers might not provide enough advertising and personal selling support to maintain a desired level of communications with potential customers. Customers demand many services from this type of company, such as installation and repair. The firm is able to serve its customers much more effectively by using its own personnel instead of a wholesaler. [See Section 6-2.]

PROBLEM 6-8 A classmate has asked you for an explanation of the Standard Industrial Classification system. How would you describe it?

Answer: The SIC system is a method created by the U.S. Bureau of the Census for classifying organizations. Each industry in the classification has been assigned a code number. Firms are assigned to the industry from which they derive most of their revenues. Two-digit code numbers identity major industries and other digits further refine the classification. [See Section 6-3.]

PROBLEM 6-9 How could a firm that markets office furniture use the SIC system to segment markets?

Answer: The U.S. Bureau of the Census and many other government and non-government organizations collect considerable data that are broken down by SIC categories. These organizations, for instance, provide figures on the number of firms in each category, their employment levels, and their sales. An office furniture company can determine what major SIC categories and subcategories purchase the greatest volume of office equipment. These could be chosen as targets for the marketing effort of the firm. [See Section 6-3.]

PROBLEM 6-10 A new sales representative for a company that sells office copiers believes that selling efforts should be directed to the purchasing agents who are employed by target customers. Do you agree?

Answer: The sales representative probably should direct selling efforts to purchasing agents *and* to various other parties who will be influential in the decision-making process. The buying center may include an office manager, secretarial supervisors, executive secretaries, financial executives, and even other parties, such as company chief executives, who might not logically be involved in the purchase of copiers. The sales representative should devote considerable effort to finding out who will be dominant in the decision to buy a particular brand and type of machine. [See Section 6-4.]

PROBLEM 6-11 Assume that you have been appointed as the marketing manager for a company that sells electronic typewriters to businesses and other organizations. What *roles* in the buying centers of targeted companies might be important in selling your product?

Answer: All of the various roles that can be part of the buying center may be important to marketing your product. For example, users, such as secretaries, receptionists, and others who work with typewriters may be a part of the buying center. Purchasing agents (buyers) certainly would be important. Executives who worry about getting correspondence and other paperwork accomplished might act as influencers. The deciders could be purchasing agents, or they could be the secretaries or their superiors or even top management. Influential gatekeepers could be secretaries or their superiors. [See Section 6-4.]

PROBLEM 6-12 A classmate has asked you for the meaning of problem recognition in industrial buyer behavior. How would you answer?

Answer: Problem recognition, as it pertains to industrial buyer behavior, occurs when someone in the company recognizes a difference between a desired condition and an actual condition that can be resolved through buying. For example, an employee of a supermarket may notice that stocks of Nabisco Shredded Wheat are often very low and decide to advise the buyer to order more inventory. Or a machinist who is employed by a precision tools manufacturer could discover that one of the company's lathes is operating very inefficiently and needs replacing. [See Section 6-4.]

PROBLEM 6-13 A financial executive for a maker of bed sheets and blankets has not been a member of a buying center to date. She has been asked, however, to help determine if the firm should purchase new mill machinery this year. In turn, she has asked you, a purchasing agent, how she should go about searching for a solution to this buying problem. How would you advise her to proceed?

Answer: She should become involved in two major search activities. The first is deciding what criteria to use in evaluating suppliers. Possible criteria are low price, fast delivery, reliable delivery, guaranteed installation and repair service, and high product effectiveness. The second search activity is to evaluate various suppliers who may be able to fulfill the criteria for the machinery. This may involve visiting with sales representatives, reading catalogs and brochures prepared by suppliers, reading advertisements, and consulting with other company personnel. [See Section 6-4.]

PROBLEM 6-14   A purchasing agent for a major shirt manufacturer buys fabrics from which the firm's shirts are made. What type of search effort is the purchasing agent most likely to use?

Answer: Habitual behavior is most likely in this case. Since the firm's business is making shirts, the decision to purchase fabrics is routine and recurring. It has been made on many occasions in the past. The purchasing agent probably places routine orders often when inventories are at a low level. Suppliers that have been used successfully in the past would likely be re-used, provided that their methods of operation, services, and policies have not been dramatically changed. Even in circumstances such as this, however, well-informed buyers keep an eye on the market, and from time-to-time, watch for better suppliers. [See Section 6-4.]

PROBLEM 6-15   Assume that you are marketing paper stock to the executives at a major publishing company. You have learned that these executives are engaged in outside search for a new paper supplier. Through what means could you attempt to convince the publishing personnel to purchase from your company?

Answer: Your firm probably already sponsors advertisements that appeal to this potential customer. But there are other things you can do. One strong possibility is to have your company sales representatives call on members of the publishing company's buying center and make persuasive presentations. Another possibility is to convince satisfied users of your paper to inform the publishing personnel of their own profitable use of your company's offerings. Still another tactic would be to get your company name to buyers through articles in trade and professional magazines read by publishers. [See Section 6-4.]

PROBLEM 6-16   Assume that you have completed a sale of a telephone system to a large department store. What post-purchase activities would you be likely to undertake?

Answer: An important activity would be to make sure that the system was installed promptly and correctly. Then you would instruct department store employees on how to use the system. This could involve several days of training sessions. You would want to check how the system was operating after a trial period of several weeks. If major operating problems had developed, these would have to be solved. Financing for the department store customer would have to be arranged, including terms that were agreeable both to the customer and to the manufacturer's financial department. In the case of breakdowns, you would need to provide for repairs. [See Section 6-4.]

7 GATHERING INFORMATION FOR MARKETING DECISIONS

THIS CHAPTER IS ABOUT

- ☑ **The Importance of Marketing Information**
- ☑ **Marketing Information Systems**
- ☑ **Steps in a Marketing Research Project**
- ☑ **Cost/Benefit Analysis of Marketing Information Projects**
- ☑ **Sales Forecasting**

7-1. The Importance of Marketing Information

You may have already come to the conclusion that marketers need considerable information in order to achieve their goals. If so, you're right. In fact, relevant information can be one of the major keys to success in marketing.

EXAMPLE 7-1: Some advertisers considered dropping television as a marketing medium when they discovered that many consumers were recording programs on VCR's and "zapping" the commercials (playing them on fast forward at many times the normal speed) on viewing. However, research showed that zapped commercials were recalled nearly as well as those watched at normal speeds—a welcome relief for television marketers!

EXAMPLE 7-2: Kimberly Clark found that many consumers disliked the inconvenience of seeking out and purchasing disposable diapers in retail stores. Given this information, the firm began a program of selling its "Huggies" by mail. The program has been very effective in marketing the brand to new mothers.

Marketers utilize information in making target customer selection, product planning, pricing, promotion, and distribution decisions.

A. Target customer selection

Target customers are those who have a need for a product or service and the income to pay for it. Marketing information on both of these variables can be uncovered by management.

EXAMPLE 7-3: Dupont concentrates the selling efforts for its Benlate soybean fungicide on target customers in southern Louisiana and the upper Mississippi Delta. The company made this decision based on information it gathered indicating that fungus-related soybean disease was greater in these areas than in any other.

B. Product planning

Marketing information is vital in determining what products to add, drop, or change, and what elements to include in packaging and branding. Failure to stay in tune with customer preferences and new moves by competitors can lead to serious declines in sales and profits. On the other hand, relevant marketing information may lead a firm to advances in sales and profits.

EXAMPLE 7-4: Nickelodeon MTV Networks acted upon information that many children, ages 8–12, resisted parents' attempts to make them bathe. Nickelodeon developed "Green Slime" shampoo and liquid soap, which were heavily promoted on the television network. The product was an instant success, as many children indicated that they wanted to be "Green Slimed."

C. Pricing

Marketing information can be very useful in arriving at price decisions. Facts on company sales, prices, and competitors' prices may be invaluable to pricing administrators. For example, most retailers "price-shop" their competitors. Managers or their employees visit rival stores and take careful notes on the prices of competing items.

D. Promotion

Marketers use large amounts of information to make promotion decisions. Sales representatives provide input on the sales concluded, number of calls made, and number of orders taken. This information is useful in evaluating the selling effort and marketing strategies. Advertising executives gather information on the effectiveness of various ads and campaigns and the usefulness of particular tactics in developing ads.

EXAMPLE 7-5: Research has indicated that female voices are just as effective as male voices in motivating sales through television commercials. Prior to this finding, the majority of commercials used male "voiceovers," because advertisers believed that a masculine voice was more effective.

E. Distribution

Marketing managers gather and employ considerable information in distribution decision making. In choosing channels of distribution, for instance, they need input on the sales and costs of various kinds of wholesalers and retailers. Likewise, information on costs and services rendered by various transportation carriers is needed in order to choose the most promising physical distribution system.

EXAMPLE 7-6: A producer of processed chili products stopped using contract-carrier trucking firms and purchased three of its own trucks. This decision was made after a study showed that maintaining its own trucks would lower the company's distribution costs and permit faster and more reliable transportation to customers.

7-2. Marketing Information Systems

Marketing information systems (MIS) are parts of the marketing organization that are used for the continuous collection and analysis of data and provision of information to marketing decision makers. Figure 7-1 outlines the major components of an MIS.

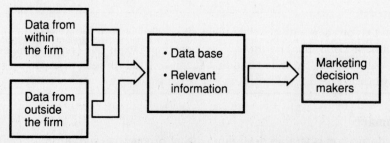

FIGURE 7-1: The marketing information system (MIS).

- **Input.** MIS personnel collect data from within the firm, such as sales data from the accounting department. They also collect data from outside the firm, such as population data from the federal government.

- **Data base.** The MIS maintain a data base, where these data are received, processed, edited, and stored. When the need arises, MIS personnel retrieve any part of the data and report it in such a way that it is meaningful to marketing decision makers. In most cases, mainframe computers and minicomputers are heavily used for these functions in the MIS, although small firms may not need these aids, relying instead on simple calculations or personal computers.

- **Output.** The output of the MIS is timely and relevant information that marketing executives need to help improve their decision making.

7-3. Steps in a Marketing Research Project

Marketing research projects are designed to gather and analyze information to improve marketing decision making. Research results are among the inputs that go into the marketing information system. Effective research should be *objective* (unbiased) and *structured* (planned in detail). This process consists of a number of well-coordinated steps, which are illustrated in Figure 7-2.

A. Identifying the problem

Managers use marketing research in order to help overcome problems. A problem exists when there is a difference between a desired situation and an actual situation. Researchers and managers should work together to make sure that the research focuses on problems that interfere with effective decision making.

Some problems are obvious—if sales are down and you know your company's product has defects, you can reasonably assume you know what the problem is. Other problems are not so obvious—you may need to look for them. **Exploratory research** is a way of identifying problems. It is a special kind of inquiry in which analysts examine *symptoms,* such as sales declines, and attempt to discover the underlying *causes* for those symptoms.

EXAMPLE 7-7: The McFaddin chain of nightclubs suffered considerable declines in sales and in profits during 1986. These declines could have been caused by some internal problem, such as poor service or unduly high prices. But these declines were symptoms of larger problems: an overall decline in alcohol consumption and the efforts of the states to raise the drinking age to 21.

B. Choosing information sources

Once a problem has been defined, researchers seek information that will be of value in solving it. Sometimes **secondary data**, which have been collected by some other organization, are adequate. These data are frequently available at low cost and can often be acquired quickly. The user of secondary data should take care to ensure that the data are current and reliable, and do in fact measure what he or she wants to measure. Some good sources of secondary data are the *Census of Population, The Statistical Abstract*, and various other publications of government agencies, foundations, trade associations, and colleges and universities.

Primary data are collected by a company's own researcher(s). There are several ways for researchers to collect primary data.

1. Surveys

One possibility is to use surveys, in which individuals are asked questions through the mail, over the telephone, or in person. These are widely used and can yield a wide variety of information. Personal interviews can lead to the acquisition of considerable in-depth information. Interviewers can explain the nature of the questioning process and can observe the interviewees. However, this form of gathering information can be costly. Mail questionnaires can be of value when many respondents who are geographically separated must be contacted. However, the response to these efforts may be low, and those who complete questionnaires may not be representative of the population at large. Telephone interviews can provide quick answers,

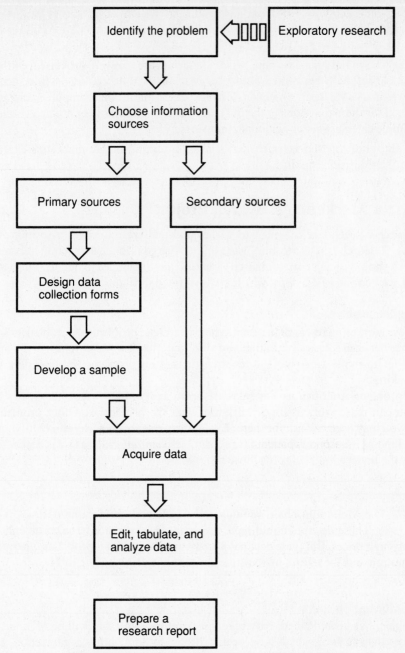

FIGURE 7-2: Steps in a marketing research project.

especially when the questions and the interviewing process is short. However, many persons are not at home when the telephone interview is attempted and some have unlisted phone numbers.

2. *Observation*

Another way to collect data is through observation, during which researchers take note of individual behavior. This can be done in person or by mechanical means. It is possible to use this method to observe consumers in their natural setting—when they are shopping, for instance—and to acquire information without interfering with their customary activities. Unlike surveys, however, observation provides little insight into consumer attitudes, opinions, and other mental states.

EXAMPLE 7-8: Marketers may use in-place video cameras to record the paths that consumers take in traveling through grocery stores, in order to gain insights into consumer shopping behavior. Mechanical counters can be used to measure the number of automobiles that pass over a given site, in order to determine the potential traffic of a location. Devices attached to television sets can be used to measure what program a set is tuned to at a given time, in order to determine which programs are most often watched.

3. Experiment

Experiments are conducted to provide evidence that one action caused a particular outcome. Figure 7-3 illustrates a typical marketing research experiment. An **independent variable**, such as an advertisement, is presented to a group of *subjects*, such as consumers. This presentation is called the *treatment*. Measures of a **dependent variable**, such as attitude toward the advertised

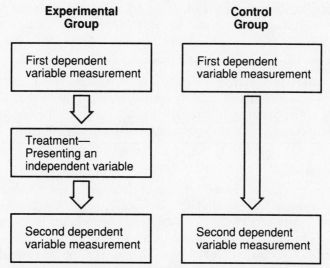

FIGURE 7-3: Design of a typical marketing research experiment.

product, are made both before and after the treatment. *The effect of the independent variable is judged as the difference in the dependent variable from before to after the treatment.* Often the performance of the group that received the treatment, called the *experimental group*, is compared to the performance of a group that did not receive a treatment, called the *control group*. Experiments cannot prove that an independent variable is the sole cause of a change in a dependent one, but they can provide considerable evidence that a particular independent variable does affect a dependent variable in predictable ways. The major drawbacks with experiments are that they can be very time-consuming and costly.

EXAMPLE 7-9: An over-the-counter drug manufacturer wanted to test the effect of a price reduction (independent variable) on sales (dependent variable) of its headache remedy. Prices were cut by 15% in six cities (the experimental group) and left unchanged in six others (the control group). In the experimental cities, sales rose by an average of 12%, while they remained unchanged in the control cities. On the basis of this evidence, the researchers may reasonably conclude that price decreases do in fact bring about sales increases.

C. Designing data collection forms

Researchers who undertake primary research are faced with the task of developing data collection forms. These are questionnaires and other guides that tell interviewers and observers what to say and do. The data collection forms should be designed to collect *only* information that will be of value in solving the research problem. They should be carefully formulated and pretested before they are actually used. Those who construct the forms should attempt to make them as clear and as simple as is feasible, in order to promote the receipt of useful information.

D. Developing the sample

It is usually impossible to collect information from every element of the population, so researchers engage in sampling. In *sampling*, researchers collect information from a small portion of the population under study. The sample selected should be as representative (typical) of the population as possible. There are two approaches to sampling that a researcher can take.

1. *Probability sampling*

In the case of *probability* sampling, the researchers know the probability that a member of the population will be included in the sample. Thus, sample statistics will tend to have the same characteristics as population measures, allowing the researchers to associate the sampling statistics to the larger population measures. One approach to probability sampling is to employ **random sampling**, in which case every member of the population has an equal chance of being chosen. This might be done by drawing names from a hat, for instance; but in actual practice, it is usually accomplished through the use of statistical tables or a computer. The major problems with probability sampling are that it can be costly and it is usually time-consuming.

EXAMPLE 7-10: A marketing researcher wants to find out how realtors react to a newly developed auto leasing plan. The researcher takes a random sample by acquiring a list of all realtors in the city under study, assigning a number to each one, and then selecting the numbers to be included in the sample through a computer program that chooses numbers randomly.

---

2. *Nonprobability sampling*

Sometimes researchers are so pressed for time or have such a small budget that they must use more informal, nonprobability samples. In this case, the researchers do not know the probability that representative members of the population will be included in the sample. Under these circumstances, the researchers *cannot* make statistical statements in association with population measures on the basis of their sample statistics. They may (*a*) use their own judgment in choosing individuals who seem to be representative of the population—this method is called a **judgment sample**; or (*b*) they may contact individuals who are easy to reach, such as a university class—this method is called a **convenience sample.** In nonprobability sampling, however, there is always the danger that informal samples may be seriously nonrepresentative of the population.

E. Acquiring the data

In acquiring data, researchers collect information through secondary sources, surveys, observations, or experiments. The analysts may be in charge of supervising, motivating, and controlling a field staff. In other instances, professional data acquisition firms are contracted to do this work. These firms are in a position to provide very good results because they maintain well-trained and well-supervised staffs.

F. Editing, tabulating, and analyzing the data

Once the data have been collected, they should be *edited* as a check for interviewer or interviewee error or dishonesty. Then the data are *tabulated*, or formed into statistics such as means, percentages, and medians. Following tabulation is *analysis*, whereby mathematical measures are used to test the significance of the statistics that have been computed. (Statistical methods of tabulation and analysis are beyond the scope of this book.)

EXAMPLE 7-11: A researcher conducts a study which shows that 11% of the men in the survey have visited a particular variety store, while only 6% of the women have been in the store. Statistical analysis can indicate if this is a significant difference or if this difference could be due to chance alone.

G. The research report

Once the data have been analyzed, they are ready for *interpretation*. This means examining them and deciding what they mean in terms of the problems that the study is examining. The interpretation results in statements of the implications of the study, and often concludes with recommendations to management.

Analysts should prepare a written report that sets forth the research process, its findings, and recommendations. This should be done carefully, as the quality of the entire research effort is likely to be judged by the report. The goal of the report should be effective communication to management as to how marketing decisions can be improved. Often the written document is accompanied by an oral report that explains the highlights of the research.

7-4. Cost/Benefit Analysis of Marketing Information Projects

Marketers would find it impractical to base *every* marketing decision on marketing research or MIS output. Information from these sources should be used only when the benefits outweigh the costs. *Cost/benefit analysis* is necessary to determine if an information acquisition project should be undertaken.

- **Cost/benefit analysis** involves estimating the money value of all the costs and benefits of an information acquisition project to determine if the benefits outweigh the costs.

Information acquisition **benefits** are defined as the difference between profits resulting from decisions made on the basis of acquired information and profits resulting from decisions made without that information. And in order to assess benefits, we have to determine the **costs**. There are four categories of costs:

(1) *Expenses*. One information acquisition cost is the expense of conducting the research or of using the MIS.
(2) *Revenue delays*. Revenue delays are unrealized revenues that the company passes up because a decision is being postponed while information is being sought.
(3) *Errors in the data*. If the information is incorrect, poor decisions can be made, resulting in lower profits than if no information had been collected.
(4) *Change in situation*. If the marketing situation changes, the research may be outdated, making the cost of having obtained it a total loss.

To complete a cost/benefit analysis, analysts prepare numerical estimates of the costs and the benefits and subtract the former from the latter. If the result is positive, the information should be collected. Otherwise, it should not.

7-5. Sales Forecasting

Forecasts of sales are special kinds of marketing information. They are very important because companies base most of their plans on the forecasts. Also, most of the control activities of the firm use input from sales forecasts. Some forecasts are for the *long run* (over one year) and are employed for decisions that will have lasting impact on the company. *Short-run* forecasts are for a year or less, and are of help in making plans that are of limited duration.

EXAMPLE 7-12: A long-run forecast might predict that a company's sales will increase by 85% over the next five years. On the strength of this forecast, management might build a new plant, lease new warehouses, and/or buy out several intermediaries. A short-run forecast might suggest a 13% increase in company sales over the next 12 months. This forecast could encourage management to build up inventories and temporarily raise prices.

There are several widely used sales forecasting techniques: *judgment of executives and sales representatives, time series analysis, regression analysis, surveys,* and *test markets.*

A. Judgment of executives and sales representatives

A company may require its experienced managers and/or sales representatives to prepare forecasts, based solely on their judgment. These individuals may have insights into the market and intuitions that allow them to predict future sales fairly accurately. On the other hand, judgment may be biased.

Some executives and sales representatives are unduly optimistic or pessimistic. Some executives may set goals too high in order to display their competence. Also, sales representatives whose quotas are based on sales forecasts may deliberately keep their forecasts low so their quotas will be easy to reach.

EXAMPLE 7-13: The Thompson Medical Company uses sales representative judgment in forecasting sales for its products, such as Dexatrim capsules. The firm has found that these estimates are reasonably accurate, although, when past estimates are compared with past sales, the actual sales tend to be higher. This being the case, Thompson's researchers adjust the sales representatives' forecasts upward to account for these biases.

B. Time series analysis

Time series analysis projects past sales into the future. Figure 7-4 illustrates the linear projection concept. An analyst first plots actual sales figures as points on a graph, then draws a straight line (or a curve) through the points, thereby reflecting the overall *direction* of past sales. If this line is extended to future years, it provides sales forecasts for these years. Some firms use mathematical techniques to produce the forecasts, rather than relying on graphical representations.

The *linear* time series technique, in which analysts simply extend past general patterns in sales to future periods, is called **trend analysis**. It is also possible to extend *cycles* (recurring patterns of advances and declines) and *seasonal patterns* (recurring advances and declines that take place in a typical year, such as increases in greeting card sales just before a holiday). The time series techniques are useful if it is expected that past events predict future events.

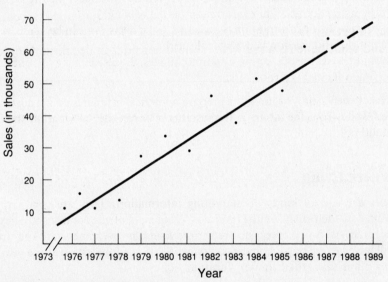

FIGURE 7-4: An example of trend analysis. The solid line represents actual data; the dashed line represents estimated data.

C. Regression analysis

In the case of regression analysis, the analyst uses the relationship of sales to some variable other than past sales to predict future sales. The sales of air conditioners may be closely related to summer temperatures, for instance. If this is the case, weather forecasts may be of value for sales forecasting. Regression analysis uses these other variables in mathematical formulas to predict future sales. It is useful when a variable is obviously closely related to sales.

D. Surveys

Surveys ask customers for their future buying plans. This method is especially valuable when introducing new products, i.e., when management has no past experience upon which to base future estimates. Surveys are more likely to be accurate for industrial than consumer markets, because industrial buyers often think out their buying plans more carefully than do consumers. Surveys are subject to error, however, as buyers cannot always predict their future purchasing.

E. Test markets

Some firms place products for sale in limited, representative markets, called test markets, and use those sales figures as indicators of sales for the market in general. If, for example, a company earns 10% of the market in representative test markets, it may assume that it will earn a 10% market share in the total market. Test markets can be expensive and time-consuming. Also, rivals may disrupt the tests; they may, for instance, reduce prices in the test market area. A further problem is that test-marketing delays action while the test is in effect. Overall, however, test-marketing is a realistic way of forecasting sales.

RAISE YOUR GRADES
Can you explain . . . ?

☑ how a manufacturer could benefit from research on target consumers, pricing, and promotion in formulating marketing strategy

☑ why a firm might be able to benefit from marketing research related to product planning and physical distribution

☑ what kinds of data inputs a wholesaler might use in an MIS

☑ what marketing research steps a marketer should undertake before introducing a new product in the market

☑ how a firm might set up an experiment to determine if one proposed ad is more effective than another in getting favorable attitudes toward a company product

☑ what costs and what benefits a marketer should consider in deciding whether a marketing research project should be undertaken

☑ why a firm might use sales representatives' judgment in producing sales forecasts

SUMMARY

1. Relevant information can be one of the major keys to success in marketing.
2. Marketers utilize information in making target customer selection, product planning, pricing, promotion, and distribution decisions.
3. Marketing information systems (MIS) are parts of the marketing organization that are used for the continuous collection and analysis of data and provision of information to marketing decision makers.
4. Marketing information systems include (1) inputs of data from inside and outside the firm, (2) data bases of relevant information, and (3) outputs to marketing decision makers.
5. Marketing research projects are designed to gather and analyze information to improve marketing decision making.
6. The steps in a marketing research project are: (1) identifying the problem; (2) choosing information sources; (3) designing data collection forms; (4) developing a sample; (5) acquiring the data; (6) editing, tabulating, and analyzing the data; and (7) preparing a research report.
7. Cost/benefit analysis is necessary to determine if an information acquisition project should be undertaken.
8. Cost/benefit analysis involves estimating the money value of all the costs and benefits of the information acquisition project to determine if the benefits outweigh the costs.
9. Sales forecasts are instrumental in all planning and control activities of marketers.
10. Among the more widely used sales forecasting techniques are judgment of executives and sales representatives, time series analysis, regression analysis, surveys, and test markets.

RAPID REVIEW

Multiple Choice

1. If Pacific Southwest Airlines seeks information that will be useful in selecting target consumers, it is likely to look for those (**a**) who have a need for the airline services, (**b**) who are in lower social classes, (**c**) who are in informal groups, (**d**) who are in lower-income groups. [See Section 7-1.]

   a

2. Information for product planning would *not* be used in order to decide (**a**) what products to add, (**b**) what products to drop, (**c**) changes in product quality, (**d**) what promotion budget to use. [See Section 7-1.]

   d

3. Pricing administrators are especially likely to seek information on which of the following: (**a**) company product performance, (**b**) competitors' product performance, (**c**) company sales, (**d**) company sales quotas. [See Section 7-1.]

   c

4. *Not* included in important information to help make promotion decisions by the Fireman's Fund Insurance Co. is (**a**) the effectiveness of company ads, (**b**) consumer desires for new kinds of policies, (**c**) number of sales calls made, (**d**) number of orders taken by sales representatives. [See Section 7-1.]

   b

5. In making distribution decisions, a company is in particular need of information on (**a**) the effectiveness of company ads, (**b**) product preferences by target customers, (**c**) services rendered by transportation carriers, (**d**) the prices of competing computers. [See Section 7-1.]

   c

6. A marketing information system for a firm is used for _____ collection and analysis of data. (**a**) continuous, (**b**) infrequent, (**c**) intermittent, (**d**) little. [See Section 7-2.]

   a

7. The MIS for a firm collects data from both (**a**) stock and real estate brokers, (**b**) public and private employment agencies, (**c**) large and small stock exchanges, (**d**) inside and outside the firm. [See Section 7-2.]

   d

8. At the data base of a firm, data are *not* (**a**) deleted, (**b**) processed, (**c**) edited, (**d**) stored. [See Section 7-2.]

   a

9. The output of an MIS for a firm is information that (**a**) is readily available, (**b**) marketing executives need, (**c**) can be analyzed by a computer, (**d**) can be acquired at a low cost. [See Section 7-2.]

   b

10. A marketing problem exists when there is a difference between an actual and a _____ situation. (**a**) problem, (**b**) necessary, (**c**) desired, (**d**) planned. [See Section 7-3.]

    c

11. _____ research is used to identify problems. (**a**) Marketing, (**b**) Exploratory, (**c**) Primary, (**d**) Empirical. [See Section 7-3.]

    b

12. _____ data are those collected by an outside organization. (**a**) Secondary, (**b**) Primary, (**c**) Survey, (**d**) Experimental. [See Section 7-3.]

    a

13. Surveys are *not* taken (**a**) by telephone, (**b**) in person, (**c**) through observation, (**d**) by mail. [See Section 7-3.]

    c

14. If a corporation conducts an experiment on how much a proposed new product might increase sales, sales is the (**a**) subject, (**b**) treatment, (**c**) control group, (**d**) dependent variable. [See Section 7-3.]

    d

15. In simple random sampling, each member of the population has a(n) _____ chance of being chosen. (**a**) definite, (**b**) equal, (**c**) great, (**d**) unlikely. [See Section 7-3.]

    b

16. When market researchers perform _____, they are using mathematical models to test the significance of statistics. (**a**) editing, (**b**) tabulating, (**c**) analysis, (**d**) interpretation. [See Section 7-3.]

    c

17. In cost/benefit analysis, one of the costs that analysts are likely to study is the expense incurred for (**a**) gathering information, (**b**) advertising, (**c**) producing the product, (**d**) packaging the product. [See Section 7-4.]

    a

18. When sales representatives forecast sales, the sales forecasts may be low because of the psychological effect of sales (**a**) expenses, (**b**) quotas, (**c**) analysis, (**d**) budgets. [See Section 7-5.]

    b

19. In the case of _____ analysis, companies project sales into the future for forecasting purposes. (**a**) trend, (**b**) survey, (**c**) test market, (**d**) regression. [See Section 7-5.]

a

20. In using _____, an analyst for the Toro Corp. might use the relationship between snow blower sales to snowfall to predict sales. (**a**) time series analysis, (**b**) test markets, (**c**) surveys, (**d**) regression analysis. [See Section 7-5.]

d

SOLVED PROBLEMS

PROBLEM 7-1 Assume that you are in charge of selecting target customers for the Minnetonka Corporation Check-Up toothpaste. What information would you seek? How would you obtain that information?

Answer: In this case, you would gather information that would help you decide which consumers have a need for the product and have the income to afford it. The first part (needs) can be determined by consumer surveys that ask a variety of people how well they are satisfied with the toothpaste they are currently using and how they feel about other brands, including Check-Up. The second part (income) may be determined by studying the income data which are available in secondary sources, such as United States Bureau of the Census publications. [See Section 7-1.]

PROBLEM 7-2 What major product planning decisions would managers for Whirlpool make, based on relevant information?

Answer: Managers for Whirlpool would use marketing information to help determine what products to add, drop, or change, and what elements to include in packaging and branding. Much of this information would come from current and prospective Whirlpool customers, who could be asked for their opinions on the company's and competitors' products and services. Also, management could use information on sales, expenses, and profits of its existing products as indicators of which products could benefit from product-development effort. Declining profits in home freezers might indicate the need for product changes, for instance. [See Section 7-1.]

PROBLEM 7-3 Assume that you are setting prices for a new running shoe produced by Nike. On what variables would you seek information?

Answer: Included in the information that would be useful are facts on company sales, prices, and competitors' prices. Sales data would indicate which Nike running shoes are selling in volume and which are not. Management could consider the prices of each type of shoe and determine which tend to bring in the most sales. These should be compared to competitors' prices, to indicate where the firm stands with respect to its competition. This analysis might indicate that Nike needs a low-priced running shoe to stay competitive. [See Section 7-1.]

PROBLEM 7-4 If you were collecting information to evaluate the selling effort of the sales force for a steel pipe distributor, what information on sales representative performance would you look for?

Answer: Included in the information that would be helpful are the volume of sales by the distributor's sales representatives, the number of calls made, and the number of orders taken. The current volume of sales could be compared to past levels and to sales of competitors, to provide an overall indication of how well the sales force is performing in the steel pipe industry. The number of calls made would help in assessing the extent to which sales representatives are working diligently to cover the market. Data on the number of orders taken would furnish evidence as to how productive are individual sales representatives and how efficient the sales force is as a whole. [See Section 7-1.]

PROBLEM 7-5   If a company that mass-markets soups is in the process of selecting channels of distribution and physical distribution systems, what are some of the major kinds of information that it needs?

Answer: Marketers for a company that mass-markets soups can use inputs on the sales and costs of various kinds of wholesalers and retailers in selecting channels of distribution. Some wholesalers might be too small or too costly to fulfill the company's needs. This mass marketer needs middlemen who can carry large amounts of product in an efficient manner. Management can use information on the costs and services rendered by various transportation carriers in order to choose the most promising physical distribution system. A decision might be made, for example, to choose a trucking company that provides fast and economical pickup and delivery and long-distance transportation. [See Section 7-1.]

PROBLEM 7-6   A fellow student has read about marketing information systems in a business magazine and wonders what they are. What would you tell him?

Answer: Marketing information systems (MIS) are parts of the marketing organization that are used for continuous collection and analysis of data and provision of information to marketing decision makers. Those personnel who work within the system are charged with the responsibility of assisting marketing managers in developing strategy and tactics. The information that they furnish must be appropriate, timely, and in a form that managers will find useful in solving marketing problems.

PROBLEM 7-7   Assume that you are setting up a data bank for a newly formed MIS in a large canning company. What functions should your data bank perform?

Answer: At the data base of the MIS, provision should be made to receive, process, edit, and store information. For a large firm, this will require a staff of personnel who are well acquainted with the canning industry and its major customers, who are experienced in data acquisition and processing, and who are familiar with the problems faced by marketing managers. It will also require extensive computer support. When the need arises, steps should be taken by the company MIS personnel to retrieve the data and report it in such a way that it is meaningful to the company's marketing managers. [See Section 7-2.]

PROBLEM 7-8   If sales are down at a national chain of retail stores, how can the firm determine the cause?

Answer: One useful way to determine the cause is to conduct exploratory research. In this special kind of inquiry, analysts would attempt to identify problems that are causing sales declines by examining symptoms, such as reductions in revenues for particular products in different parts of the country. Then the analysts would attempt to discover the underlying problems. They might find, for instance, that sales are depressed mainly in regions where large rivals are strong, and conclude that the firm should increase promotion expenditures and reduce prices in these regions. [See Section 7-3.]

PROBLEM 7-9   Assume that you are collecting information to determine if you should open a laundromat in the college area of the city. The Chamber of Commerce has given you data on local population, income, and sales. How should you evaluate these data?

Answer: Since these data have been collected by someone else, you should take care to ensure that it is current and reliable and that it truly measures what you want to measure. The Chamber of Commerce employees probably obtained the data from other sources, such as government publications or university research studies. You should carefully examine these, in order to make sure that the data are up to date and have been properly recorded. [See Section 7-3.]

PROBLEM 7-10   How could McCormick and Company conduct an experiment to see if a new container for its herbs would bring in more sales than old containers?

Answer: Researchers for McCormick and Company could place the new containers in test cities and continue to use the old containers in control cities. These two sets of sites should be "average," or representative, of the United States population as a whole. Sales could be measured over a period of time (such as six months) and comparisons made between the test and control cities. This will provide an indicator of the sales-generating power of the new container. [See Section 7-3.]

PROBLEM 7-11   Assume that you are designing a questionnaire to be sent to households to determine householder attitudes toward a shopping center. How should the questionnaire be developed?

Answer: The questionnaires should be designed to collect only information that will be of value in solving the research problem—measuring attitudes toward the shopping center. They should be carefully formulated and tested by the researchers before they are actually used to acquire data. Those who construct the forms should attempt to make these as clear and simple as is feasible, in order to promote the receipt of useful information by those who will be making decisions regarding the shopping center. [See Section 7-3.]

PROBLEM 7-12   Assume that you are conducting research for a consulting firm. You are in a hurry to conduct the study because the management of the client firm must make a quick decision as to whether or not to bring out a new product variation. What informal sampling methods might you employ?

Answer: Two informal sampling methods could be used. One is to employ judgment in choosing individuals who seem to be representative of the population (a judgment sample). Your judgment might suggest that if 300 attendees at a trade show were surveyed, the research results would be representative. Another alternative would be to contact individuals who are easy to reach (a convenience sample). In employing this method, you might survey members of a club, one or more college classes, or consumers who shop in a mall. [See Section 7-3.]

PROBLEM 7-13   A confused classmate has asked you to explain the difference between analysis and interpretation. How would you respond?

Answer: The classmate should be told that analysis involves using statistical measures to test the significance of statistics that have been computed. It might be used, for instance, to determine if the average price of a company product sold in retail stores is higher than the average price of a competitor. On the other hand, interpretation involves examining data and deciding what they mean, in terms of the problems that the study is examining. The interpretation results in statements of the implications of the study and often in recommendations to management. An interpretation might be that company prices are too high and that these should be lowered to gain market share. [See Section 7-3.]

PROBLEM 7-14   A lumber wholesaler is considering a marketing research project and wants a cost/benefit analysis undertaken. How can benefits be measured?

Answer: The lumber wholesaler can measure the information benefits by estimating the difference between company profits resulting from decisions based on the information, and profits resulting from decisions made without the information. This would require that the researcher prepare estimates of sales, costs, and profits under both conditions. These estimates are only forecasts, not known facts, but they are really the only effective way of measuring the expected value of the research project. [See Section 7-4.]

PROBLEM 7-15   What are the possible major costs of a marketing research project that a company might conduct to assess changes in advertising appeals?

Answer: One possible cost element is the expense of conducting the research or of using the MIS. Another is revenue delays, which are unrealized revenues that the company passes up because a decision is being postponed while information is sought. A third cost element might be errors in the data—incorrect information can lead to faulty decisions, resulting in less profit than if no information were collected. Finally, the situation may change, making the research outdated. [See Section 7-4.]

PROBLEM 7-16   What decisions should a large retailer base on short-run and long-run forecasts?

Answer: Short-run forecasts are for a year or less and can help in making plans that are of limited duration. Retailing management can make decisions such as how much to spend for advertising next year, whether prices for certain goods should be changed, and whether to offer coupons to consumers, based on such forecasts. Long-run forecasts are used in making decisions that will have lasting effects on the company. The retailer might decide to change its store interiors, use more truck (rather than rail) freight, or to construct new warehouses, based on long-run forecasts. [See Section 7-5.]

PROBLEM 7-17   A chain of auto supply stores is considering using the judgment of executives, sales managers, and sales representatives to make sales forecasts. What are the advantages and disadvantages of this method?

Answer: The executives, sales managers, and sales representatives may have very good insights and intuitions that allow them to predict future sales fairly accurately. Those who have long experience in the company and industry may be particularly valuable for this purpose. On the other hand, their judgment may be biased. Some executives and sales representatives are unduly optimistic or pessimistic, and this is reflected in their forecasts. Also, sales representatives whose quotas are based on sales forecasts may deliberately keep their forecasts low, so their quotas will be easy to reach. This is especially likely in a very competitive industry, such as auto supply retailing. [See Section 7-5.]

PROBLEM 7-18   A classmate has asked you to explain the difference between trend analysis and regression analysis. How would you respond?

Answer: You can explain to the classmate that, in the case of trend analysis, analysts project past sales into the future. It is assumed that overall patterns of change in sales will not be altered with the passage of time. For regression analysis, the analyst uses the relationship of sales to some other variable to predict future sales. This could involve using estimates of expected snowfall to project future sales of snow-mobiles and skis. [See Section 7-5.]

PROBLEM 7-19   When would you most likely use surveys, rather than another forecasting technique?

Answer: You would most likely use surveys when introducing new products, i.e., when management has no past experience upon which to base future estimates. Statistics-based techniques cannot be employed under such circumstances. You might also use surveys when dealing with industrial buyers. Surveys are more likely to be accurate for industrial than consumer goods, because industrial buyers tend to be more informed and often have thought out their buying plans more carefully. This puts them in a position to estimate their future purchases fairly accurately. In addition, they may be more willing than the consumer to participate in the survey. [See Section 7-5.]

PROBLEM 7-20   What are the advantages and disadvantages of test markets as a sales forecasting technique for consumer goods firms?

Answer: Some consumer goods firms may place products for sale in test markets and use those sales figures as predictors of sales for the market in general. This is a realistic method of forecasting, since it is based on what actually happens in the market. However, test markets tend to be expensive and time-consuming. Also, rivals can disrupt a test, for example, by reducing prices in the test markets. A further problem is that action is delayed while a test is in effect. Finally, outside forces, such as weather, labor union strikes, and sudden changes in consumer buying plans can distort the test results. Overall, though, they are a realistic way of forecasting. [See Section 7-5.]

PART III
MARKETING DECISION MAKING:
THE MARKETING MIX

8 PRODUCT MANAGEMENT

THIS CHAPTER IS ABOUT

- ☑ **Goods and Services as Sources of Satisfaction**
- ☑ **Types of Goods and Services**
- ☑ **Product or Service Development Activity**
- ☑ **The Product Life Cycle**
- ☑ **Width and Depth Strategies**
- ☑ **Product Positioning**
- ☑ **Packaging**
- ☑ **Labeling, Branding, and Trademarks**

8-1. Goods and Services as Sources of Satisfaction

Why do people buy Wendy's hamburgers, Bufferin analgesics, Kodak cameras, and H & R Block tax services when there are many other goods and services to spend their money on? The answer is that consumers do not see goods and services as things of value for their own sake, but as *bundles of satisfaction*, or sources of benefits. As long as consumers believe that a bundle is worth the time, money, and effort they must invest in it, they will make a purchase. This being the case, marketers view products broadly, as benefits offered, rather than as mere physical items.

EXAMPLE 8-1: Nike running shoes are physical entities. But, when purchasing Nikes, a consumer doesn't buy just the physical item; rather, the consumer buys what the product promises or what satisfactions it can deliver. Nike has managed to satisfy consumer needs by offering such benefits as comfort and safety. Some of its former competitors, who have failed to offer these or similar benefits, are now bankrupt.

8-2. Types of Goods and Services

Goods and services (referred to hereafter as "goods" for convenience' sake) are the major output of our economy. As you have already learned, goods are classified either as consumer or industrial, depending on the purpose for which the goods are purchased. Marketers further classify goods into types that illustrate general purchasing patterns. Recognizing these patterns helps in planning a marketing strategy for each type of good.

A. Types of consumer goods

There are four types of consumer goods.

1. Convenience goods

Convenience goods are those goods which consumers are not willing to go to much trouble to buy. Instead of shopping for a particular item, they buy whatever is most easily obtainable. Consumers purchase convenience goods on a frequent basis and pay a low price for them.

Examples of convenience goods are candy bars, chewing gum, disposable lighters, pocket combs, and pencils.

Marketers of convenience goods usually make their offerings available to consumers in a large number of locations. This makes it easy for buyers to acquire the items they want with a minimum of effort.

2. Shopping goods

Shopping goods are offerings on which consumers spend considerable effort, often comparing prices and quality of a number of products in order to make the best buy. Generally, consumers shop infrequently for these items and pay relatively high prices for them. Examples of shopping goods are men's suits, sailboats, expensive cameras, and cars.

Most manufacturers of shopping goods distribute their products to fewer retailers than do convenience goods producers. These manufacturers realize that retailers are more likely to mount strong promotional campaigns for the goods if they have less competition.

3. Specialty goods

Specialty goods are items for which the consumer is willing to expend considerable effort to acquire a preferred brand. Rather than seeking the best buy, the consumer will travel great distances and spend a lot of time in order to find a preferred item. Many of these goods are expensive. Some examples of specialty goods are high-fashion women's clothing, VCR's, and health foods.

The producers of specialty goods stock their offerings in only a few retail establishments in a given city. This encourages the retailers to work hard at selling the goods—they know they have no immediate competitors and will not share sales with rivals.

4. Unsought goods

Unsought goods are items that most consumers are not eager to purchase. Unsought goods satisfy negative needs, so consumers often put off buying these offerings until the last minute. Examples of unsought goods are tooth fillings, life insurance, and burial plots.

Since most retailers and wholesalers are not willing or able to stock these goods, producers often find that they must do the retailing and wholesaling work themselves. Further, they may need to use incentives such as low prices and high-pressure selling techniques in order to produce adequate sales.

B. Types of industrial goods

There are five types of industrial goods.

1. Installations

Installations are expensive goods that organizations acquire in order to produce goods and services. These goods are primary factors that determine how much the buying organization can produce. Buyers' accountants *depreciate* the cost of installations over the lifetime of the asset, rather than treating the cost as a one-time expense. Examples of installations are milling machines, casting machines, and blast furnaces.

High-level executives and senior sales representatives play a major role in selling installations. Months may pass before the marketer and the buyer complete the negotiations on a particular sale. After the buyer has placed an order, employees of the marketing company usually strive to ensure that the product is properly delivered, installed, and maintained in operating condition.

2. Accessories

Accessories are similar to installations, except that they have shorter lives, are less expensive, and do not determine the production capacity of the buying company. Workers use accessories in combination with installations for production purposes. Examples of accessories are factory maintenance and repair tools and welding machines.

Marketers of accessories often employ wholesalers. They usually set firm prices, and are not likely to negotiate prices as installations producers often do. Accessory marketers conduct much of their promotion effort in business and trade magazines.

3. Raw materials

Raw materials are goods that marketers sell in their natural state. They become part of the buyer's product. Buyers treat the cost of raw materials as an *expense*, not as a depreciation item. Raw materials may be either *agricultural* or *nonagricultural*. Some examples of agricultural raw materials are corn and livestock; some examples of nonagricultural raw materials are crude oil, coal, and bauxite.

Middlemen, such as grain elevator operators, collect agricultural raw materials and sell them to industrial buyers. Most of the marketing decisions relating to these products have to do with warehousing and storage.

In the case of nonagricultural raw materials, producers normally sell directly to buyers without the aid of wholesalers. Negotiations between buyer and seller over prices and product characteristics are common.

4. Parts and processed materials

Parts and processed materials are goods that are purchased in a finished or partially finished condition. These goods become part of the buyers' products, and their purchase is treated by buyers as an expense. Examples of parts and processed materials are integrated circuits for television sets, chips for computers, batteries for automobiles, and flour for bakeries.

Marketers of parts and processed materials usually sell directly to buyers, often through long-term contracts. Buyers and sellers determine prices and product characteristics through personal contact, so advertising is less important for these goods than it is for other kinds of goods.

5. Operating supplies

Operating supplies are goods that buyers use in carrying out their business activities. These items do not become part of the buyers' products, have low unit prices, and are treated as expenses. Examples of operating supplies are computer paper, lubricating oil, grease, and water.

Producers of operating supplies utilize wholesalers extensively because their orders are scattered among large numbers of firms that purchase in small quantities. Price competition in this industry is intense.

8-3. Product or Service Development Activity

• In order to remain profitable, companies must introduce new products to the market.

Products don't just happen. Rather, they come into existence as a result of careful management, thought, and research. This brings us to a discussion of what activities are needed for successful new product development. In this context, a product is "new" if the firm has not offered it previously. There is a six-step process that firms follow to help determine what products they should add to their offerings.

A. Producing ideas

The first step in new product or service development to create *ideas*. Ideas may come from inventors, customers, competitors, employees, sales representatives, suppliers, and others.

EXAMPLE 8-2: A 3M Company researcher was attempting to formulate a new superglue, but the substance he developed was just not very adhesive: it stuck, but it didn't *stay* stuck. So, instead of changing the formula for his adhesive, he thought about *new* uses for a glue that wouldn't stick. And he came up with gummed note pads. The company introduced these pads to the market (as Post-Its) and was very successful in selling them, both as consumer and as industrial goods.

B. Screening

The second step in new product or service development is *screening*. When marketers screen, they evaluate the ideas that they have formulated earlier and eliminate those that seem to have little chance of earning a profit. Many marketers make use of checklists, which list and rate desirable product characteristics. Figure 8-1 shows a hypothetical checklist which a bank might use in

	Rating				
	Very Good	Good	Average	Poor	Very Poor
Production cost	_____	____	_____	____	_____
Distribution cost	_____	____	_____	____	_____
Fills needs of customers	_____	____	_____	____	_____
Differs from competitors' offerings	_____	____	_____	____	_____
Fits company image	_____	____	_____	____	_____
Does not violate the law	_____	____	_____	____	_____
Employees can sell it	_____	____	_____	____	_____
Will not use up too much cash	_____	____	_____	____	_____
Does not require much investment	_____	____	_____	____	_____
Does not put customer at risk	_____	____	_____	____	_____
Enhances consumer welfare	_____	____	_____	____	_____
Totals	_____	____	_____	____	_____

FIGURE 8-1: Hypothetical screening checklist. Marketers check a scale for each characteristic. Totals appear at the bottom.

screening for a proposed new credit card. Some companies will further consider only those products that receive at least a minimum number of "very good" or "good" ratings, or a minimum score, depending on the system they use.

C. Economic evaluation

The third step in new product or service development is *economic evaluation*. Marketers carry out an economic evaluation of product or service ideas that successfully pass the screening stage. This evaluation involves estimating expected sales and costs, in order to produce forecasts of profits, return on investment, and breakeven levels.

EXAMPLE 8-3: The Kentucky Fried Chicken (KFC) Corporation introduced a chicken nuggets product in 1984, several years after McDonald's and other fast-food chains had introduced similar products. KFC did not introduce nuggets until it had thoroughly estimated future sales and costs, and was reasonably sure that it could earn satisfactory profits. The nuggets turned out to be very profitable for the company.

D. Development

The fourth step in new product or service development is further *development* of the actual product. Marketers transfer product ideas that pass economic evaluation into a development stage, during which they decide exactly what kind of product to produce. In this stage, a company may develop *prototypes* or actual models of the proposed product in limited quantities.

EXAMPLE 8-4: Beatrice/Hunt-Wesson Foods decided to move Wesson corn oil into development in 1985 because this product had produced a highly positive economic evaluation. The firm produced small quantities of this "all-natural, cholesterol-free" product in order to determine consumer reactions to such an offering. Numerous consumers liked the corn oil, so management decided to subject it to testing.

E. Testing

The fifth step in new product or service development is *testing*. In the case of testing, marketers find out how well a proposed new offering will actually sell in the marketplace. Usually, this involves selling or "test-marketing" the offering in a small number of typical cities to determine if sales are large enough to justify full-scale production. Test markets can be very useful because they actually measure sales results.

EXAMPLE 8-5: Village Inn Pancake House restaurants experienced severely declining revenues in the mid-1980's. Management felt that its dessert menu was too limited and might be turning off some consumers. The firm therefore introduced pies in Arizona, Florida, and Nebraska test markets. Sales of pies increased total revenues by over 37% in the test markets, so management decided to market pies nationally, and was elated by the results.

F. Commercialization

The sixth step in new product or service development is *commercialization*. In the commercialization stage, the company makes a full-scale introduction of a product that has survived test-marketing. The introduction may be national or it may be limited to certain regions. Limited introduction may occur when the firm is strapped for cash or is not convinced that the product will sell well in all portions of the national market.

EXAMPLE 8-6: Gilroy Farms, a leading supplier of onion and garlic products, conducted a test market which indicated that bottled garlic would sell well in minced and crushed forms. The firm needed to extend its offerings to meet retailer demands for a garlic product that was convenient for consumers. In 1985 the firm commercialized the bottled product in selected regions of the country. It stocked the product, along with appropriate recipes, in the fresh-produce sections of supermarkets. The new offering quickly met with the approval of supermarket buyers and consumers.

8-4. The Product Life Cycle

Once a new product has been commercialized, it enters into the so-called *product life cycle*, which is made up of the various stages of the product's life in the marketplace. A study of these stages can help marketers make effective product decisions. There are four stages in a product life cycle: introduction, growth, maturity, and decline (see Figure 8-2).

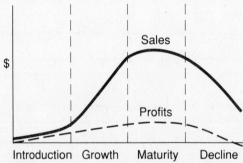

FIGURE 8-2: The product life cycle shows changes in sales and profits with the passage of time.

A. Introduction

The first stage in the product life cycle is *introduction*. During the introduction stage, the product is new and sales grow slowly. Profits are usually nonexistent or minimal during this stage because of high initial costs and low sales. Companies spend considerable sums attempting to convince consumers to try the new product.

EXAMPLE 8-7: The toothpaste market is highly competitive. Over the years, competitors have introduced many new products in an attempt to wrest control of the market from the leader, Procter and Gamble's Crest. In 1985, Colgate-Palmolive introduced Dentagard plaque-fighter, a toothpaste that controls plaque formation on teeth. Sales were strong, but profits were low as the firm struggled to establish itself as an industry leader.

B. Growth

The second stage in the product life cycle is *growth*. After a product becomes well known and customers start to buy it, the product enters the growth stage. During this stage, sales grow rapidly and profits appear. Rival companies may enter the market. Management attempts to develop promotion that attracts buyers to the company brand and away from competing brands. The company may consider dropping prices or improving distribution.

EXAMPLE 8-8: As of 1986, a Miles Laboratories' product, "Within" multivitamins with calcium and extra iron, was in the growth stage of the product life cycle. The company sponsored a $3.5 million advertising campaign on three television networks and offered cents-off coupons. These efforts were necessary to battle competitors who claimed that their vitamins had more dietary and nutritional benefits.

C. Maturity

The third stage in the product life cycle is *maturity*. At maturity, sales grow slowly, then begin to fall, and profits decrease. High promotion expenses are needed to combat rivals. To protect profits, management may seek to find new uses for the product or new selling appeals.

EXAMPLE 8-9: When sales of Arm and Hammer baking soda declined, management sought new uses for the product. It came up with the idea of promoting the product as a refrigerator, freezer, and cat litter deodorant. Sales increased substantially.

D. Decline

The fourth stage in the product life cycle is *decline*. During the decline stage, sales and profits fall from previous levels. Often, consumer desire for the product decreases and competition increases. The company may experience very low profits or may actually suffer losses. Management may drop the product or may attempt to revive it through such means as promotion, price-cutting, or product improvement.

EXAMPLE 8-10: Mattel, Inc.'s Barbie dolls sold in great volume in the 1960's. Then, during the late 1970's and 1980's, sales fell from previous levels, to such a point that management feared that this once very popular product might have to be dropped. However, management decided in 1984 to gamble on a pumped-up advertising campaign for the dolls. This effort increased sales significantly and helped produce a turnaround that saved the company from bankruptcy.

Eventually, every offering will slip into decline. Some new items fail prematurely, however. In many cases, products fail because management did not "read the market" correctly—that is, management did not accurately interpret what consumers actually wanted. In other cases, competition may turn out to be more severe than management expected. Finally, a number of brands fail because costs exceed those anticipated by management. Careful planning can reduce the occurrence of premature failure to a considerable extent.

8-5. Width and Depth Strategies

Many companies offer numerous products and services. Beatrice Companies, for example, markets Tropicana juices, Peter Pan peanut butter, Hunt's barbeque sauce, La Choy Chinese Foods, Orville Redenbacher popcorn, Culligan water treatment, Samsonite luggage, Rusty Jones rust preventive, and Avis car rental, among other goods and services. We say that Beatrice has a *wide product mix*, which is made up of many *product lines*.

- The **product mix** is the total of all goods and services that a company offers.
- **Product lines** are combinations of similar items within a product mix, such as a line of men's clothing.

A. Width

A *wide product mix* is one that is made up of many product lines. Having a wide product mix is a strategy that enables the marketer to satisfy numerous groups of target consumers and to diversify, so that the company is not overly dependent on just one or a few product lines.

EXAMPLE 8-11: K-Mart offers a wide product mix. This strategy attracts many different kinds of consumers into the store and permits "one-stop shopping," so that buyers can satisfy many needs under one roof.

B. Depth

A *deep product mix* is one that is made up of a variety of offerings within product lines. Having a deep product mix is a strategy that allows marketers to specialize in satisfying many consumers' needs for a certain type of product. Most successful men's clothing stores, for example, have enough depth—various brands, sizes, and styles—to satisfy many consumers' needs. The more depth a company has, the more likely it is that it will be able to build a reputation as a specialist in particular lines.

EXAMPLE 8-12: Bookstore chains such as B. Dalton have considerable depth. A consumer, for instance, will find in a B. Dalton store many recipe books with a variety of titles, themes, prices, and lengths.

8-6. Product Positioning

Product positioning refers to the alignment of a firm's products and services in relation to one another and to those of competitors, *in the minds of consumers*. A company can position products according to product characteristics, target consumers, or target benefits. Effective positioning distinguishes the product as unique and clearly different from others in the eyes of target consumers.

EXAMPLE 8-13: American Honda positions its motor scooters as more fashionable, "hip," and trendy than other scooters and motorcycles. It promotes the idea that having a Honda makes the owner special and different from others. It would appear that this positioning strategy has worked, since the company holds about 80% of the U.S. motor scooter market, most of which it gained in a little over 18 months.

8-7. Packaging

Marketers can differentiate their products from those of competitors through effective packaging. Packaging fulfills three essential functions.

A. Product protection

Packages help *protect* products and consumers. Protection is needed while products are stored in warehouses, displayed in retail stores, and held by consumers. Protection is also needed when products are being shipped.

EXAMPLE 8-14: Some companies realize that they must provide considerable protection for their products. Silverette brand paper clips are enclosed in sturdy cardboard boxes that cannot be easily destroyed and do not allow product leakage. Anacin bottles are "childproof"—hard to open. Since the Tylenol poisoning scare in 1983, many manufacturers have moved to sealed packaging for over-the-counter drugs.

B. Assisting in product use

Well-designed packages help consumers use products effectively. Well-designed packages resist falling over or spilling, are not difficult to open and close, and are not too heavy or bulky.

C. Promoting the product

Packages play a role in *promoting* the product. Packages can help promote the product through attractive design, pleasing use of color, and interesting promotional messages. Or they can be of value for their own sake, as when jam jars serve as drinking glasses.

EXAMPLE 8-15: Nabisco Shredded Wheat boxes have attention-getting colors and illustrations. In addition, they feature recipes for snacks that consumers can make using Shredded Wheat. Hershey's chocolate covered almond Solitaires appear in slender streamlined packages that are suggestive of the color of the chocolates contained inside.

8-8. Labeling, Branding, and Trademarks

The final three important elements of product management are labeling, branding, and using trademarks.

A. Labeling

Labeling refers to information written on the product, its package, or on tags or other materials that go with the product. Labeling's most basic function is to identify the product. Labels also indicate such things as what is in the product, how it works, how it was made, dangers associated with the item, and the name and location of the manufacturer. Some labels merely give the brand name of the offering. Others specify a grade, such as "Choice" meats or provide basic product information.

B. Branding

Branding is what a company does to identify its products and services and to distinguish them from competitors' offerings. **Brand names** are parts of brands that can be communicated orally, such as "Coke." Some brand names are extremely valuable because consumers have developed a deep-seated loyalty to them. Examples are Coca-Cola, Ford, Tide, Crest, Winchester, L & M, and Hershey.

If the marketer has numerous products that are closely related in type and quality, it may use a *family brand*, such as Kellogg's. Or it may employ an *individual brand* for each item. Brands that producers own are termed *manufacturers' brands*, while those that wholesalers or retailers own are *private brands*. Yet another strategy is to use *generic brands*, where the product itself is labeled and no specific brand name is offered.

C. Trademarks

Trademarks are symbols or words that a firm has exclusive legal rights to. Owners of trademarks have filed an application with the U.S. patent office. They must use the symbols or words for five years before the patent office will grant a trademark. This means that other companies cannot use the trademark or even a similar one.

If a trademark becomes *generic*—that is, if consumers come to use it to refer to products in general, rather than to a particular company's brand—the company may lose its trademark. This loss has taken place in the cases of aspirin and nylon.

RAISE YOUR GRADES
Can you explain . . . ?

☑ what is meant by saying that buyers purchase "bundles of satisfaction"

☑ why some product offerings are classified as industrial goods while others are classified as consumer goods

☑ how a marketing department can test a proposed new product for its acceptance among potential customers prior to product introduction

☑ how the marketing strategy of a company should change as a company brand moves from the introductory stage to other stages in the product life cycle

☑ how a company can tell if it has adequate product width or depth or both

☑ why some products are enclosed in very colorful packages, even though this increases company costs

☑ The difference between a company's brand, label, and trademark

SUMMARY

1. Consumers purchase goods and services in order to obtain bundles of satisfaction; that is, to satisfy their needs.
2. There are four types of consumer goods: convenience goods, shopping goods, specialty goods, and unsought goods.
3. There are five types of industrial goods: installations, accessories, raw materials, parts and processed materials, and operating supplies.
4. New product development consists of producing and screening product ideas, economic evaluation, development, testing, and commercialization.
5. There are four stages in the product life cycle: introduction, growth, maturity, and decline.
6. The *width* of a product mix is determined by the number of different lines a company offers, whereas *depth* refers to the variety of offerings that are available within individual product lines.
7. Product positioning refers to the alignment of a firm's products and services in relation to one another and to those of competitors, in the minds of consumers.
8. Packages protect the product, assist in product use, and help promote the product.
9. Labels, brands, and trademarks are used to identify products and set them apart from the competition.

RAPID REVIEW   Answers

Short Answer

1. Consumers buy goods and services *not* as things of value for their own   *satisfaction*
   sake, but as "bundles of _____." [See Section 8-1.]
2. Bubble Yum chewing gum, RCA VCR's, and Curtis Mathes television sets   *consumer*
   are types of _____ goods. [See Section 8-2.]
3. Specialty goods such as Cadillacs are items that consumers are willing to   *substantial*
   spend _____ effort to acquire. [See Section 8-2.]

4. Fork lift trucks, sugar beets, and engine alternators are types of _____ goods. [See Section 8-2.] *industrial*

5. When marketing personnel for General Electric evaluate new product ideas and eliminate those with little chance of profit, they are _____ products. [See Section 8-3.] *screening*

6. _____ evaluation of a new product involves estimating expected sales and costs, in order to produce forecasts of profits, return on investment, and breakeven levels. [See Section 8-3.] *Economic*

7. At the _____ stage of the product life cycle, sales grow rapidly and profits appear. [See Section 8-4.] *growth*

8. The stage of the product life cycle during which sales and profits fall is called _____. [See Section 8-4.] *decline*

9. If a company product line lacks _____, then it does not offer enough variety to satisfy most consumers' needs. [See Section 8-8.] *depth*

10. The management of the Kellogg Company is a firm believer in _____ _____, which can help differentiate the product from others in the minds of consumers. [See Section 8-6.] *product positioning*

11. The three essential functions of _____ are to protect the product, promote the product, and assist in product use. [See Section 8-7.] *packaging*

12. Any information written on the product, its package, or on tags or other materials that go with the product is called _____. [See Section 8-8.] *labeling*

13. Apple Computer, like many other producers, uses branding in order to _____ its products. [See Section 8-8.] *identify*

14. A manager might seek to obtain trademarks for company products because they have _____ protection. [See Section 8-8.] *legal*

15. For many years, managers of Coca Cola Company have feared losing their right to exclusive use of the word "Coke." If this trademark becomes _____, the company may lose it. [See Section 8-8.] *generic*

16. A brand, such as Del Monte, that is used with more than one company product is called a _____ brand. [See Section 8-8.] *family*

17. Brands owned by wholesalers or retailers, such as K-Mart's "Focal" photographic film, are called _____ brands. [See Section 8-8.] *private*

18. Brands owned by producers, such as "Mr. Coffee" coffeemakers, are called _____ brands. [See Section 8-8.] *manufacturer's*

SOLVED PROBLEMS

PROBLEM 8-1 In what sense is the purchase of a new car actually the purchase of a "bundle of satisfaction"?

Answer: When purchasing a car, consumers do not buy a combination of steel, aluminum, rubber, plastic, and other materials. In reality, they are buying transportation, appearance, status, reliability, economy, self-esteem, a means of keeping costs down, and other such benefits. In other words, a car is purchased not as a thing of value for its own sake, but rather to satisfy certain needs; thus, it can be called a "bundle of satisfaction." [See Section 8-1.]

PROBLEM 8-2 How can an item be both a consumer and an industrial good?

Answer: Some products are both, depending on the purposes of purchasers. A personal computer purchased to keep inventory and other records and to serve as a word processor for a small business is an industrial good. The buyer acquires it for business purposes. The same product is a consumer good if consumers acquire it for personal use—to write personal letters, store recipes, prepare income tax returns, prepare family budgets, and the like. [See Section 8-2.]

PROBLEM 8-3 Do you consider hamburger to be a shopping good or a convenience good?

Answer: Individuals buy convenience goods with a minimal expenditure of effort and time. But when consumers buy shopping goods, they are willing to spend considerable effort comparing one shopping good with another. Generally, shopping goods tend to be more expensive than convenience goods. Hamburger can be considered a shopping good. Many consumers compare the price and quality of this product from one store to another. They consider the price per pound and various quality factors, such as the meat's fat content and appearance of freshness. [See Section 8-2.]

PROBLEM 8-4 Most marketing textbooks indicate that marketers should strive to satisfy the needs of consumers. Yet some marketers try to sell unsought goods, even though consumers are not eager to purchase them. Why?

Answer: Consumers need a number of unsought goods, even if they are not eager to purchase them. Marketers must heavily promote unsought goods, because these goods satisfy negative needs, such as medical and dental care, life insurance protection, and preplanned funeral arrangements. Increasingly, marketers of unsought goods, such as dentists and lawyers, are involved in advertising and in other forms of promotion such as publicity. In addition, marketers of unsought goods are taking steps to make their offerings more convenient, as by locating their offices in shopping centers. [See Section 8-2.]

PROBLEM 8-5 Motor carriers such as Allied Van Lines purchase considerable quantities of over-the-road trucks. What category of industrial goods are trucks for these firms? Why?

Answer: Over-the-road trucks are installations for motor carriers. For these firms, the trucks are expensive items used to provide services. They determine how much service the firms can furnish, so they are very important purchase items, accounting for as much as 80% of the trucking firm's capital. Typically, accountants depreciate truck purchase costs, rather than charging these as expenses. Depreciation is necessary because the useful life of the trucks extends over many years. [See Section 8-2.]

PROBLEM 8-6 Assume that you are in charge of product planning for a company. You realize the fundamental importance of producing ideas and screening, and need to hire personnel to carry out these two functions. What abilities would you seek in the persons hired?

Answer: The function of those who produce ideas will be to come up with an extensive list of possible new products. The firm should consider hiring persons who can look at traditional products in creative new ways. On the other hand, screening is more analytical than producing ideas and consists of eliminating alternatives that probably will not be profitable. Here, the firm needs persons with quantitative skills as well as experience in the industry and considerable "common sense." [See Section 8-3.]

PROBLEM 8-7 Assume that you are in charge of test marketing at a company that makes personal care products. A new employee has asked for an explanation of the purpose of test marketing. How would you respond?

Answer: Managers at personal care firms use test marketing to find out how well proposed new products will sell in the marketplace. They place the product being tested in retail stores located in test cities that are believed to be typical of the population in general. Then they measure sales levels to determine if these are sufficient to justify product introduction. Typically, these test market studies are given careful attention by management, especially for large income producing products such as toothpaste and bath soap. [See Section 8-3.]

PROBLEM 8-8 In 1985 the American Cyanamid Company spent $6 million on advertising for a new tray-bait roach insecticide called "Combat." Why would the company spend so much on promotion during the introductory state of the product life cycle?

Answer: The Combat roach insecticide was new to the market, and many consumers were not aware of its existence or of the particular bundle of benefits it offered. Competition is extensive in this industry, so the company had to change consumer buying habits—luring target customers away from rivals. Sales were low, so the firm had to take action to persuade consumers to initially purchase and then repurchase the new offering. [See Section 8-4.]

PROBLEM 8-9   A popular oven cleaner is now in the maturity stage of the product life cycle. Several years ago, this product was in the growth stage. Compare the likely status of this product during these two stages of the product life cycle.

Answer: During the growth stage of the oven cleaner, sales were growing rapidly and profits appeared, as increasing numbers of consumers became aware of and used the product. Rivals probably entered the market. During the current maturity stage of the product, sales growth has probably slowed and in fact begun to fall, with profits therefore decreasing. Management may need to take steps to increase sales and profits at this stage. This is particularly the case because oven cleaners have lost ground due to the popularity of self-cleaning ovens and microwave ovens. [See Section 8-4.]

PROBLEM 8-10   During the decline stage of Barbie dolls, the Mattel Company increased advertising to increase sales. What other actions could management have taken?

Answer: The Mattel company could have decreased its prices, so that Barbie dolls were more competitive in the marketplace. However, this could have set off a price war with competitors. Or it could have altered the product in some way to make it more appealing, perhaps by making Barbie's features more youthful. Another possible action would have been to seek distribution in additional retail stores, especially toy stores, thus increasing the doll's visibility in the market. Or the firm could have changed its advertising themes to appeal more successfully to its consumers. Finally, the company could have dropped the doll altogether, without trying to keep it in the marketplace. [See Section 8-4.]

PROBLEM 8-11   Explain the difference between product width and product depth. Provide examples of each strategy.

Answer: Product width refers to the number of product lines that a company offers. The Procter and Gamble Company, for instance, has a very wide product line, which includes detergents, toothpastes, soft drinks, disposable diapers, and paper towels. In contrast, product depth refers to the variety of offerings that are available within individual product lines. The Rocket manufacturing company, for example, has only one product (WD-40) which is a metal lubricant; this company has no depth. Most clothing and sporting goods stores, which offer a variety of brands, styles, colors, etc., offer considerable depth. [See Section 8-5.]

PROBLEM 8-12   How does McDonald's position itself with respect to Burger King? Support your answer with examples.

Answer: McDonald's positions itself as a "family" eating place, more so than does Burger King. Its stores, complete with miniature playgrounds, appeal strongly to children. Similarly, its advertisements, many of which feature Ronald McDonald and appear on Saturday morning television are child-oriented. Many of the company sandwiches and drinks are designed specifically for youngsters. Finally, the chain's prices are designed so that they are within the budget of the average family. [See Section 8-6.]

PROBLEM 8-13   How can packages, such as those used for E.J. Brach, and Sons candies, promote the products they contain?

Answer: Packages may have attractive design and color, and be interesting promotion pieces in themselves. Brach Candies are packaged in such a way that they have eye appeal and are very suitable as gifts. Illustrations on the packages are designed to make the candies appear to be very appealing. On special occasions, such as Valentines Day and Christmas, this company creates colorful holiday boxes, which make the product "special" for the time of year. [See Section 8-7.]

PROBLEM 8-14   What packaging functions do toothpaste tubes provide?

Answer: Toothpaste tubes protect the product from unsanitary elements and leakage. They assist in product use by being flexible, easy to store, and easy to squeeze. They also promote the product through attractive color and design and through information printed on the package. [See Section 8-7.]

PROBLEM 8-15   What labeling might you use for "Wear-Me-Now" shirts?

Answer: Information such as material content, size, washing and ironing instructions, "Made in the U.S.A." (appeals to patriotism), and the brand name could appear prominently on the label. This information would identify the product, differentiate it from competitor's offerings, and make its use more effective. [See Section 8-8.]

PROBLEM 8-16   What kinds of information are contained in labels?

Answer: Many labels list product ingredients, as in the case of processed foods such as cereals. Others provide directions as to how the product should be used, as with chainsaws. Some labels specify how a product is made (e.g., handmade, for authentic Navajo rugs). Or labels may warn of dangers associated with misuse of the product (prescription and over-the-counter drugs are examples). The name and location of the manufacturer may appear on labels. Some labels even provide a grade for the product. [See Section 8-8.]

PROBLEM 8-17   What is the purpose of branding?

Answer: Firms use branding to help identify their products and services and to distinguish them from competitors' offerings. For example, consumers are able to distinguish Coca-Cola from Pepsi-Cola and other beverages and to appreciate differences in the products. Consumers can readily see, through the prominent display of brand names, which company's offerings they are examining. The brand name on the bottle and on bottle caps, as well as distinctive colors and lettering, differentiate one firm's products from the others. Furthermore, the benefits of advertising that one firm undertakes go to its *own* products and not to those of competitors. [See Section 8-8.]

PROBLEM 8-18   Distinguish between brands and brand names.

Answer: Brands are words, marks, or symbols that identify company products or services. The Gannett Corporation, for example, is the owner of the *USA TODAY* newspaper brand name and its symbol, which is a globe with horizontal lines drawn to the side. Brand names, such as Tropicana orange juice, are parts of brands that can be communicated orally. Symbols or marks, then, are parts of brands but not of brand names. [See Section 8-8].

PROBLEM 8-19   What is a trademark?

Answer: Trademarks are brands that have been given legal protection by the United States Patent Office. Mars, Inc., for example, has a trademark for its M&M's candies. This means that the company enjoys exclusive use of the brand, and this can be protected through the courts. Competitors cannot use the trademarks that a firm owns.

PROBLEM 8-20   What happens to a trademark that becomes generic? Can you think of some trademark brands that have come to have a generic meaning?

Answer: A generic trademark is one that, over a period of time, consumers come to use to refer to a product class in general, rather than to a specific brand. If a brand offered by a company is highly successful, buyers may associate it with the offerings of many companies and the original company loses its identification with the offering. The company can lose its trademark if it becomes generic, as in the case of aspirin and nylon. [See Section 8-8.]

9 PRICING GOODS AND SERVICES

9-1. The Meaning of the Term *Price*

• **Price** is the amount of money that is given in exchange for a good or service.

Actually, price is a more complicated subject than many realize. For example, a 48-ounce package of Carnation powdered milk costs less per ounce than a 36-ounce package. The price of movie admission is sometimes less during the day than at night. Supermarkets sometimes run specials near the end of the week, charging lower prices during those days than at the beginning of the week. And some service stations charge less for a cash purchase than for a credit card purchase. As you can see, pricing decisions depends on many factors.

• There is an **equilibrium**, or state of balance, between what consumers pay and what they obtain.

This concept is illustrated in Figure 9-1. Consumer A wants a high-quality television set and is willing to pay for it. She visits a conveniently located, nicely decorated Curtis Mathes dealer. The sales personnel are very friendly and helpful; and, after she purchases a set for $1,295, the store's employees assist her in arranging for financing and delivery.

Consumer B is on a restricted budget. She visits a warehouse-like "box store." Once inside the store, she finds few sales personnel, so she must shop for herself. She selects a set that is much like the set Consumer A purchased, except that it costs $595 and has a shorter warranty. After paying cash for the set, she takes it home in the trunk of her car and installs it herself. In each case, the price the consumer pays is in balance with the quantity and quality of goods and services being offered.

• Differences in what consumers are willing to pay for goods and services offer opportunities for market segmentation.

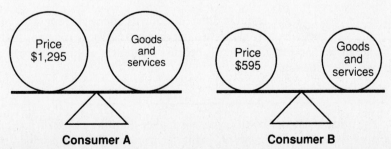

FIGURE 9-1: There is an equilibrium between prices and consumer goods and services.

Some firms, such as K-Mart and Wal-Mart, aim at bargain-conscious consumers. Other firms, such as Tiffany's (jewelers) and Saks Fifth Avenue, aim at those who want more and are willing to pay to get it. The industrial goods market can be segmented in much the same way.

EXAMPLE 9-1: Northwestern Mutual Life Insurance Company sells two types of life insurance plans for key executives of companies. Term insurance plans are inexpensive, but do not have cash values when the policies terminate. On the other hand, whole life policies have cash values, but are more expensive than term. Each of the two types of policies appeals to a particular segment of the market.

9-2. Major Factors to Consider in Setting Prices

Marketers must consider four main factors when setting prices: demand, cost, competition, and the law.

A. Demand

Marketers must consider *demand* when setting prices; that is, they must consider the price levels that consumers are able and willing to pay. In general, the lower the price, the higher the demand. The relationship between demand and price is illustrated in Figure 9-2 in the form of a **demand curve**, where price is plotted against quantity purchased. The demand curve in Figure 9-2 shows that a vending machine operator can sell more soft drinks by lowering the price per can. This demand curve, which shows that quantity purchased rises as prices fall, is an example of *elastic* demand.

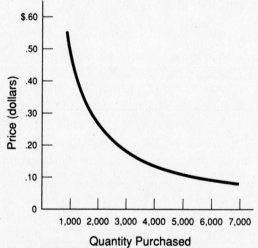

FIGURE 9-2: Demand curve for soft drinks sold in vending machines.

- If the percentage change in quantity sold exceeds the percentage change in price, demand is called **elastic**.

- If the percentage change in quantity sold does *not* exceed the percentage change in price, demand is called **inelastic**.

An organization that has been successful in differentiating its offerings from those of rivals is likely to have an *inelastic* demand, which would have a flat demand curve. This means that it may be able to charge a higher price than that of its rivals because customers will be willing to pay the higher price for that particular offering.

EXAMPLE 9-2: The price of Perrier bottled water is higher than the prices of its competitors. The company has managed to build up an image of quality and prestige for this product, mainly through advertising, that allows it to sell large volumes at high prices.

---

note: It should *not* be assumed that all consumers will buy more of a good or service as its price decreases, as Figure 9-2 suggests. In some cases (e.g., headache remedies), consumers believe that, "you get what you pay for," and will buy a high-priced item because they believe the price signals high quality.

B. Cost

Marketers must consider the overall *cost* of providing a product when setting prices. Ordinarily, companies will not sell an offering for less than its cost. Costs, then, tend to place a floor on prices. But there are two kinds of costs. Some costs are *fixed*—they do not change as the firm increases or decreases its output. An example is rent for a warehouse building. Other costs are *variable*—they increase or decrease as the output of the company changes. An example is labor—more wages must be paid to produce a higher volume of goods. Most managers will not allow prices to fall below variable costs. Figure 9-3 provides a graphical example of fixed and variable costs.

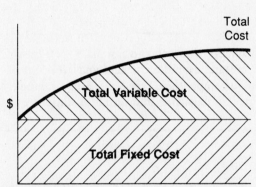

FIGURE 9-3: Example of fixed and variable costs of producing goods and services.

FIGURE 9-4: The most profitable price is often the one for which the difference between total revenue and total cost is greater than that for any other price.

Determining the "right" price is not always easy. A useful objective is to find a price for which the difference between *total revenue* (price × output) and *total cost* is greater than for any other price. In Figure 9-4, that price is labeled "*X*." This price *X* will bring in more profit than any other price.

C. Competition

When competition is strong, a firm may have to set prices at levels that are not much above costs. On the other hand, when competition is weak, nonaggressive, or even nonexistent, management may choose to set prices at higher levels.

EXAMPLE 9-3: During the 1970's, IBM had few competitors for its personal computers, and most consumers felt that this brand was clearly superior to others. As a result, the firm was able to set prices well above costs. In the 1980's, however, many competitors brought out personal computers that were comparable to IBM's, but sold at much lower prices. The company was forced to cut its prices drastically.

D. The law

There are a number of legal restrictions on pricing (many of which are discussed in Chapter 2, Section 2-1). Generally, marketers cannot use prices to gain monopolies and cannot make pricing agreements with competitors. Prices on goods sold to buyers other than consumers should be equal (*nondiscriminatory*), unless the company can justify price differences, as by showing that it costs less to serve one customer than it does to serve another. Marketers must familiarize themselves with pricing laws and must usually engage competent attorneys to advise on complex legal issues.

9-3. The Effect of Company Policies on Price

- **Company policies** are general rules or guidelines that indicate what kinds of decisions company employees should make in order to fulfill company objectives.

An important responsibility of marketers is to develop pricing policies. The best pricing policy is that which fulfills the objectives of the company's overall marketing strategy most closely. If, for instance, the objective is to provide high-income consumers with fashionable china dinnerware (as in the case of Lenox china), a high price may be appropriate. On the other hand, a firm that strives to furnish low-income consumers with average-quality pliers and other hand tools may select a policy of low prices.

Pricing policies differ considerably from one firm to another because of differences in company objectives. Some retailers have a policy of providing **leaders** (prices lower than normal) to entice customers into the store. Others attempt to keep all of their prices lower than those of competitors. Some companies offer prestige or very high-quality products and services and have a high-price policy relative to rivals. Still others have a policy of maintaining their prices near industry averages. Their policy is not to "rock the boat" by starting a price war.

EXAMPLE 9-4: True Value Hardware stores serve consumers who want to purchase well-known manufacturers' brands (such as Corning, West Bend, Sunbeam, Hamilton Beach, and Norelco) of household goods at prices that are lower than those of many competitors. True Value aims at middle-income consumers and advertises the prices of its offerings in magazines and on radio stations that appeal to this segment.

9-4. The Strategic Use of Price in Marketing

Each company has a particular strategy for the use of price. In some companies, prices do not have much of a role in marketing strategy. The company's costs are approximately the same as those of rivals and there may be little incentive to charge more or less than they do. Also, if the company sells a product with little advantage over its competitors, it may simply keep prices near industry averages. In other industries, such as the comic book industry, customary prices are the rule . Management also may fear that lower prices could start a price war or arouse government officials to bring charges of anti-competitive actions.

Other firms are aggressive in pricing. Those who have a cost advantage over rivals or whose products have a considerable advantage may take this stance. Managers whose target markets want low prices often use the price element of the marketing mix forcefully.

Whether or not price should be used as an aggressive element in the marketing mix depends considerably on overall strategy. If a firm is appealing to a price-conscious target customer, and its managers believe that the firm can outdo its rivals in delivering a low price, price may be used as an important strategic tool.

EXAMPLE 9-5: The Brown and Williamson Corporation produces Sir Walter Raleigh pipe tobacco, which is priced below many of its rival products. Consumers who desire an economical product are likely to purchase this tobacco. The company produces in large volume, keeping unit costs low and permitting low prices.

9-5. Price-Level Policies

There are a number of policies that determine the general price level at which a company will market a product.

A. Pricing below competition

When a pricing-below-competition policy is in effect, a firm sets its prices lower than those of its rivals. This policy is most likely to be effective if a firm's costs are lower than those of competitors.

Then management is in a position to appeal to target customers who seek low prices. An elastic demand situation favors this policy.

B. Pricing above competition

With a pricing-above-competition policy, a firm maintains its prices at a level above those of its competitors. This may be an effective policy when demand is inelastic, as it is for many prestige and high-quality goods. Some consumers will pay more if they feel that high quality is associated with high price.

EXAMPLE 9-6: Many consumers are willing to pay higher prices for branded rather than generic prescription drugs. They believe that branded goods are superior.

C. Pricing at a competitive level

A pricing-at-competitive-levels policy is intended to meet competition, that is, to set prices at or only slightly above or below those of rivals. This may be an effective policy if the product does not have a strong advantage over competition or when management wants to prevent price wars.

EXAMPLE 9-7: Large household moving firms, such as Mayflower and National Van Lines, set their prices at competitive levels. The companies in this industry realize that price cuts could lead rivals to charge lower prices, resulting in lower revenues for all.

D. Cost-plus pricing

In the case of cost-plus pricing, managers first determine costs per unit. To this, they add a percentage **margin**, designed to furnish a profit. The result of these calculations is the price. This policy is easy to apply and simple to understand. Firms that stock many items, such as retailers, often employ it. The principal disadvantage of cost-plus pricing is that costs may not be related to demand, resulting in poor price selections and decreased revenues.

EXAMPLE 9-8: When the Santa Fe Railroad experienced increases in the cost of labor, the firm increased its rates for transportation of agricultural products. This increase caused a number of grain dealers to switch to truck transportation.

E. Return-on-investment pricing

When a firm uses a return-on-investment pricing policy, it sets prices at a level designed to produce a desired profit which is a percentage of invested capital. This policy requires that managers first determine total investment costs, and then calculate the prices that are likely to produce the desired rate of return.

In order to use return-on-investment pricing, a firm must be good at forecasting the sales and costs that are associated with various prices. This is a difficult task, one that many small-business managers find impossible.

F. New product pricing

When a company introduces a new product, it may use a *skimming* or a *penetration* price.

   (1) **Skimming.** Skimming involves assessing prices that are high relative to company costs. Management is likely to use this strategy if demand is inelastic and there are few potential competitors.
   (2) **Penetration.** Penetration pricing involves charging a low price relative to company costs. Management is likely to use this strategy when demand is elastic and the likelihood of competition is strong.

EXAMPLE 9-9: In 1986, the Compaq Company brought out its new personal computer—the Deskpro 386—which incorporated a chip that gave it the power of a large microcomputer. This product had a feature that no competitor could match, so the price of the Deskpro 386 was set at two to three times the price of other, existing personal computers. The relatively high price of this PC is an example of a skimming price.

G. Odd-even pricing

In the case of odd-even pricing, the marketer assesses prices that end in odd numbers, such as $4.95 or $1.99. Many retailers follow this policy. They believe that such prices give target customers the illusion of a bargain; $1.99, for example, appears to be (significantly) cheaper than $2.00.

H. Price lining

Some retailers use price lining. They have a few established prices (such as $59.95, $79.95, $99.95, and $139.95 for women's dresses), and fit the items they buy for resale into those price categories. This policy is based on the assumption that consumers have various price categories in mind and buy from each of these, instead of looking for an individual price for each item. Using price lines makes price calculations and choices simple for sales clerks and consumers.

9-6. Discount and Allowance Policies

Marketers grant *discounts* and *allowances* to customers who are willing to give up benefits that they would otherwise receive, or who are willing to perform specified activities.

A. Quantity discounts

Quantity discounts are price reductions given to customers who agree to purchase minimum quantities. There are two kinds of quantity discounts.

(1) **Cumulative quantity discounts** are price reductions given to customers who purchase certain minimum quantities during a specific time period, such as a year. The discounts are used to induce customers to place most of their business with the firm and can be helpful in reducing the company's selling, storage, and shipping costs.

(2) **Noncumulative quantity discounts** are provided to customers who buy minimum quantities in a single order. They help reduce the marketer's costs, as small orders are very expensive to handle.

B. Cash discounts

Cash discounts are price reductions given to customers who pay their bills within a specified time period. Those customers who pay within ten days of the date of billing, for example, may be given a discount of two percent. This can reduce the amount of money that the marketer ties up in non-interest-bearing accounts receivable. Further, liberal cash discounts can be a way of attracting customers.

C. Functional discounts

Companies pay wholesalers and retailers **functional** or **trade discounts** to compensate them for the marketing activities that they perform. Those wholesalers or retailers who perform for companies extensive marketing functions, such as advertising, transportation, and personal selling, tend to receive large functional discounts. A functional discount may also be offered if a company is eager to attract the business of a particular channel member; that is, someone who handles the product between the company and the end user.

EXAMPLE 9-10: The Fairacres Farm Cooperative suggests that channel member supermarkets charge $1.79 for a ten-pound bag of their potatoes. This is the usual price for this product at the retail level. The supermarkets receive a functional discount of 20 percent for doing this. This means that they pay Fairacres $1.43 (80% of $1.79).

D. Promotional allowances

Marketers give **promotional allowances** to wholesalers and retailers to compensate them for the promotion activities that they undertake. Promotional allowances may take the form of price reductions, free goods, or cash payments. We can list two types of allowances:

(1) **Cooperative advertising allowance**. Money paid to a channel member for part of the advertising of a product is called a cooperative advertising allowance.
(2) **Push money allowance**. Money paid to retail sales people for selling a company's offerings is called a push money allowance.

9-7. Geographic Pricing Policies and Procedures

Marketers can handle freight costs to customers in various ways. Marketers can cover delivery costs, or customers may pay delivery costs—or some combination may be used. However they are handled, the price of a product must take into account the geographic pricing policies of the company.

A. FOB pricing

The term *FOB* indicates who pays the freight and who owns the goods. There are two types of FOB pricing.

(1) **FOB point of origin** means that the buyer pays for the transportation charges and takes ownership at the seller's plant. This policy makes transportation costs lower for buyers located near the producer and higher for those located farther away. It is useful for marketers who want to remain competitive in the region near a plant.
(2) **FOB destination** means that the seller pays the transportation charges and owns the goods until they arrive at the buyer's location. This policy makes the marketer more competitive in places located far from the plant.

B. Uniform delivered prices

Under **uniform delivered prices**, all customers, regardless of their location, pay the same final price. This makes a company more competitive in areas far from the plant, and less competitive than it would ordinarily be in nearby regions. This policy is often used for products that are not heavy or bulky and therefore have low transportation costs.

C. Zone pricing

Under **zone pricing**, all buyers in a particular zone (geographical area) pay the same price. The zone-pricing method is often used because it makes the calculation of transportation charges to buyers a simple process. Mail-order companies often use this technique.

D. Freight absorption

Firms that use **freight absorption** pay for some of the freight to customers who are located at a distance. A company that uses a freight-absorption policy will normally absorb (pay) enough freight cost to make the final price to far-away customers the same as that charged by competitors. It is useful to marketers who have desirable customers located far from the plant.

E. Basing point prices

When **basing point prices** are used, customers are charged for freight from some location, called a *basing point*, to their site. The basing point may or may not be the place from which the goods were actually shipped. Sometimes there are two or more basing points and the customer pays the freight from the nearest one. Using this system simplifies geographic pricing and may result in extra profits to the marketer, especially when the basing point is further from the customer than is the actual point of origin for the goods. The courts have declared that basing point pricing is illegal when it is used by two or more firms to fix prices.

RAISE YOUR GRADES
Can you explain . . . ?

☑ why there is an equilibrium or balance between what consumers pay for a product and what they obtain
☑ how demand, cost, competition, and the law combine to determine the prices of a good or service
☑ how company policies help determine the specific price that a company will charge for individual offerings
☑ why some marketers are not aggressive pricers
☑ why some brands are priced at levels above the competition
☑ why some companies provide functional discounts to retailers
☑ why a manufacturer might use freight absorption pricing

SUMMARY

1. Price is the amount of money that is given in exchange for a good or service.
2. There is an equilibrium, or state of balance, between what consumers pay and what they obtain.
3. Differences in what consumers are willing to pay for goods and services offer opportunities for market segmentation.
4. Marketers must consider four main factors when setting prices; demand, cost, competition, and the law.
5. Company policies provide general rules or guidelines for setting prices that fulfill company objectives. Thus, pricing policies differ considerably from one firm to another.
6. Firms differ according to the extent to which they use price as an element of their marketing mix.
7. There are a number of widely used pricing policies: pricing below, above, and at a competitive level; cost-plus pricing; return-on-investment pricing; skimming or penetration pricing for new products; odd-even pricing, and price lining.
8. Marketers grant discounts and allowances to customers who are willing to give up benefits or perform certain activities. These can take the form of quantity discounts (cumulative or noncumulative), cash discounts, functional or trade discounts, and promotional allowances, such as cooperative advertising or push money allowances.
9. There are a number of geographic pricing policies that determine who will pay the freight for goods shipped to customers. These include FOB pricing (point of origin or destination), uniform delivered pricing, zone pricing, freight absorption pricing, and basing point pricing.

RAPID REVIEW   Answers

Short Answer

1. Price refers to the amount of money that is given in exchange for a _____ or _____ . [See Section 9-1.]   *good, service*
2. There is a(n) _____ between what consumers pay and what they obtain. [See Section 9-1.]   *equilibrium*
3. In many cases, higher prices for a product can be expected to _____ the quantity sold. [See Section 9-2.]   *decrease*
4. If the percentage increase in the quantity of Yugo automobiles sold exceeds the percentage decrease in price, demand is said to be _____ . [See Section 9-2.]   *elastic*
5. Those costs that do not change as a firm increases or decreases its output are called _____ costs. [See Section 9-2.]   *fixed*

6. When competition is strong, as it is in the dry cereal industry, a firm such   *low*
   as Kellogg's may set prices at _____ levels, relative to costs.
   [See Section 9-2.]

7. What customers are able and willing to pay determines the _____   *demand*
   for a product. [See Section 9-2.]

8. Company policies provide guidelines for fulfilling company   *objectives*
   _____. [See Section 9-3.]

9. _____ prices are sometimes used to entice customers into super-   *Leader*
   markets. [See Section 9-3.]

10. The best pricing policy for a firm is one that follows the company's overall   *marketing*
    _____ _____ most closely. [See Section 9-3.]   *strategy*

11. If a company's costs are approximately the same as those of its rivals,   *little*
    there may be _____ incentive to charge more or less than they
    do. [See Section 9-4.]

12. A company is likely to pursue a policy of pricing below competition on   *elastic*
    goods for which demand is _____. [See Section 9-5.]

13. Pricing above competition may be a good policy for _____   *prestige*
    goods. [See Section 9-5.]

14. When using a cost-plus pricing policy, a company sets prices by adding a   *margin*
    _____ to unit costs. [See Section 9-5.]

15. When a company uses skimming for a new product, its prices are   *high*
    _____, relative to company costs. [See Section 9-5.]

16. _____ _____ discounts are given to customers who   *Noncumulative*
    buy minimum quantities in a single order. [See Section 9-6.]   *quantity*

17. _____ discounts are given to Mobil Corporation customers   *Cash*
    who pay their bills within a specified time period. [See Section 9-6.]

18. In the case of FOB _____ _____ _____   *point of origin*
    pricing, the retail buyer pays the transportation charges. [See Section 9-7.]

19. Under _____ _____ pricing, all customers regardless   *uniform delivered*
    of their location, pay the same final price. [See Section 9-7.]

20. Using _____ _____ pricing, a company attempts to   *freight*
    set freight rates so that the final price to buyers is equal to that of its   *absorption*
    competitors. [See Section 9-7.]

SOLVED PROBLEMS

PROBLEM 9-1   A hardware store owner has informed you that price is a more complicated subject
than most people realize because many factors influence pricing. Do you agree?

Answer: The hardware store owner is correct. Price depends on many factors, including the location
(and delivery charges) of the buyer, the quantity purchased, the date when the purchase is made, when
the bill is paid, if the offering is acquired for cash or credit, what business activities the buyer does for the
seller, among other factors. Because each company has its own unique pricing policies and procedures, it
is difficult to transfer knowledge from one firm to another. [See Section 9-1.]

PROBLEM 9-2   Viking Jewelers carries high-quality products, is located in a prestigious site, provides
many customer services, and has a tastefully designed store interior. What type of prices is this store
likely to change for its goods and services? Why?

Answer: Viking Jewelers realizes that there is an equilibrium or state of balance between the prices that
its customers pay and the benefits that they obtain. Its customers pay high prices for the status, extensive
services, and pleasing atmosphere that the store provides. If customers desire lower prices, they will

have to forgo some of these benefits. Discount jewelers often have nonprestige locations, limited customer services, and rather plain store interiors which may not be carpeted or tastefully designed. [See Section 9-1.]

PROBLEM 9-3 Assume that an executive for a new airline has studied cost, competition, and the law in setting fares for overseas flights. What other major factors should the firm consider before setting its prices?

Answer: The airline executive should consider demand, which is a very important factor in fare setting. Usually, lower fares will stimulate the demand for airline seats while higher fares reduce demand. If the demand is very high, i.e., when many people are flying for business or personal purposes, the airline can raise fares without losing revenues. When demand is down, e.g., when a hostage takeover discourages air travel or the economy is depressed, the airline may be forced to lower some or all of its fares. If demand is higher during certain times of the day (such as late mornings), the firm may charge higher fares than for less popular flying times. [See Section 9-1.]

PROBLEM 9-4 The management of a major video equipment company believes that demand is elastic for its 8-mm videocassette recorders. What does this tell management about the best price level that it should charge?

Answer: It appears that low prices would be an effective strategy for this company's 8-mm videocassette recorders. Such prices are associated with percentage increases in demand that are greater than the percentage increases in price. In this case, low prices should produce high total revenues. Company executives will have to examine costs before making a decision, however. If unit costs are not substantially higher when the firm's output increases, the lower prices will in fact be the most profitable ones. This is likely for a large firm, which has considerable capacity to produce. [See Section 9-2.]

PROBLEM 9-5 You have been asked to advise a friend about how to set prices for a janitorial service for office buildings that he is establishing. You have been given considerable information on the expected costs of the operation. How should you use this information in helping your friend set prices?

Answer: Your friend's costs should put a floor on the prices of his janitorial service company. This cost would be a limit below which his prices normally should not go. He may decide to use either total or variable cost for this purpose. It is possible that he might price below cost for a short time, in order to gain clients. This is a very competitive industry, so such a strategy may be effective. Eventually, however, the prices must be raised so that costs are covered and there is a contribution to profit. [See Section 9-2.]

PROBLEM 9-6 A small picture frame manufacturer has put together information on the revenues and costs associated with various price levels for its products. How can this information be used to determine the best price?

Answer: The picture frame company management should seek out the price that offers the largest difference between total revenue and total cost. This is the optimum price. If, however, this industry is a very dynamic one, in which demand and cost levels are subject to changes over time, management should periodically re-examine cost and revenue estimates to determine if the optimum price level has changed. [See Section 9-2.]

PROBLEM 9-7 A major supermarket chain has a policy of providing high-quality goods and services and projecting an image of quality. It has a pricing policy of keeping many prices high, relative to those of competitors, and using leaders to entice customers into company stores. Why shouldn't this firm do away with pricing policies and allow individual store managers to set prices as they see fit?

Answer: Policies serve as general rules or guidelines for the store managers. They indicate what kinds of decisions the managers should make in order to fulfill company objectives. Without policies, individual store managers might, intentionally or unintentionally, make pricing decisions that conflict with company objectives. This chain has, as an important objective, the provision of high-quality goods and services, and an image of quality. Price cutting by individual store managers could seriously weaken this image and suggest to consumers that the firm's marketing efforts are not well-coordinated. [See Section 9-3.]

PROBLEM 9-8 A ski shop owner is very aggressive in pricing, attempting to undercut competitor prices whenever possible. The owner believes that all businesses follow this pricing policy. Do you agree?

Answer: The ski shop owner is not correct. In some businesses, prices do not play much of a role in marketing strategy. If company costs are approximately the same as those of rivals, if the products have little or no differential advantages, if industry customary prices are in effect, or if management fears price wars, it is best to avoid extensive use of an aggressive pricing policy. This ski shop probably has lower costs than its competitors have, or the owner is willing to accept lower profits per unit sold than its rivals are. These circumstances would make the aggressive pricing strategy of the owner appropriate. But other firms might find that it runs counter to company objectives. [See Section 9-4.]

PROBLEM 9-9 A producer of high-quality furniture has costs that are near the industry average. Demand is inelastic for these products. Would you recommend pricing below competition?

Answer: Pricing below competition would probably not be recommended for this furniture manufacturer. Its costs are near the industry average, so low prices could lead to dangerously low profit levels. Further, demand is inelastic, so price reductions would not bring about substantial increases in revenue. If management can find ways of reducing costs or making demand more elastic (advertising or product improvements are possible options), pricing below competition could be an effective strategy. [See Section 9-5.]

PROBLEM 9-10 Managers at H.J. Heinz Company set the prices of Weight Watcher's frozen meals above the prices of most competitive brands. Is this a good strategy? After all, Heinz may lose business to its competitors.

Answer: It may be a good strategy for the H.J. Heinz company. Demand for its Weight Watcher's frozen meals probably is fairly inelastic, since the firm produces and aggressively promotes a very high-quality product, which has an excellent image in the industry. Further, some consumers may associate higher prices with higher quality in the low-calorie frozen foods industry, making the Heinz strategy especially profitable. [See Section 9-5.]

PROBLEM 9-11 A cousin of yours plans to open and manage a bookstore and has asked for your advice concerning whether or not to use a cost-plus pricing policy. What factors should your cousin consider in making this choice?

Answer: The cost-plus pricing policy may be a good one for a bookstore, at least until the manager has worked in the store long enough to establish experience in pricing and related elements of the marketing mix. Cost-plus pricing is easy to apply and simple to understand. It is not as time-consuming as are many other methods. It is often used by bookstore managers who stock many items. However, the store owner should realize that costs may not be related to demand, in which case ineffective price selections are possible. The owner should be prepared to change at least some of the prices derived from cost-plus calculations. [See Section 9-5.]

PROBLEM 9-12 The potential bookstore owner mentioned in Problem 9-11 is also considering return-on-investment pricing. Would you recommend this policy?

Answer: In order to use return-on-investment pricing, the bookstore owner must be good at forecasting the sales and costs that are associated with various prices. This is a difficult task, one that many small business managers cannot do well. Since the manager is new to the business, it may be best to avoid using this policy, at least until the owner acquires experience. In the meantime, the owner could benefit by learning, perhaps through a college class, what sales and cost forecasting techniques are available and how to use them. [See Section 9-5.]

PROBLEM 9-13 Recently, a cosmetics company introduced a new mascara that is irritant-free for contact-lens wearers. Demand for the product appeared to be inelastic and there were no major competitors at the time. What pricing policy could the company have used to introduce this new product?

Answer: A skimming policy would have been a good choice for introducing this new mascara. In the case of skimming, management assesses prices that are high, relative to company costs. This policy is in order when demand is inelastic, which is probably the case for a new product that has a special appeal—like being irritant-free for contact-lens wearers. The lack of competition would also support a skimming policy. If consumers do not like the product as well as management expects, or if competitors enter the market, the company may be forced into price reductions. [See Section 9-5.]

PROBLEM 9-14 The Lettuce-Spray Company provides noncumulative quantity discounts to retailers who buy minimum quantities of its Heavenly salad dressings. What benefit does the company derive as a result of the discount?

Answer: The major benefit is to reduce Lettuce-Spray's costs. Small orders for Heavenly salad dressing can cost nearly as much as large ones, because a large proportion of the costs of getting and filling an order are fixed. Small order are therefore less desirable. The discount will lead some buyers who order in small quantities to avoid patronizing Lettuce-Spray. Small businesses, in particular, are likely to follow this course of action. Further, the discount will force some buyers into ordering large quantities less frequently, rather than ordering small quantities more frequently. [See Section 9-6.]

PROBLEM 9-15 Assume that you are the owner/manager of a small music store. You sell musical instruments on credit but find that the credit purchases have become excessive. How might you reduce your accounts receivable?

Answer: You could offer cash discounts to the music store customers who pay in cash at the time they receive the merchandise or who pay their bills within a specific time period, such as 10 days or 30 days. This will result in savings to customers who pay their bills rapidly, as well as savings in the amount of money that your store ties up in non-interest-bearing accounts receivable. [See Section 9-6.]

PROBLEM 9-16 Assume that you are the marketing manager for a small cannery. You desire to get more food stores to stock your canned vegetables. How might you accomplish this?

Answer: The cannery could provide more discounts or higher discounts than do most major competitors in the canned vegetables field. It may turn out that the food stores who take advantage of the discounts will be larger firms, since many small customers are unable to comply with the conditions that such discounts require. Appealing mainly to larger customers (such as supermarket chains) may be very profitable, because these companies can provide large sales volumes to the cannery at a low cost. [See Section 9-6.]

PROBLEM 9-17 How might a company get supermarkets to help promote its products?

Answer: A company could provide promotion allowances to supermarkets to compensate them for the promotion activites that they undertake. The allowances may take the form of price reductions, free goods (such as one case free with every 12 cases purchased), or cash payments. Also, a company could pay for part of the middlemen's advertising for its products. [See Section 9-6.]

PROBLEM 9-18 A New York City producer of high-quality handbags and accessories has many large retail outlets in Southern California and hopes to gain more. What geographic pricing policy could help this company achieve its objective?

Answer: The company should quote FOB destination prices. Here, the seller pays the transportation charges and owns the goods until they arrive at the buyer's location. This makes the firm competitive in places located far from the plant, such as Southern California. Management may also decide to absorb some of the freight going to that market. This could help the firm become more competitive in Southern California, but it may have to charge higher prices to customers located in other markets to subsidize the freight absorption. [See Section 9-7.]

PROBLEM 9-19 A marketing executive for a company headquartered in Chicago believes in using uniform delivered prices to retailers for the company's skin care lotion. A financial executive disagrees. What argument can the marketing executive make to support his position?

Answer: The marketing executive can logically argue that, with uniform delivered prices, all customers, regardless of their location, pay the same price for the skin care lotion. This makes the firm competitive in areas far from the plant, such as Seattle and San Diego. This policy is common for products such as lotion that are heavy or bulky relative to their unit prices and that have low transportation costs. [See Section 9-7.]

PROBLEM 9-20 A North Dakota producer of baked goods (mainly cookies and crackers) that are sold throughout the United States wants to make its freight charges low enough to compete with large and aggressive rivals in Minnesota and Illinois. What geographical pricing policy should the North Dakota producer use?

Answer: The North Dakota producer probably should use a freight absorption pricing policy. In this case, the producer pays for some of the freight to customers who are located at a distance, especially if they are situated near its major rivals. The baked goods producer should pay enough of the freight to make the final price to target customers the same as that charged by competitors. This policy is useful to marketers who have important customers located far from manufacturing plants. The North Dakota firm is in this situation. [See Section 9-7.]

10 PHYSICAL DISTRIBUTION

THIS CHAPTER IS ABOUT

- ☑ **The Systems Concept of Physical Distribution**
- ☑ **The Major Components of the Physical Distribution System**
- ☑ **Advantages of Effective Physical Distribution**
- ☑ **Trends in Physical Distribution**

10-1. The Systems Concept of Physical Distribution

Many people believe that marketing is mainly concerned with promotion. They are often surprised to learn that it includes physical distribution as well. Yet this is a very important aspect of marketing.

- **Physical distribution** is the efficient movement of finished goods from producers to customers.

Through physical distribution, marketers create *time* and *place utility* for customers:

- **Time utility** means making goods available *when* they are needed.
- **Place utility** means making goods available *where* they are needed.

EXAMPLE 10-1: The Lockheed Corporation creates *time utility* if it delivers radar jammers to the United States Navy on the date that the Navy wants them. The Sunkist Cooperative creates *place utility* by making California oranges available in Boston.

Physical distribution in a company is a *system* of interrelated parts that work together toward one or more common goals. The parts of a physical distribution system are interrelated because what happens to one part affects the others. Normally, the common goals are to provide customers with the goods they desire at the time when and place where they want them, all at a reasonable cost. The most useful goals are those that are specific enough to provide guidance to physical distribution personnel.

EXAMPLE 10-2: A small waterbed producer has a goal of delivering its products at least one day faster than any competitor. To achieve this goal, it uses two of its own trucks and has modern, efficient warehouses located near major retail customers. This combination of resources allows the producer to handle and dispense orders quickly.

The systems concept allows marketers to make *tradeoffs* between parts of the physical distribution system. Tradeoffs mean that costs in one part of the system may be increased to provide decreased costs in other parts or to improve customer services.

EXAMPLE 10-3: The Ford Motor Company ships automobile parts from Michigan to assembly plants in California by air freight. On one hand, this is an expensive mode of transit. On the other hand, rapid transportation lowers inventory costs and improves production scheduling to the degree that total costs are reduced.

10-2. The Major Components of the Physical Distribution System

There are three major components of a physical distribution system. These are *warehousing and storage*, *transportation*, and *location*.

A. Warehousing and storage

Warehousing consists of holding and caring for goods after they have been produced and before they are delivered to customers. The two major subdivisions of warehousing are *storage* and *breaking bulk*.

1. Storage

Storage means keeping items in inventory. If products are produced and consumed at different times, storage must bridge this gap.

EXAMPLE 10-4: Consumers buy fireworks, skis, Christmas cards, and turkeys primarily at certain times of the year. However, producers of these items must operate steadily throughout the year to minimize production costs. Hence, their products must be stored as they are produced. Other products, such as oranges, are produced at one time of year and stored for consumer use throughout the year.

Marketers also store goods to accumulate large lots that receive low transportation rates. Railroads, trucks, and other carriers quote lower per unit rates for large than for small shipments.

In determining how much inventory to carry, marketers focus their efforts on two factors: customer service and cost. These two factors work in opposite directions. High levels of inventory allow the firm to fill customer orders rapidly and minimize the danger of **stockouts** (being out of stock when orders come in). But large inventories drive up inventory costs, such as interest, spoilage, or obsolescence expenses. Most firms therefore try to invest in intermediate levels of inventory, which will permit reasonable customer service at costs that are not excessive.

EXAMPLE 10-5: A plumbing and heating wholesaler could store an inventory of 500 two-inch galvanized valves, which should be enough to prevent stockouts. However, storing 500 valves would result in an annual inventory cost of $1,100. Thus, the wholesaler has elected to hold an inventory of 300 valves. This quantity reduces inventory costs to $710 and still keeps stockouts to an average of three per month, which management feels is not too much.

---

2. Breaking bulk

Breaking bulk means moving large shipments to a warehouse (or warehouses) located near markets. These shipments are then broken down at the warehouse into individual orders for customers, as shown in Figure 10-1. The producer can ship in large quantities to the warehouse, thus achieving low transportation rates. Rapid delivery to customers is then possible, since the warehouse is located near customers. Also, a large quantity of merchandise flows through the warehouse, which should be large enough to support specialized and efficient equipment and personnel.

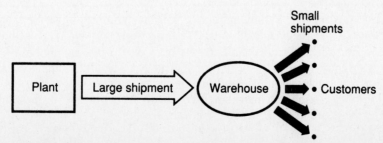

FIGURE 10-1: The breaking bulk system of warehousing and storage.

B. Transportation

Transportation involves moving products from the plants or warehouses of the seller to the receiving facilities of the buyer. Marketers can achieve an advantage over competitors by providing fast, reliable, low-cost delivery and by offering specialized transportation services.

Carriers are companies that furnish transportation services. **Shippers** are marketers who are the customers of carriers. When shippers own their own transportation equipment (such as trucks), they are called **private carriers**. The major objective for entering into private carriage is to obtain superior transportation services.

For most marketers there are several modes (types) of transportation that are feasible.

(1) **Railroads**. Railroads are most useful for heavy and bulky goods that are shipped over long distances. Their costs per *ton mile* (moving one ton of freight one mile) are relatively low. However, rail freight is slower than air freight and can be less efficient than moving goods by truck. Rail freight requires the movement of goods from railroad freight terminals to buyers' warehouses. Damages in transit can be considerable. And some railroads are subject to high pilferage rates.

EXAMPLE 10-6: Most coal-mining companies move the coal that they have excavated by rail freight. The rates are low, and these firms are not heavily concerned with speed in transit.

---

(2) **Trucks**. Trucks are of the most value in moving small shipments of manufactured goods over short distances. Damages in truck transit are less than those for rail. Trucks can reach any points that have roads, and can furnish pickup and delivery service. However, they are less economical than railroads for long hauls (over 400 miles) and for carrying heavy and bulky commodities.

(3) **Airlines**. Airlines offer one primary advantage for hauling freight—speed. Their rates are high, but may be counterbalanced by savings in inventory costs or efficiency in serving customers. Airlines are often used for small, expensive, and/or emergency items. Their major weaknesses are their high costs and limited capacity.

(4) **Water**. Water carriers are best for moving heavy and bulky items, such as gravel and grain, over long distances at low costs. They are slow, however, and can operate only part of the year in some regions because the water may freeze. Also, they can serve only areas that have navigable waterways and good port facilities.

(5) **Pipelines**. Pipelines can only be used for transporting fluid (gas or liquid) products, such as natural gas and oil. Most of the major pipelines are owned by oil and gas producers. In a few cases, grains can be mixed with water, forming a slurry, which can be fluid enough to be transported by pipeline. This mode of transportation is capable of carrying large volumes at a low cost. It is, however, inflexible, as products can only be transported where pipelines have been built.

(6) **Combined modes of transportation**. Sometimes different carriers cooperate with one another. Goods may be transported **piggyback**, in which loaded truck trailers are moved on railroad cars, thereby reducing the costs to the shipper. The same thing can be accomplished by **fishyback**, which involves moving loaded truck trailers or railroad cars by ship. Many bulk goods are loaded into large *containers* which can be transported by one carrier, such as a truck, and then transferred to another carrier, such as a railroad, with a minimum of loading and unloading effort.

(7) **Freight forwarders**. The various modes of transportation quote lower rates per hundredweight for large shipments. Railroads have lower rates for *carloads* (normally over 40,000 pounds) and trucks for *truckloads* (sometimes over 5,000 pounds). Also, carload and truckload shipments tend to be more efficient than smaller shipments. Because of the difference between large-volume and small-volume rates, *freight forwarders* are specialized businesses that consolidate many small shipments from various shippers into carload and truckload movements. This allows the shippers to enjoy lower rates and often faster shipment.

C. Location

Marketers must decide in which cities and on which sites within cities to locate retail stores and warehouses. There are three major factors that they must consider in making this decision.

1. Demand

For some firms, such as grocery stores, demand is a very important location criterion. They must be situated in a place that allows them to provide customer satisfaction through their locations. Often these firms locate where there is substantial traffic, such as near major traffic arteries or centers of employment.

EXAMPLE 10-7: Convenience stores, such as 7-11 and Pic-Quik, locate in neighborhoods and near thoroughfares that are convenient to large numbers of their customers. The intent is to minimize the amount of time that shoppers must spend traveling to and from the stores.

---

2. Cost

Another important determinant of location for many manufacturers is cost. Warehouses are often located in places where rents are low or where low-cost transportation, either from the plant to the warehouse or from the warehouse to customers, is available. In addition, some retailers seek low-rent locations within cities.

EXAMPLE 10-8: Discount stores, army surplus stores, pawn shops, and lumber yards often locate in low-rent, remote sites. Management seeks low costs and knows that many potential customers will drive to a hard-to-reach site, because their desire to purchase is strong.

---

3. Competition

A firm may choose to locate in a particular place because its competitors have adopted certain strategies. For example, a warehouse may be located in a certain city because the firm can serve customers from the warehouse faster than its competitors. Retailers sometimes seek out locations that are more likely to attract customers than its competitor's locations, or that appeal to customer shopping patterns.

EXAMPLE 10-9: Kinney shoe stores are deliberately located near competing shoe store outlets. Management realizes that most customers prefer to shop around from one shoe store to another before committing to a purchase. Thus, by locating near competitors, they stand a better chance of getting the return customer than if they were located in less accessible areas.

10-3. Advantages of Effective Physical Distribution

There are several situations in which a company can acquire an advantage over competitors by performing physical distribution more effectively than its rivals do. This is particularly so in the case of industries whose products are essentially the same as those of their rivals.

EXAMPLE 10-10: The products of one steel mill are essentially the same as those of its competitors. USX, a large steel company, realizes this, so it attempts to compete through inexpensive, reliable, and reasonably fast transportation. It uses rail freight to serve many customers, and it makes sure that the railroads it uses have good track records.

Another advantage of effective physical distribution is that many sales representatives can emphasize rapid delivery as a strong selling point. If Company A can promise a shipment in one week, whereas Company B cannot provide delivery for two weeks, Company A may outdo Company B in sales. Rapid delivery is especially important in industries whose customers need goods available quickly in order to preserve the value of those goods.

EXAMPLE 10-11: Wonder Bread is delivered very rapidly after it has been produced, so it will be fresh when it appears on retail shelves. Many consumers want fresh bread and are even willing to pay a premium price to get it.

When competitors are weak in physical distribution, there is a special incentive for a firm to excel in this field. Rivals who have unreliable delivery schedules or who damage goods in transit are particularly vulnerable, and may be easily outdone by a firm whose physical distribution is excellent.

10-4. Trends in Physical Distribution

Physical distribution is in a continuous state of flux. Managers must work to stay abreast of changing ideas and improved methods, as new opportunities for servicing customers better or reducing costs are always developing.

- Some carriers have improved their equipment and service so that they can satisfy shippers better than competing carriers.

Shippers should always be alert for improved carrier service. They should review their current carriers and research new ones to compare prices, delivery schedules, and other factors important to serving their customers well.

EXAMPLE 10-12: The Union Pacific Railroad is one of the more progressive lines in the industry. It has taken many measures to prevent the delay of shipments caused by traffic congestion in terminals and has developed a system to get shipments on a train in a reasonable time. The company can thus offer faster delivery than many railroad and truck competitors who are weaker in these areas.

- Government regulation of the transportation industry became much less rigorous after 1980 than it was prior to 1980.

In the 80's carriers were permitted to provide a number of services that were once prohibited, such as delivering to new cities or over new routes. Also during the 80's many shippers were able to get rate concessions or new services that were once not available. This trend should continue.

- Physical delivery equipment is continually being improved.

New truck designs have reduced wind resistance to improve fuel economy. Railroad cars have been redesigned so that they do not jar—and damage—goods being transported as much as they commonly did in the past. Many warehouses have been partially or fully automated to bring about reductions in costs and rapid, trouble-free loading and unloading. Containers are being designed for an expanding list of goods and are becoming more standardized from one country to another. Developments such as these can lead to effective cost reductions and improvements in service performance.

- Managers are discovering new ways of managing physical distribution to improve services and cut costs.

Computer technology has been applied to transportation, warehousing and storage, and location in ways that were not possible several years ago. These include finding the most economical transportation routes and identifying low-cost inventory levels. Computer applications can be expected to become even more pronounced in the future.

RAISE YOUR GRADES

Can you explain . . . ?

☑ how physical distribution creates time and place utility for customers
☑ why the systems concept of managing physical distribution activities is successful
☑ how manufacturers can help prevent stockouts of their products in supermarkets
☑ why many large companies engage in breaking bulk
☑ why many producers of bulky goods use railroads to transport their offerings
☑ why numerous companies use trucks to transport items from warehouses to retail stores
☑ why many fast-food restaurants are situated in high-traffic locations

SUMMARY

1. Physical distribution is the efficient movement of finished goods from producers to customers, providing time and place utility for customers.
2. Physical distribution in a company is a system of interrelated parts that work together toward one or more common goals.
3. The systems concept allows marketers to make tradeoffs between parts of the physical distribution system to decrease costs or to improve customer services.
4. There are three major components of the physical distribution system: warehousing and storage, transportation, and location.
5. Warehousing and storage refers to the holding and housing of goods between the time they are produced and the time they are shipped to customers. Companies may either store inventories, or they may move large shipments to warehouses near markets—a process, known as breaking bulk.
6. Transportation consists of moving products from the plants or warehouses of the seller to the receiving facilities of the buyer. The major modes of transportation available to marketers are railroads, trucks, airlines, water, pipelines, and combined modes (such as piggyback or fishyback); freight forwarders, who consolidate small shipments into carloads or truckloads, may also be used to move products.
7. Location refers to the determination of where stores and warehouses should be located. The three major factors in making the location decision are demand, cost, and competition.
8. Effective physical distribution can offer an advantage over competitors when the products of a company are essentially the same as those of its rivals, when customers want rapid delivery that competitors cannot provide, or when competitors are especially weak in physical distribution.
9. Physical distribution is constantly improving because many factors such as improved equipment and service, less government regulation, computer technology, and other developments can bring about cost reductions and improvements in service performance.

RAPID REVIEW   Answers

Multiple Choice

1. Physical distribution consists of moving finished goods to (**a**) warehouses, (**b**) customers, (**c**) retail outlets, (**d**) rail depots for loading. [See Section 10-1.]   *b*
2. When a company makes its products available where they are needed, this is an example of (**a**) time utility, (**b**) possession utility, (**c**) production utility, (**d**) place utility. [See Section 10-1.]   *d*
3. The physical distribution system for a company consists of a grouping of   *b*

_____ parts. (a) independent, (b) interrelated, (c) uncoordinated, (d) unrelated. [See Section 10-1.]

4. Physical distribution components work together to achieve (a) undamaged shipments of bottles, (b) safe storage of products, (c) common goals, (d) well-located distribution centers. [See Section 10-1.]

c

5. When the physical distribution system of a company increases costs in one area to decrease costs in another or to improve customer services, it is making a(n) (a) tradeoff, (b) substitution, (c) replacement, (d) offset. [See Section 10-1.]

a

6. Foster Grant sunglasses are sold most heavily in the spring, but the company produces them year-round. During the rest of the year, the company keeps its products in (a) warehouses, (b) shipment docks, (c) storage, (d) retail outlets. [See Section 10-2.]

c

7. If a company maintains high levels of inventory, it is likely to have (a) stockouts, (b) high costs, (c) slow customer service, (d) slow delivery. [See Section 10-2.]

b

8. Which of the following is *not* an advantage of breaking bulk? (a) low rental rates for warehouses, (b) low transportation rates, (c) fast delivery to customers, (d) efficient warehouse equipment. [See Section 10-2.]

a

9. Which of the following is *not* a means whereby a company can achieve an advantage over rivals through transporting its products? (a) fast delivery, (b) few damages in transit, (c) low production training costs, (d) providing specialized transportation services. [See Section 10-2.]

c

10. Shippers who own their own trucks are called (a) private carriers, (b) personal carriers, (c) personal shippers, (d) jobbers. [See Section 10-2.]

a

11. Railroads are especially useful to firms for transporting (a) bulky goods, (b) small shipments, (c) nonbreakable goods, (d) emergency goods. [See Section 10-2.]

a

12. Damages in transit are especially a problem to shippers who use (a) trucks, (b) airlines, (c) railroads, (d) water. [See Section 10-2.]

c

13. Trucks are of the most value to companies when moving small shipments of manufactured goods over (a) long distances, (b) places inaccessible by water, (c) rough roads,(d) short distances. [See Section 10-2.]

d

14. High transportation rates that an airline charges may be counterbalanced by savings in _____ costs to shippers. (a) transportation, (b) production, (c) inventory, (d) payroll. [See Section 10-2.]

c

15. A disadvantage to shippers who use water carriers is (a) high transportation rates, (b) slow transportation, (c) uneconomical rates for long distances, (d) inability to move bulky items. [See Section 10-2.]

b

16. When using piggyback transportation, a trucking company arranges for the movement of truck trailers by (a) ship, (b) railroads, (c) caravan, (d) tractors. [See Section 10-2.]

b

17. Which of the following is *not* a major factor that a company should consider in locating its stores? (a) demand, (b) cost, (c) competition, (d) railroad freight rates. [See Section 10-2.]

d

18. Companies usually try to locate warehouses in places with (a) high automobile traffic, (b) low rents, (c) high prestige, (d) extensive computer facilities. [See Section 10-2.]

b

19. When competitors have essentially the same product as those of another company, that company can still achieve an advantage over competitors through (a) faster delivery service, (b) offering a different product, (c) better sales reps, (d) ad campaigns. [See Section 10-3.]

a

20. Government regulation of transportation became _____ in the 1980's than it was in the years prior to 1980. (a) more stringent, (b) less stringent, (c) more detailed, (d) more widespread. [See Section 10-4.]

b

SOLVED PROBLEMS

PROBLEM 10-1 Assume that you have been appointed as the physical distribution (PD) manager for a tannery located in southeastern Missouri. You are attempting to specify the more important objectives of your job. What are the major kinds of utility (satisfaction) you would try to provide to company customers?

Answer: The major kinds of utility for a tannery physical distribution manager would be time utility (making goods available to customers when they are needed) and place utility (making goods available where they are needed). In order to accomplish these goals it would be necessary to determine the desired characteristics of the tannery warehouses and where they should be located. Another important decision is what kind of transportation media to use (probably a combination of trucks, railroad, and barges). Finally, it would be necessary to specify the most desirable inventory levels and kinds of material handling systems to be used. [See Section 10-1.]

PROBLEM 10-2 A classmate has read that physical distribution in a company makes up a system and asks you why this is important to the company. How would you answer?

Answer: The classmate should be advised that a system is a grouping of parts that are interrelated and work together toward one or more common goals. (The respiratory system in the human body is a good example of a system that has many parts working to achieve a common goal.) This definition also applies to physical distribution. The parts are interrelated—a change in one part brings about changes in others. If a company switches from rail to air transportation, for instance, its inventories could decline. All parts work together toward a common goal, serving customers at reasonable costs. [See Section 10-1.]

PROBLEM 10-3 MacIntyre Cosmetics is a leading producer of perfumes and other cosmetics. What specific kinds of physical distribution goals should it have, and what are some of the problems this company will have in achieving these goals?

Answer: MacIntyre Cosmetics' goals should be to provide customers with the cosmetics they desire at the time and place that they want them, all at a reasonable cost. Since this company must sell through many types of wholesalers and retailers, each of which has different physical distribution requirements, these goals are very complex and often difficult to achieve. One retail customer, for instance, may demand rapid transportation while another may stress very tightly coordinated physical handling procedures. This company will make many tradeoffs to achieve its goals. [See Section 10-1.]

PROBLEM 10-4 A food wholesaling company executive has stated that it is profitable to make tradeoffs between parts of the company physical distribution system. What does this mean?

Answer: The food wholesaling company executive means that the systems concept encourages the firm to make tradeoffs between parts of the physical distribution system. This means that costs in one part may be increased to provide (1) decreased costs in other parts or (2) improved customer service. The company, for example, might increase inventory costs by shipping goods infrequently, in order to decrease transportation costs by shipping by railroad carload or by truckload. [See Section 10-1.]

PROBLEM 10-5 An automobile plastics sales representative has stated that the plastics company makes a major effort to avoid stockouts. How can it do this?

Answer: The automobile plastics company can maintain high levels of plastic inventories, which will allow the firm to minimize dangers of stockouts, i.e., being out of stock when orders come in from the automobile producers. Another means of avoiding stockouts is to provide rapid transportation to warehouses and other points where goods are held by customers. Company managers may decide that the firm should invest in its own fleet of trucks for this purpose, rather than using common or contract carriers. [See Section 10-2.]

PROBLEM 10-6   A photographic supplies producer has informed you that the only reason for holding inventories is storage. The producer is experiencing high transportation costs and slow delivery to customers. Can inventories be used to remedy this situation?

Answer: The photographic supplies producer takes a very limited view of the function of inventories. Breaking bulk—moving large shipments to warehouses located near markets—is a very important reason for inventories in a number of industries, including photographic supplies. Producers can ship in large quantities to warehouses and receive low transportation rates from the carriers. Then, rapid deliveries to customers are possible. [See Section 10-2.]

PROBLEM 10-7   How can a large appliance manufacturer achieve differential advantage over competitors in the transportation of its refrigerators and other major appliances?

Answer: A large appliance manufacturer can achieve differential advantage by transporting refrigerators in a manner that provides customers with the benefits they seek. Good benefits to provide are fast, reliable delivery and low damages in transit. The manufacturer might, for instance, provide specialized services, such as reinforced packing materials to keep goods from damage while being moved. If this company can achieve an excellent track record for providing fast and reliable transportation services to all customers, both large and small, it may gain a differential advantage over its competitors. [See Section 10-2.]

PROBLEM 10-8   The K-9 Treet Company is considering using railroads to transport its dry dog food to retailers. Would you recommend this course of action? If not, what would you suggest?

Answer: Rail freight probably would not be the best alternative for shipping dry dog food, for several reasons. (1) Rail freight is most useful for heavy and bulky goods that are shipped over long distances. (2) Rail freight is slower than air and many truck shipments. (3) Rail freight requires the movement of goods from railroad freight terminals to buyers' warehouses. (4) Damages in rail-freight transit can be considerable. All of these factors suggest that the K-9 Treet Company should use truck, rather than rail, transportation. [See Section 10-3.]

PROBLEM 10-9   Should the Sechrist Company move its packaged coffee from plants to warehouses by trucks? Most of its warehouses are located within 300 miles of a plant and receive frequent, small shipments.

Answer: Truck transportation may be of value for transporting packaged coffee for several reasons. This medium is most effective in moving small shipments of manufactured goods over short distances, which is the case for the Sechrist Company. Damages in truck transit are generally less than those for rail. Truck carriers perform pickup and delivery functions, relieving the producer of this activity. Finally the coffee probably will be delivered faster than if railroads were employed. [See Section 10-2.]

PROBLEM 10-10   A product manager for a packaged drink mix producer has wondered if air freight might be useful in reducing physical distribution costs from the plant to the warehouse. This company keeps its inventories at low levels. Would you recommend this move?

Answer: Air freight would not reduce transportation costs for this packaged drink mix producer. Airline rates are very high, so airlines are mainly used for expensive and emergency items. The main advantage of these carriers is that they are fast, permitting inventory reductions. But, in this case, the high fares would not be compensated for by reductions in inventory, since the company already maintains low inventory levels. [See Section 10-2.]

PROBLEM 10-11   A Minnesota grain wholesaler is considering using barges to transport wheat to New Orleans, rather than using a railroad. What possible problems could this wholesaler encounter with water transportation?

Answer: The grain wholesaler should be aware of the fact that barge carriers are slow. It may take many days, or even weeks, to reach New Orleans. Also, these carriers can operate only during that part of the year when the water is not frozen. Finally, they can serve only those areas with adequate waterways and port facilities, which means that if the Minnesota company shifts to other destinations, water carriage may not be adequate. The overall advantage of water carriage for this firm is its low cost, which may largely compensate for all of these disadvantages. [See Section 10-2.]

PROBLEM 10-12 Assume that you are one of the managers of a new fast-food chain. What factors should you consider when choosing locations for building restaurants?

Answer: The major factors that your fast-food chain should consider are demand, cost, and competition. Demand is important, so the best location might be where large numbers of people pass or accumulate, such as on a major street, near schools or factories, or in downtown business districts. Cost considerations might lead the firm to select a low-rent site, even if there is a sacrifice of traffic volume. Competition might lead the company to choose a location that is not near major rivals. [See Section 10-2.]

PROBLEM 10-13 A beer distributor (wholesaler) is wondering what factors to consider in locating a warehouse. What would you suggest?

Answer: As with other kinds of firms, the major factors to consider are demand, cost, and competition. Demand is not as important to a beer distributor as it would be to other kinds of firms, so long as the location is such that it permits rapid and low-cost delivery. Cost is very important in this competitive industry, so the warehouse should be situated where rental rates are low. Competition is not a strong factor in locating a beer distributor warehouse because it is not necessary that a warehouse be situated far from rivals. [See Section 10-2.]

PROBLEM 10-14 The owner of a ladies' clothing store has asked you for advice on where to locate. What would you recommend?

Answer: A good strategy would be to locate near competing ladies' clothing stores, perhaps in the same malls or in the same neighborhood. Many clothing buyers like to look in several stores before making a purchase and avoid stores that are isolated. In addition, the store owner would want to avoid sites with rentals that are too high, that lack the desired image, or have inadequate traffic. Among the better locations are malls that draw in large numbers of customers who would be among the clothing store's desired target customers. [See Section 10-2.]

PROBLEM 10-15 Would you recommend that a lumber mill attempt to compete with its rivals through physical distribution? Why?

Answer: It would be a good idea to consider physical distribution as a competitive element for a lumber mill. Lumber is a somewhat basic commodity, as it does not differ materially from one mill to another. The firm could differentiate itself from rivals through fast or reliable delivery, few stockouts, or flexible pickup and delivery service. A good physical distribution system could offset similarities in the basic product. [See Section 10-3.]

PROBLEM 10-16 A manufacturer of small electric motors has used railroads for making shipments to customers for over 20 years. This manufacturer strives for fast delivery and low inventory levels. Should management consider a change?

Answer: Yes, the manufacturer should consider a change. The transportation industry is in a state of flux, and the railroads are no exception to this. Management methods, equipment, regulation, and other factors change continually. The producer's management should realize that conditions may have changed in 20 years and should look for desirable new alternatives in rail and motor freight. Changes may be in order. It may be, for example, that a switch to truck transportation will permit faster delivery of the motors to customers or will reduce inventory and warehousing costs. [See Section 10-4.]

MIDTERM EXAM
(Chapters 1–10)

Part 1: Multiple Choice (50 points)

1. Which of the following is *not* a major kind of utility that marketers provide?
   - (a) time utility
   - (b) money utility
   - (c) place utility
   - (d) possession utility

2. An important element in the modern definition of marketing is the fact that _____.
   - (a) marketing creates exchanges
   - (b) marketing is a business activity
   - (c) marketers direct the flow of goods from consumers to producers
   - (d) producers buy goods for personal satisfaction

3. The study of marketing as a participant in the overall society is called _____.
   - (a) global marketing
   - (b) mega-marketing
   - (c) micro-marketing
   - (d) macro-marketing

4. Approximately _____ of the typical firm's expenses are used to cover marketing costs.
   - (a) one-fourth
   - (b) one-third
   - (c) one-half
   - (d) three-fourths

5. According to the marketing concept, the company's major goal is to serve customer needs and _____.
   - (a) earn a profit
   - (b) pay reasonable wages
   - (c) award high taxes
   - (d) increase company wealth

6. Which of the following is *not* part of the marketing strategy?
   - (a) the kind of customer the firm seeks
   - (b) the customer needs the firm attempts to satisfy
   - (c) the combination of marketing functions that management uses to satisfy customers
   - (d) the techniques that management uses to select productive workers

7. The _____ consists of those forces outside the company that have an important effect on the success of the marketing strategy.
   - (a) marketing mix
   - (b) environment
   - (c) exchange process
   - (d) micro marketing strategy

8. In scanning the environment, which of the following aspects of competition need *not* be carefully considered?
   - (a) the number of competitors
   - (b) competitor strengths and weaknesses
   - (c) the strategies of competitors
   - (d) competitor hiring processes

9. A marketer with good sources of supply may be able to attain _____.
   - (a) low advertising rates
   - (b) low mortgage rates
   - (c) large shares of market
   - (d) liberal credit terms

10. Marketing tactics are more _____ than are strategies.
    - (a) long-run in nature
    - (b) subject to change
    - (c) general in nature
    - (d) permanent

11. Marketers who practice segmentation seek out subgroups of target customers _____.
    - (a) who have high incomes
    - (b) who seek different benefits
    - (c) whose needs are similar
    - (d) whose needs are different

12. If there are many segments and each segment consists of only a few consumers, management may be well advised to _____.
    (a) produce marketing mixes that appeal to a combination of subgroups
    (b) produce a large number of marketing mixes
    (c) increase the costs of segmentation
    (d) create a unique marketing mix for each customer

13. A major advantage of market segmentation to the firm is that it _____.
    (a) increases marketing costs
    (b) can produce customer satisfaction
    (c) increases brand loyalty for rival products
    (d) may aim at the wrong segments

14. Which of the following is *not* a requirement that a company should meet if segmentation is to be successful?
    (a) there must be subgroups who will react similarly to marketing programs
    (b) the firm must be able to reach targeted subgroups
    (c) there must be information permitting managers to differentiate their products
    (d) segmentation should be more profitable than not segmenting

15. Which of the following is *not* a major source of demographic data?
    (a) transportation carriers
    (b) government agencies
    (c) universities
    (d) companies

16. To constitute a market, individuals or organizations must have the _____ to buy a product or a service.
    (a) desire
    (b) savings
    (c) borrowing power
    (d) credit worthiness

17. Industrial markets consist of those who buy to satisfy the requirements of _____.
    (a) their families
    (b) the organization they work for
    (c) their husbands and wives
    (d) their children

18. Decreases in the U.S. population growth rate are partially attributable to the fact that women are doing all of the following *except* _____.
    (a) marrying at later ages
    (b) pursuing careers
    (c) having smaller numbers of children
    (d) marrying more frequently

19. The area of the country which has the largest population is _____.
    (a) East-North-Central
    (b) Pacific
    (c) East-South-Central
    (d) New England

20. In the United States, there has been a strong movement of population from _____ to _____ areas.
    (a) warmer, colder
    (b) high income, low income
    (c) rural, urban
    (d) urban, rural

21. Consumer behavior does *not* consist of the activities wherein individuals decide _____ to buy goods and services.
    (a) whether
    (b) when
    (c) from whom
    (d) not

22. If a problem faced is not great or if the problem has arisen many times in the past, consumers may act _____.
    (a) habitually
    (b) irrationally
    (c) by gathering research information
    (d) through considerable information search

23. Which of the following are perceived by consumers and produce responses intended to satisfy drives?
    (a) cues
    (b) reinforcement
    (c) utilities
    (d) traces

24. Which of the following is *not* an element of consumer minds, according to psychoanalytic theory?
    (a) the id
    (b) the superego
    (c) the ego
    (d) the gestalt

25. According to the diffusion of innovation theory, the _____ are the first to try a new offering.
    (a) early majority
    (b) early adopters
    (c) innovators
    (d) laggards

26. The demand for industrial goods is _____.
    (a) derived from consumer goods demand
    (b) derived from government expenditures
    (c) derived from taxes
    (d) derived from bond sales

27. The definition of industrial goods emphasizes that these products are _____.
    (a) purchased to satisfy individual needs
    (b) purchased to satisfy organization needs
    (c) purchased to satisfy family needs
    (d) not purchased on credit

28. A useful and widely used means of classifying industrial buyers is the _____ system.
    (a) Buyer Profile Analysis
    (b) Industrial Purchaser Category
    (c) Specific Intermediate Correspondence
    (d) Standard Industrial Classification

29. In the buying center of an industrial buyer, influencers _____.
    (a) provide information for evaluating goods
    (b) have formal authority to make purchases
    (c) use the goods and services that are purchased
    (d) control the flow of information into the buying center

30. If an industrial buyer finds a product bought previously to be satisfactory and decides to continue to purchase it, this is called _____.
    (a) new task buying
    (b) continual task buying
    (c) straight rebuy
    (d) modified rebuy

31. Marketing information is *not* vital for which one of the following product planning decisions?
    (a) determining what products to add
    (b) determining what products to drop
    (c) determining what elements to include in packaging
    (d) determining what production workers to hire

32. Which of the following is *not* part of a marketing information system?
    (a) data from within the firm
    (b) data from outside the firm
    (c) relevant information
    (d) income flows

33. _____ is a special kind of research used to identify problems.
    (a) Primary research
    (b) Preapproach research
    (c) Exploratory research
    (d) Comprehensive research

34. When researchers contact respondents who are easy to reach, this is called a _____ sample.
    (a) judgment
    (b) convenience
    (c) probability
    (d) cluster

35. Which of the following is *not* a marketing research cost?
    (a) salaries to sales managers
    (b) expenses of conducting research
    (c) revenue delays
    (d) errors in the data

36. Marketers view products broadly, in terms of the _____ they offer, rather than as mere physical items.
    (a) prices
    (b) attitudes
    (c) warranties
    (d) benefits

37. Shopping goods are those which consumers _____.
    (a) spend considerable effort in buying
    (b) are not willing to go to much trouble to buy
    (c) prefer over all other brands
    (d) are not eager to purchase

38. In the economic evaluation stage of the product or service development activity, marketers _____.
    (a) decide what kind of product to produce
    (b) estimate expected sales and costs
    (c) eliminate ideas by screening
    (d) create ideas for new products

39. Which of the following is *not* a way marketers can position products?
    (a) according to product characteristics
    (b) according to target consumers
    (c) according to transportation costs
    (d) according to target benefits

40. _____ are brands that have received legal protection, so that other firms cannot use them.
    (a) Family brands
    (b) Individual brands
    (c) Trademarks
    (d) Private brands

41. Differences in consumers with regard to what they will pay opens up opportunities for _____.
    (a) transportation cost reduction
    (b) selling cost reduction
    (c) market segmentation
    (d) sales forecasting

42. A _____ shows how many units a marketer can sell at various prices.
    (a) demand curve
    (b) supply curve
    (c) cost curve
    (d) profit curve

43. Costs that increase or decrease as the output of the company changes are called _____.
    (a) fixed costs
    (b) variable costs
    (c) altering costs
    (d) recurring costs

44. Leader prices are used _____.
    (a) to avoid price wars
    (b) to give prestige to company brands
    (c) to entice customers into stores
    (d) to keep prices higher than those of competitors

45. Producers provide _____ discounts to wholesalers and retailers to compensate them for the marketing activities that they perform.
    (a) cash
    (b) quantity
    (c) cooperative
    (d) functional

46. Which of the following is *not* a component of physical distribution?
    (a) warehousing and storage
    (b) transportation
    (c) location of stores
    (d) pricing

47. The systems concept encourages marketers to make _____ between parts of the physical distribution system.
    (a) tradeoffs
    (b) declines
    (c) costs
    (d) advances

48. Marketers attempt to set inventory levels high enough to avoid the danger of _____.
    (a) depletions
    (b) fines
    (c) stockouts
    (d) accumulations

49. Trucks have an advantage over railroads in moving _____.
    (a) large shipments
    (b) small shipments
    (c) bulky goods
    (d) goods over long distances

50. Which of the following is *not* a trend in the improvement of physical distribution equipment?
    (a) truck tractors have less wind resistance
    (b) railroad cars do not jar goods as much as they once did
    (c) Many warehouses are automated
    (d) containers are becoming less standardized

Part 2: Short Answer (50 points)

1. Those managers who pursue the _____ concept believe that the organization should emphasize efficiency in producing and distributing goods and services.

2. Taken together, the major marketing functions make up what is called the _____ _____ of the firm.

3. Advertising is _____ communication aimed at large groups.

4. The part of the marketing mix that deals with the physical movement of goods is called _____ _____.

5. _____ _____ _____ are the paths of ownership that items take in moving toward potential customers.

6. A _____ _____ consists of an overall plan to achieve company goals.

7. Marketing managers aim their efforts at particular potential customers, called _____ _____.

8. The rate of technology is _____ at an increasing rate.

9. The _____ consists of the behavior of production, income, employment, and prices.

10. To be effective, marketing strategies should be _____ with each other.

11. _____ _____ consists of developing and carrying out marketing programs that are aimed at subgroups of the total market.

12. One of the major requirements that a company should meet if segmentation is to be successful is that it should be more _____ than a no-segmentation strategy.

13. _____ consist of statistical facts about target customers.

14. _____ segmentation involves creating subgroups based on psychological characteristics.

15. _____ segmentation focuses on subgroups made up of potential customers that are attracted to the same elements of the marketing mix.

16. A _____ is made up of individuals or organizations who have the money and the desire to buy a product or service.

17. _____ markets are made up of those who buy goods and services for personal use and the satisfaction of personal desires.

18. The number of individuals who live in a particular place at a given time is measured by _____ figures.

19. Those persons who were born shortly after World War II are called the _____ _____ generation.

20. The stages in the family _____ _____ are based on age, marital status, and number of children.

21. In making purchase decisions, most consumers first recognize a _____.

22. The _____ theory of consumer behavior assumes that consumers are rational and aware of their needs and wants.

23. Consumers have _____, such as hunger, that seek satisfaction.

24. _____ theory looks at how consumers perceive their environment.

25. _____ groups are those from which consumers seek guidance for proper behavior.

26. In the case of _____ marketing, the firm serves customers through its own personnel, rather than through wholesalers.

27. Industrial buyers include both business and _____ organizations.

28. The Standard Industrial Classification (SIC) system classifies industrial buyers based on where the bulk of their _____ originate.

29. Those persons who are involved in an industrial goods purchasing decision are members of the _____ _____.

30. For industrial buyers, a problem exists when there is a significant difference between a desired condition and a(n) _____ _____.

31. In helping to select target customers, marketing information can indicate which individuals have a need for the product and have the _____ to afford it.

32. _____ _____ systems are used for continuous collection and analysis of data and provision of information to marketing decision makers.

33. _____, unlike surveys, provides little insight into customer attitudes, opinions, and other mental states.

34. In the case of _____ sampling, the researcher knows the probability that a member of the population may be included in the sample.

35. In the case of _____ _____ forecasting, analysts project past sales into the future.

36. Consumers do not see goods and services as things of value for their own sake but as bundles of _____.

37. Installations determine how much the buying organization can _____.

38. At the _____ stage of the product life cycle, sales grow rapidly and profits appear.

39. The _____ _____ is the total of all goods and services that the company offers.

40. Well-designed packages help consumers _____ products effectively.

41. To a large extent, there is a(n) _____ or situation of balance between what consumers pay and what they obtain.

42. If a percentage change in quantity sold for a product exceeds a percentage change in price, demand is called _____.

43. If a firm has a cost advantage over rivals, it is likely to charge _____ prices than they do.

44. In the case of cost-plus pricing, marketers add a _____ to their costs per unit, in order to attain a profit.

45. If goods are sold FOB point of origin, the _____ pays for the transportation charges at the seller's plant.

46. Physical distribution consists of the efficient movement of _____ _____ from producers to customers.

47. A physical distribution system is a grouping of parts that are interrelated and that work together toward one or more common _____.

48. _____ means moving large shipments to warehouses located near markets and making smaller shipments into individual orders for customers.

49. The major factors that marketers consider in location decisions are demand, _____, and competition.

50. Many companies can attain differential advantage over rivals through physical distribution, especially when their products are _____ _____.

ANSWERS

Part 1: Multiple Choice (50 points)

1. **(b)** [Section 1-1]	18. **(d)** [Section 4-2]	35. **(a)** [Section 7-4]
2. **(a)** [Section 1-2]	19. **(a)** [Section 4-2]	36. **(d)** [Section 8-1]
3. **(d)** [Section 1-3]	20. **(c)** [Section 4-2]	37. **(a)** [Section 8-2]
4. **(c)** [Section 1-3]	21. **(d)** [Section 5-1]	38. **(b)** [Section 8-3]
5. **(a)** [Section 1-4]	22. **(a)** [Section 5-1]	39. **(c)** [Section 8-6]
6. **(d)** [Section 2-1]	23. **(a)** [Section 5-3]	40. **(c)** [Section 8-8]
7. **(b)** [Section 2-1]	24. **(d)** [Section 5-3]	41. **(c)** [Section 9-1]
8. **(d)** [Section 2-1]	25. **(c)** [Section 5-4]	42. **(a)** [Section 9-2]
9. **(d)** [Section 2-1]	26. **(a)** [Section 6-2]	43. **(b)** [Section 9-2]
10. **(b)** [Section 2-2]	27. **(b)** [Section 6-1]	44. **(c)** [Section 9-3]
11. **(c)** [Section 3-1]	28. **(d)** [Section 6-3]	45. **(d)** [Section 9-6]
12. **(a)** [Section 3-1]	29. **(a)** [Section 6-4]	46. **(d)** [Section 10-1]
13. **(b)** [Section 3-2]	30. **(c)** [Section 6-4]	47. **(a)** [Section 10-1]
14. **(c)** [Section 3-2]	31. **(d)** [Section 7-1]	48. **(c)** [Section 10-2]
15. **(a)** [Section 3-4]	32. **(d)** [Section 7-2]	49. **(b)** [Section 10-2]
16. **(a)** [Section 4-1]	33. **(c)** [Section 7-3]	50. **(d)** [Section 10-4]
17. **(b)** [Section 4-1]	34. **(b)** [Section 7-3]	

Part 2: Short Answer (50 points)

1. production [Section 1-4]	26. direct [Section 6-2]
2. marketing mix [Section 1-5]	27. nonbusiness [Section 6-1]
3. mass [Section 1-5]	28. revenues [Section 6-3]
4. physical distribution [Section 1-5]	29. buying center [Section 6-4]
5. Channels of distribution [Section 1-5]	30. actual condition [Section 6-4]
6. marketing strategy [Section 2-1]	31. income [Section 7-1]
7. target customers [Section 2-1]	32. Marketing information [Section 7-2]
8. expanding [Section 2-1]	33. Observation [Section 7-3]
9. economy [Section 2-1]	34. probability [Section 7-3]
10. coordinated [Section 2-3]	35. time series [Section 7-5]
11. Market segmentation [Section 3-1]	36. satisfaction [Section 8-1]
12. profitable [Section 3-2]	37. produce [Section 8-2]
13. Demographics [Section 3-4]	38. growth [Section 8-3]
14. Lifestyle [Section 3-4]	39. product mix [Section 8-5]
15. Marketing attribute [Section 3-4]	40. use [Section 8-7]
16. market [Section 4-1]	41. equilibrium [Section 9-1]
17. Consumer [Section 4-2]	42. elastic [Section 9-2]
18. population [Section 4-2]	43. lower [Section 9-4]
19. baby boom [Section 4-2]	44. margin [Section 9-5]
20. life cycle [Section 4-4]	45. buyer [Section 9-7]
21. problem [Section 5-1]	46. finished goods [Section 10-1]
22. economic [Section 5-2]	47. goals [Section 10-1]
23. drives [Section 5-3]	48. Breaking bulk [Section 10-2]
24. Gestalt [Section 5-3]	49. cost [Section 10-2]
25. Reference [Section 5-4]	50. the same [Section 10-3]

11 MARKETING INTERMEDIARIES AND CHANNEL MANAGEMENT

THIS CHAPTER IS ABOUT

☑ **Channels of Distribution**
☑ **The Use of Intermediaries—Wholesalers and Retailers**
☑ **Establishment of Channels of Distribution**
☑ **Management of the Channels of Distribution**
☑ **Types of Wholesalers**

11-1. Channels of Distribution

You may have wondered why Pepsi Cola is served in Burger King restaurants, whereas Coca Cola is available in McDonald's, or why K-Mart carries Fruit of the Loom T-shirts, whereas Wal-Mart does not. These patterns exist because of *channel-of-distribution* decisions.

• A **channel of distribution** is the network of companies that carry out marketing activities as goods and services move from producers to customers.

The channels convey *title* to goods.

EXAMPLE 11-1: The channel of distribution for General Foods' Tang breakfast drink is from the producer General Foods to wholesalers to grocery stores. On the other hand, the channel of distribution for General Electric dishwashers is from G.E. direct to retail stores.

Channels of distribution are not the same as *physical* distribution. Figure 11-1 illustrates the difference between channels of distribution and physical distribution. In this example, the channel of distribution, which is like that used for Dr. Scholl's foot care products, extends from manufacturer to wholesalers to retailers to customers. The physical distribution pattern, on the other hand, is made up of product movements through carriers from one *location* to another.

11-2. The Use of Intermediaries—Wholesalers and Retailers

Each producer must decide whether or not to use **middlemen**—wholesalers and retailers—in the channel of distribution. If a company decides to use middlemen, it must determine what kind and how many.

• **Wholesalers** are companies that earn most of their revenues from sales to retailers, other wholesalers, manufacturers, and nonprofit organizations.

• **Retailers** are firms that earn most of their revenues from sales to consumers.

EXAMPLE 11-2: Sysco, Inc., is a food wholesaler. It provides food supplies to organizations such as college student union cafeterias. Safeway is a retailer. It furnishes food and other items to consumers in its supermarkets.

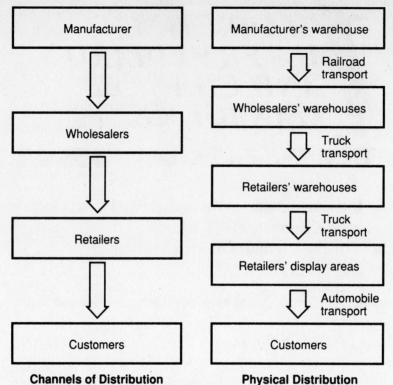

Channels of Distribution   **Physical Distribution**

FIGURE 11-1: There is a difference between channels of distribution and physical distribution.

Middlemen are often called **intermediaries** because they act as links between producers and those who use the product or service. A producer will use intermediaries when those intermediaries can carry out desired marketing activities more effectively than can the producer itself. Some of the more important marketing activities that intermediaries can perform are listed below.

(1) **Product planning.** Wholesalers and retailers find out what items their customers want; then they acquire these items from producers. Often, wholesalers and retailers are better judges than producers as to what offerings are in demand because they are in constant contact with customer needs. In this sense, intermediaries assist in generating *production utility*.

(2) **Financing.** Wholesalers and retailers often provide credit to their customers, making it unnecessary for producers to perform that service. Through financing, intermediaries provide *possession utility*.

(3) **Transportation and storage.** Many wholesalers and retailers provide delivery to customers. In addition, they operate warehouses and keep inventory. This relieves the producer of performing these functions, which it may not be able to do as effectively as an intermediary can. By providing transportation and storage, intermediaries assist in generating *time and place utility*.

(4) **Selling.** Wholesalers and retailers can often do a better job of selling goods to customers than producers can. They know the local market—and the target customers who are located in it—as well as specific customer needs and preferences. This selling function helps generate *possession utility*.

(5) **Taking title to goods.** Many wholesalers and retailers invest funds in inventory, thereby reducing the amount that producers must divert to this function. This results in *possession utility*, and is especially important when interest rates are high and inventory-carrying costs are expensive.

(6) **Consulting.** Wholesalers and retailers provide specialized advice to producers in such areas as advertising and pricing. Their experience and expertise can be invaluable to manufacturers.

(7) **Evaluating credit risks.** Wholesalers and retailers are often in a better position to evaluate the credit-worthiness of buyers of the product, because they are closer to the customers in the channel of distribution. Producers are not in a position to investigate the credit of, say, retailers who are large in number and widely dispersed. Producers are in great need of assistance in this task.

Intermediaries do not come without costs, of course. They may be reimbursed by **margins**, which are differences between the price they pay for items and the price they charge customers. Or they may receive **commissions**, which are percentages of their sales provided by producers.

A producer balances the amount of reimbursement it must provide intermediaries with the value of the services that these intermediaries offer. If the services of an intermediary are of greater value to a producer than the costs, the producer is likely to employ intermediaries. Often, intermediaries can serve the market more efficiently than manufacturers because they enjoy *economies of scale*. Since they serve many producers, intermediaries are able to attain economies. In addition, many wholesalers and retailers maintain specialized equipment and personnel and, as a result, are able to keep costs low.

11-3. Establishment of Channels of Distribution

When manufacturers design channels of distribution, they must decide what kinds of intermediaries and the number of each kind that will be needed. In order to do this, they consider the marketing strategy of the firm and the effectiveness of various kinds of intermediaries in carrying out that marketing strategy.

EXAMPLE 11-3: The Marvel Tool Company produces crescent wrenches, which are sold through hardware stores to consumers who want high-quality tools. These stores are effective in reaching "serious" tool buyers. A network of aggressive wholesalers serves these hardware stores at a low cost to Marvel. These wholesalers have established contacts with the retailers and have earned their respect as good judges of what will sell. By using the wholesalers, Marvel can effectively reach retailers without having to employ a sales force.

A. The number and patterns of channel levels

The number of levels in a channel of distribution depends on the producer's circumstances. Some producers may use channels with multiple levels. They may, for instance, sell to wholesalers, who sell to other wholesalers, who sell to retailers or industrial buyers. Other producers may go to the other extreme and employ **direct distribution**, selling directly to consumers or industrial buyers. Figure 11-2 illustrates various patterns that can be used in the channel of distribution.

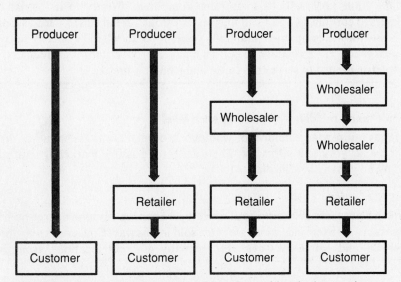

FIGURE 11-2: There are various combinations of levels that producers can choose to use in the channel of distribution.

Direct distribution is most desirable under the following circumstances:

• When the producer wants to control marketing activities closely, rather than delegating them;
• When the products are perishable and must be moved to market quickly before they lose value;

- When the products are technical in nature and the producer's employees have specialized selling and service knowledge that intermediaries lack;
- When target customers are few and located near one another, so the producer can serve them at a reasonable cost;
- When products are purchased in orders of sufficient size to support the costs of having a sales force;
- When the products are heavy or bulky, so that using intermediaries would produce high physical distribution costs;
- When good intermediaries are not available;
- When the producer is strong enough financially to support a sales force and other costs of direct distribution.

The opposite set of circumstances favors indirect distribution through intermediaries.

EXAMPLE 11-4: IBM distributes its mainframe computers direct to industrial users for several reasons. Direct distribution allows the firm to control marketing activities closely. The products are technical in nature, and are purchased in large orders. Finally, the firm is strong enough financially to support a sales force and the other costs of direct distribution.

B. The number of channels

Sometimes companies use more than one channel of distribution. Multiple channels may be the best marketing strategy when multiple products are offered, and especially when the products differ substantially in such factors as their technical nature, bulk and weight, and perishability. Also, if the same product is sold in two or more markets that differ significantly, multiple channels of distribution may be employed.

EXAMPLE 11-5: While IBM sells its mainframe computers directly to industrial buyers, it sells personal computers to consumers and small businesses through retail stores, such as Computerland. It would be very costly for the company to maintain a sales force to sell PC's directly to consumers. IBM has found it to be much more effective to sell its smaller products through retailers, who have the facilities and expertise needed to serve consumers and small businesses.

C. Deciding how many middlemen to use at each level

A producer may utilize a large number of wholesalers or retailers in its channel of distribution, or it may restrict the network to a select few. There are three possible marketing strategies to consider when deciding how many intermediaries to use.

1. Intensive distribution

Producers who use intensive distribution sell their offerings through a large number of retail or wholesale units. Convenience goods are often sold in this way. Consumers want products such as chewing gum and soft drinks available in many different locations, from gas stations to drugstores.

2. Exclusive distribution

Producers who employ exclusive distribution use only one wholesaler or retailer for each geographic area served. This allows the producer to select only the best-qualified intermediaries, who are then motivated to sell the product because they have an exclusive distributorship. Also, it is less costly for the producer to utilize only a few intermediaries, rather than a large number. Producers of specialty items often pursue this strategy.

EXAMPLE 11-6: The Curtis Mathes Corporation utilizes exclusive distribution. Each retailer has a geographic area of a city (or a whole city, if its population is small) within which no other Curtis Mathes dealer is located.

3. Selective distribution

Selective distribution is a strategy that is a compromise between intensive and exclusive distribution. Producers limit the number of intermediaries to those they believe have the most potential, but do not grant exclusives. This strategy can reduce costs and produce high levels of sales. Distributors are aggressive in promoting the product because they know that not many rivals sell it, but there are enough distributors to sell the product effectively. This strategy is common for shopping goods and specialty goods.

EXAMPLE 11-7: Goodyear Tire and Rubber follows a selective distribution strategy for its automobile tires. The tires are stocked in a limited number of retail stores and gas stations which produce sales levels beyond certain minimum levels established by Goodyear.

D. Selecting individual intermediaries

When faced with the task of deciding what specific wholesalers and retailers to use, each producer must first determine what marketing activities must be performed by the intermediary, then find the one(s) who can best perform these activities. Producers must also balance the costs of using each prospective wholesaler or retailer with the value of their services. A very able wholesaler, for example, may be too expensive for a firm to use. Of course, some intermediaries are not willing to stock the producer's offerings, so it may be necessary for management to use second- or third-choice intermediaries, or even to sell direct to customers.

EXAMPLE 11-8: Foster Grant realizes that the wholesalers it uses to sell sunglasses to retailers must be able to perform a number of marketing activities well. These include aggressive selling, stocking display materials, and carrying inventory. The firm carefully assesses potential wholesalers before asking them to stock its products.

11-4. Management of the Channels of Distribution

After a channel of distribution has been developed, management must administer it on a day-to-day basis. Channel objectives must be developed and steps taken to ensure that all members of the channel coordinate their efforts in moving toward these objectives.

The **channel captain** is the leader of the channel, responsible for settling conflicts and remedying poor performance.

In many cases, the channel captain is the producer, but may be a retailer or wholesaler. Often, it is simply the most powerful member of the channel that is the captain.

EXAMPLE 11-9: The J.C. Penney Company is the channel captain for many of the products it sells. This giant retailer is more powerful than many of the manufacturers that serve it. The producers are heavily motivated to sell their products through Penney stores and are willing to allow this company to make most channel decisions.

Sometimes conflicts arise in the channels. Retailers may demand higher margins, for example, or producers may become angry with retailers, arguing that they are not selling sufficient volumes of their products. It is the job of the channel captain to minimize and overcome such conflicts.

The channel captain should continually be alert for evidence of poor performance on the part of other firms in the network. Once evidence of poor performance is uncovered, remedial action should follow. If, for example, some wholesalers are not performing well, the remedial action may be moderate, involving an attempt to motivate particular wholesalers to perform better; or it may be more extreme, involving the replacement of some marginal wholesalers.

11-5. Types of Wholesalers

There are many kinds of wholesalers. Producers attempt to select those whose operations are most compatible with the marketing activities that need to be performed.

A. Service wholesalers

Service wholesalers carry out all or most of the marketing activities important to a producer. These wholesalers are the most numerous and handle a larger volume of business than any other category of wholesalers. They are most suitable for producers who do not want to perform much of the marketing function themselves. Service wholesalers receive their compensation through margins.

EXAMPLE 11-10: The Valley Pump Company is a Texas producer of pumps used primarily in the oil industry. The firm's expertise is mainly in production, not in marketing. It employs six wholesalers to accomplish most of its marketing objectives.

Some independent retailers have banded together into organizations that do the wholesaling for themselves. Called **voluntary chains**, these organizations achieve the advantages of large service wholesalers while maintaining member independence.

B. Limited-function wholesalers

Another category of wholesalers consists of limited-function enterprises, which perform only some of the marketing activities important to a producer. Some limited-function wholesalers, for instance, do not grant credit, carry inventories, or carry wide lines of merchandise. A particular type is the **agent**, which does not take title to the goods carried, as do service wholesalers. Although some limited-function wholesalers receive their compensation through margins, agents earn a commission, which is a percentage of their sales of a producer's items. Agents assume many of the marketing activities of producers and can offer a good way of entering new markets. There are three main types of agents.

1. Manufacturer's agents

Manufacturer's agents carry numerous brands in each product class, but sell only a part of the output of each supplier. They have limited authority in setting prices and terms of sale. Such agents are especially valuable when a producer wants to introduce new products or sell goods in areas where customers are small or few. Manufacturer's agents are also useful when it is difficult for a producer to cover the expenses of its own sales force.

2. Selling agents

In contrast to manufacturer's agents, selling agents sell all of a producer's output of one or more items. These firms have considerable authority in setting prices and terms of sale. They undertake virtually all of the major marketing activities for some producers and become what amounts to the marketing department of the producer.

3. Brokers

Brokers are specialists in buying and selling. Their job is to bring buyers and sellers together. Brokers, in contrast to other kinds of agents, do not deal with buyers and sellers on a continuing basis. Rather, they are used for one or several related transactions only. Their major resource is the extensive information that they possess about the market—information that can be invaluable to buyers and sellers.

RAISE YOUR GRADES

Can you explain . . . ?

☑ how a channel of distribution differs from physical distribution
☑ what marketing activities an intermediary might perform for a large producer
☑ why a large manufacturer might decide to employ direct distribution
☑ why intensive distribution is appropriate for many convenience goods
☑ how a manufacturer might go about the process of selecting specific intermediaries
☑ why large producers are the channel captains for many of the goods they carry
☑ why a very small producer might decide to use service wholesalers

SUMMARY

1. Channels of distribution are networks of companies that carry out marketing activities as goods and services move from producers to customers.
2. Middlemen serve as intermediaries in the channel of distribution because they link producers with those who use their product or service.
3. Middlemen include wholesalers and retailers. Wholesalers gain the bulk of their revenues from sales to retailers, other wholesalers, manufacturers, and nonprofit organizations; retailers obtain most of their revenues from sales to consumers.
4. Intermediaries can carry out a number of marketing activities in the channels of distribution, such as product planning, financing, transportation and storage, selling, taking title to goods, consulting, and evaluating credit risks.
5. A producer balances the amount of reimbursement it must provide intermediaries with the value of the services that they provide.
6. Producers may use several levels in the channel of distribution or they may use direct distribution, depending on the circumstances they face.
7. Producers may use more than one channel of distribution if their products or markets differ significantly.
8. Producers may use intensive, exclusive, or selective distribution, depending on their product strategy.
9. In selecting specific intermediaries, the best policy is to determine what marketing activities are to be performed and then to select the intermediary who can best carry them out.
10. The channel captain is the leader of the channel and should carry out its duties in such a way that all parties work in a coordinated manner.
11. Service wholesalers carry out a wide range of marketing activities for producers.
12. Limited-function wholesalers perform fewer marketing activities for producers than service wholesalers. However, there can be advantages to using limited-function wholesaler such as manufacturer's agents, selling agents, and brokers.

RAPID REVIEW   Answers

Short Answer

1. Channels of distribution consist of _____ of companies that   *networks*
   carry out marketing activities as goods and services move from producers
   to consumers. [See Section 11-1.]
2. The major middlemen that can be included in the channel of distribution   *wholesalers,*
   for a company are _____ and _____. [See Sec-   *retailers*
   tion 11-2.]

3. Which of the following is *not* a customer of wholesalers—consumers, retailers, wholesalers, or nonprofit organizations? [See Section 11-2.] — *consumers*

4. Middlemen are called _____ because they serve as links between producers and those who use their products or services. [See Section 11-2.] — *intermediaries*

5. Wholesalers engage in product planning by finding out what items their _____ want. [See Section 11-2.] — *customers*

6. The difference between the price a wholesaler pays for an item and the price it charges customers is called a _____. [See Section 11-2.] — *margin*

7. When establishing channels of distribution, producers first consider the _____ _____ of the firm. [See Section 11-3.] — *marketing strategy*

8. A firm that does not use wholesalers or retailers is engaged in _____ distribution. [See Section 11-3.] — *direct*

9. _____ distribution may be most desirable for a company when its products are technical in nature. [See Section 11-3.] — *Direct*

10. A company is likely to use more than one _____ if its markets differ significantly. [See Section 11-3.] — *channel*

11. When using _____ distribution, a company sells its products through many retailers. [See Section 11-3.] — *intensive*

12. Exclusive distribution for a company is often useful for _____ goods. [See Section 11-3.] — *specialty*

13. Producers select specific intermediaries by determining what _____ activities must be performed by the channel and then finding middlemen who can best accomplish these. [See Section 11-3.] — *marketing*

14. The member of a channel of distribution that has the most power is often called the _____ _____. [See Section 11-4.] — *channel captain*

15. _____ wholesalers carry out all or most of the marketing activities important to producers. [See Section 11-5.] — *Service*

16. Wholesalers that perform only some marketing activities are called _____ _____ wholesalers. [See Section 11-5.] — *limited-function*

17. A(n) _____ does not take title to goods. [See Section 11-5.] — *agent*

18. The form of compensation paid to a wholesaler that is based on a percentage of the sales of a producer's goods is called a _____. [See Section 11-5.] — *commission*

19. The type of wholesaler that sells all of a producer's output of one or more products is called a(n) _____ _____. [See Section 11-5.] — *selling agent*

SOLVED PROBLEMS

PROBLEM 11-1 A classmate does not understand the difference between channels of distribution and physical distribution. How would you explain the difference?

Answer: Channels of distribution are networks of companies that carry out marketing activities as goods and services move from producers to consumers. Wholesalers and retailers are important elements in many of these networks. Physical distribution refers to physical flows of products and services, as through transportation facilities and warehouses. Physical distribution managers make decisions in fields such as selecting transportation modes and deciding on the best inventory levels. [See Section 11-1.]

PROBLEM 11-2 An Arkansas law places a tax on the inventories of retailers but not those of wholesalers. This brings about considerable confusion on the part of intermediaries who sell goods at both retail and wholesale levels. How can an Arkansas business tell if it is subject to the tax?

Answer: An Arkansas business is a wholesaler if it is a company that receives the bulk of its revenue from sales to retailers, other wholesalers, manufacturers, or nonprofit organizations. As long as the firm does not gain 50 percent or more of its sales from consumers, it is a wholesaler. Retailers are companies that receive the bulk of their revenues from sales to consumers. [See Section 11-2.]

PROBLEM 11-3 A small manufacturer of ball-point pens has heard that wholesalers can assist producers in this industry with product planning. How do wholesalers carry out this function?

Answer: Wholesalers can assist producers of ball-point pens in a number of ways. They find out what items (color, shape, style, etc.) their customers want and then acquire these items from producers. Often, wholesalers are better judges than producers as to what offerings are in demand, because they know their customers' needs—they are closer to the market. If changes in the ball-point pen market take place—if, for example, customers suddenly show a distinct preference for fat red pens with nylon tips instead of thin blue pens with steel tips—wholesalers are in a position to quickly detect these changes and report them to producers. [See Section 11-2.]

PROBLEM 11-4 Why might executives of the Greyhound Corporation believe that wholesalers can do a better job of selling soap pads to supermarkets than can Greyhound personnel?

Answer: Executives of the Greyhound Corporation are aware that wholesalers know the market for soap pads in the geographic areas they serve. Wholesalers are acquainted with retailers and their personnel and have insights into local markets that most manufacturers do not possess. Some act more like divisions of the producers whose products they sell than as independent businesses. [See Section 11-2.]

PROBLEM 11-5 A pet supplies wholesaler receives a commission of 20 percent on all dog and cat collar sales of a producer's brand up to $2 million in sales, and a commission of 30% for all sales above $2 million. The wholesaler sells $2,500,000 of the producer's goods. What is the commission?

Answer: The commission is

$$\begin{aligned} \$2{,}000{,}000 \times .20 &= \$400{,}000 \\ +\$\ 500{,}000 \times .30 &= \$150{,}000 \\ \hline \text{Total commission} &= \$550{,}000 \end{aligned}$$

[See Section 11-2.]

PROBLEM 11-6 A manufacturer of processed cheese has boasted in its advertisements: "We do not use wholesalers. This allows us to save money because we do not have to pay them. The savings are passed on to consumers in lower prices." Criticize this statement.

Answer: The processed cheese manufacturer may be making statements in the advertisement that are not true. Producers balance the amount of reimbursement they pay wholesalers with the value of the services that they provide. If the services are not of greater value than the costs, they are not likely to employ wholesalers in the channel. Basically, wholesalers are used for processed cheese because they can carry out physical distribution, promotion, and product planning activities more effectively than can producers. [See Section 11-2.]

PROBLEM 11-7 Assume that you have joined the marketing department of a newly incorporated producer of lawn furniture that plans to distribute its products nationally at an intermediate price. The marketing manager has assigned you the task of establishing channels of distribution for company products. What kinds of decisions would you have to make?

Answer: It would be necessary to determine what kinds of wholesalers and retailers to utilize for the lawn furniture, and the number and kind that would be needed. In order to do this, you should consider the marketing strategy of the firm and the effectiveness of various kinds of intermediaries in carrying out marketing strategy. A typical producer might use up to two dozen wholesalers and several hundred variety store, discount store, and department store retailers. [See Section 11-3.]

PROBLEM 11-8 A large cosmetics company introduced a line of skin care products in 1988. In your opinion, should the firm have employed direct distribution?

Answer: Direct distribution probably would not have been a good alternative for this company. Target consumers for most skin care products are large in number and are geographically dispersed throughout the United States. In addition, most skin care purchases do not amount to a large dollar volume. Good intermediaries are available for the introduction of skin care products. [See Section 11-3.]

PROBLEM 11-9 Should a large aluminum company use direct distribution in selling aluminum to airplane producers such as McDonnell-Douglas?

Answer: Yes. First, the aluminum products that an airplane manufacture would buy are technical in nature; i.e., these products must meet exacting specifications to satisfy the user's needs. Aluminum company employees have the specialized selling and service knowledge that intermediaries might lack. They have detailed training and experience relating to company products and services. Further, they are aggressive sellers of company brands. They do not spread their attention over multiple brands, as intermediaries might do. Target customers are few and located near one another. Also, most order sizes are large and the products are bulky. Finally, a large firm probably has the financial resources to market directly. [See Section 11-3.]

PROBLEM 11-10 The Sara Lee Corporation markets both PayDay candy bars and Jimmy Dean Steak & Biscuits. Should both of these products be sold through the same channel of distribution?

Answer: PayDay candy bars and Jimmy Dean Steak & Biscuits should not both be sold through the same channel of distribution. The two products differ substantially from each other and require different marketing strategies. The candy bars are convenience goods, while the Steak & Biscuits are shopping goods. Each of the two offerings has a different set of target consumers. The same channel could not be used to effectively market both offerings. [See Section 11-3.]

PROBLEM 11-11 The Ralston Purina Company produces Pro Plan, which is a high-quality and high-priced, seven-formula line of dog and cat foods. Would you recommend intensive distribution for this product?

Answer: No. Intensive distribution would not be a good idea for Pro Plan dog and cat food. This product line is expensive and is made up of specialty goods. Consumers would not expect to find it in a large number of conveniently placed locations. Many retailers would not have a need for a product line with such a narrow market. In fact, consumers can buy Ralston Purina's Pro Plan only from pet stores and veterinarians. [See Section 11-3.]

PROBLEM 11-12 Do you recommend that the A.H. Robbins Company use intensive distribution for its ChapStick Petroleum Jelly Plus lip protector?

Answer: Intensive distribution would be useful for Chapstick Petroleum Jelly Plus lip protector. It is a convenience good for most target consumers, so widespread distribution is desirable. Large numbers of geographically dispersed consumers buy the product and want it available in easy-access locations, such as food stores and drug stores. [See Section 11-3.]

PROBLEM 11-13 Assume that you are employed by the Very Incredible Products Company, producer of Wrinkle Free, an aerosol spray that removes wrinkles from cloth. Your job is to select individual intermediaries for inclusion in the channel of distribution. How would you go about selecting wholesalers and retailers?

Answer: The first step is to determine what marketing activities must be performed by the channel of distribution. These would include advertising, sales promotion, physical distribution, and price determination. Then you should make a search for middlemen who can best carry out these activities. It would be necessary then to determine the costs of using each prospective wholesaler or retailer, as these costs should be balanced with the abilities of each. [See Section 11-3.]

PROBLEM 11-14 Revlon is the channel captain for some of the products that it produces. What should it do, in order to manage the channels effectively?

Answer: Revlon must administer the channels on a day-to-day basis. It should develop channel objectives, such as specific market share goals, and take steps to ensure that all members of the channel coordinate their efforts in moving toward these objectives. This may require considerable diplomacy on the part of the sales force. It should attempt to minimize conflicts, such as those between wholesalers and large retailers. The company may have to take remedial action when problems occur, such as providing product information to retailers whose employees are not well-informed about Revlon products. [See Section 11-4.]

PROBLEM 11-15 A medium-sized producer of sheet metals is considering whether or not to use a service or a limited-function wholesaler. This firm has little expertise in marketing. What would you recommend?

Answer: A service wholesaler probably would be best for the sheet metal producer. If management has little expertise in marketing, it may want to utilize a wholesaler that will virtually take over the marketing function, with the exception of product planning. If this is the case, a service wholesaler would be appropriate. On the other hand, the firm may want to retain primary responsibility for some of the functions, such as promotion and transportation. Then a limited-function wholesaler might be the better choice. [See Section 11-5.]

12 RETAILING DECISIONS

THIS CHAPTER IS ABOUT

☑ **The Function of Retailing**
☑ **Kinds of Retailers**
☑ **The Wheel of Retailing Theory**
☑ **Managing a Retail Store**

12-1. The Function of Retailing

Retailing is a surprisingly complex field. Success demands considerable knowledge and insight into a number of fields. Many retailers fail each year, indicating that success can be hard to come by.

• **Retailing** consists of the activities involved in selling goods and services to consumers.

Retailers are firms that receive the majority of their revenues from serving consumers. They act as contacts between consumers and other members of the channel of distribution, as Figure 12-1 indicates. If retailers fail to satisfy consumers, even the best marketing efforts of producers and wholesalers will be canceled out.

FIGURE 12-1: Retailers serve as contacts between consumers and other channel members.

• Retailers act as representatives of consumers in their interactions with producers and wholesalers.

Retailers make an effort to acquire a combination of goods that meet the needs of their customers, to make these available where and when they are wanted, to inform consumers about them through promotion, and to furnish desired services. Thus, they provide *time*, *place*, and *possession utility* to customers.

EXAMPLE 12-1: A customer of Osco sporting goods stores can obtain all of the items needed, at various price levels, for beginning, intermediate, or advanced skiing. These items include skis, poles, boots, mountings, gloves, clothing, and accessories. The ski equipment is made available in convenient displays, and well-informed sales personnel are available to give advice on purchases. Credit is also available to customers who desire it.

• Producers and wholesalers depend on retailers to represent them by effectively carrying out marketing activities for their products.

These marketing activities fall into the now familiar categories of product, price, place, and promotion. Retailers are effective in accomplishing these activities because they are specialists. They can operate at reasonable cost levels because of specialization and, if they are large, because they enjoy economies of scale. These economies result from spreading fixed costs over large numbers of products sold. If manufacturers and wholesalers tried to do the retailing themselves, this would require very large or, in some cases, staggering investments.

- Many sellers of services to consumers operate in a manner that is similar to retailing.

Sellers of services to consumers include plumbers, hair salons, banks, some hospitals, accounting firms, restaurants, motion picture theaters, equipment rental companies, and other profit-seeking service companies; other sellers of services include government agencies, universities, and other nonprofit organizations. All of these deal with consumers; hence many retail theories and research findings are usable by these organizations.

EXAMPLE 12-2: Although it is a government agency, many of the activities of the U.S. Postal Service are essentially retailing in nature. Its consumers are those who desire various mail services. Officials of the agency make product (service), price (mailing fee), place (delivery and hours of operation), and promotion (some advertisements) decisions. They are in competition with various rivals, such as UPS and Federal Express.

12-2. Kinds of Retailers

There are several ways of classifying retailers. These are by *ownership, benefits sought by customers, width of product line, activities carried out,* and *type of customer shopping effort.*

A. Ownership

When classified by ownership, retailers can be independents, chains, association of chains, or franchises.

1. Independents

Independents are very common in the retailing field. An independent is owned separately—it is *not* a member of a chain. Owners of independents are their own bosses. Independent retailers tend to develop close relations with their customers and offer products and services that these customers desire, rather than aiming at the mass market like chains. Numerous jewelry stores, drug stores, boutiques, hair salons, and restaurants are independents.

2. Chains

Chains are members of companies that own multiple outlets. Areas of retailing in which chains are numerous are department stores, grocery stores, variety stores, motels, and fast-food restaurants. Many of these are very large. Safeway, Inc., the J.C. Penney Company, Holiday Inns, Inc., Sears Roebuck and Company, and Wendy's are all chain organizations.

Because chains are large, they can operate very efficiently. They buy goods in large quantities, thus receiving volume discounts. They develop standardized ways of doing things throughout all units of the chain that help keep their costs down. Because they have multiple units, they are not dependent on the economic health of any one community—losses in some areas can be made up for by gains in others. Because of their large size, they can also hire specialists for various marketing activities, such as advertising.

3. Associations of independents

Associations of independents come together in order to enjoy some of the advantages of chains and yet remain independent. **Cooperative chains** are independent retailers that arrange to do their own wholesaling, giving them many of the strengths of chains, such as buying power. **Voluntary chains** are like cooperative chains, except that a wholesaler starts and manages the group. AG (Associated Grocers) stores are a cooperative chain. Shopco is a voluntary chain.

4. Franchises

Frandises operate somewhat like voluntary chains. A **franchisor** (commonly a producer) makes agreements with **franchisees** (retailers). The franchisor agrees to let franchisees use the company name, get consulting and other advice, and buy operating supplies. The franchisee agrees to do certain things, such as make a minimum investment, pay the franchisor a percentage of sales (called a *royalty*), and operate according to rules laid down by the franchisor. Hertz Rent-a-Car, McDonald's, Dunkin' Donuts, and Holiday Inns are all franchise organizations.

B. Benefits sought by customers

Retailers can be categorized by the benefits that their customers seek.

(1) **Economic shoppers.** Economic shoppers want stores to offer products that are seen as a good buy for the price—i.e., they want quality goods and services and low prices. They may be willing to go to considerable effort (such as driving long distances) to get to such outlets.

(2) **Personalizing shoppers.** Personalizing shoppers look for outlets that are hospitable and friendly. They enjoy talking with friendly store personnel. Many small independents attract this category.

(3) **Ethical shoppers.** Ethical shoppers select certain retailers because they want to support small businesses or businesses that are locally owned and operated. They tend to avoid chains.

(4) **Apathetic shoppers.** Apathetic shoppers want to minimize the time and effort spent in shopping, which they do not like. They look for fast shopping trips and convenience, such as that obtained through quick checkouts and easy parking.

EXAMPLE 12-3: Some retailers are successful in segmenting the market toward a particular type of benefits-sought customer. Seven-Eleven stores pursue the apathetic shopper. Many department stores, such as Dayton-Hudson, target personalizing shoppers. Discounters, such as Target Stores, focus on economic shoppers. Some small businesses aim at the ethical category.

C. Width of product line

Retailers differ according to how wide their product lines are.

(1) **General merchandise retailers.** General merchandise retailers offer a wide product line. They satisfy a variety of needs under one roof. Many retailers have engaged in what is called **scrambled merchandising**. They have added new lines to their traditional ones to attract new customers and more fully serve old ones, thus becoming general merchandise retailers. Often the new lines they bring in have larger markups than traditional ones.

EXAMPLE 12-4: Many supermarkets, such as Skaggs Alpha Beta, have added nonfoods, making them general merchandise retailers. They sell sporting goods, automobile supplies, toys, household utensils, and gift items. Discounters, such as K-Mart, have added food items. They carry numerous canned and some packaged goods. Service stations, such as Conoco, also carry convenience foods, soft drinks, and tobacco products.

---

(2) **Limited-line retailers.** Limited-line retailers have only one or several similar product lines. They offer less width but more depth in their product lines than do general merchandise stores. This means that they are more specialized and better able to provide the selection that discriminating shoppers want. For example, a consumer who desires to examine a variety of running shoes before making a selection can do so in Osco sporting good stores.

(3) **Specialty store retailers.** Specialty store retailers specialize in one or two segments of a product line so that they provide considerable depth but not much width. They excel in satisfying the particular needs of target customers. Their sales personnel are often very knowledgeable about the product line and serve as useful advisors to customers. Many import, gift, newspaper, book, and high-quality clothing stores are specialty stores.

D. Activities carried out

Another way of categorizing retailers is according to the activities that they perform. There are several major kinds of outlets.

(1) **Discounters.** Discounters operate on a high inventory turnover and low margin basis. They seek an advantage over rivals by offering low prices. They offer fewer services than other stores, such as salesclerk help, in order to keep costs down. Other savings are achieved by buying in large volumes and standardizing store operations. K-Mart, Wal-Mart, and Target are all discount stores.

(2) **Supermarkets.** Supermarkets also seek high inventory turnovers and low margins. Their wide product lines include both foods and nonfoods (which typically have higher margins than foods). Like discounters, the stores are large in size. Each store is organized by departments (such as produce and meat) with a departmental manager.

(3) **Department stores.** Department stores are large and stock many product lines. Their inventory turnover is low and their prices high relative to those of many competitors. They offer numerous customer services, such as credit and salesclerk advice. Like supermarkets, they are organized and operated by departments (such as furniture and men's wear). Many have a large parent store in a city and operate satellite stores in surrounding shopping centers.

(4) **Variety stores.** Variety stores are much like department stores, except that they typically are smaller and have fewer services and lower prices. Most of their product lines consist of manufacturer's brands. They employ fewer sales personnel and generally do not have the prestige image of department stores.

EXAMPLE 12-5: Service Merchandise Company stores are variety stores that are ordinarily located in shopping centers. They stock a wide product line, ranging from sporting goods to toys, but their lines have less depth than do most department stores.

---

(5) **Direct marketing retailers.** Direct marketing retailers do not have sites where consumers go to shop. Rather, these retailers include mail order, telephone, vending machine, and personal selling at customers' homes (door-to-door and party plans). These retailers have grown in recent years, providing considerable consumer convenience. A recent development is in-home shopping, where consumers see items on television and phone in orders.

EXAMPLE 12-6: Mary Kay, Inc., is a direct marketing retailer that has a large sales force of "consultants" who call upon consumers and offer a wide variety of cosmetic and personal care items, mainly for women.

---

(6) **Miscellaneous.** There are many other kinds of retailers defined by the activities they perform. These include clothing stores, gasoline filling stations, and tire stores. Most are specialty shops or limited-line outlets.

(7) **Shopping centers.** Shopping centers are combinations of a number of retail outlets that coordinate their activities in order to attract customers. There are several types of shopping centers.

- *Enclosed malls.* Large, enclosed malls are usually in suburban locations, where they draw considerable traffic. They offer the advantages of protection from bad weather, a wide product line, convenience of parking, and a recreational atmosphere. Center managers work with store managers to develop special events and sales and to maintain the facility.

- *Neighborhood shopping centers.* These feature mainly convenience goods and services. They are frequently built around a supermarket or large variety store. Their main focus is to serve consumers who are located in nearby neighborhoods.

- *Community shopping centers.* Most of these sell convenience goods, services, and a limited amount of shopping goods. They are likely to include a department store outlet, variety stores, clothing stores, and a number of convenience goods units. They serve a broader region than neighborhood centers and often attract numerous motorists who are driving by the center on the way to or from work or other activities.

- *Regional shopping centers.* These usually include convenience, shopping, and specialty goods stores. They are large in size and provide both depth and breadth of shopping assortments for consumers. Many are enclosed malls and include at least one full-line department store. These centers serve a large geographic region, often attracting consumers who have driven a number of miles for a visit.

E. Shopping effort

Retailers can be classified according to the effort that they expect customers to expend.

(1) **Convenience stores.** Customers shop in convenience stores because these stores are conveniently located and furnish easy shopping. These stores offer the advantages of ample parking space, a layout that makes shopping easy, displays that permit prompt selection, quick checkouts, and locations near target consumers' homes and places of work.

(2) **Shopping stores.** Shopping stores consist of outlets that consumers compare to other stores before deciding which one to patronize. Managers of these stores should make comparison shopping easy by locating *near* competitors, sponsoring comparative ads, and developing an image of high product and service quality.

(3) **Specialty stores.** Specialty stores target consumers who have a strong positive attitude toward them and are willing to expend considerable effort to buy there. Rather than relaxing their efforts because of a good image, though, specialty stores must stay alert for ways to maintain their preferred position.

EXAMPLE 12-7: Baskin-Robbins ice cream outlets are popular specialty stores. The company does not, however, relax its efforts to please customers. It continually brings out new flavors, while keeping popular older ones. In 1986, the outlets were extensively remodeled to provide a more pleasant in-store eating atmosphere.

12-3. The Wheel of Retailing Theory

The **wheel of retailing theory** is useful in describing and predicting new developments in retailing. According to this theory, when a new kind of retailer enters the market, its development is characterized by stages, as shown in Figure 12-2. A newcomer X first enters the market with low costs, low margins, and few services for consumers. The newcomer then captures large portions of the market from established retailers. With success, the newcomer then upgrades its stores, thereby incurring higher costs which require higher prices. This stage is followed by a new wave of newcomers Y and Z, who come into the market with low costs, etc. These newcomers succeed, upgrade, and take away market share from the initial newcomer. This process continues with time—the wheel keeps turning.

12-4. Managing a Retail Store

Managing a retail store requires decisions in a number of areas, each of which is very important to success. These areas include location, the store building and interior, promotion, merchandising, and pricing.

A. Location

The location of the retailer can be an important determinant of its success, particularly for convenience and shopping stores. The type of target consumer and the desires of those consumers are major factors in determining location. Retail establishments might locate downtown, in shopping centers, or in **strips** (groups of stores that are clustered together along streets and roads but do not work together in a cooperative fashion, as shopping center stores do). Or a retail establishment might choose to be free-standing (away from other buildings). But in each case the choice of location would be dictated by the types of customers the retailer is seeking and the needs of those customers.

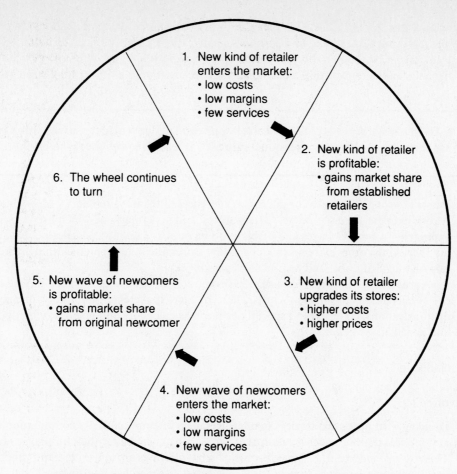

FIGURE 12-2: The wheel of retailing theory is useful in describing and predicting developments in retailing.

EXAMPLE 12-8: Pic-Quik convenience stores are located in neighborhoods that are near target consumers—on high-traffic streets near places of work and shopping—because these retailers are seeking convenience shoppers. Sak's Fifth Avenue locates in prestigious sites, because it pursues status-seeking customers. Kinney shoe stores locate near other shoe stores to facilitate comparisons with rivals by customers who are seeking bargains.

B. Store building and interior

The store building and its interior should be designed to meet customer expectations. Building and interior design can have a major impact on store image, which is critical for success.

EXAMPLE 12-9: Zale's jewelry stores are located mainly in shopping centers. Their physical facilities help create an image of high-quality products at moderate prices, and they maintain extensive sales help to foster that image. The stores are very modern and well maintained. Displays are arranged tastefully, while "sale" signs suggest savings for customers.

C. Promotion

Like producers, retailers rely mainly upon advertising, personal selling, and sales promotion to communicate with potential customers.

(1) **Advertising.** Retailers use advertising to inform consumers of what is in the store, provide information on prices, and to maintain a positive image. Many, especially independents, use local media, such as radio and newspapers, extensively. The focus of their advertising depends on the type of target consumer they seek and on their marketing strategy.

EXAMPLE 12-10: Walgreens ads mainly feature low prices. They appeal to those who seek a variety of goods at reasonable cost. Many of their products are used as leaders to entice consumers into company stores.

---

(2) **Personal selling.** There are considerable differences in the ways retailers use personal selling. At one extreme are discounters, variety stores, and supermarkets, which use the **self-service approach**—where packages and displays do most of the selling and sales people are few in number. At the other extreme are department stores and high-fashion clothing stores, which rely on knowledgeable and helpful sales personnel.

(3) **Sales promotion.** Many retailers use sales promotion (a) to draw consumers into the store and (b) to encourage consumers to buy. These retailers make extensive use of displays, sales, demonstrations, contests, and specialities (such as calendars and give-away ball-point pens and pencils).

D. Merchandising

In retailing, product planning activities are usually called **merchandising**. Several major functions are involved.

(1) **Deciding what goods and services to offer.** Retailers attempt to offer a combination of goods and services that will meet the desires of target consumers better than those of competitors. This requires judgment, keeping records of what offerings are in demand and which are not, and marketing research. Buyers for stores select the merchandise to be offered. They are among the more important company personnel.

(2) **Selecting suppliers.** Suppliers can be wholesalers or producers. These organizations usually employ sales personnel who provide considerable information about their companies' products and services to retailers. Some buyers visit central markets, such as the Furniture Market in Chicago, where suppliers maintain information-provision booths, displays, and sales personnel.

(3) **Working with suppliers.** Retailers negotiate with suppliers in order to obtain benefits that meet their specific needs. Sometimes they are able to obtain price reductions or other favors if they are good customers or have substantial buying power.

Retailers should watch and keep records of the sales of particular items and the performance of suppliers. Over a period of time, patterns can change, resulting in the need for changes in goods and services offered and in suppliers.

E. Pricing

Retailers, like producers, consider demand, cost, and competition in setting prices. Many retailers use markup or cost-plus pricing. They mark items down when sales are not up to expectations. Some, like discounters, use pricing as a very important variable in the marketing mix.

RAISE YOUR GRADES

Can you explain . . . ?

☑ how retailers serve as contacts between manufacturers and their customers
☑ why some independent stores are able to attract customers away from major chains
☑ why independent retailers sometimes decide that it is in their best interest to join a cooperative chain

☑ why apathetic shoppers often patronize convenience stores
☑ why some consumers patronize specialty shops on a frequent basis
☑ why shopping stores often locate near other shopping stores
☑ how retail buyers go about deciding what goods to offer

SUMMARY

1. Retailing consists of the activities involved in selling goods and services to consumers.
2. Retailers act as representatives of consumers in their interactions with producers and wholesalers.
3. Producers and wholesalers depend on retailers to represent them by effectively carrying out marketing activities for their products.
4. Many sellers of services to consumers operate in a manner that is similar to retailing.
5. Retailers can be classified by ownership as independents, chains, associations of independents, and franchises.
6. Retailers can be classified according to the benefits sought by customers. These classifications are economic, personalizing, ethical, and apathetic shoppers.
7. Classifying retailers according to the width of their product lines results in general merchandise, limited line, and specialty store classes.
8. Retailers can be classified according to the activities they perform as discounters, supermarkets, department stores, variety stores, direct marketing retailers, miscellaneous, and shopping centers.
9. According to shopping effort put forth by customers, retailers can be classified as convenience, shopping, and specialty stores.
10. The wheel of retailing theory describes and predicts new developments in retailing, as novel retailers enter the market with low costs, experience cost increases with growth, and are challenged by new novel retailers.
11. Retailers should be located according to the type and desires of the target consumer that is sought.
12. The store building and its interior should be designed to meet customer expectations.
13. Retailers use advertising, personal selling, and sales promotion to carrying out their promotion objectives.
14. In merchandising, retailers determine what goods and services to offer and what suppliers to employ.
15. Like producers, retailers consider demand, cost, and competition in setting prices.

RAPID REVIEW   Answers

Short answer

1. Retailers receive the majority of their revenues from serving _____. [See Section 12-1.]   *consumers*

2. Retailers provide time, place, and _____ utility to customers. [See Section 12-1.]   *possession*

3. Many sellers of _____ operate in a manner that is very similar to retailing. [See Section 12-1.]   *services*

4. Numerous _____ develop very close relationships with their customers. [See Section 12-2.]   *independents*

5. _____ are not dependent on the economic health of any one community. [See Section 12-2.]   *Chains*

6. _____ chains are started and managed by wholesalers. [See Section 12-2.]   *Voluntary*

7. Franchisors usually expect franchisees to pay _____ to them. [See Section 12-2.]   *royalties*

8. A chain discounter is likely to appeal to _____ shoppers. [See Section 12-2.]   *economic*

9. _____ shoppers are likely patrons of convenience stores. [See Section 12-2.]   *Apathetic*

10. _____ merchandising has resulted in many stores becoming general merchandising stores. [See Section 12-2.]   *Scrambled*

11. Specialty outlets provide considerable _____, but not much width in their product lines. [See Section 12-2.]   *depth*

12. _____ stores operate on a high turnover, low-price basis. [See Section 12-2.]   *Discount*

13. Avon is an example of a _____ _____ retailer. [See Section 12-2.]   *direct marketing*

14. A wide product line, convenience of parking, and a recreational atmosphere are all advantages of _____ _____. [See Section 12-2.]   *shopping centers*

15. Location is not as important for _____ stores as it is for convenience and shopping stores. [See Section 12-2.]   *specialty*

16. _____ are likely to use local newspapers as advertising media. [See Section 12-4.]   *Independents*

17. Discounters, variety stores, and supermarkets often use the _____ approach to personal selling. [See Section 12-4.]   *self-service*

18. Retailers rely most heavily on sales promotion, personal selling, and _____ to carry out their promotion objectives. [See Section 12-3.]   *advertising*

19. Retailers consider demand, cost, and competition when determining _____. [See Section 12-3.]   *price*

SOLVED PROBLEMS

PROBLEM 12-1 How do retailers such as Kroger supermarkets act as representatives of consumers?

Answer: Retailers such as Kroger supermarkets make an effort to acquire a combination of goods that meet the needs of their specific customers. In Kroger's case, the goods include a combination of foods and nonfoods that appeal to middle-income families. The firm makes the goods available in carefully selected locations and provides physical distribution functions in such a way that the products are fresh and undamaged. Kroger informs its target customers about its product mix through advertising and instore promotion. It furnishes the services, such as carry-out services, that consumers desire. [See Section 12-1.]

PROBLEM 12-2 Why would a company that produces sports clothing use established retailers to sell to consumers, rather than doing the retailing itself?

Answer: A producer of sports clothing depends on retailers, such as sporting goods and variety stores, to represent it in carrying out marketing activities in which retailers have specialized expertise. Further, the firm would need a very substantial investment if it chose to do its own retailing. Individual retail stores can carry many lines and represent numerous producers, and enjoy economies of scale, as a result. The retailers are in a position to effectively carry out pricing, advertising, personal selling, and physical distribution functions. They have expertise in serving particular classes of consumers in specific regions of the country. [See Section 12-1.]

PROBLEM 12-3 How are chain stores such as Dairy Queen able to operate so efficiently?

Answer: Chain stores such as Dairy Queen are able to buy goods in large quantities, receiving volume discounts on items such as ice cream ingredients, meat, and hamburger buns. They have developed specialized routine ways of doing things, such as making sundaes and milk shakes and cleaning ice cream dispensing machines, thereby keeping costs down. Because of their large size, they can also afford to hire skilled specialists for the various marketing jobs, such as creating advertising campaigns. [See Section 12-2.]

PROBLEM 12-4 What do franchisors require of their franchisees?

Answer: Franchisees must make a minimum investment in the business. They are required to pay the franchisor a percentage of sales (normally around five percent), called a royalty. They must operate according to rules laid down by the franchisor. These rules cover areas such as how products should be handled, how advertising is to be conducted, and the physical appearance of the store. [See Section 12-2.]

PROBLEM 12-5 A friend who has lived in a small town all of her life is planning to open a flower shop there. Which benefits-sought-by-customers category would you advise her to target?

Answer: Ethical shoppers probably would be the best target for this flower shop. These consumers want to support small businesses and firms that are locally owned and operated. Since the friend has lived in the town all of her life, she could probably attract many of these individuals. She may find that a large proportion of the local community would like to see her succeed. [See Section 12-2.]

PROBLEM 12-6 Assume that you have taken a position with a firm that is about to go into business as a chain discount operation. The company will offer many manufacturer's and private brands at low prices. It will aggressively attempt to build market share, first regionally and then nationally. What benefits-sought-by-customers category would you choose?

Answer: Economic shoppers are the superior choice for the chain discount firm. These consumers want products that are seen as a good buy for the price—quality goods and services at a reasonable cost. They are willing to forgo extensive services and luxurious retail environments, as well as convenience, if they can obtain low-priced products that are of adequate quality. [See Section 12-2.]

PROBLEM 12-7 The owner of a Chinese food restaurant has come to you for advice. He has always appealed to personalizing shoppers—those who enjoy friendly service and a congenial atmosphere. He feels, however, that many potential restaurant patrons are apathetic shoppers. Should he attempt to appeal to both groups?

Answer: Probably not, because the desires of these two groups are very different. Personalizing shoppers look for friendly and hospitable restaurants. They enjoy talking with friendly personnel. Apathetic customers, however, want to minimize the time and effort involved in eating in a restaurant. They look for speed and convenience and might not like restaurant employees who want to chat. [See Section 12-2.]

PROBLEM 12-8 A small gift shop is located in a neighborhood where a large variety store with a gift department has just opened. The owner of the small store has asked you for advice on what to emphasize in advertisements to prevent the loss of customers to the variety store. What would you suggest?

Answer: The gift store owner probably should stress the depth of the product line, which a variety store cannot match because of its neglect of low-margin and low-turnover items. The gift shop advertisements should inform potential customers that they are more likely to find the specific item they want in the gift store than in a variety store. The advertisements could also feature the knowledgeable and helpful personnel of the store. [See Section 12-2.]

PROBLEM 12-9 If you were offering a new lawn furniture line that would sell at relatively high retail prices, would you most likely choose to sell it through discounters, department stores, or some other kind of outlet, such as specialty stores?

Answer: Department stores probably would be the best choice for the new lawn furniture line. They specialize in items with low inventory turnover and high prices, as is the case with the lawn furniture. Discounters operate on a high-turnover, low-price basis. Generally, department store personnel can be expected to provide a higher degree of customer service. This is important because the line is new and needs selling support to compensate for its lack of consumer recognition. [See Section 12-2.]

PROBLEM 12-10 Assume that you are about to establish a new bookstore business and are considering locating in an enclosed mall. What are some of the major reasons why customers might be attracted to the mall, rather than some other location?

Answer: Malls are very good locations for bookstores. Many malls have a relaxed and cordial atmosphere that is compatible with the image the bookstore seeks. In addition, malls provide protection from both hot and cold weather, so consumers seek them out. Convenient parking is usually available. Mall managers feature special events and sales, which can pull in shoppers. The largest segment of the population that malls attract are well-educated women, a group which is a target for many bookstores. [See Section 12-2.]

PROBLEM 12-11 Neiman Marcus department stores are specialty stores, in the minds of many, but not all, target consumers. Does this mean that management can relax its efforts to satisfy consumers and compete aggressively with rivals, and enjoy its good image and financial position?

Answer: Neiman Marcus executives should not relax their efforts to satisfy consumers and remain competitive just because of the strong positive attitudes of consumers. To do so would open the door for aggressive rivals to move in and capture markets that this department store controls. The executives should be on the alert for methods to maintain their preferred position. They may have to change portions of the product line, alter the physical format of some departments, bring out new advertising themes, or adopt new pricing and credit policies from time to time. [See Section 12-2.]

PROBLEM 12-12 What are some of the major benefits that convenience stores should provide for their customers, in light of the fact that many are in the "apathetic" category?

Answer: Convenience stores must offer benefits that make shopping quick and easy. They should furnish ample parking space, layouts that make shopping simple, displays that promote fast product selection, and quick checkouts. They must also have locations that are near homes, places of work, or other travel destinations of target customers. Many offer prepared food (such as sandwiches) because they have found that large numbers of target consumers are dissatisfied with slow service in fast-food restaurants. [See Section 12-2.]

PROBLEM 12-13 A law firm that serves large corporate clients has engaged you as a consultant to choose a location for its main office. What kind of a location would you seek?

Answer: A law firm such as this one would want a prestigious location, perhaps in a high-rent office building or a professional suite. It might be situated near the headquarters of some of its larger clients, although convenience would be of less importance than it would be, say, for most convenience stores. Sites in both downtown business areas and well-to-do suburbs should be investigated. The firm probably would be less concerned about avoiding expensive leases or rentals than would, say, most retail stores. [See Section 12-4.]

PROBLEM 12-14 What kind of a store building and interior would you advise for shoe stores that cater to middle-income consumers?

Answer: Shoe stores are shopping stores, so the store building and interior should make comparison shopping as easy as possible. This can be accomplished by having displays that enable shoppers to fully examine a wide range of merchandise. Management may want to devote most of the space in the building to displays and to minimize the amount of space used for storage and office purposes. The building and interior should create an image of high shoe quality and extensive service to customers. [See Section 12-4.]

PROBLEM 12-15 Assume that you are opening a music store in a shopping mall. What kind of advertising media would you seek?

Answer: For the music store, local media would be best in reaching potential customers in the community. Strong possibilities are local newspapers and radio. Both of these are low in cost and reach a large proportion of the local residents. The specific media chosen should be those that will reach the target consumer. If the main target consumer is teenagers, for example, a radio station that emphasizes rock music may be a good choice. [See Section 12-4.]

PROBLEM 12-16 Would you recommend the self-service approach to personal selling for a department store?

Answer: Self-service would not be appropriate for a department store. Customers who patronize such stores rely on knowledgeable and helpful sales personnel. They are willing to pay relatively high prices in exchange for the prestige associated with a department store and for the services that such stores furnish, but others (such as variety stores) do not. Many customers would react negatively to self-service—their expectations would not be met. [See Section 12-4.]

PROBLEM 12-17 If you were in charge of merchandising for a tire store, what would be your major objective in choosing goods to offer?

Answer: The best merchandising policy would be to select a combination of goods that would meet the desires of target customers better than that of competitors. This would require a study of what benefits target customers want, and how well they are able to obtain these benefits to solve their problems. It also would require an analysis of the strengths and weaknesses of competing tire dealers' products and a comparison of these with the products sold in your store. [See Section 12-4.]

PROBLEM 12-18 A recent college graduate has decided to set up a kitchen and bath shop near the college campus. How could he obtain information that would allow him to select the best suppliers?

Answer: The best source of information for the kitchen and bath shop would be the sales personnel that the suppliers employ. He should rely heavily on them to gain a comprehensive and meaningful overall idea of what goods are available. If he is able to attend a trade show to meet with representatives of the suppliers, this will provide additional information. He should be encouraged to write to prospective suppliers, requesting brochures, price lists, and other pertinent information. Also, he can visit with other businesses who have purchased from various suppliers and solicit their opinions. [See Section 12-4.]

13 PROMOTION DECISIONS

THIS CHAPTER IS ABOUT

☑ **Promotion Strategies**
☑ **Promotion Messages**
☑ **Promotion as a Communications System**
☑ **Major Promotion Methods**
☑ **Promotion Goals**
☑ **The Promotion Budget**

13-1. Promotion Strategies

What do these four situations have in common?

A Whirlpool dishwasher commercial points out that the product leaves dishes and glasses spotless and stain-free.

A sales representative convinces a hardware store owner to stock Skil bench power saws in the store.

A spokesman for the Buick division of General Motors sends a press release to the news media describing the new Buick line.

A supermarket sets up an end-of-aisle display for Orchard Sun Fruit Beverage in 40 company stores.

You may have recognized that all four are *promotion* efforts.

• **Promotion** consists of marketing communications with target customers.

Promotion is one of the four P's of the marketing function. Marketers may aim promotion directly at consumers or industrial buyers, as in the case of the Whirlpool ad described above. Or they may target intermediaries who sell to consumers or industrial buyers, as with the hardware store example.

A. Types of promotion strategies

1. *Pull promotion strategy*

A **pull promotion strategy** is one in which marketers direct most of their efforts toward selling *consumers*—getting them to demand or "*pull*" the product from retailers, who must in turn demand the product from wholesalers and producers. In many cases, a pull promotion strategy calls for substantial expenditures on advertising.

2. *Push promotion strategy*

Marketers direct **push promotion strategies** toward *wholesalers and retailers*. The idea is to get them to stock and aggressively sell the product, so that sales to the consumer will result. Many push strategies rely more on personal selling than on advertising.

B. Forms of promotion strategies

Promotion strategies may involve either *mass communication* or *interpersonal communication*.

1. Mass communication

In the case of *mass communication*, marketers direct their messages to large numbers of receivers. They obtain little feedback (communication) from the receivers as to how well their messages are getting across. This is an effective way of reaching large numbers at a low cost per individual contacted.

2. Interpersonal communication

Interpersonal communication is direct from one person to another. When a sales representative talks with a prospect, for example, two-way communication is possible. This is a costly method in terms of the expense that is required per individual contacted. On the other hand, it can be very effective, since interpersonal communication can capture considerable attention and interest.

13-2. Promotion Messages

• Many promotion messages are designed to *inform* customers about something a marketer is doing.

When the Buick division of General Motors introduces a new product, for instance, promotion is useful in spreading the news. Other instances when promotion provides information may occur when the marketer wants to tell customers that it is offering a sale, has moved to a new location, provides a new or special service, or has discontinued a service it formerly offered.

EXAMPLE 13-1: La Quinta Motor Inns. Inc., uses advertisements to inform potential guests that its service includes rooms that are soundproof, to "keep the noise of the world outside." This service has special appeal to business travelers, many of whom desire a good night's rest after a trying day's work away from home.

• Other promotion messages are designed to *persuade* the customer, rather than just to inform.

The objective of persuasion is to guide the behavior of potential customers so that they will take actions suggested by the marketer. Normally, marketers do this by promising rewards that customers will receive if they act in the ways the promotion dictates. Efforts to persuade are very common among marketers today.

EXAMPLE 13-2: Dale Carnegie & Associates advertisements carry the message that its sales courses will reward enrollees with the insights needed to be successful in selling. These ads urge sales representatives to attain that reward by filling out registration forms attached to the advertising brochure.

• A third objective of promotion messages is to *remind* customers of a product.

This reminder function is most common for large companies that have been in existence for many years. Already well known companies must periodically remind target customers of the existence of their products and the benefits they offer. Without reminder promotion, customers may be lost to aggressive rivals.

EXAMPLE 13-3: Wrigley's chewing gum advertisements serve mainly to remind consumers of the existence of the product line. There is no point in informing consumers about it, as virtually everyone is aware of its existence. Similarly, persuasion is not necessary because many consumers already use the gum. Consumers are simply reminded about it from time to time, so that they do not forget.

13-3. Promotion as a Communications System

Communication involves transmitting symbols that carry meaning to other parties, resulting in the sharing of ideas. Obviously, promotion is a form of communication. An understanding of the communications process, then, can benefit those who are involved in promotion. It can point out effective ways of informing, persuading, and reminding.

Figure 13-1 provides a graphic description of a **communications system**. It is made up of a source, message, channel, receiver, feedback, and noise.

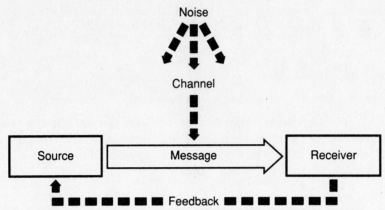

FIGURE 13-1: Graphic depiction of a communications system.

- The *source* is the party who desires to do the communicating—the marketer, in the case of promotion.
- The source forwards a *message* through a *channel*, which is a method of transmitting information, such as advertising or personal selling. If the communication is effective, the information received by the *receiver* is the same as that intended by the source.
- *Noise* can interfere with transmission, however. It is made up of factors that interfere with the message in the channel. Noise can be physical, e.g., when a jet airplane sound blocks out a sales representative's appeal; or it can be mental, e.g., when a consumer is worrying about paying the electric bill and does not pay attention to an advertisement.
- Finally, *feedback* consists of the flow of information from the receiver to the source. The source uses this information to assess how well the communication process is working. A sales rep, for instance, may notice that a potential customer is interested in the safety features of the riding lawn mower that the rep is attempting to sell. This might lead the rep to go to considerable lengths in discussing the product's excellent safety record.

EXAMPLE 13-4: General Mills' sales representatives (sources) call on retailers and wholesalers (receivers) to convince them to carry company products. These reps attempt to develop persuasive messages that will bring about this behavior. Noise (such as competing sales personnel) may interfere with this process, however. The sales representatives rely on feedback—listening to and observing potential customers—to determine if their messages are getting across.

13-4. Major Promotion Methods

The major promotion methods are advertising, personal selling, sales promotion, publicity, and public relations.

A. Advertising

Advertising consists of mass communication that is paid for by an identified sponsor and directed toward groups. Since the receivers of advertising are groups, marketers cannot fashion messages according to the needs and desires of individual target customers. Also, advertising feedback is not as quick or accurate as it is for personal selling, since sales personnel can directly observe how well their messages are getting across. Advertisements always name the sponsor and are paid for.

Various media are employed by advertisers, including magazines, newspapers, radio, television, direct mail, and signs. Essentially, this is an effective way to reach large numbers of potential customers at a low cost per receiver.

EXAMPLE 13-5: General Foods has used advertising very effectively for its Sanka Brand Decaffeinated Coffee. Television and magazine ads emphasize the good flavor and aroma of the coffee along with the fact that it does not keep drinkers awake at night. They describe the brand as having a "smooth and satisfying taste." The well-designed advertisements have enabled the brand to become the top-selling decaffeinated coffee in the world.

B. Personal selling

Personal selling involves person-to-person communication between sales representatives and their receivers, called *prospects*. Unlike advertising, personal selling allows interaction between the source and the receiver. Sales representatives can tailor their messages to the unique characteristics of each prospect and, by listening and observing, can attain quick and accurate feedback that will permit them to change their messages if necessary.

Personal selling is by far the most powerful promotion technique. It is much harder to dismiss a sales representative than it is to ignore a television commercial or sales promotion message. However, it is the most expensive method in terms of cost per receiver reached. Considering these factors, firms with customers who place large orders, including many industrial goods sellers, rely most heavily on this method.

EXAMPLE 13-6: Sales representatives for the Siemens Corporation sell high-technology telephone systems to businesses, government agencies, and nonprofit organizations such as school systems. The representatives spend many hours with potential buyers, attempting to convince these prospects to purchase Siemens systems. These reps are obviously effective, as Siemens is one of the more profitable companies in the industry.

C. Sales promotion

Sales promotion consists of a variety of company-sponsored promotion activities that supplement advertising and personal selling. These activities are impersonal and can be directed at industrial buyers, consumers, or intermediaries. Most are nonrecurring; that is, they last for a specific time period and then are dropped or changed. Some types of sales promotion are retail store displays, free samples, premiums, coupons, contests, trading stamps, and free product samples.

EXAMPLE 13-7: The Reader's Digest Association sponsors sweepstakes contests that are aimed at potential subscribers to the *Reader's Digest*. Contest entrants fill out forms that they receive in the mail, registering them for the sweepstakes. The objective is to persuade these entrants to become subscribers, which the contest literature urges them to do.

D. Publicity

Publicity is similar to advertising except that it is free and tends to pertain to newsworthy events. The most common kinds of publicity are news releases, feature stories about companies, and photographs. Publicity is heavily controlled by the news media rather than by the marketer. The firm can send a story to the media or invite them in for a press conference, but the news media can choose to ignore the publicity effort or even change the message from that which the marketer intended. Thus, publicity can be both positive and negative.

EXAMPLE 13-8: Hasbro, Inc.'s, Alphie II learning computer for preschool children received many favorable news stories in magazines and newspapers in 1986. The media recommended it to parents for their children. This favorable publicity helped increase sales of the Alphie II. During the same year, the media carried negative stories on Tonka action toys, citing that some had a spotty safety record. This negative publicity was partly responsible for a decrease in sales of action toys.

E. Public relations

Public relations are communications activities directed at the public at large, the press, government, employees, and other groups, in an attempt to develop a favorable image of a company. A public relations effort is not intended, at least directly, to produce sales. Public relations activities include such things as lobbying, sponsoring athletic teams, creating floats for parades, conducting plant tours, and using promotion messages to persuade members of the public that they should hold a particular opinion.

EXAMPLE 13-9: During 1986, the Hormel Company was locked in a very hostile strike with workers in its Austin, Minnesota, meat processing plant. Both the company and the union used newspapers and radio stations to present their respective sides of the story to the public.

13-5. Promotion Goals

Every company should have *promotion goals* to guide its promotion programs. Once developed, goals help answer questions such as what methods and media to use, how much to spend, and what messages to carry. Companies use both general and detailed goals.

A. General goals

General goals represent what management wants promotion to accomplish in affecting its audiences. There are five general goals.

(1) **Reach.** An important goal is to expose an adequate number of target customers to a message—to "reach" them. In doing this, management defines target customers, determines their number, and then chooses methods and media that will most effectively reach the intended audience.

EXAMPLE 13-10: In 1986, Nike, Inc., introduced Street Socks, an aerobic dancing and casual athletic shoe with a low price (under $30). The company ran advertisements in *Runner's World* in order to reach target customers.

(2) **Attention.** As a goal, attention consists of getting members of a target audience to focus their minds on the message. This can be difficult because targets are bombarded with many sources competing for their attention. Literally thousands of advertisements, sales promotion vehicles, sales representatives, and editorial features compete for attention in the media. Thus, marketers often try to design promotions so that targets will see them as being strikingly different from other phenomena in the environment. Advertisements may use humor, unusual-looking models, color, or loud sounds to attract attention. Or marketers may appeal to curiosity or the desires of targets to achieve important needs.

EXAMPLE 13-11: Sales representatives of AT&T computers find out, through questioning, just what data processing and data base management needs customers have. Then they focus their sales presentations directly on these needs. This approach is effective in capturing the attention of potential buyers.

(3) **Understanding**. Understanding takes place when receivers interpret messages in the manner that the source intended. The major points of a message should be clearly highlighted and presented in an appealing and interesting manner. The message should be clear and not overly difficult to comprehend. Simplicity of presentation is important to understanding.

EXAMPLE 13-12: Ads for Crest toothpaste point out in a few words that its gel toothpaste helps keep tartar from building up on teeth. They illustrate this by showing a dental pick just above a toothbrush topped with Crest. The point that the company intends to convey is obvious.

---

(4) **Changing attitudes**. Changing attitudes is an important goal for many promotion messages. Attitudes are positive or negative states of readiness to respond in a particular way. For example, a customer may have a positive attitude toward Almond Joy candy bars and a negative attitude toward Diet Center weight reduction centers. Changing negative attitudes can be very desirable to the marketer, since a negative attitude increases the probability that target customers will purchase the promoted brand in the future.

EXAMPLE 13-13: Ads for Check-Up Plaque Fighting Gum indicate that it is "clinically proven to remove plaque when you can't brush." Management realizes that this ad will not cause large numbers of consumers to rush out and purchase the brand. But such an ad may make attitudes toward Check-Up more favorable and increase the chance that consumers will buy the gum in the future.

---

(5) **Action**. Numerous promotion efforts strive for action as their goal. Sales calls are designed specifically to result in consumer purchase. This is also the case for a variety of sales promotion efforts, such as displays. Some ads, particularly those of retailers, urge the target customer to "buy now." Without action, there would be no sales.

B. Specific goals

Specific goals should specify the target customers and the effect that the firm expects to produce through promotion. Specific goals should be sufficiently detailed to point out what actions promotion personnel should take when decisions are required. The general goals only indicate the overall impression that the company wants to make on consumers.

EXAMPLE 13-14: A GTE Corporation specific goal might be to use personal selling to convince 20 food processors that they can reduce expenses by installing Sprint telephone systems in their plants. Another specific goal for GTE would be to use advertising on television to convince 20,000 middle-income households that Sprint is a durable and dependable product (this is an example of attitude change).

13-6. The Promotion Budget

There are a number of ways in which firms determine how much to spend on promotion. A firm may allocate a percentage of sales for promotion, match the promotion expenditures of competitors, use informed judgement, employ the objective method, or it may use a combination of any or all of these.

A. Percentage of sales

A widely used technique is to allocate a certain percentage, say two percent, of the current or projected year's expected sales to promotion. A percentage of sales is easy to calculate and helps ensure that the firm will be able to pay for promotion expenses incurred. Logically, however, it is shaky because companies may need extra-large promotion budgets when sales are low and may not need such large budgets when sales are high. This method may produce results whose effects are the opposite of what a company needs.

B. Matching competitors

Organizations can allocate an amount for promotion that approximates the amounts spent by major rivals. A variation of this method is to spend slightly more than rivals do. This method may be useful in protecting the firm's market share and is of value for industries in which competition is fierce. However, the promotion needs of one company may have no relation to those of competing companies. Further, rivals may not have used good judgment in determining their budget levels, so imitating them is not necessarily wise.

C. Judgment

If a company employs marketing executives who have considerable knowledge and experience, it may set promotion budgets that are based on the informed judgment of those executives. An executive who is well-informed on such matters as company objectives and what competitors are expected to do may be able to provide good judgment-based estimates. Judgment is certainly useful in producing budgets, but it can also be in error since it is subjective and subject to bias. For this reason, it is best used in combination with other methods.

D. The objective method

The objective method involves first determining specific promotion objectives and then setting a budget that is expected to permit the company to attain these objectives. This method is logical, as the amount spent is based on how much is needed to reach intended goals. The objective method can take more time and effort than other methods because promotion managers must plan their future actions in detail. However, it can result in very well thought-out budget levels.

EXAMPLE 13-15: A variety store promotion objective is to convince 50,000 consumers to visit the store at least once in a year's time. Based on past experience, management feels that 500,000 consumers must be reached with newspaper ads to accomplish this. The total cost of the ads is $78,000. This figure would represent the promotion budget.

In practice, it is often most useful for firms to use a variety of methods to set the promotion budget. When this is done, the shortcomings of one method can be offset by the strengths of others. A combination of the objective method with one or more of the other methods discussed above is known to produce very effective results.

RAISE YOUR GRADES

Can you explain . . . ?

☑ why marketers use promotion to help achieve their goals
☑ what kind of "noise" might interfere with the messages of a sales representative when he or she is attempting to sell products to a customer
☑ why marketers are willing to spend millions of dollars for advertising
☑ what kinds of promotion marketers use to assist in carrying out promotion goals
☑ why some firms spend considerable effort seeking publicity for their products, activities, and companies
☑ how marketers can develop promotion budgets that are likely to be of value in carrying out their objectives

SUMMARY

1. Promotion consists of marketing communications with target customers.
2. A pull promotion strategy is designed to sell consumers on a product.
3. A push promotion strategy is designed to sell wholesalers and retailers on a product.
4. Promotion strategies may involve either mass communication or interpersonal communication.
5. Promotion messages are designed to inform, persuade, or remind customers about a company's product.
6. The study of communications systems is useful in understanding promotion. A communications system is made up of a source, message, channel, receiver, feedback, and noise.
7. The major promotion methods are advertising, personal selling, sales promotion, publicity, and public relations.
8. Advertising consists of mass communication that is paid for by an identified sponsor and directed toward groups.
9. Personal selling involves person-to-person communication between sales representatives and their receivers, called prospects.
10. Sales promotion consists of a variety of company-sponsored promotion activities that supplement advertising and personal selling.
11. Publicity is similar to advertising except that it is free and pertains to newsworthy events.
12. Public relations are communications activities directed at the public at large, the press, government, employees, and other groups, in an attempt to develop a favorable image of the company.
13. Every company should have promotion goals to guide its promotion programs.
14. General goals point out what management wants promotion to accomplish in affecting its audiences. The major general promotion goals are reach, attention, understanding, changing attitudes, and action.
15. Specific goals should specify the target customers and the effect that the firm expects to produce through promotion.
16. There are several methods by which firms may determine a promotion budget:

    - the percentage-of-sales method, which involves allocating a certain percentage of the current or projected year's expected sales to promotion;

    - the matching competitors method, which involves allocating an amount for promotion that approximates the amounts spent by major rivals;

    - the judgment method, which employs the judgment of experienced marketing executives who can determine how much to spend;

    - the objective method, which involves allocating a budget based on reaching specific promotion objectives.

    A combination of the objective method with one or more of the other methods discussed above is known to produce very effective results.

RAPID REVIEW   Answers

1. A promotion strategy aimed at convincing consumers to purchase a product is called a **(a)** mass communication appeal, **(b)** one-on-one approach, **(c)** pull promotion strategy, **(d)** push promotion strategy. [See Section 13-1.]   *c*

2. When the National Livestock & Meat Board runs ads calling beef "real food for real people," it is striving to **(a)** inform, **(b)** persuade, **(c)** remind, **(d)** conduct personal selling. [See Section 13-2.]   *b*

3. When a General Mills sales representative informs a supermarket buyer that the firm has developed a salt-free version of its Pop-Secret microwave popcorn, the sales rep is striving to **(a)** inform, **(b)** persuade, **(c)** remind, **(d)** advertise. [See Section 13-2.]   *a*

4. A firm that sends out sales representatives is the **(a)** source, **(b)** receiver, **(c)** channel, **(d)** feedback in a communications system. [See Section 13-2.]   *a*

5. Feedback in a communications system runs from the receiver to the (a) channel transmitter, (b) sales representative, (c) customer, (d) source. [See Section 13-3.]   *d*

6. In a communications system, the message is carried by a (a) receiver, (b) channel, (c) source, (d) carrier. [See Section 13-3.]   *b*

7. Anything that interferes with effective communication is called (a) interference, (b) noise, (c) static, (d) blockage. [See Section 13-3.]   *b*

8. Advertisements are aimed at (a) sources, (b) small groups, (c) large groups, (d) individuals. [See Section 13-4.]   *c*

9. One of the major promotion methods that is most effective for reaching a large number of customers at a low cost per receiver is (a) advertising, (b) personal selling, (c) publicity, (d) sales promotion. [See Section 13-4.]   *a*

10. An advantage of using sales representatives for promotion is quick and accurate (a) action, (b) information, (c) sales responses, (d) feedback. [See Section 13-4.]   *d*

11. Which of the following is *not* sales promotion: (a) a Campbell Soup Company retail display, (b) a Delco battery coupon, (c) a Clorox Company contest, (d) an American Dairy Association television commercial. [See Section 13-4.]   *d*

12. When *Sportsweek* magazine provides free promotion (news) about a new kind of catcher's mitt produced by the Spaulding Company, this is an example of (a) advertising, (b) sales promotion, (c) publicity, (d) public relations. [See Section 13-4.]   *c*

13. Carter Hawley Hale department stores is trying to develop a favorable image of the company when it promotes through (a) publicity, (b) public relations, (c) advertising, (d) sales promotions. [See Section 13-4.]   *b*

14. "Reach" is one of the _____ goals of a company. (a) general, (b) specific, (c) indivisible, (d) summary. [See Section 13-5.]   *a*

15. Advertisements are designed so that they are different from other advertisements in order to attain the goal of (a) reach, (b) attention, (c) understanding, (d) action. [See Section 13-5.]   *b*

16. _____ toward a product are states of readiness to respond in a certain way. (a) Images, (b) Exposures, (c) Attitudes (d) Emotions. [See Section 13-5.]   *c*

17. Specific promotion goals for firms should specify (a) the target customer, (b) the pricing strategy, (c) physical distribution tactics, (d) channels of distribution strategy. [See Section 13-5.]   *a*

18. The _____ method of calculating a promotion budget could easily cause a firm to spend small amounts on promotion when it should be spending large amounts. (a) percentage-of-sales, (b) matching competitors, (c) judgment, (d) objective. [See Section 13-6.]   *a*

19. The _____ method of determining the promotion budget is used in combination with other methods. (a) percentage-of-sales, (b) matching competitors, (c) judgment, (d) objective. [See Section 13-6.]   *c*

20. The _____ method of determining the promotion budget requires that executives base the amount spent on how much is needed to reach intended goals. (a) percentage-of-sales, (b) matching competitors, (c) judgment, (d) objective. [See Section 13-6.]   *d*

SOLVED PROBLEMS

PROBLEM 13-1 "All promotion is used to convince people to do things that they really do not want to do." How would you react to this statement?

Answer: The statement is incorrect. It assumes that all promotion has the objective of persuading. This is not the case, as many promotion efforts are designed to inform and remind. Information objectives are very common for personal selling, and reminder objectives are very common for advertising. In addition, attempts to convince consumers to do things they really do not want to do are likely to be ineffective. Hence, relatively few successful companies attempt this. They realize that, in the long run, such strategies will undermine customer confidence in them, and may create outright hostility. [See Section 13-2.]

PROBLEM 13-2 "Promotion of goods and services such as Dial soap is merely one form of communication." How would you react to this statement?

Answer: This statement is true. Promotion of Dial soap is a form of communication. Sources (mainly sales representatives and advertising personnel) transmit messages (such as, "Aren't you glad you use Dial?") to receivers (target customers) over channels (sales presentations and advertisements). Promotion encounters noise (such as telephone calls that interrupt sales presentations and the advertisements of competitors). In addition, Dial promotion is improved by feedback from sales personnel and from marketing researchers. It shares these elements with other kinds of communication. [See Section 13-3.]

PROBLEM 13-3 Would you recommend that Lockheed Corporation make extensive use of advertising in promoting its fighter planes?

Answer: Advertising would not be a good promotion technique for Lockheed fighter planes because it is a form of mass communication, directed toward groups. Obviously, large groups are not the market for fighter planes. The firm needs to fashion messages according to the needs of individual target consumers. In the defense industry, air forces of various countries are the targets. They require individualized messages, such as those available through personal selling. It is very important that the methods and media form chosen reach the target market. [See Section 13-4.]

PROBLEM 13-4 Assume that you have developed a set of exercises that have proven to be beneficial for people with backaches. You have written about and illustrated the exercises in a 60-page booklet that you want to sell directly to backache victims. What would be the most effective promotion method to use?

Answer: Advertising would be the best method of promoting your booklet. It is an effective way of reaching large numbers of potential customers at a low cost per receiver. You must sell large numbers of the booklet in order to make profits because printing costs are mainly fixed. This means that if you only sell 100 booklets, the cost per unit might be $40, but if you sell 1000, the unit cost might be $5. Personal selling to individual backache victims would not reach a sufficient number of target customers and would be a slow and costly method. Of course, personal selling could be used for doctors, chiropractors, and physical therapists. They, in turn, might promote the booklet to their patients. [See Section 13-3.]

PROBLEM 13-5 A sales representative has mentioned to you that she benefits by receiving feedback from prospects. What does she mean by feedback?

Answer: Feedback is information which the sales representative receives from the prospect as to how the message is getting across. The sales representative can obtain quick and accurate feedback through careful listening and observing. This will assist her in determining when to feature new benefits or how to answer objections. If she is skilled in this process, she will be able to help prospects determine their needs and how best to satisfy them. [See Section 13-4.]

PROBLEM 13-6 Managers of the High Sierra Condominium Complex have found that it is difficult to sell their condominium units. Many potential buyers have reservations because the units are expensive and they have heard stories about some complexes going bankrupt. What promotion media would you recommend that High Sierra use in attempting to sell the units?

Answer: Personal selling would be best for High Sierra. It is the most powerful of all the promotion techniques. Individuals experience more difficulty in dismissing a sales representative than they do in ignoring an advertising or sales promotion message. Sales representatives can be very persuasive and can answer particular questions and doubts that specific prospects raise. This is especially important for High Sierra, because its units are expensive and some consumers have heard stories about condominium complexes that have become bankrupt. It will take considerable persuasion to convince them to buy. [See Section 13-4.]

PROBLEM 13-7 "Modern marketers rely more on sales promotion than they do on advertising and personal selling in promoting their goods and services." Do you agree with this statement?

Answer: The statement is incorrect. In most companies, sales promotion is used to supplement, rather than to substitute for, advertising and personal selling. It is not ordinarily a good replacement for these two techniques. Displays, coupons, contests, store demonstrations, trading stamps, and other sales promotion methods must take a back seat to the work of sales representatives and advertising personnel—the vital links in communicating with target customers. [See Section 13-4.]

PROBLEM 13-8 Assume that you own and manage a new specialty restaurant that offers Croatian food. You would like to contact local newspapers and radio stations to obtain publicity for your business. What are the dangers in such a strategy?

Answer: Your restaurant can send a story or news release to a newspaper or local radio or television station or invite members of the media in for a press conference. These efforts may result in favorable publicity for your restaurant. However, the media may ignore your publicity effort (they probably will if it does not appear to be newsworthy) or change the message from that which you intended. Further, publicity can be negative, as well as positive. Media personnel may accent features of your restaurant, such as its age, that are not favorable to you and that you would rather not have mentioned. [See Section 13-4.]

PROBLEM 13-9 Assume that you have been placed in charge of public relations for a large public accounting firm. What might your duties include?

Answer: Your major objective would be to develop a favorable image of the accounting firm in the eyes of the public at large, the press, government, employees, and other groups. Specific possibilities might include lobbying, possibly sponsoring athletic teams and parade floats, working for the local United Way effort, arranging free tax preparation advice for the elderly, and using promotion messages to convince members of the public that they should hold a particular opinion on tax law changes. [See Section 13-4.]

PROBLEM 13-10 How should management of Alfalfabets, a health-food restaurant, go about designing their "reach" general promotion goals?

Answer: First, the management of Alfalfabets restaurant should define target consumers as specifically as is possible. At present they make an attempt to appeal to consumers who are health-conscious (the salad bar contains nutritious food and the sandwiches are low in calories). In addition, it is necessary for management to estimate the total number of target consumers in the area. Following this, management should select media (such as college newspapers) that will contact the largest number of the intended audience (made up of target consumers). [See Section 13-5.]

PROBLEM 13-11 How can a vacuum cleaner manufacturer create advertisements that capture the attention of target consumers?

Answer: In order to create vacuum cleaner ads that capture the attention of target consumers, this firm should design its advertisements so that consumers see them as being different from other aspects of the advertising environment. They may use humor, unusual-looking models, color, loud sounds, or interest-catching musical effects. Or they may attempt to make consumers curious about the advertisement or the product. Another good approach is to conduct research among target consumers, discover the needs of target consumers which might be satisfied through their vacuum cleaners, and then emphasize these needs through its advertisements. [See Section 13-5.]

PROBLEM 13-12   A novice sales representative believes that the most important general promotion goal is to develop customer understanding of the company and its products. How would you advise the rep to go about attaining this goal?

Answer: In his presentations, the sales representative should make sure that the major points of the message are clearly highlighted and presented in an interesting manner. The message should be clear and not overly difficult to understand. He should cover those aspects of the company and its products that will be of genuine interest to the prospect and avoid aspects that the prospect does not care about. He should stress ways in which the company and its products can bring important benefits to prospects. [See Section 13-5.]

PROBLEM 13-13   Why would American Express want to develop promotion programs with "attitude change" as a general goal?

Answer: Attitudes are positive or negative states of readiness to respond in a particular way. Attitude change can be very desirable to American Express, since it increases the probability that its target consumers will use its services in the future. Some target consumers may have negative attitudes toward American Express or toward credit cards in general. These consumers may believe that it is too costly or too time-consuming to obtain a credit card. The company should focus on problems that target consumers may encounter (such as losing cash while traveling) and how American Express can help solve such problems (such as providing loans to cardholders during emergencies. [See Section 13-5.]

PROBLEM 13-14   How would a company such as Rexall Drugs pursue the "action" general promotion goal?

Answer: The action goal in this case consists of getting consumers to purchase Rexall goods—to "buy now." Thus, the fulfillment of this goal results in the inflow of cash into the company. Many Rexall products are sold on the basis of their low prices, relative to competing stores. Company advertisements give the impression that consumers can save money if they take action while the low prices (often sale prices) are still in effect and while the goods are available. They suggest that waiting to make a purchase may result in a lost opportunity. [See Section 13-5.]

PROBLEM 13-15   The promotion manager for a manufacturer of teen skin care products has stated, "Our promotion goals are to achieve reach, attention, and favorable attitudes toward our products." Are these sufficient goals to guide the company's promotion activities?

Answer: The promotion manager has not provided sufficient goals to guide the company promotion activities. Firms need general goals, such as those that the promotion manager has stipulated. In addition, they require specific goals to guide their promotion programs. The specific goals should specify the target customers and the effect that the firm expects to produce through promotion. An example of a useful specific goal is "to make 300,000 teenagers from middle-income families in the eastern half of the nation aware of the company's new acne prevention lotion." [See Section 13-5.]

PROBLEM 13-16   Assume that the Abex Corporation (a producer of hydraulic valves and motors for airplanes and space vehicles) sets its promotion budget as four percent of next year's projected sales. Do you approve of this method of developing the budget?

Answer: The method is easy to calculate and it helps ensure that Abex will be able to pay for the promotion expenses incurred. Logically, it is shaky, however, because the Abex Corporation may need large promotion budgets when sales are low and may not need as much promotion when sales are high. Yet this method may lead to the opposite results. For example, if the company loses a large contract for airplane motors to competitors, it may need promotion *increases* in the budget, even though sales would drop. [See Section 13-6.]

PROBLEM 13-17 Would it be wise for a fast-food restaurant to set its promotion budget simply by planning to spend one-half of the amount that its major competitor spends for promotion?

Answer: This method can be useful in protecting the restaurant's market share and is of value in an industry such as fast foods where competition is intense. However, the promotion needs of the restaurant may have no relation to those of its major competitor. This firm, for example, may be in need of promotion programs that will allow it to generate large increases in cash flow. Its rival may not have such a need if its cash flow position is secure. Further, the rival may not have used good judgment in setting its budget level, in which case imitating it would not be wise. [See Section 13-6.]

PROBLEM 13-18 Would you approve if a ball-point pen manufacturer based its promotion budget on the judgment of a committee of three senior executives with a total of 50 years of experience in the writing instruments industry?

Answer: The ball-point pen company executives are probably well informed on such matters as company objectives and what competitors may be expected to do. In this case, they may be able to furnish good, judgment-based estimates. However, their judgment may be in error, since it is subjective and subject to bias. Their feelings about how consumers will react to company promotions may be colored by generally optimistic or pessimistic attitudes which do not reflect true evaluations of consumer behavior. For this reason, the company should use this method in combination with other methods. [See Section 13-6.]

PROBLEM 13-19 Would it be wise for a large toy manufacturer's promotion budget to be based on the objective method?

Answer: Basically, the objective method is a sound one that should be considered by the toy company. This technique requires first determining the company promotion objectives and then setting a budget which is expected to permit reaching the objectives. This is logical, as the amount spent is based on how much is needed to reach intended goals. It makes use of the judgment of company executives but does so in a way that minimizes their biases. At the same time, it takes into account expected actions which competing toy makers might take. [See Section 13-6.]

PROBLEM 13-20 If the promotion budget for a company were based on the objective method, what problems do you think that the firm might face?

Answer: The objective method could take more time and effort than other methods because promotion managers must plan their future actions in detail. They must develop clear-cut promotion objectives and research the market and the promotion media carefully in order to determine the best ways of implementing these objectives. However, the process can result in very well thought out budget levels for the company. [See Section 13-6.]

14 ADVERTISING STRATEGY AND TACTICS

14-1. The Uses of Advertising

Advertising has been defined as mass communication that is paid for by an identified sponsor and directed toward groups. You probably are better acquainted with this than with most marketing functions, because advertising is apparent virtually everywhere you go and provides a continuous barrage of messages. Most people, however, are not aware of the uses of this tool by marketers. Figure 14-1 outlines the uses of advertising that are discussed below.

A. Primary and secondary demand

Some marketers attempt to build **primary demand**—demand for the product rather than a company brand—through advertising. This may be the case when the advertiser already has a large share of the industry market or is an organized group.

EXAMPLE 14-1: The Potato Board, an organization financed by potato farmers in the United States, designs advertising to induce consumers to eat this vegetable. Some ads proclaim it as "Today's hottest diet food," and go on to explain that the potato is low in calories and has many vital nutrients.

Most advertisers, however, aim at stimulating **secondary demand**, which is demand for a particular *brand*. They try to establish an advantage for their brands over others. If they were to emphasize primary demand, the effects of their efforts would be to benefit competitors as well as themselves.

EXAMPLE 14-2: The Emhart Company ads feature the idea that its Thermogrip brand hot glue gun is a non-messy way to glue that sets in 60 seconds with no clamping, no mixing, and no harmful fumes. The ads further relate that it works on any porous material and will not clog up.

B. Institutional and product advertising

Institutional advertising is used to boost the image of a company in the minds of target customers or others. Institutional advertising does not try to sell a particular product or service, but to build goodwill for the sponsor. Such advertising may say that a particular company cares about society, provides many jobs, or is a good citizen.

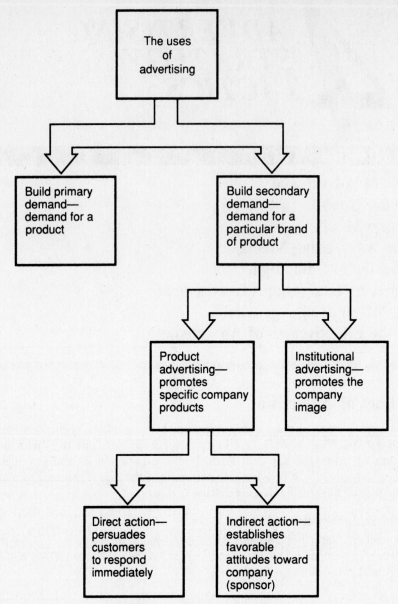

FIGURE 14-1: The uses of advertising.

EXAMPLE 14-3: Jack Daniels ads portray the company as one that employs homespun, rural Tennessee people who are devoted to their work, to tradition, and to a relaxed lifestyle.

Product advertising is used to promote specific company products and may take two forms.

 (1) **Direct action** ads attempt to convince target customers to respond immediately, e.g., by encouraging consumers to "purchase [our brand] today." Many retail ads are of this type.
 (2) **Indirect action** ads try to establish favorable attitudes toward the sponsor, on the assumption that such favorable attitudes will lead to future purchases.

EXAMPLE 14-4: Hormel's Dinty Moore beef stew ads are of the indirect action type. They try to develop an attitude that their beef stew is good for kids. The ads show children involved in strenuous play activities and proclaim "Looks like a Dinty Moore day."

14-2. Advertising Goals

Since advertising is one kind of promotion, it can have the general goals of *reach*, *attention*, *understanding*, *attitude change*, and *action* (as discussed in Chapter 13). As in the case of all promotion, advertising should also have specific goals that specify the target customer and the effect that the firm expects to produce through advertising.

EXAMPLE 14-5: A small producer of waterbeds has a general advertising goal of using television ads to reach 10,000 potential customers and convince 500 of them to visit a company factory outlet store to inspect the merchandise. The specific expected goal is that 50 sales to target customers will result from the store visits.

A company may need to change advertising goals over time. These goals are seldom permanent. When overall company objectives, the marketing strategies of competitors, or the desires of target customers shift, advertising goals may require revision.

14-3. Advertising Media

There are a number of *media*, or promotion channels, that advertisers can use. The major categories are print, broadcast, direct mail, and miscellaneous.

A. Print media

Print media are magazines and newspapers, which convey messages visually.

1. Magazines

Magazines are a medium capable of reaching many different kinds of target customers. Some, such as *Reader's Digest*, reach a national audience. The *Digest* and many others also have regional editions. Other magazines, such as *Arizona Highways*, target a specific geographic area. Still other magazines such as *PC User* and *Junior Miss* are available to contact special interest groups.

Magazine reproduction quality is very good, so product illustration can be made very colorful and appealing. Their messages can be longer and more complex than those on radio or television. Consumers read and reread magazines, and may even pass them on to others. Some have prestige value. Some can be used to target special segments.

Magazines have some disadvantages, however. Some are very expensive media. Also, a magazine often has a long *closing period*—i.e., there is a long wait between the time when an ad is given to the magazine and time it is actually published. Finally, advertisers may also experience **waste circulation**, when individuals who are not target customers read the magazine.

2. Newspapers

Newspapers reach almost every home and many businesses and nonprofit organizations. Many members of a family or organization read them. Their messages can be longer and more complex than those on radio or television. This medium is useful in reaching particular markets, such as cities or parts of cities. Also, newspaper closing periods are short.

Newspapers also have disadvantages. A local newspaper is not a good medium for reaching a large regional or national market. The printed copies do not reproduce illustrations as well as do magazines. Also, newspapers are not kept and reread as much as magazines. Finally, some do not offer the prestige of television and some magazines.

B. Broadcast media

Broadcast media consist of radio, which conveys messages orally, and television, which conveys messages both orally and visually.

1. Radio

Radio, which is widely used by both small and large advertisers, is often used to reach local markets. This medium reaches virtually everyone, so it is a means of contacting a mass market. It also can be used to reach particular segments, since different individuals listen to different kinds of programs and at different times of day. Advertising time can be purchased at low rates, and closing periods are very short.

A problem with radio is that the message is short. If the target is not affected *during* the commercial, the effect of the message is lost. Further, radio appeals only to the sense of hearing. It cannot take advantage of visual communication, like television and print media.

2. Television

Television reaches large numbers of consumers, particularly during "prime time" (7:00 to 10:00 or 8:00 to 11:00 PM). Marketers can reach specific groups by choosing appropriate networks, stations, times of day, and programs.

Television appeals to the senses of sight and sound, so it can produce very high-impact ads. Finally, advertising on television probably adds to the prestige of the sponsor and its product or service.

Television can be very expensive. Like radio, it cannot convey lengthy messages. Also, it is not as effective in reaching select potential markets as are some other media.

EXAMPLE 14-6: Procter and Gamble can reach large numbers of nonemployed women with Tide ads by placing commercials on The Edge of Night—a daytime drama show. Stroh can contact young sports fans with commercials on ESPN (the sports network).

C. Direct mail

A company that uses direct mail forwards letters, fliers, brochures, catalogs, and other promotion pieces directly to target customers. Many companies do not need to use independent media—their only channel is the mail. Direct mail has minimal waste circulation because firms can use mailing lists made up solely of likely prospects for the product. This mode is free from such distractions as other ads in a magazine. Finally, the marketer can use only production quality that meets its exact needs.

The negative side of direct mail advertising is that some prospects consider direct-mail pieces a nuisance and discard them before reading. It may be difficult, or prohibitively expensive, to get a good mailing list for some products. Also, some mailing lists rapidly become obsolete. The cost per contact can be high relative to other media.

D. Miscellaneous

There are several other kinds of advertising media available to marketers.

(1) *Outdoor advertising*. Outdoor advertising is available through billboards and signs. **Billboards** are owned by media companies and are rented to advertisers. They can remind consumers to make a purchase while on a shopping trip or while driving to and from work. They reach large numbers of consumers economically. **Signs** are smaller than billboards and are owned by advertisers. A weakness of both media is that the message must be very short or consumers will not have time to read it. Also, drivers and their passengers are subject to many distractions while in an automobile.

(2) *Transit advertising*. Transit advertising consists of ads placed inside or outside of taxis, buses, streetcars, and railroad cars. It provides communication exposure to specific groups, such as commuters, who may be good targets for certain advertisers. Transit advertising is a low-cost method of advertising.

(3) *Specialty advertising*. Specialty advertising consists of messages on novelty or useful articles, such as pens, calendars, and matches. Hallmark calendars, for example, are given out free each year. These items can be useful to remind target customers about the company and its products. Like transit advertising, specialty advertising is a low-cost medium. Sometimes it takes on unique forms—sky writing and banners, and the Goodyear Blimp.

14-4. Choosing Advertising Media

One of the most important decisions that marketers make is choosing advertising media. Many are available and the choice is not easy. The major factors to consider are advertising goals, media circulation, the message, and the cost of the media.

A. Advertising goals

The major determinant of which media are best is the advertising goal or goals. These specify the nature and size of the target customer and the intended effect of the message on the target. Advertising goals are based on promotional goals, which are general in nature.

EXAMPLE 14-7: Assume that American Express wants to inform 500,000 upper-middle-income consumers that it will extend manufacturers' warranties on products bought with its credit card. A logical choice of advertising vehicle would be *Forbes* magazine, which reaches large numbers of consumers in the upper middle-income bracket.

B. Circulation

Obviously, the best media are those with readers, listeners, or viewers who are target customers of the marketer. The media themselves, along with a number of outside agencies, collect and publish data on *circulation*, which is the number of readers, listeners, or viewers reached by a medium. The circulation data include information on the nature of the target audience.

EXAMPLE 14-8: *TV Guide* reaches a much larger number of working women than does *McCalls*. Thus, *TV Guide* is a more attractive advertising medium for such things as womens' suits, frequent flyer programs, and convenience foods, which appeal more to the working woman.

C. The message

The medium should be compatible with the advertising message. It should fit the public image and editorial content of the message. Of course, what is compatible with one message may not be so with another.

EXAMPLE 14-9: An ad for a new Goodyear high-performance tire would be appropriate in *Auto Week*. An ad for a new Pillsbury cake mix might appear in *Family Weekly*. An ad for Epsom computer printers might be well placed in *U.S. News and World Report*.

D. Cost of the media

Both total cost of advertising and cost per individual contacted are important criteria to consider when choosing advertising media. The total cost of some media exceeds the budgets of many companies; small businesses, for example, avoid network television because the total cost of advertising on that medium is so high. But the total cost is not the only factor to consider. Larger companies often advertise on television, despite the high total cost, because that medium reaches so many people. A measure of cost and reach, **cost per contact**, is the total cost divided by the number of readers, listeners, or viewers. Many advertisers calculate **cost per thousand**, which is cost per contact times 1,000. For example, for used cars the cost per thousand of the *Los Angeles Times* is very low but it would be very high for direct mail.

14-5. The Advertising Campaign

An **advertising campaign** consists of a coordinated program, including a number of advertisements, that have a common goal or goals and are scheduled to be completed within a specified time.

In practice, an advertising campaign can involve a number of activities. For instance, when Chrysler is introducing a new car, it may issue a press release and have a news conference on one day, introduce radio commercials on another, use television commercials several days later, follow up with newspaper and magazine ads shortly after this, and then continue this effort for several months.

Advertising campaigns can be advantageous to the marketer. All ad efforts within the campaign are focused on the same goals, so they emphasize common buyer benefits and reinforce one another. The advertising efforts are coordinated so that they fit a schedule that has been designed for maximum effectiveness. The various ad activities are treated as part of a system, rather than as a series of disjointed functions.

EXAMPLE 14-10: Merrill Lynch (a national stockbroker) conducted an advertising campaign in late 1986, intended to convince investors to confer with Merrill Lynch financial consultants about the advantages of purchasing municipal bonds through the company, because of a newly passed tax law. Ads appeared in *Nation's Business*, *The Wall Street Journal*, *Business Week*, and on ABC television. Their common theme was, "Some municipals will be stars after tax reform. Will yours?"

14-6. Techniques of Designing Advertisements

There are several techniques available to ensure that an advertisement will have the intended impact on target customers. These include appeals, layout, illustrations, headlines, and text.

A. Appeals

Every advertisement and every campaign should have one or more **appeals**, which are the motives of target consumers to which the ads are directed. Many different appeals are available, including saving money, saving time, impressing others, succeeding in careers, improving appearance or health, and assisting others.

Appeals serve as a central idea to which every element in the advertisement should contribute. Marketers should take great care in the selection of appeals. Even those that are catchy and seem to be capable of attracting attention and interest may not be appropriate to the advertising goals.

EXAMPLE 14-11: Some U.S. Sprint ads carry the appeal of being able to converse with others without being interrupted by annoying and distracting noises.

B. Layout

Layout in an advertisement refers to the way in which the various parts are positioned with regard to one another. Well-designed layouts can be useful in capturing attention and interest and in developing product image.

EXAMPLE 14-12: Walgreens ads feature a crowded layout, which is intended to create the impression of low prices and specials. Tiffany Jewelers ads use few words and considerable white space, however, as a means of creating a status image.

C. Illustrations

Illustrations are drawings, photographs, graphs, paintings, charts, and other visual devices that can be used to gain attention and interest. They can also be used to promote target customer understanding and to help create an image for the product or company.

EXAMPLE 14-13: Campbell Soup Company Le Menu dinner ads show attractive photographs of the dinners on a plate on a table—ready to be eaten. The photos are intended to make the product appear to be irresistibly delicious.

D. Headlines

Headlines are employed to capture attention and interest and to break up long passages of printed material. Effective headlines often stimulate curiosity, as with "What a neat idea" for Wrinkle Free. Others promise benefits, as with Maxwell House instant coffee's "Instant Relaxation."

E. Text

The **text** is the written or spoken portion of the ad that follows the headline—it is the central part of the advertising message. Good text is clear in meaning and easy to comprehend. It does not attempt to present too many ideas, as a complicated message is likely to overwhelm the audience. Text should not be too long, and it should be both believable and interesting.

14-7. Utilizing Advertising Agencies

A. The uses of advertising agencies

Numerous marketers employ **advertising agencies**, specialists in preparing advertisements and advertising campaigns, to carry out their programs. Agencies sometimes design entire campaigns, assisting in developing goals, selecting and making contacts with media, choosing appeals, and designing individual ads. In fact, some agencies assist in developing marketing plans that extend into the areas of product, place, and price, rather than just creating promotion. In addition, agencies commonly perform marketing research services for their clients. The major functions of agencies, however, are to design advertisements and campaigns and to place ads with the media.

B. The cost of using advertising agencies

Many agencies charge commissions. They frequently obtain 15 percent of the amount that an advertising medium bills for the advertising. That is, the agency charges advertisers the full amount due the medium; then it witholds 15 percent when paying the medium.

Some advertisers do not favor commissions. They would rather pay fees for the specific services that they want performed, rather than a commission for a range of services, many of which may not be wanted. Fees are specific amounts for particular jobs, rather than percentages of advertising billings.

C. The benefits of using advertising agencies

Agencies can offer a number of benefits to marketers. Agencies have specialized personnel in various aspects of advertising, such as choosing media, art, and writing, which the advertiser may not employ. Agencies have experience and insight as a result of their past experiences with other accounts. They can bring fresh insight and understanding to a marketer who may be bogged down in traditional and uninspiring methods. The discounts that the media offer agencies are also offered to local, but not to national, advertisers. This provides a strong stimulus to national advertisers to use agencies, since the media costs are the same, regardless of whether or not they use an agency.

14-8. Testing the Effectiveness of Advertising

Marketing executives should always test the effectiveness of their advertising. Testing is useful in making advertising as effective as possible and in demonstrating the value of advertising to upper management.

A. When to test

1. Pretests

Pretests are undertaken *before* a full audience is exposed to the advertising. These tests are useful in predicting if the advertising will be successful, and in revealing aspects that should be changed in order to make it more successful. Sometimes pretests involve comparisons between two or more advertisements; for example, a sample audience of consumers may be asked to indicate which of two commercials is the most attention-getting.

2. Posttests

Posttests are taken *after* a full audience has been exposed to the advertising. If the response is positive, management may decide that the effort should be continued as planned. If the response is negative, the advertising may be changed or discontinued.

B. What to test for

1. *Reach*

Management can measure the reach of a medium by examining data on the number of print copies sold, the number of persons living in a viewing or listening area, or the number of persons tuned into various television and radio stations at various times. Another way of measuring reach is through readership or listenership surveys. Here, interviewers ask consumers if they have read, viewed, or listened to specific advertisements. Some research firms specialize in conducting such tests, employing staffs of skilled interviewers.

2. *Attention*

Attention can be measured by interviewing target customers and then asking them the degree to which they recognize or recall each ad. This can be done as a pretest, in which a sample group of target customers reads, hears, or sees the advertisement and then evaluates it. Or a sample of target customers may be asked for indications of recognition or recall after the ad has been run (a posttest).

3. *Understanding*

Recall tests are a useful method of measuring understanding. It is assumed that target customers will recall what they understand. Another means of measuring understanding is to ask target customers how much they comprehend about a message they recently read, heard, or viewed.

4. *Changing attitudes*

In order to measure attitude change, marketers need gauges of attitudes toward the brand or company both before and after the appearance of an ad. **Attitude scales** are a useful means of measuring attitude changes. A typical scale includes questions such as:

Armstrong Solarian Floors Are

Colorful	_____ _____ _____ _____ _____ _____ _____	Drab
Durable	_____ _____ _____ _____ _____ _____ _____	Not durable
Comfortable	_____ _____ _____ _____ _____ _____ _____	Not comfortable
Natural-looking	_____ _____ _____ _____ _____ _____ _____	Artificial-looking

---

Most measures of attitude and attitude change contain 15 to 20 such scales.

5. *Action*

The last measure of effectiveness is to assess the behavior or actions of the target customers. Some marketers use a very simple method to test action: they look at sales figures before and after the appearance of an ad or campaign. If revenues go up, there is evidence of effectiveness. This method is called a **sales test**. The problem with the sales-test approach is that outside factors, such as the weather, competitor ads and prices, changes in incomes, and labor union strikes, may affect sales. Also, many people will hear or see an ad but may not make a purchase for a long time. These outside factors can be at least partially accounted for by comparing sales-figure changes in cities or areas where the ads appeared with figures in areas where the ads did not appear.

EXAMPLE 14-14: A producer of dishwasher detergent schedules an ad campaign from March to May in Chicago, but does not run the campaign in Detroit. From March to May, sales increase by 20% in Chicago, but remain flat in Detroit. This campaign may be judged a success.

Another measure of action is to assess target customer **intentions to buy**. This involves interviewing those who have been exposed to an ad or campaign and those who have not been exposed (either as a pretest or posttest) and comparing their interview results. Questions such as the following can be asked:

- I'm 99% sure I'll buy it. _____
- I'm 95% sure I'll buy it. _____
- I'm 90% sure I'll buy it. _____
- I'm 75% sure I'll buy it. _____

C. Which tests are most useful?

Marketers must use their own judgment and weigh their own circumstances to determine which of the tests of effectiveness to use. Obviously, the best test or tests to use are those that measure the effectiveness of ads in achieving the advertising goals. For example, if the goal is action, a sales test or intention-to-buy test may be best. Also, the amount of money the marketer has available for research is a factor. Finally, some find that a particular test is beyond their means and settle for a less expensive one.

RAISE YOUR GRADES

Can you explain . . . ?

☑ why many marketers attempt to build secondary rather than primary demand with their advertisements

☑ why common advertising goals are to attain reach, attention, understanding, attitude change, and action on the part of customers

☑ why many retailers advertise extensively in newspapers

☑ why a firm might choose radio as an advertising medium

☑ what is meant by the term "advertising campaign," as it is used by marketers

☑ how marketers decide what appeals to feature in their advertisements

☑ how a firm can decide whether or not to use advertising agencies to assist in its promotion efforts

☑ how marketers can measure attitude changes brought about by their advertisements

SUMMARY

1. Advertising can be used to build primary demand (for a particular product) or secondary demand (for a particular brand of product).
2. Institutional advertising is used to build the image of the company in the minds of target customers or others.
3. Product advertising is used to promote specific company products.
4. Advertising can have the same general and specific goals as other types of promotion.
5. A company may need to change advertising goals over time.
6. The main types of media that advertisers can use are print media (magazines and newspapers), broadcast media (radio and television), and direct mail.
7. When choosing advertising media, marketers should consider advertising goals, media circulation, the advertising message, and the cost of the media.
8. An advertising campaign consists of a coordinated program, including a number of advertisements, that have a common goal or goals and are scheduled to be completed within a specified time.
9. The techniques used to design advertisements are effective appeals, layout, illustration, headlines, and text.
10. Advertising agencies are specialists in preparing advertisements and advertising campaigns.
11. Marketing executives should always test the effectiveness of their advertising, using pretests or posttests.

12. The reach of a medium can be measured by examining viewing or listening data about the medium or by conducting surveys.
13. Attention can be measured by interviewing target customers and then asking them the degree to which they recognize or recall each ad.
14. Understanding can be measured through recall tests.
15. Changing attitudes can be measured by gauging attitudes toward the brand or company both before and after the appearance of an ad.
16. Action can be measured by assessing the behavior of the target customers, either with sales tests or intention-to-buy surveys.
17. Marketers must determine which of the tests of effectiveness to use.

RAPID REVIEW   Answers

Short Answers

1. If Welch Foods, Inc., sponsored ads designed to convince Americans to drink more grape juice, it would be attempting to build _____ demand. [See Section 14-1.]   *primary*

2. When Procter and Gamble sponsors ads to increase sales of Luvs diapers, they are trying to build _____ demand. [See Section 14-1.]   *secondary*

3. If Milton Bradley sponsors ads that attempt to build the image of the company, rather than to sell products, this is called _____ advertising. [See Section 14-1.]   *institutional*

4. When AT & T sponsors ads designed to convince consumers to subscribe to its "Reach out America" reduced-charge telephone service, this is an example of _____ advertising. [See Section 14-1.]   *product*

5. A Purina Cat Chow ad states that the product provides all of the nutrition your cat needs to have a healthier, happier life. This is an example of _____ advertising. [See Section 14-1.]   *indirect action*

6. Changes in overall company objectives could require that a company change its advertising _____. [See Section 14-2.]   *goals*

7. If a small, local barber shop took out an ad in *Mechanics Illustrated*, it would experience considerable _____ circulation. [See Section 14-3.]   *waste*

8. The time between when the *Washington Post* receives an ad from a company and the time it publishes the ad is called the _____ period. [See Section 14-3.]   *closing*

9. _____ could *not* be used by the Drackett Products Company to carry a long and complicated message about Drano drain opener: radio, newspapers, magazines, direct mail. [See Section 14-3.]   *Radio*

10. The major factors that True Value Hardware Stores should consider in deciding whether to advertise in *Country Living* or *House and Garden* magazine are its goals, the media circulation, the message, and the _____. [See Section14-4.]   *cost*

11. The Hershey Food Corporation would most likely *not* allocate all of its advertising to a single newspaper because its _____ is not large enough. [See Section 14-4.]   *circulation*

12. A ladies dress shop probably would *not* advertise in *Gentlemen's Quarterly* magazine because of the incompatibility of its _____. [See Section 14-4.]   *message*

13. In calculating cost per thousand for a television station, the Corning Glass Works managers would divide _____ by the total number of viewers times 1,000. [See Section 14-4.]   *total cost*

14. An advertising campaign for Swanson's Great Starts frozen breakfast sandwiches consists of a number of ads with a common _____. [See Section 14-5.]   *goal*

15. Ads for Sears Roebuck and Company "Discover" credit cards emphasize its convenience and low cost. These are both advertising _____. [See Section 14-6.]

appeals

16. The commissions that advertisers pay to ad agencies are approximately _____ percent. [See Section 14-7.]

15

17. _____ of effectiveness are taken *after* advertisements have been shown to the public. [See Section 14-8.]

Posttests

18. Managers for General Foods can measure the _____ of *Family Circle* magazine by examining data on the number of copies sold. [See Section 14-8.]

reach

19. If Fruit of the Loom managers want to measure the effectiveness of an ad for men's t-shirts as a means of changing attitudes, _____ are useful for this purpose. [See Section 14-8.]

attitude scales

20. A problem with sales tests of advertising effectiveness is that some people may hear or see an ad, but not _____ for a long time. [See Section 14-8.]

purchase

SOLVED PROBLEMS

PROBLEM 14-1   Would you recommend that Gaines Foods, Inc., conduct an ad campaign designed to convince dog owners that a diet of table scraps is a poorly balanced diet for pets?

Answer: You probably should not make this recommendation. Gaines is only one of many producers of dog food, yet it would be paying for an entire advertising campaign to benefit *all* pet-food producers. The company probably does not have a large enough share of the market to justify stimulating primary demand. The benefits of such a program would go to its competitors as well as to Gaines, so the funds would not be applied where they can do the most good; namely, to build demand for Gaines products. [See Section 14-1.]

PROBLEM 14-2   In 1986 the Norfolk Southern Railway conducted an ad campaign which carried the message that this was an aggressive, dynamic, responsible, and alert company that is dedicated to industrial leadership. It is difficult to imagine freight shippers running out and using the railroad after seeing the ad. Was it a waste of money?

Answer: The ad was not a waste of money. It was an institutional advertisement, with the objective of building goodwill for the Norfolk Southern Railway, rather than to generate demand for railroad freight services. Goodwill is useful in influencing government officials, voters, journalists, and others to support rules and regulations which are favorable for Norfolk Southern. It can also be valuable for a number of other purposes, including winning customers, hiring talented employees, and maintaining stock prices. [See Section 14.1.]

PROBLEM 14-3   The General Motors Acceptance Corporation runs ads detailing the benefits of leasing automobiles over buying them. It is doubtful that these ads would induce target customers to make immediate leases. What is GMAC's objective if it is not to build an immediate demand for leases?

Answer: This is an indirect action advertisement. It attempts to establish favorable attitudes toward the leasing offerings of GMAC, on the assumption that these will lead to revenues at some time in the future. The ad is not intended to convince target customers to respond immediately, as many supermarket and car-dealers' promotions are. GMAC managers know that if they are effective in changing attitudes, revenue increases can be expected in the future for leased cars. [See Section 14-1.]

PROBLEM 14-4   A car rental dealer has informed you that the advertising goal of the company is to reach as many consumers as possible. Is this an adequate goal?

Answer: This is not an adequate goal for the car rental dealer. It is much too general. Appropriate goals are more specific. They identify the target customer and indicate the effect that the firm expects to produce through advertising. An example of an adequate goal is "to convince 1,000 business travelers in Pittsburg to rent an automobile from the company during the next fiscal year." [See Section 14-2.]

PROBLEM 14-5 You have just been hired as the advertising manager for a local, independent department store. The president of the firm indicates to you that the store's advertising goals, which were determined and written in 1947, should be studied carefully to guide your efforts. What would your first action be?

Answer: Your first action should be to study and evaluate the department store advertising goals. Since they were constructed in 1947, they are probably due for revision. Department stores have changed substantially since 1947, growing more competitive and more dynamic. Changes in overall company objectives, the economy, marketing strategies of competing department stores, or the desires of target consumers may dictate a change in goals. Many department stores are currently sponsoring direct-action ads, for example, but this practice was not common in 1947 when department store competition was less severe. [See Section 14-2.]

PROBLEM 14-6 Hayworth Industries, Inc., could use the *Popular Mechanics* magazine to advertise its cordless irons. Would you recommend this medium?

Answer: Hayworth Industries, Inc., could select a better medium for its cordless iron advertisements. This product is more likely bought by women than by men. Yet the readership of *Popular Mechanics* is made up mostly of men, so that a considerable portion of the advertising dollar will be wasted. A medium directed more toward women such as *Good Housekeeping, Woman's Day,* or the *Ladies Home Journal* would be a better choice. [See Section 14-3.]

PROBLEM 14-7 An office equipment company is thinking about using magazines to advertise its new line of stylish office furniture. Would you recommend this medium?

Answer: Magazines could be a very good medium for several reasons. Their reproduction quality is very good—important to a company whose product's appearance is part of an appeal to customers' desire for prestige and success. The message can be long and complex, which is often necessary for a new line of office furniture. Many target customers reread magazines and pass them on to others, which can help in providing audience exposure to the new line. Finally, some magazines such as *Business Week* and *Fortune,* have prestige value and can be used to target special segments, such as business managers and owners. [See Section 14-3.]

PROBLEM 14-8 Evaluate the effectiveness of newspapers as an advertising medium for a sandwich meat product.

Answer: This could be a good medium for advertising a sandwich meat product. Newspapers reach almost every home and this type of product must have a broad market. Many members of the family read these publications. Their messages can be longer and more complex than one aired on radio or television. Newspapers can also be useful in reaching particular markets, such as specified large cities. Their closing periods are short. However, a newspaper is not a good medium for reaching the national market in a short time period. The printed copies do not reproduce as well as do magazines, nor are they kept and reread as often as magazines. [See Section 14-3.]

PROBLEM 14-9 Would you recommend radio advertising for a line of stainless flatware?

Answer: Radio probably would not be a good medium for a line of stainless flatware. Radio ad messages last for only a short time and cannot be complex, yet a good ad message for flatware cannot be effective without going into some detail on the composition and nature of the product. Further, radio appeals only to the sense of hearing. It cannot take advantage of visual communication, which is helpful in selling stainless flatware. Photographs, drawings, and even television pictures would be more capable of conveying the kind of image that this company requires. Women's magazines, such as *Good Housekeeping,* would be good media. [See Section 14-3.]

PROBLEM 14-10   If you were the advertising manager for International Games, Inc., would you consider the use of television to promote a new card game?

Answer: Television reaches large numbers of viewers, so it could be a good medium for advertising a new game. By selecting appropriate stations and times of day, the firm may reach a selective target audience. Television appeals to both the senses of sight and sound, so it can create high-impact ads. For example, it can show people having fun while playing the card game. It adds prestige to the sponsor and to the game, which may have appeal to consumers who want to feel that they are playing the "in" game. [See Section 14.3.]

PROBLEM 14-11   Would you recommend that a pharmaceutical company use direct mail in attempting to interest medical doctors in prescribing a new arthritis pain killer?

Answer: Direct mail may be a good choice for the pharmaceutical company. This medium is free from distractions and can be produced at a high quality level that will impress doctors. Research has indicated that many doctors read direct mail pieces and often devote considerable time to them. Another possible medium for this firm would be medical journals. [See Section 14-3.]

PROBLEM 14-12   A bank president who is a friend of the family has informed you that, "Our bank chooses advertising media that have the largest circulation. Nothing else is really of importance in promoting bank services." Do you agree with this means of choosing media?

Answer: The bank president's approach is very simplified. Yet a number of small firms pursue this strategy, perhaps believing in the strategy that "bigger is better." In selecting media, the bank should consider a number of factors in addition to circulation. The advertising goals are very important. If the bank strives to attract customers from particular income groups or social classes, for instance, it should use media that reach these groups. Other important elements for the bank to consider are the nature of the message and the cost of the media. [See Section 14-4.]

PROBLEM 14-13   A lumber yard owner and manager who is a friend of yours uses advertising extensively. Yet he does not believe in using campaigns. Rather, each individual advertisement is treated as an independent activity. Should he consider the use of campaigns?

Answer: The use of campaigns is likely to improve the promotion efforts of the lumber yard. Campaigns can coordinate the individual advertisements of this firm, so that they contribute to the company goals. Each ad can be scheduled so that it fits in with others and is presented at the most opportune time. In a campaign the various advertising activities are treated as part of a system, rather than as a series of disjointed functions. If, however, the lumber yard advertises only infrequently or if its individual advertisements deal with entirely different products, management may decide that campaigns really are not justified. [See Section 14-5.]

PROBLEM 14-14   You have secured a part-time position at a local variety store and have been placed in charge of creating advertisements. The store manager has asked you to prepare an advertisement for a new line of women's coats that the store is introducing. How would you begin this task?

Answer: The first step would be to create one or more appeals for the new line's advertisement. These appeals, which are the motives of target consumers to which the ad will be directed, will serve as a central idea to which every element in the advertisement should contribute. Possible appeals are that the coats are very stylish, or comfortable, or low in price; or the coats may be advertised as specifically designed for particular groups, such as women college students. [See Section 14-6.]

PROBLEM 14-15   Continuing with your advertising job (as explained in Problem 14-14 above), what rules would you follow in writing the text of the advertising?

Answer: The text should be clear in meaning and easy to understand. This means that it should be written in everyday language and in a logical manner. It should not attempt to present too many ideas, nor have an excessive number of appeals (many coat ads have only one appeal). It should not be so long that it will discourage reader interest. Finally, it should be believable and interesting; for example, it might describe a concrete benefit that coat purchasers will enjoy. [See Section 14-6.]

PROBLEM 14-16   The owner of a new t-shirt shop that is located in a large suburban mall is thinking about using advertising agencies; however, she is not exactly sure what these companies do for their clients. What would you tell her about the functions that are performed by agencies?

Answer: You could inform the shop owner that advertising agencies are specialists in preparing advertisements and advertising campaigns. They prepare plans for campaigns, assist in developing goals, select and make contacts with media, choose appeals, and design individual ads. Some assist in formulating overall marketing plans and conduct marketing research. The t-shirt shop, unless it is much larger than most, is probably not large enough to afford the services of an agency, unless the agency itself is a one- or two-person shop that specializes in serving small clients. [See Section 14-7.]

PROBLEM 14-17   Why might a large company prefer to pay fees rather than commissions to its advertising agency?

Answer: A company may not want a wide range of services provided by the agency. Rather, it may want to pay fees only for the specific services it wants performed. The firm may prefer to carry out many activities, such as developing promotion objectives and marketing research, for itself. This is likely for a large firm that probably has a well-developed advertising department. [See Section 14-7.]

PROBLEM 14-18   A knitwear company has developed a new long-lasting men's sock and is in the process of producing an ad campaign for the new offering. Why might it use pretests for the ads?

Answer: Pretests will be useful to the knitwear company in predicting if the campaign will be successful and in revealing aspects that should be changed in order to make it more successful. The researchers can try out several versions of each men's sock advertisement, discover the strengths and weaknesses of each one, and choose the one that is most effective. This process takes much of the risk of failure away from the company and allows management to focus its attention on other areas of the new product introduction that are more risky. [See Section 14-8.]

PROBLEM 14-19   A baby food company has developed an advertisement that is designed to appeal to mothers. It points out that the baby food is very tasty and contains natural ingredients. How might the company assess consumer understanding of the ad?

Answer: The baby food company might decide to use recall tests, which are based on the assumption that mothers will recall what they understand. A sample of these consumers could be asked to read the advertisement or view it on television, and later be quizzed on how much they remember. Another means of measuring understanding would be to ask a sample of mothers how much they comprehended about baby food advertisements they have recently read, heard, or viewed. If the comprehension for the new baby food ad is high, compared to other brands, it may be judged effective. [See Section 14-8.]

PROBLEM 14-20   A friend of yours who owns a bookstore recently ran an ad in the campus newspaper. Sales rose 10 percent for the week after the ad, compared to the previous week. Does this prove that the ad was effective?

Answer: The sales increase does not prove that the ad was effective. Outside factors, such as the weather, competitor ads and prices, changes in incomes, the closing of a competing bookstore, cancellation of a big event such as a rock concert, even sheer chance, may account for the bookstore's revenue increase. Also, a number of people may have read the advertisement but may not make a purchase for a long time. The effect of the promotion on them will not be registered by the sales increase. Further, other elements of the bookstore's marketing strategy—those in addition to the campus newspaper promotion—may have contributed to the rise in sales. These include changes in the bookstore's displays, the addition of popular new books to inventory, or price changes. [See Section 14-8.]

15 PERSONAL SELLING ACTIVITIES

THIS CHAPTER IS ABOUT

☑ **The Importance of Personal Selling**
☑ **The Steps Involved in Personal Selling**
☑ **Planning for Future Sales Representative Needs**
☑ **Recruiting, Selecting, and Training Sales Representatives**
☑ **Motivating Sales Representatives**
☑ **Compensating Sales Representatives**
☑ **Controlling Sales Performance**

15-1. The Importance of Personal Selling

You have probably had contact with a large number of **sales representatives**—those who are responsible for *personal selling*.

- **Personal selling** is a means of promotion that involves interpersonal communication between two or more people.

Sales representatives are able to tailor their activities to the unique wants of particular **prospects** (i.e., potential customers). Further, they can modify their messages as they receive feedback from prospects.

EXAMPLE 15-1: If a Procter and Gamble sales representative is unable to interest a grocery store buyer in canned Folgers coffee, the rep may still be able to sell the retailer Folgers in brick packs (airtight foil and plastic packages). If the buyer is unimpressed by the fact that brick packs cost less than cans, the buyer may be swayed by their size, which takes up less shelf space than cans.

- An effective sales representative can persuade prospects that they will achieve desired goals by purchasing particular goods or services.

Persuasion is an important element of personal selling. The ability to convince others to change their thoughts and actions is crucial to making a sale.

EXAMPLE 15-2: A sales representative for the Hearst Corporation may be able to persuade members of Remington Arms to buy a full page ad in *Sports Afield* if the managers are convinced that it will increase sales of their 12-gauge shotguns.

- Sales representatives can adjust their messages to particular prospects, modify them according to feedback, answer objections, ask for an order, and try again if turned down.

Because sales representatives can tailor their appeals to specific prospects and specific situations, no other form of promotion has such a high success rate. Thus, personal selling is the major source of revenues for many companies, including IBM, Lockheed, General Dynamics, and American Hospital Supply.

• Sales representatives can act as consultants and problem solvers for their clients and prospects.

Sales representatives may offer advice on inventory, storage procedures, pricing, advertising, and many other functions. They first attempt to discover the needs of prospects, then they try to satisfy these needs. In short, they serve the customer.

EXAMPLE 15-3: A GTE Sprint sales representative may be able to save a prospect company which makes many telephone calls thousands of dollars per year by convincing the prospect to use Sprint's WATS long distance telephone system.

• Sales representatives can be either *order getters, order takers*, or *missionary reps*.

(1) **Order getters.** The job of order getters is to win new customers and get old customers to buy more. This means that they must be very persuasive and highly motivated.

(2) **Order takers.** Order takers essentially serve existing customers. They call on these parties, with whom they are often very well-acquainted, and take orders on a routine basis.

(3) **Missionary sales representatives.** Missionary sales representatives do not actually take orders. It is their responsibility to call on potential customers and assist them with such things as display, advertising, and pricing. They are used to build goodwill with customers.

15-2. The Steps Involved in Personal Selling

The major steps in personal selling are prospecting, the preapproach, the approach, the presentation, answering objections, closing, and serving customers after the sale. These steps are shown in Figure 15-1.

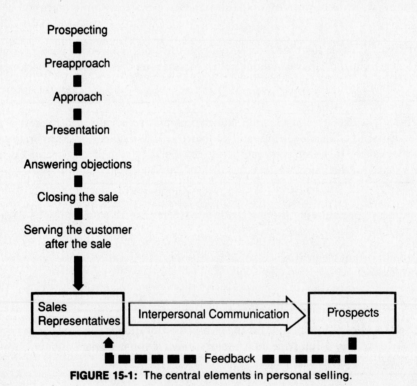

FIGURE 15-1: The central elements in personal selling.

A. Prospecting

Prospecting consists of developing a list of potential customers who have the ability and the need to purchase company offerings. There is no point in calling on those who cannot afford to make a purchase. Likewise, it is a waste of time to attempt to sell to someone who has no need for the item.

Past customers are usually good prospects themselves, and often serve as sources for new prospects. Sometimes they are willing to refer sales representatives to friends and/or business acquaintances. Sales reps may also rely on advertisements to draw inquiries from potential customers. Frequently, however, representatives can locate good prospects through simple observation.

EXAMPLE 15-4: A White Truck Company representative notices that an independent trucker has a truck that is often sidelined for repairs. The rep may decide that this trucker would be a good prospect for a new truck, especially if the truck came with an outstanding warranty.

B. The preapproach

In the **preapproach**, sales representatives gather information about the characteristics and needs of the prospects upon whom they'll call. For examples, reps who sell industrial goods and reps who sell consumer goods to intermediaries must collect information on a prospect's business needs—and should have some prior knowledge of a buyer's personal characteristics. If the preapproach is done well, a good sales representative will be able to act as a problem solver and consultant for a prospect.

EXAMPLE 15-5: A Xerox sales representative makes a thorough analysis of the copying needs of prospective customers before attempting to sell them a Xerox unit. The analysis indicates what is copied, how much, and the quality of reproduction that the prospect desires. After completing the analysis, the representative is in a position to recommend a particular Xerox product that will fit the needs of a particular customer.

C. The approach

The **approach** consists of the first 60 seconds or so of a presentation and sets the stage for the rest of the presentation. It is very important to make a good first impression, as first impressions tend to be permanent and will influence the success of the prospective business relationship. In the approach, it may be necessary to be diplomatic with a *gatekeeper*, such as a secretary, in order to gain permission to see the prospect. It is also wise to get an appointment with a prospect ahead of time.

D. The presentation

In the **presentation** a sales representative attempts to convince the prospect to purchase a good or service. Many sales representatives follow the **AIDA formula** in making the presentation: this stands for getting *Attention, Interest, Desire*, and *Action*. The first two, attention and interest, can often be captured by promising a benefit or by arousing curiosity. Desire may be stimulated by showing how company offerings can satisfy a need. Action can be encouraged by urging that the prospect take specific steps to acquire the product.

A sales representative should use information gathered in prospecting and the preapproach in order to identify the needs of prospects. Another source of information is *feedback*—listening to and observing the prospect during the presentation.

E. Answering objections

From time to time prospects will raise *objections* to what the representative has said. Objections are useful indicators of what the prospect is thinking. When objections arise, the representative should listen carefully, and then respond by clarifying the objections, demonstrating that they are not true, or even by turning an objection into a selling point.

EXAMPLE 15-6: Suppose a prospect of a Minnesota Woolen Mills representative states, "That color is not in fashion this year." The representative may reply, "That's true, but if you check the fashion lines for fall, you'll see it has made a comeback and is expected to be the most popular color of the season."

F. Closing

In **closing**, the sales representative asks for the order. If the earlier stages have been handled well, the close may come about very easily. Specific useful closing techniques include

- summarizing the benefits already covered;
- assuming that the prospect will buy and asking, "Which model do you want?";
- comparing the product (favorably) to those of competitors;
- pointing out that a purchase should be made immediately or the prospect will lose an opportunity.

EXAMPLE 15-7: After summarizing the benefits of leasing a car, a new car dealer's sales representative may point out to an executive client that a lease should be made right away before the lease rate increases.

G. Serving customers after the sale

Sales representatives should not take an order and then forget about the customer. Ignoring the customer after a sale can result in customer dissatisfaction and the rep's inability to sell again to that customer in the future, as well as bad word-of-mouth publicity for the rep and the company. Some sales reps, such as computer sales reps, are very involved in post-closing activities: they help to install the product and assist in training customer employees to use the product. Other sales reps may not be so actively involved, but they should still pay attention to customers after a sale. Sales representatives should call back on customers after a sale to make sure that problems have not arisen and that customer needs are being met. This practice will help ensure good long-term relationships. It may also help reinforce buyers' attitudes that a good purchase has been made.

EXAMPLE 15-8: A Century-21 real estate sales representative makes it a point to call back on clients who have purchased a home a few days after the closing. The rep congratulates the new owners on making a good purchase, answers any questions they may have about it, and generally attempts to be helpful. This rep is one of the top sellers for the company.

15-3. Planning for Future Sales Representative Needs

Sales managers are those individuals who direct and guide the sales force. One of their principal duties is to plan for future sales representative needs; that is, they must decide how many and what kind of sales representatives to hire. To do this, they have to answer some questions.

(1) *How many?* Sales forecasts are useful in planning for sales force needs. If sales are expected to rise substantially, management is likely to hire new personnel. Also, changes in company marketing strategy may signal the need for new hires. For example, in 1986, the Brunswick Corporation decided to engage in more aggressive selling of its door control systems for the transportation industry. This required increasing its sales force by over 10 percent. Finally, Sales managers need to plan for replacements. Some representatives may retire, resign, be promoted, or be fired. To the extent possible, these should be anticipated and planned for.

(2) *What kind?* In deciding what kinds of people to hire, management should carefully compile and study **job descriptions**, which highlight the major duties and responsibilities of the selling positions. Also, much can be learned by studying the characteristics of current top performers and attempting to hire new people with these characteristics.

EXAMPLE 15-9: A chemical company that sells herbicides and pesticides to farmers has discovered that its better sales representatives have college degrees and were raised on a farm. The company seeks such individuals in its hiring programs.

15-4. Recruiting, Selecting, and Training Sales Representatives

A. Recruiting

Recruiting is the process of promoting job openings to possible applicants. A company can advertise job openings in newspapers and magazines, conduct interviews on college campuses, contact other companies or other departments within the company, use employment agencies, or screen those who come to the company looking for jobs. The best procedure is that which will reach the kinds of applicants wanted. Recruiters must be effective in getting individuals interested in working for a particular company. It cannot be assumed that all of the persons management wants to hire are interested in the company.

EXAMPLE 15-10: Maytag recruiters visit college campuses in seeking prospects for selling jobs. Much of their interviewing time with students is devoted to "selling" the company to those students.

B. Selecting

Selecting involves deciding which of the job applicants to hire. Sales managers study application forms, recommendations, and test results, and they conduct personal interviews for this purpose. Personal interviews are especially important, as they can reveal how well applicants work with others and the extent to which they are effective communicators.

EXAMPLE 15-11: The Halliburton (oil field supplier) company does not extend a job offer to applicants until they have been exposed to three interview sessions. The interviewers look for evidence of maturity, ability to communicate, listening ability, intelligence, personality, and forcefulness.

C. Training

Training is important for both new and existing sales representatives. New hires are taught such things as how to sell, how to serve prospects, and facts about the company, its products, and its competitors. Existing representatives need training in new methods of selling, changes in company goals and policies, and new products. Some training programs for existing representatives are designed mainly to motivate and inspire sales performance.

Training programs may employ several techniques, such as lectures, role playing, or on-the-job training. *Lectures* can be used to provide basic information about the company, its products, and the industry. Many firms use *role playing*, in which trainees develop selling skills by practicing on others who act as prospects. Discussion groups, meetings, and study of written materials at home can also be useful. *On-the-job training* is often employed; in this case, new hires literally learn selling by doing it, often under the observation of a senior sales representative. Some large organizations employ specialized trainers who have considerable expertise in training. Smaller companies usually have experienced sales people and sales managers do the training.

EXAMPLE 15-12: The J. Silver Company, a plumbing and heating wholesaler, uses on-the-job training for new sales representatives. After receiving basic instruction on company products, policies, and selling techniques, new recruits call on prospects with a senior representative. When the seniors feel that newcomers are ready to sell alone, they allow the new reps to do so.

15-5. Motivating Sales Representatives

• **Motivation** consists of developing the incentive or drive that leads sales representatives to perform adequately and to improve their performance.

There are several important means of motivation. One is through the *compensation system*, in which effective performance results in higher pay and more or better fringe benefits. Nonfinancial techniques can be of value as well. Representatives may be given more status, privileges, or responsibility as a reward for good performance. Finally, when sales representatives are informed that their performance is of substantial importance to the firm, they may be motivated to high performance. Like other employees, representatives like to have feedback from management as to exactly what is expected of them and how well they are performing. The provision of this kind of information can be a very useful motivating factor.

EXAMPLE 15-13: General Motors dealers' sales representatives are honored by their dealerships through various awards, including "salesperson of the week" and "salesperson of the year." The awards are based on how many automobiles are sold and overall dollar sales. Individual representatives consider the awards to be very prestigious and compete aggressively for them.

Of course, not all representatives have the same needs and desires. What motivates one may have little impact on another. Some seek security; others want high financial rewards, status, or achievement. Sales managers should be careful listeners and observers in order to learn what the specific needs and desires of each representative are. Informed managers are in a position to motivate others through the best means. If a manager can find ways that representatives can satisfy their own needs and those of the company through the same actions, the result can be a highly motivated sales force.

15-6. Compensating Sales Representatives

One of the more useful means of directing and motivating sales representatives is through **financial compensation**—the money earnings reps receive. Sales managers are responsible for determining how much to pay the sales force and what compensation method to employ.

A. Amount of compensation

The job description, which sets forth the duties and responsibilities of salespersons, is useful in determining the amount of compensation. If it calls for substantial skills, compensation may have to be high. If the duties are very routine and commonplace, lower compensation may be permitted. The pay that representatives receive should be high enough, in comparison to that at other companies, to attract effective sales representatives and to allow them a comfortable standard of living. It should be reasonably related to the compensation of others in the company.

EXAMPLE 15-14: IBM's job descriptions require that their new hires have potential, in terms of sales ability, human relations, and financial and technical ability. The firm hires only very highly qualified applicants. Its pay scale is set to attract such individuals, who can earn upwards of $50,000 annually after several years with the company.

B. Compensation methods

There are several compensation methods for sales representatives.

(1) *Straight salary.* Some firms pay representatives a *straight salary*, i.e., a fixed amount per year. This method provides security to employees and allows management to assign nonselling duties to the sales force. (Reps are sometimes reluctant to perform non-sales-related functions if they are paid on commissions.) Straight salary is particularly advantageous if sales fluctuate considerably so that a commission on sales results in widely varying income.

(2) *Straight commission.* Other companies pay *straight commissions*, usually a percentage of sales or gross margin generated by the representative. This method furnishes considerable incentive for the rep to produce. Many sales representatives prefer this method because their earnings are limited only by their abilities and motivation.

(3) *Salary plus commission.* The most popular compensation method is salary plus commission. Sales representatives receive a base salary, which serves as a cushion for lean periods. On top of this they receive a commission. This plan can furnish the advantages of both straight salary and straight commission with few of the disadvantages.

EXAMPLE 15-15: Sales representatives for the Eaton Manufacturing Company receive a salary for their first year with the firm. After this period, they are allowed to continue on salary or switch to salary plus commission. Over 80% opt for salary plus commission, as they can always earn more with commission than through a straight salary.

(4) *Draw.* Some representatives who receive commissions also have a *draw*. A draw is a loan against future commissions that reps can receive when their sales are not high enough to produce a specified level of commissions.

EXAMPLE 15-16: A sales representative earns a 10% commission on sales. She has a draw of $3,000 per month. If she sells $20,000 worth of merchandise in a month, her commission would be $2,000, so she can draw $1,000. If her sales are $30,000 or more, the commission is at least $3,000 and she cannot draw funds.

C. Expense accounts

Expense accounts are payments or reimbursements made to cover the work-related expenses of members of the sales force, such as food, lodging, entertainment, travel, and laundry. An expense account may be either *per diem*, a fixed amount per day, or *itemized*, with specific limits for each expense item, such as $5 for breakfast and $10 for lunch.

15-7. Controlling Sales Performance

In controlling sales performance, sales managers set up standards of desirable performance, compare actual performance with the standards, and take remedial action when necessary. Many standards of performance are specified as **quotas** or targets. Sales quotas, for instance, are amounts against which actual sales are compared. Other standards can be set in terms of gross margin, number of sales calls made, or total number of calls resulting in a sale.

Managers can compare sales representatives with one another, to their own past performances, or to quotas. When performance falls short of the standards, management is advised that a problem exists and further fact-finding is in order. The fact-finding may reveal that the representative in question needs further supervision, training, motivation; or it may result in dismissal in extreme cases.

RAISE YOUR GRADES

Can you explain . . . ?

☑ why numerous companies use sales representatives to sell their products and services, rather than relying only on advertising

☑ how sales representatives might serve as consultants for their customers

☑ how sales representatives might obtain a list of prospects that are good potential customers

☑ why marketers should plan for future sales representative needs

☑ where marketers might be able to find good recruits for selling positions

☑ why many companies provide training for experienced as well as new sales representatives

☑ how sales managers can determine how much to pay their sales representatives

☑ how sales managers can control the performance of their sales forces

SUMMARY

1. Personal selling is a means of promotion that involves interpersonal communication between two or more people.
2. Effective sales representatives can persuade prospects that they will achieve desired goals by purchasing particular goods or services.
3. Sales representatives can adjust their messages to particular prospects, modify them according to feedback, answer objections, ask for an order, and try again if turned down.
4. Sales representatives can act as consultants and problem solvers for their clients and prospects.
5. Sales representatives can be either order getters, order takers, or missionary reps.
6. There are seven steps in personal selling:

   - prospecting, which involves developing a list of prospects who have the ability and the need to purchase company offerings;
   - preapproach, which involves gathering information about the characteristics and needs of the prospects that will be called upon;
   - approach, which consists of the first 60 seconds or so in the presentation and sets the stage for the remainder of the presentation;
   - presentation, in which the representative attempts to convince the prospect to purchase a good or service;
   - answering objections made by prospects;
   - closing, when the sales representative asks for the order;
   - serving customers after the sale.

7. Sales managers can anticipate and plan for future sales representative needs based on changes in sales levels, changes in marketing strategies, retirements, resignations, promotions, or dismissals.
8. Sales managers can decide what kinds of people to hire by establishing job descriptions and studying the characteristics of their top performers.
9. Recruiting refers to promoting job openings to possible applicants drawn from a number of sources, such as advertisements, campus interviews, other companies, etc.
10. Selecting involves deciding which of the job applicants to hire, based on application forms, recommendations, test results, or personal interviews.
11. Training is an important function for both new and existing sales representatives. They are taught such things as how to sell, how to serve prospects, and facts about the company, its products, and its competitors.
12. Training programs may employ several techniques, such as lectures, role playing, or on-the-job training.
13. Motivation consists of developing the incentive or drive that leads sales representatives to perform adequately and to improve their performance.
14. Sales managers should attempt to learn what the specific needs and desires of each representative are in order to develop effective methods of motivation, both financial and nonfinancial.
15. Compensation decisions require determining how much to pay sales representatives and the method of compensation.
16. The job description is useful in determining the amount of compensation.
17. There are several methods of compensation that sales managers can choose from, including straight salary, straight commission, salary plus commission, or a draw against commission.
18. Expense accounts are payments made to cover work-related expenses of the sales force.
19. Sales performance is controlled by setting up standards, comparing actual performance with the standards, and taking remedial action when necessary.

RAPID REVIEW   Answers

Multiple Choice

1. When employees practice personal selling, they are engaged in (**a**) impersonal communication, (**b**) interpersonal communication, (**c**) mass communications, (**d**) public relations. [See Section 15-1.]

2. When sales representatives try to convince others to change their thoughts and actions, they are attempting (**a**) bribery, (**b**) good public relations, (**c**) persuasion, (**d**) the approach. [See Section 15-1.]

c

3. Sales representative for the Crown Cork and Seal Company direct their communictions to (**a**) suppliers, (**b**) channels, (**c**) producers, (**d**) prospects. [See Section 15-1.]

d

4. Sales representatives can modify their messages when they receive (**a**) feedback, (**b**) noise, (**c**) marketing research, (**d**) publicity. [See Section 15-1.]

a

5. Sales representatives develop a list of possible clients who have the ability and the need to purchase company products when they are (**a**) approaching, (**b**) prospecting, (**c**) presenting, (**d**) selling. [See Section 15-2.]

b

6. The AIDA formula does *not* include (**a**) attention, (**b**) action, (**c**) intentions, (**d**) desire. [See Section 15-2.]

c

7. Asking for an order is part of (**a**) the closing, (**b**) the presentation, (**c**) answering objections, (**d**) serving customers. [See Section 15-2.]

a

8. When a machine company's sales representatives serve customers after a sale, they would *not* be expected to (**a**) ensure that problems have not arisen, (**b**) assist in installing the machines, (**c**) help train customer employees in machine use, (**d**) engage in prospecting. [See Section 15-2.]

d

9. _____ forecasts should be considered when planning for future sales representative needs. (**a**) Cost, (**b**) Sales, (**c**) Inventory, (**d**) Time deposits. [See Section 15-3.]

b

10. Sales representative replacements are necessary for all of the following *except* (**a**) resignations, (**b**) retirements, (**c**) promotions, (**d**) new hires. [See Section 15-3.]

d

11. Promoting job openings to possible applicants for sales positions is called (**a**) recruiting, (**b**) prospecting, (**c**) advertising, (**d**) interviewing. [See Section 15-4.]

a

12. In selecting new sales representatives, companies are likely to rely heavily on (**a**) physical examinations, (**b**) psychological tests, (**c**) personal interviews, (**d**) character references. [See Section 15-4.]

c

13. A training program for new and inexperienced sales representatives would probably *not* include (**a**) how to sell, (**b**) how to serve prospects (**c**) facts about the company, (**d**) company stock yields. [See Section 15-4.]

d

14. If some sales trainees practice on others who act as prospects to develop selling skills, this is called (**a**) on-the-job training, (**b**) role playing, (**c**) trial and error, (**d**) study groups. [See Section 15-4.]

b

15. An important means of motivating sales representatives is the (**a**) compensation system, (**b**) forecasting system, (**c**) pricing system, (**d**) sales promotion system. [See Section 15-5.]

a

16. Sales managers can improve their ability to motivate sales representatives through (**a**) well designed advertisements, (**b**) sales promotions, (**c**) listening techniques, (**d**) customer relations programs. [See Section 15-5.]

c

17. The document which is of value to sales managers in determining how much to pay sales representatives is the (**a**) job application, (**b**) resume, (**c**) warehouse receipt, (**d**) job description. [See Section 15-6.]

d

18. The compensation plan that provides the most incentive for sales representatives is the (**a**) straight salary, (**b**) straight commission, (**c**) expense account, (**d**) draw. [See Section 15-6.]

b

19. Standards of desirable performance are used by sales managers to help control (**a**) sales representatives, (**b**) sales quotas, (**c**) sales performance, (**d**) sales. [See Section 15-7.]

c

20. Targets to help control sales performance can include all of the following *except* (**a**) quotas, (**b**) number of calls made, (**c**) motivation training, (**d**) past performance. [See Section 15-7.]

c

SOLVED PROBLEMS

PROBLEM 15-1 A fellow student has indicated to you that personal selling is an activity that involves one person—the sales representative. How would you react to this statement?

Answer: The student's answer is incomplete. Personal selling involves interpersonal communication between two or more parties—the sales representative and one or more prospects. It is a two-way form of communication. Thinking about personal selling as one-way communication is wrong because it ignores the important role of the representative in listening to prospects, observing their actions, and reacting to these, in order to adjust the message to the individual prospect. The best salespeople work with prospects as joint problem solvers, rather than just as speakers. [See Section 15-1.]

PROBLEM 15-2 How can a film company's sales representative use persuasion as a means of successful selling?

Answer: The film company's sales representative can use persuasion to convince prospects to change their thoughts and actions regarding company products. In this case, the representative attempts to persuade prospects that they can achieve desired goals by purchasing particular products. For example, this salesperson might be able to induce a buyer for a drug store chain to stock the company's film because it has a higher margin or a more rapid turnover than competing brands and will contribute more to profits. Or the buyer might be convinced that the brand will increase store traffic. [See Section 15-1.]

PROBLEM 15-3 A freight company manager has come to you for advice. To stimulate company sales, he can either hire an additional sales representative or conduct more advertising. What are some of the arguments that favor adding a sales representative?

Answer: One argument that you could raise is that personal selling is probably the major source of revenue for the freight company. Sales representatives can tailor their message to particular prospects, modify them according to feedback, answer objections, ask for an order and, if turned down, communicate further to recoup and obtain the order. Sales representatives can act as consultants and problem solvers for the freight company prospects. After orders are obtained, the reps can take steps to ensure that customers are satisfied with the service; for example, they can respond to questions or arrange for credit. Many freight customers will patronize a particular company only after conducting extensive negotiations with a salesperson. [See Section 15-1.]

PROBLEM 15-4 Why should a computer sales representative who calls on retail stores engage in prospecting?

Answer: A computer sales representative should use prospecting to eliminate calls on retail stores or industrial buyers who cannot make a purchase because they do not have the ability or the need to purchase the company's hardware or software. This saves valuable time and permits the representative to concentrate efforts on good prospects. In addition, prospecting provides an opportunity to gather useful information on the computer needs of the prospect. [See Section 15-2.]

PROBLEM 15-5 Assume that you are a sales representative for a truck company. Your customers are firms that maintain truck fleets. Would you bother to conduct preapproaches?

Answer: You are well advised to conduct preapproaches. In this case, you would gather information about the characteristics and needs of fleet buyers. This information might include the sizes of the fleet companies, the volume of their shipments, and the size of individual shipments. Or you might want to know if they provide pickup and delivery service. Insights on these and related variables would assist you in acting as a problem solver and consultant for potential purchasers of your company's trucks. [See Section 15-2.]

PROBLEM 15-6 How can a sales manager be sure that a company's sales representatives obtain information to identify prospect needs that can be used as input into the presentation?

Answer: Sales representative should use information gathered in prospecting and in the preapproach in order to identify client needs. Salespersons should be required by the company to devote considerable attention to these two processes, so they can take advantage of the resulting large amounts of useful information on prospect needs. Another source of information reps can rely on is listening to and observing the prospect during the presentation. The company should stress this in its training programs for new recruits and its continuing training for veteran members of the sales force. [See Section 15-2.]

PROBLEM 15-7 A major appliance sales representative has asked you how to go about closing a sale. What would you advise?

Answer: The sales representative might summarize the benefits of the appliances that have been covered in the presentation. These benefits might include high performance, minimum energy usage, reasonable price, and extensive warranties. Or the representative could assume that the prospect will buy and ask "what model, color, grade, (or some other variation) do you want?" Comparing the products favorably against those of a competitor and then asking for a sale is another effective closing technique. Finally the representative could point out that an order should be made in the near future, or the prospect will lose an opportunity, such as a bargain price. [See Section 15-2.]

PROBLEM 15-8 How can a computer sales representative serve customers after the sale?

Answer: The computer sales representative may help to install the product and to show the buyer how to use it for word processing, database management, or other purposes. Also, he or she can call back on customers after a sale to make sure that problems have not arisen and that customer needs are being met. Problems in the use of hardware and software, in servicing the computers, in billing, and in fulfilling the requirements for warranties, should be handled before customer dissatisfaction sets in. [See Section 15-2.]

PROBLEM 15-9 You are the new sales manager for a food wholesaler and have to hire several new representatives. How would you determine the desired characteristics of the new hires?

Answer: You should begin by carefully studying job descriptions for the food wholesaler's positions. These job descriptions should highlight the major duties and responsibilities of members of the sales force. The nature of these duties and responsibilities determines what kinds of new people to hire. If, for example, sales representatives are required to develop many new accounts, then recruits with good persuasion abilities should be hired. Also, much can be learned by studying the characteristics of current top performers and attempting to hire people with these characteristics. If the more productive salespersons have business administration degrees, for example, this would suggest hiring others with such degrees. [See Section 15-4.]

PROBLEM 15-10 You are a sales recruiter for a meat processing company. Where might you recruit new sales representatives?

Answer: There are a number of possibilities that you could use. One is advertising in newspapers and trade magazines. These could be useful in getting members of competing meat processing company sales forces to inquire into the jobs. New recruits could also be sought through interviews on college campuses. These can produce large numbers of well-prepared job applicants. You could rely on contacts with other companies or other departments within your own company. In addition, you might use employment agencies who have proven themselves in the past. Finally, you could consider those who approached the company looking for jobs who have shown considerable initiative and interest in the firm. [See Section 15-4.]

PROBLEM 15-11 How might Digital Equipment Corporation sales managers go about selecting individuals to extend job offers to, out of their list of recruits?

Answer: Digital sales managers can study application blanks to weed out obviously unqualified recruits. They can look at recommendations from previous employers to identify major strengths and weaknesses of the applicants. Tests can be administered to discover aptitudes and personality characteristics that are important in selling Digital products. Also, the sales managers can rely on personal interviews. These are especially useful, as they help reveal how well applicants work with people and communicate with others. [See Section 15-4.]

PROBLEM 15-12 What training methods should a food processing company consider for new representatives?

Answer: The company could use lectures to provide basic information on the company and the food processing industry. Role playing, in which trainees practice on others who act as prospects, can be used to develop selling skills. Also, trainees can be provided with written materials about the company, its policies, and its products, for study at home. Another possibility is on-the-job training, in which new hires literally learn selling by doing it, often under the observation of a senior sales representative. This kind of training prepares new representatives for the intense competition that they will face in this industry. [See Section 15-4.]

PROBLEM 15-13 A sales manager wants to motivate representatives to better performance. How might this be done?

Answer: One possibility is through a compensation system in which sales representatives are paid more for better work. Commissions, for example, furnish more financial rewards to members of the sales force who are productive than to nonperformers. Or, if the firm uses salaries, it can award raises or promotions to the most productive employees. Also, bonuses can be presented to those whose accomplishments were substantial. The company should find nonfinancial incentives to be of value as well. The sales manager should make an effort to be observant and learn the needs of individual members of the sales force. This makes it possible to furnish the kind of need satisfaction that each one desires. [See Section 15-5.]

PROBLEM 15-14 How can a sales manager for a restaurant supply wholesaler determine how much to pay the members of the sales force?

Answer: The sales manager should study job descriptions for the company's sales representatives, which set forth the duties and responsibilities of salespersons. If this document calls for substantial skills, education, or experience, compensation may have to be reasonably high. If the duties are commonplace, lower compensation may be permitted. The pay that representatives receive should be high enough to attract effective sales representatives and to allow them a comfortable standard of living. It should be reasonably related to the compensation of others in the company and in the industry. The restaurant supply industry generally offers high compensation levels compared to many other industries. [See Section 15-6.]

PROBLEM 15-15 An office supply company pays its representatives by straight salary. What are the advantages of this to the sales representatives?

Answer: A straight salary provides security to the employees, who otherwise would have to worry about earning commissions when customers are not buying office supplies. This system also allows salespersons to do nonselling activities without losing income. Since sales fluctuate considerably in this industry, a straight salary is advantageous. It is useful in attracting new employees, who may seek stability in earnings, and may not be convinced of the advantages of commission plans. At a later point in their careers, the representatives may want commissions, however, because this may allow them to earn more. [See Section 15-6.]

PROBLEM 15-16 A small appliance wholesaler pays a straight salary to the members of the sales force. Management is considering converting to a straight commission system. What are the arguments for such a conversion?

Answer: A straight commission would furnish considerable incentive for the wholesaler's sales force to produce. This may be appropriate in a very competitive industry, such as small appliances. Many of the sales representatives who are capable of selling in volume will like this method because their earnings are limited only by their abilities and motivation. Less productive employees may not like the straight commission. The wholesaler probably should allow new members of the sales force a salary or some other guarantee for a limited time period such as a year. When they are experienced, they can be shifted to commissions. [See Section 15-6.]

PROBLEM 15-17 An office supply wholesaler now provides a draw of $5,000 per month for each sales representative. The firm pays a 10% commission on sales. If a sales representative's sales are $40,000 in a month, how much can she draw?

Answer: The commission is 10% of $40,000, or $4,000. Since the draw is $5,000, she can draw $1,000 during this month. The office supply wholesaler may require that this be paid back, perhaps at the end of the year, or it may be a guaranteed draw, which need not be paid back by the representative. [See Section 15-6.]

PROBLEM 15-18 A water heater sales manager has a sales force that calls on large stores in the midwest. What steps should be taken to control the sales force?

Answer: First, the sales manager should set up standards of desirable performance. For water heaters, some possible standards would be sales, sales as a percentage of quota, profits, expenses, number of sales calls made, and number of calls that result in sales. The next step would be to compare actual performance with the standards. This requires information from sales representative reports and company records. Finally, the sales manager should take remedial action when necessary. This may involve additional sales representative motivation, supervision, or disciplinary action. [See Section 15-7.]

PROBLEM 15-19 What are some of the standards that a chewing gum company could use to control sales representatives?

Answer: One of the possible standards which the chewing gum company might use to control sales representatives is a system of quotas, or targets. For example, each territory might be assigned a sales quota. This sets forth the expected sales volume for the salesperson assigned to that territory and would be a good standard for the company. If this firm must keep its costs under control because unit profit margins are not high, then gross margin would be another useful standard. Since new accounts are important to any firm, another valuable standard would be the number of new accounts that each salesperson can open. Also, standards should be set for nonselling activities, such as checking on customer credit worthiness. [See Section 15-7.]

PROBLEM 15-20 In controlling sales representatives, a sales manager can compare individual performance in various ways. What are the three major ways?

Answer: The sales manager may compare the performance of each sales representative with that of the sales force as a whole. This involves computing averages and comparing them to individual performance measures. For example, each salesperson's sales as a percentage of quota can be compared to the company average. This allows managers to identify top- and low-level achievers and to indicate where remedial steps might be taken. In addition, the sales manager can compare the output of each member of the sales force with his or her own past achievements. This is useful in indicating trends in performance over time. Finally, the sales manager can compare individual performance measures with quotas, providing a basis for comparing individual work with company plans and expectations. [See Section 15-7.]

16 INTERNATIONAL MARKETING

THIS CHAPTER IS ABOUT

☑ **The Significance of International Marketing**
☑ **Environmental Factors in International Marketing**
☑ **The International Marketing Mix**
☑ **Kinds of Participation in International Marketing**

16-1. The Significance of International Marketing

International marketing means marketing efforts that extend across national boundaries. International marketing includes arrangements by which companies manufacture products in this country to sell abroad (called **exporting**), or arrangements by which companies produce and sell products overseas, or have foreign firms do the manufacturing and selling for them. One special kind of international marketing is called **multinational marketing**, which refers to companies that market in *many* countries. Coca Cola and IBM are two well-known multinational marketing companies.

EXAMPLE 16-1: Bayer AG is one of the largest international marketers in the world. This West German company's Bayer aspirin is the best-selling pain reliever in Argentina, Brazil, Spain, and Korea. It ranks second in West Germany and is widely sold in many other nations. In the United States and Canada, its marketing efforts are handled by Sterling Drugs, a U.S. pharmaceutical company.

A look at some export statistics furnishes some idea of the significance of international marketing to U.S. firms. Figure 16-1 presents data on exports from the United States to other countries. It indicates

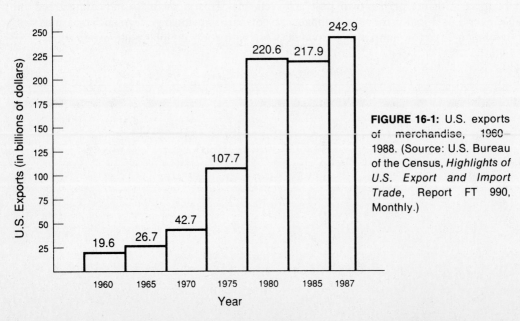

FIGURE 16-1: U.S. exports of merchandise, 1960–1988. (Source: U.S. Bureau of the Census, *Highlights of U.S. Export and Import Trade*, Report FT 990, Monthly.)

that the volume of exports is very large and is growing rapidly. It does not, however, reveal everything about U.S. marketers' operations as it covers only exports and not earnings secured by U.S. firms from overseas factories. However, the export figures suggest that U.S. firms are growing increasingly dependent on foreign markets for their financial success. Firms that ignore these markets pass up high potential profits.

Certain goods account for a higher percentage of U.S. exports than do others. Figure 16-2 sets forth the distribution of exports by commodity groups in 1987. Machinery and transportation equipment clearly lead the list. This includes such products as motor vehicles, aircraft, computers, and power generating machinery. "Other manufactured goods," the second largest category, includes iron and other metals, textiles, and clothing.

The areas of the world do not purchase U.S. exports equally. Figure 16-3 points out that Asia is the largest customer for American goods. This is followed by North America and Europe. Statistics for individual countries reveal that the most exports go to Canada. This is followed by Japan, the United Kingdom, and Mexico.

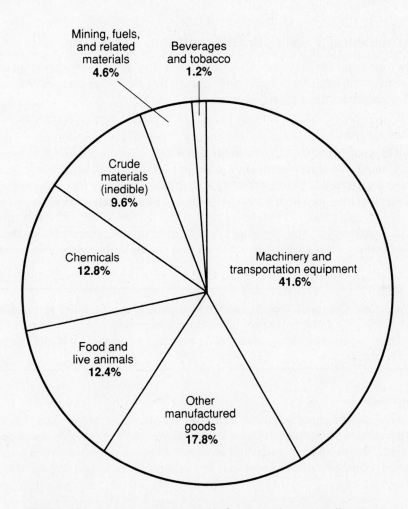

FIGURE 16-2: Percent distribution of U.S. exports by commodity groups, 1987. (Source: U.S. Bureau of the Census, *Highlights of U.S. Export and Import Trade*, Report FT 990, 1988.)

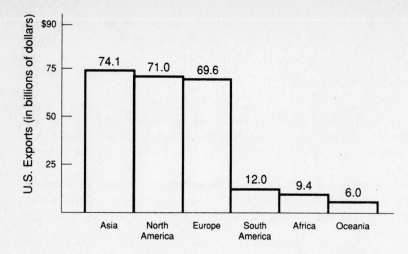

FIGURE 16-3: U.S. exports by continental areas, 1987. (Source: U.S. Bureau of the Census, *Historical Statistics*, Series U-317-394.)

16-2. Environmental Factors in International Marketing

Marketers have found that the environments within which they do business vary from one country to another. This requires adjustments in marketing strategy. Let's examine some of the more important environmental variables and their impact on marketers.

A. Competitors abroad

The amount of competition that U.S. marketers face abroad varies considerably from one country to another. Competition is very intense in some countries, requiring that a firm stay one step ahead of others in order to succeed. In other countries, an organization may face little competition. A firm may even enter a market with little or no competition, but attract rivals as soon as it enjoys profits. What was once a very good, near-exclusive market can become filled with other firms. Managers often seek out markets with limited competition, as these can be more profitable than competitive markets. Only strong firms should attempt to compete in the more competitive arenas.

EXAMPLE 16-2: Coca Cola and Pepsico have been successful in obtaining permission to sell their drinks in China. They enjoy a near monopoly there, as the government policy is to have only two foreign soft drink makers in the country. The companies do not need to compete with RC Cola, Shasta, Dr. Pepper, and other brands.

B. Technology abroad

Some countries already enjoy advanced technologies, which can benefit U.S. firms that market there. The advantages of marketing in a country whose technology is highly developed can be high product quality, low production costs, and efficient movement of goods. When technology is not well developed, transportation of goods can be a real problem, as fast and reliable transit is not available.

EXAMPLE 16-3: Transportation of goods in Bulgaria can be very difficult. The roads there are narrow and in poor condition. Railroad service is subject to frequent breakdowns, irregular schedules, and damaged goods brought about by poor handling methods.

Even communication can be a problem in some foreign countries. The telephone and postal systems in some areas of the world are unreliable, making it difficult for marketing managers to communicate with other managers, customers, suppliers, and government officials.

C. Suppliers abroad

Industrial marketers who purchase goods from foreign countries must seek out countries with adequate supplies of power, raw materials, and finished goods. In less developed nations, management may not find it easy to acquire supplies that are of the desired quality and price—or it might be difficult to locate supplier firms that can be depended upon to maintain production and delivery standards. On the other hand, various countries, such as West Germany, have well-managed suppliers which are able to attract industry as a result of their efficiency.

EXAMPLE 16-4: In 1986, the Ford Motor Company decided to produce a new automobile (with the brand name Tracer) in Taiwan for sale in Canada. One of the major reasons why Ford chose this location was that Taiwan is a large supplier of auto parts and components, which were needed for the new offering.

D. Economies abroad

Prosperous foreign economies often provide a ready market for American products. Countries that enjoy economic prosperity have high levels of income and employment, as well as highly developed facilities for communication, production, and distribution. Consumers there purchase a variety of goods and services, many of which are luxuries. Marketers are especially attracted to countries that have a large middle class, providing a mass market for numerous goods and services. On the other hand, economies are subject to downturns, and a country can lose prosperity. What was once a good market may deteriorate rapidly.

EXAMPLE 16-5: A number of oil-producing countries, including Venezuela, Norway, and Mexico, lost much of their attractiveness as markets when crude oil prices fell in the mid-1980's. The currencies of these countries declined in value and their consumers lost purchasing power, making these countries less attractive as targets.

E. Social forces abroad

The strategies that international marketers adopt should be compatible with the cultures and business customs of other countries. Languages, religions, values, and tastes vary considerably from country to country. A product that is very successful in one country may be unprofitable in another. Consumer tastes do change, however, opening up new opportunities.

EXAMPLE 16-6: American foods had never been popular in France until the early 1980's, when many French consumers discovered traditional American dishes such as chicken fried steak, french fries, and hamburgers. Makers of frozen dinners found that many consumers were eager to try TV dinners, which had once been looked down upon in that country.

Business customs in foreign countries often differ from those in the United States. American marketers need to adjust their methods of operation when they are abroad. Even small gestures can be important. For example, European executives interpret a long-lasting handsake as warm and personable, and a short, typically American one as unfriendly and cold.

F. Government abroad

Governments have a strong effect on the profitability of doing business in other countries. The governments of many countries have regulations on such factors as the right to do business, taxes, currency movements, competition, credit practices, accounting practices, and employment.

In a number of countries, gifts or "bribes" to government and corporate officials are regarded as normal business procedure—they are needed in order to obtain business. However, the United

States Corrupt Foreign Practices Act forbids major bribes. This difference of opinion with respect to what constitutes proper business procedure can be a barrier to companies who desire to operate in certain countries.

Some governments are friendly to American businesses and even encourage them to build facilities locally. Others take a different stance and erect barriers to "invasions" by foreigners. These barriers are erected mainly to protect local businesses and their employees and to strengthen the local economy.

EXAMPLE 16-7: The government of Japan has many regulations that make it difficult for foreign firms to sell goods and services there. It has erected **tariffs** (taxes on imports) that are prohibitively high for some goods. Legal restrictions prohibit the sale of many goods in the country unless a foreign firm has a Japanese partner. It is a complex process for non-Japanese marketers to comply with all of the inspection, paperwork, and other requirements that this government imposes on importers.

16-3. The International Marketing Mix

It should come as no surprise that the marketing mix for international marketing is the same as for domestic marketing—it involves product, price, place, and promotion.

A. Product

Many U.S. marketers sell the same product in other countries as they do in their homeland. Called an **identical product strategy**, this strategy permits companies to keep production costs low and to introduce abroad only those products that have a proven track record in the United States. This is a somewhat conservative strategy—one that is designed to avoid the risk of bringing out an untried new product in a foreign land.

EXAMPLE 16-8: The Schering-Plough Corporation is the producer of Interferon, a protein that fights infection and has promise for fighting cancer and AIDS. This product, produced both in New Jersey and in Ireland, is sold throughout the world. Its composition is the same, regardless of where it is sold.

A problem with the identical product strategy is that it does not conform to the modern marketing concept. Consumers in different countries often have different needs and desires. As a result, many companies have found that products must be specifically designed to meet the needs and desires of consumers in individual nations and even regions within nations.

EXAMPLE 16-9: In many countries in South America, Africa, and Asia, consumers wash their clothes in streams, rather than in washing machines. They prefer bar to powdered or flaked soap for this purpose. Whereas American companies produce powdered or flaked soap for consumers in this country, they have to develop a bar soap for sale in these other countries.

B. Price

As in the United States, international marketers should consider demand for the product, cost, competition, and government regulations in arriving at prices. Since these variables vary from one country to another, price differences exist, some of them quite substantial.

EXAMPLE 16-10: Consumers in China have much less income than those in the United States. Also, production costs are low because low wages are paid to labor. There is little competition among soft drink makers in the country, and the government regulates prices closely. Consequently, prices for Pepsi Cola are approximately 15 cents per 12-ounce bottle, below the price in most other countries.

C. Place

Marketers new to a foreign country quickly discover that physical distribution and channel of distribution facilities and operations in other countries can differ considerably from those in the United States. Transportation and storage equipment and methods are very primitive in some nations, such as India. Also, accepted channels of distribution may bear little resemblance to familiar ones in the United States or even to those in other foreign countries served by the firm.

D. Promotion

As in the United States, marketers employ promotion to communicate with target customers. The specific ways in which they use advertising, personal selling, and sales promotion often differ, however. Generally, the best promotion techniques are those that are widely accepted by target customers, business executives, and government officials in a specific country. In personal selling, this means observing local unwritten rules of behavior. In advertising and sales promotion, it means adjusting to local target customer characteristics and industry practices.

EXAMPLE 16-11: Many of the residents of Guatemala are illiterate—they can neither read nor write. This being the case, magazine and newspaper advertising is severely limited, and radio is a very popular advertising medium.

Governments in many foreign countries regulate promotion rigorously. They place limitations on what products may be advertised, what media can be used, and even what claims can be made. Since these regulations are often subject to sweeping changes, international marketers must stay abreast of the latest developments in promotion legislation.

EXAMPLE 16-12: The government of Chile prohibits advertisements that are made outside of the country. The Soviet government does not allow promotion that makes overly strong claims. It prefers ads with messages such as: "Eat more beef."

EXAMPLE 16-13: In France, wholesalers are widely used to distribute consumer goods. Direct marketing from the manufacturer to the retailer is rare. If a U.S. producer approaches a French retailer and attempts a direct sale, its sales force probably will be told to go through a wholesaler.

16-4. Kinds of Participation in International Marketing

There are various ways that marketers may participate in international marketing. Companies may become—

- **exporters**, which produce goods in the United States and distribute those goods abroad;
- **foreign producers**, which produce and distribute goods abroad;
- **licensors**, which license the right to produce or distribute goods to foreign companies.

U.S. firms may also enter into a—

- **joint venture**, in which a firm forms a partnership with a foreign company to share production and distribution responsibilities.

or U.S. firms may establish—

- **subsidiaries**, in which a firm sets up an independent company in a foreign country. Subsidiaries are not considered branches of the parent company.

The kind of participation that is best depends on the nature of the company and its objectives. Firms that are new to international business or that expect to sell only a small portion of their output abroad are often exporters. Many of the large, multinational U.S. firms are foreign producers; they have found that this method of operation helps reduce production costs, appeals to governments of other countries, and often meets with the approval of local consumers. Companies that view international trade as a sideline to their domestic business often adopt licensing agreements and joint ventures. Large companies often establish subsidiaries for much the same reasons as those that apply to foreign producer operations.

RAISE YOUR GRADES

Can you explain . . . ?

☑ why companies should carefully look at competition before entering a foreign market
☑ the impact that the economy of a foreign country can have on a U.S. firm doing business in that country
☑ why some firms have been unsuccessful in exporting U.S.-produced articles to foreign countries
☑ why some firms sell different products abroad than they sell in the United States
☑ why U.S. firms may not be active in exporting to some low-income countries
☑ why prices for some products may be lower in South America than in the United States
☑ why many firms may use wholesalers for products sold abroad, but do not use them in the United States

SUMMARY

1. International marketing means marketing efforts that extend across national boundaries.
2. Export figures suggest that U.S. firms are growing increasingly dependent on foreign markets for their financial success.
3. Certain goods account for a higher percentage of U.S. exports than others. Machinery and transportation equipment lead the list.
4. The areas of the world do not purchase U.S. exports equally. Asia is the largest customer for American goods.
5. International marketers often seek out foreign markets with limited competition.
6. International marketers often seek out countries where advanced technology is available.
7. Industrial marketers who purchase goods from foreign countries must seek out countries with adequate supplies of power, raw materials, and finished goods.
8. International marketers often seek to sell their products in countries with prosperous economies.
9. International marketers must adopt strategies that are compatible with the cultures and business customs of other countries.
10. International marketers must become very familiar with the government regulations of countries in which they try to do business.
11. International marketers should be sure that their product conforms to the needs and desires of their consumers abroad.
12. As in the United States, international marketers should consider demand for the product, cost, competition, and government regulations in arriving at prices.
13. International marketers should be aware that physical distribution and channel of distribution facilities and operations in other countries can differ considerably from those in the United States.
14. International marketers should use promotion techniques that are widely accepted by the target customers, business executives, and government officials in another country.
15. There are various ways that marketers can participate in international marketing, either as exporters, foreign producers, licensors, partners in joint ventures, or by establishing subsidiaries.
16. The kind of participation in international marketing that is best depends on the nature of the company and its objectives.

RAPID REVIEW Answers

Short Answer

1. International marketing means marketing efforts that extend across _____ _____, as when AT&T sells telephone switching equipment in France. [See Section 16-1.]

   national boundaries

2. When a company produces a product in the United States and sells it in Canada, this is called _____. [See Section 16-1.]

   exporting

3. Companies that market in many countries are called _____ marketers. [See Section 16-1.]

   multinational

4. The commodity group that accounts for more U.S. _____ than any other is machinery and transportation equipment. [See Section 16-1.]

   exports

5. Only strong firms should attempt to compete in highly _____ regions. [See Section 16-3.]

   competitive

6. When the _____ of a country is not well developed, transportation can be a real problem for marketers. [See Section 16-2.]

   technology

7. In less _____ countries, marketers may not find it easy to acquire supplies that are of the desired quality and price. [See Section 16-2.]

   developed

8. Countries with a prosperous _____ often have high levels of income, high levels of employment, and well developed communication facilities. [See Section 16-2.]

   economy

9. The strategies that international marketers adopt should be compatible with the _____ and _____ _____ of foreign countries. [See Section 16-2.]

   cultures business practices

10. The right to do business in a country, credit practices, or accounting practices could be subject to _____ regulation in other countries. [See Section 16-2.]

    government

11. Some governments respond negatively to American business and erect _____ to entering their country. [See Section 16-2.]

    barriers

12. The _____ _____ for international marketing is the same as for domestic marketing. [See Section 16-3.]

    marketing mix

13. The identical product strategy may be advantageous to a firm because it allows the company to keep its _____ costs down. [See Section 16-3.]

    production

14. A problem with the identical product strategy is that it does not conform to the _____ _____. [See Section 16-3.]

    marketing concept

15. _____ differences exist from one country to another because of variances in demand for a product, cost, competition, and government regulation. [See Section 16-3.]

    Price

16. Competition for headache remedies is not as strong in Australia as it is in England. This may prompt an American pharmaceutical company to sell headache remedies for a _____ price in Australia than in England. [See Section 16-3.]

    higher

17. Transportation and storage equipment and methods are very _____ in nations such as India. [See Section 16-3.]

    primitive

18. Personal selling by American sales representatives in Belgium should observe local unwritten rules of _____. [See Section 16-3.]

    behavior

19. _____ regulations may limit what products may be advertised, what media can be used, and even what claims can be made. [See Section 16-3.]

    Promotion

20. When an American company forms a partnership with an overseas company, this is called a _____ _____. [See Section 16-4.]

    joint venture

SOLVED PROBLEMS

PROBLEM 16-1 A friend informs you that IBM has set up a plant to produce and sell computers in England. Your friend says that this is an example of *exporting*. How would you respond to this statement?

Answer: The friend's view is incorrect. IBM's plant is not an example of exporting, which takes place when companies manufacture products in this country to sell abroad. If the IBM plant is located in England, not in the United States, its flow of products from the plant to customers does not cross national boundaries. The plant will hire English workers and probably obtain many of its supplies from that country. At least some of the profits, however, will flow back to the United States. [See Section 16-1.]

PROBLEM 16-2 A Connecticut-based producer of industrial aircraft tools recently expanded its sales efforts from the United States to Canada. According to the company president, "We are now a multinational corporation." Do you agree with this statement?

Answer: The president of the company is incorrect. Multinational marketers sell their goods and services in many countries. In contrast, this company sells only in the United States and Canada. It is not a multinational company. Multinationals are often called "world companies." They buy and sell, hire workers, and obtain money from a large number of countries. They view the entire world as a place to do business. [See Section 16-1.]

PROBLEM 16-3 In recent years, Motorola has expanded its efforts to export company brands to foreign countries. Part of the reason for this drive has been the impression on the part of Motorola executives that United States exports have increased substantially since 1960. Is this a correct impression?

Answer: Yes. Exports from the United States to foreign countries have risen more than tenfold since 1960. Motorola's contention is correct. A good portion of this growth, however, has taken place in the "machinery and transportation goods" category, while this company's major products are in other categories. Unless this firm is willing to diversify into new product lines, it should be wary about using total export figures as an indicator of how well its offerings will sell abroad. [See Section 16-1.]

PROBLEM 16-4 Assume that you are the marketing manager for a food company, and are responsible for overseas sales of cookies. You have asked a United States government official for assistance in expanding overseas sales. The official has indicated, "You food companies do not need help—You already account for the lion's share of United States exports." How would you answer this statement?

Answer: The government official is incorrect. Food and live animals make up only 12.4% of United States exports. Other categories, such as "machinery and transportation equipment" and "other manufactured goods" are much larger. Further, food companies may run into a great deal of stiff competition and regulation by government officials abroad. Tariff barriers in many countries, such as Japan and France, may make it difficult for them to compete. Other countries may attempt to protect their agricultural industry from foreign competition by setting up stiff import quotas for food products. [See Section 16-1.]

PROBLEM 16-5 A fellow student ventures an opinion that most of the exports of the United States go to Mexico and South America. How would you react to this opinion?

Answer: Essentially, the student is incorrect. Most exports go to Asia, North America, and Europe. The largest customers of the United States are Canada, the United Kingdom, and Mexico. Increasingly, United States firms are turning to Asia and Canada for export growth because these areas are becoming larger importers. In contrast, Mexico and South America are shrinking as export markets, as their purchasing power is falling. [See Section 16-2.]

PROBLEM 16-6 A small producer of computer software is considering selling its products in Western Europe. The marketing manager has heard that competition for software sales is substantial there and has asked for your advice as to whether or not to target that area. What would your advice be?

Answer: The marketing manager should consider other less competitive markets. Large and small firms, both American- and foreign-based, compete vigorously for software sales in Western Europe, especially in wealthy countries such as West Germany and Sweden. It would be difficult for the small firm, with a relatively unknown reputation, to penetrate and stay in this market. [See Section 16-2.]

PROBLEM 16-7 What warnings on entering foreign countries would you make to a producer of yogurt, which depends on fast delivery to serve customers?

Answer: The yogurt producer probably should avoid nations where technology is not well developed. When this is the case, fast and reliable transportation of goods is often not available. Trucks and trains may be subject to frequent breakdowns and departures from their schedules. Because of inefficiencies in telephone, telegraph, radio, and the postal system, shipments may arrive late or at the wrong destination. Refrigerated cars and trucks may be in short supply and may not maintain desired temperatures. Mechanics and other technicians may be in short supply. All of these factors pose difficulties for the yogurt marketer. [See Section 16-2.]

PROBLEM 16-8 Harper Corporation is looking for new countries in which it can manufacture and sell toys. What would you advise them regarding the existence of suppliers in foreign countries?

Answer: Harper is in need of supplies of power, services, raw materials, and finished goods. It should avoid countries where the suppliers cannot furnish stocks that are of the desired quality and price. This may lead management to locate its manufacturing operations in well-developed countries, such as France or Italy, and to avoid less highly developed countries, such as Spain. Suppliers are too important to a firm to locate in a site where they are inadequate. [See Section 16-2.]

PROBLEM 16-9 Currently, the economy of Taiwan is growing at a rapid pace. Consumer incomes are expanding, leading to increased revenues for Taiwanese retailers. Overall, the market appears to be healthy. Would you recommend that the Sundance Corporation locate large numbers of its convenience stores in that country?

Answer: Sundance might consider locating its convenience stores in Taiwan, since an expanding economy can be a strong market for new retail outlets. It does appear that Taiwan's economy is very healthy. However, the firm should attempt to determine if this economic trend is a permanent condition. If the economy slides downward, the company may be left with unprofitable stores. [See Section 16-2.]

PROBLEM 16-10 In 1987, a sports shoe manufacturer introduced a new shoe for those who pursue walking as a form of exercise. The shoe's initial sales in the United States were very encouraging. Based on this early sales picture, should the firm introduce the shoes into England?

Answer: Not necessarily. The shoes may not sell well in England, despite their success in the United States. Consumer values and tastes differ considerably from one country to another. The firm should conduct research to determine possible sales success in England before embarking on a major marketing campaign there. [See Section 16-2.]

PROBLEM 16-11 A neighbor has invented a pocket-held hand-warming device and is convinced it would be in high demand by hunters and other outdoor sports enthusiasts in cooler climates, such as Sweden, Germany, and Norway. He would like to introduce the product to several such countries but feels that their governments may have regulations that would pertain to the product. What advice would you provide?

Answer: The inventor of the hand warmer should look into regulations on what documents are necessary in order to obtain permission to do business in the cool-climate countries. Consideration should be given to what the governments will allow in terms of shipping their currency into the United States and converting it into dollars. Rules on what is legal and what is illegal competition in each country should also be analyzed. Government regulations of credit should be examined; for example, some countries may impose maximum interest rate levels. Some accounting practices that are legal in the United States must be altered for other countries. [See Section 16-2.]

PROBLEM 16-12   Assume that executives at a meat processing company decided to introduce hot dogs in Spain. Would you expect this to be a profitable strategy?

Answer: In all likelihood it would not. It cannot be assumed that offerings that are popular in the United States will be heavily consumed in foreign countries. Consumers in different countries often have different needs, desires, and tastes. Spaniards may not be heavy consumers of hot dogs and other sausage-type foods. [See Section 16-3.]

PROBLEM 16-13   What factors should a chewing gum company consider in pricing its sugarless bubble gum for sale in Canada?

Answer: The chewing gum company should consider demand for the brand. If it appears to be very popular, prices may be set well above cost levels. On the other hand, low demand may signal the need for small profit margins. Cost is another important factor. Management should set the price at levels sufficient to cover expected costs and result in a profit. Competition should also be considered. The heavier the competition by other gum producers, the lower the price should be. Finally, the company should look for Canadian laws that will affect pricing, such as regulations on price discrimination. [See Section 16-3.]

PROBLEM 16-14   For several decades, leading food producers have developed highly nutritious food products that were designed for areas such as the southern part of Africa, where malnutrition is high. What advertising medium would most likely be effective in such areas?

Answer: Radio would be a good choice for the food products. Many consumers in these countries own or have access to radios and spend hours each day in listening. They are very much attracted to this medium and pay attention to radio commericals. Large numbers are illiterate, so they could not read written advertisements in magazines, newspapers, and billboards. Television ownership is very limited, so this medium probably would not be effective. [See Section 16-3.]

PROBLEM 16-15   In the United States, Wembley crackers are widely sold through wholesalers. Would this necessarily be the case in selling to Indonesia or South Korea?

Answer: It would not necessarily be the case. Channel of distribution facilities and operations in other countries can differ considerably from those in the United States. This is especially the case in the food industry. The company may discover that these differences force it to use different channel systems in different countries where the product is sold. [See Section 16-3.]

PROBLEM 16-16   Assume that a U.S. company wants to set up an office in Denmark out of which its sales representatives could operate. This office would act as an independent company, and not as a branch of the parent company. Would the office properly be called an exporter?

Answer: No. When an overseas operation acts as an independent company, rather than a branch of the parent company, it is called a subsidiary and not an exporter. Since the overseas operation is independent, major decisions are made by management in the foreign country, rather than in the home country (the United States). Also, profits tend to remain in the foreign country. These arrangements make the operations quite different from export arrangements. [See Section 16-4.]

PROBLEM 16-17   If a food processor in the United States enters into a partnership with a wholesaler in South Korea, this is called a subsidiary arrangement, according to a fellow student. Comment.

Answer: The student is incorrect. This is not a subsidiary arrangement. It is a joint venture. The South Korean unit is an independent company that has entered into a partnership agreement with the U.S. food processor. It is not owned or managed by the U.S. firm, as would be the case for a subsidiary operation. [See Section 16-4.]

PART IV
PLANNING AND
CONTROLLING
MARKETING EFFORTS

17 *MARKETING MANAGEMENT*

THIS CHAPTER IS ABOUT

- ☑ **What Is Marketing Management?**
- ☑ **Developing Marketing Plans**
- ☑ **Organization**
- ☑ **Motivation**
- ☑ **The Control Process**
- ☑ **Major Control Techniques**

17-1. What Is Marketing Management?

Marketing management is the *development* and *implementation* of marketing plans. Plans are necessary to anticipate the future. Without plans, a company may be forced to take emergency actions that are not well thought out. Essentially, plans consist of two sets of ideas: a set of objectives and a set of ideas regarding how those objectives might be attained.

EXAMPLE 17-1: In 1986, Sears executives were involved in developing a line of childrens' apparel under the McKids brand, to be introduced in stores during the fall of 1987. The firm planned to advertise in *American Baby* magazine with coupons to reach new mothers. The Sears infant departments were the most profitable of all the departments, but were losing market share to specialized retailers such as Children's Place. The goal of the new brand and advertising effort was to make Sears the market leader in childrens' apparel.

Figure 17-1 outlines the major ingredients of marketing management. It indicates that the process begins in the present and is oriented toward the future. Various ways of carrying out the development and implementation processes are listed in the figure and discussed further in the sections below.

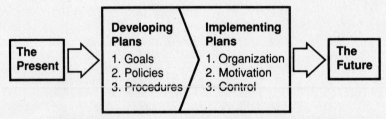

FIGURE 17-1: The essentials of marketing management.

17-2. Developing Marketing Plans

A. Goals, policies, and procedures

Marketing planners develop goals, policies, and procedures.

- **Goals** are the objectives or targets of the planning unit.

A firm should have broad overall marketing goals as well as narrower goals that support the overall goals for individual marketing functions and departments. In turn, all marketing goals should contribute to overall company goals.

EXAMPLE 17-2: A company may have a goal of earning 20% on invested capital. To help achieve this, the marketing department may have a goal of attaining a 10% share of the market for middle-income families. To support this, the advertising department may have a goal of increasing target consumer awareness of company products by 25%.

- **Policies** are guidelines for company personnel to follow in carrying out their activities.

Policies furnish answers to questions as to what course of action is appropriate when various conditions arise. In addition, they help to ensure that all marketing personnel take actions that are consistent with the actions of others. Well-developed policies contribute to the attainment of goals. As with goals, there are broad policies for the whole firm and more specific ones for individual departments and marketing functions.

EXAMPLE 17-3: The J.C. Penney Company has a policy that "the consumer comes first." This policy requires that company employees make a major effort to satisfy consumers. At the individual store level, this policy is translated into more specific policies; for instance, customers are permitted to return defective goods and sales personnel are required to treat customers with courtesy.

- **Procedures** are specific means used to carry out goals and policies.

Procedures are detailed guides for company personnel and are often set up as *rules*. At the J.C. Penney Company, for example, when a customer brings in an item for a refund, the sales clerk is required to fill out a refund slip in a specified way.

B. Long- and short-run plans

Firms have goals, policies, and procedures for both the long run and the short run. Most managers classify the long run as more than one year and the short run as one year or less.

1. Long-run plans

Long-run plans tend to be general. They are top management's ideas on what a company should be doing during a broad span of years. These plans are not changed often, as they are intended to set for the firm a consistent course of action that is not subject to abrupt change. When these plans *do* change, they reflect a major change in a firm's goals.

EXAMPLE 17-4: Prior to 1986, Federal Express was not heavily involved in international package delivery. During that year, however, the firm decided to make a full commitment overseas. Management decided to fashion a new marketing attack against the industry leader, DHL Worldwide Express. Federal Express planned to begin its new program in Japan and requested permission from that government to provide services there. The new program involved reassigning employees to the worldwide effort and acquiring ad agencies in Japan.

---

2. Short-run plans

Short-run plans specify management's intentions more specifically than do those for the long run. They also are designed to support long-run plans.

EXAMPLE 17-5: Dove Enterprises, Inc., a pet supply wholesaler, lost market share in 1986 because of price cutting by competitors. The company met this threat with a short-run plan involving company price reductions on 30% of its items, advertising increases of over 20%, and an incentive program whereby dealers could receive free goods when they placed an order with Dove.

17-3. Organization

Organization involves deciding who will be responsible for various activities needed to achieve company goals. In a one-person company, there is no need for organizing since one person does everything. As a firm gets larger, however, people tend to specialize in certain ways. One person may be responsible for selling, another may be in charge of product planning, and another in charge of physical distribution. As a company continues to grow, it may reach the stage where its infrastructure is like that shown in Figure 17-2, which sets forth a typical organization pattern for a manufacturer. In this pattern, individuals specialize by *function*. Not all companies have the same pattern as that shown in the figure, but many have a similar arrangement.

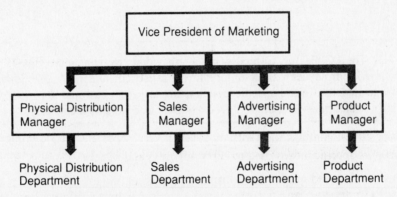

FIGURE 17-2: Typical organization plan for a manufacturer.

EXAMPLE 17-6: At the Dezurich Company, a large producer of industrial valves, there are two departments below the vice president of marketing. One is headed by the sales manager and another by the manager of marketing services, which the company defines as all marketing functions other than sales. This arrangement is used because sales is a very important ingredient to company success.

The departments within a company may be organized in various ways. One type of organization is *geographically* based; for example, there may be a regional sales manager for each of the north, south, east, and west divisions of a company's sales force. Or, if a company's products differ substantially, there may be sales managers organized by *product*. Or, if the types of customers served are quite different, the sales managers may be organized by *type of customer*.

EXAMPLE 17-7: At IBM, sales managers are organized by type of product. One group sells mainframe computers, another typewriters and associated equipment, and a third sells small computers.

17-4. Motivation

Managers carry out most of their plans through others—their *subordinates*. This means that the effectiveness of managers is largely based on their ability to *motivate* these personnel. **Motivation** involves influencing employees' attitudes toward their work, the company, and their superiors so that they will work diligently toward company goals.

A. Financial incentives

Employees are not likely to be highly motivated if they feel that their wages, salaries, or commissions are unduly low, relative to others in the company, community, or other companies. Financial incentives reflect a group of motivating factors: they support a standard of living, are status symbols, and tell employees how much the company values their services.

EXAMPLE 17-8: The Unisys Corp. (producer of computers) pays its marketing employees salaries that are higher than those they might receive from its competitors. The firm has developed a reputation for high motivation, based primarily on the earning levels which these individuals receive.

B. Nonfinancial incentives

Nonfinancial incentives can be just as important as financial ones. There are several types of nonfinancial incentives.

(1) *Employee participation.* Often a useful means of motivation is to allow employees to participate in making decisions that affect them. This can be much more effective than just treating employees as robots who receive and carry out orders.

(2) *Variety of tasks.* Some firms, such as General Motors, have found that providing employees with variety in their work can be a useful motivator. If individuals perform the same tasks day after day, they are likely to become disenchanted and bored with their work. This can be avoided through variety.

(3) *Positive communication.* Employees are more likely to be motivated if they know just what their goals are and how well they are performing in accomplishing these goals. This means that positive communication with managers is very important. Those employees who do not know where they stand in the company are not likely to be highly motivated.

EXAMPLE 17-9: The Joseph E. Seagrams & Sons distillery has developed high levels of motivation in its marketing staff. Each employee is fully informed, orally and in writing, about just what his or her duties and responsibilities are. Also, employees are kept informed in depth, on a regular basis, on how well management believes the employees are performing.

---

(4) *Individual goal achievement.* To a large extent, employees will be motivated to high performance if they feel that they can attain important individual goals by contributing to company goals. An employee who enjoys status, for instance, may be highly motivated by a prestige office and a title. Another who values close interpersonal ties may be motivated by a manager who takes a strong interest in employee well-being. Others who are very security-conscious may seek assurance that the company desires to keep them on the payroll. If individuals feel that contributing to company goals will help them achieve these personal goals, they are likely to be motivated.

17-5. The Control Process

One of the more important means of implementing marketing plans is through the use of a *control process*. A good control process requires setting up criteria of desirable performance, measuring actual performance against the criteria, and taking remedial action when necessary.

• **Criteria of desirable performance** are standards against which marketing managers can compare performance.

These standards of desirable performance are generally based on the goals of the company, such as attaining a certain market share, maintaining customer satisfaction, or staying on top of technological advances.

EXAMPLE 17-10: One of General Motors' major goals is to increase its share of the automobile market. This being the case, market share is an important criterion of performance. An important goal of AT&T is to obtain an adequate return on invested capital. It is logical then that return on invested capital is a criterion of performance.

- **Measuring actual performance against criteria** involves making provisions for flows of information about performance.

Firms can analyze a variety of information for the purpose of comparing actual performance to the criteria of performance. A reporting system may inform management about such variables as sales, costs, share of market, profits, and other variables, broken down by geographic area, territory, product, type of customer, and other categories.

- **Remedial action** is necessary when actual performance falls significantly below the criteria of desirable performance. Remedial action may require a variety of decisions, depending on the nature and size of the difference between the criteria and performance. Ordinarily, a company will not take remedial action until it has examined the facts carefully.

EXAMPLE 17-11: In 1986, the Kodak Company took remedial action because its costs, sales growth, and earnings were below desired levels. The company slashed its workforce by 10%, purchased Fox Photo, Inc. (a photo finisher), and added new products, ranging from printers to optical memory systems. The new products were added to make the company less dependent on a few offerings, which a careful managerial investigation revealed to be a cause of lower than acceptable sales and profits.

17-6. Major Control Techniques

Marketers use a number of techniques for control purposes. Among the more important are budgets, market share analysis, sales analysis, cost analysis, and the marketing audit.

A. Budgets

Budgets are financial plans for a specific future time period, such as a year. Control involves comparing the financial plans with actual expenditures. A company may budget $2,500,000 for advertising in a given year, but find that actual expenditures are $2,900,000. This discrepancy may lead to investigations revealing the need for changing advertising media, advertising agencies, or the frequency with which ads are placed. If the discrepancy between budgeted and actual figures is very small, management may ignore it.

Marketers have budgets for a number of variables. These include sales, selling expenses, advertising expenses, and administrative expenses. The levels of performance set forth in the budgets are *expected* levels—representing good, but reasonable, performance by the company and its subdivisions. Some budgets are for the firm as a whole. Others are for segments, such as divisions, product groups or territories.

EXAMPLE 17-12: The Allegheny International, Inc., Corp. discovered in 1986 that its administrative expenses were running 40% above budgeted levels. This led management to freeze executive salaries, reduce headquarters staff by over 50%, and sell company jets and limousines.

B. Market share analysis

Market share analysis is a process whereby management computes company sales as a percentage of total industry sales. Ordinarily, this is done both for the total firm and for important segments, such as particular divisions, product groups, products, and geographic areas. Then management compares market share with target levels, past levels, and the market share of rivals to decide if remedial action may be needed.

EXAMPLE 17-13: Near the beginning of 1986, U.S. Sprint Communication held only 4% of the market for long-distance telecommunications. By the end of the year, the firm had tripled its share. This led management to add more services, such as private networks. It also elected to continue its ad campaign. Management decided that the marketing plan, which had worked so well to date, should not be changed.

C. Sales analysis

Sales analysis involves breaking down sales by important segments of the business, such as by division, product or product group, type of customer, or geographic area. Sales analysis is based on the idea that often a small number of segments may account for a large share of company sales. Those segments which have low sales relative to criterion levels are flagged for possible remedial action. On the other hand, segments with high sales may be given larger budgets, in order that they might contribute still more to company sales.

The criteria for sales by company segment may be quotas established by managerial judgment, or they may be based on past sales. Or, management may simply compare each segment with the others to see which ones are contributing the most revenues.

EXAMPLE 17-14: An office products producer has four divisions. In 1987, the sales of each were as follows:

Division A	$24,300,000	Division C	$5,900,000
Division B	$11,200,000	Division D	$2,700,000

Clearly, Division A is bringing in the bulk of company sales. Management should make sure that it receives an adequate budget and managerial attention, since its failure could seriously damage the company. Similarly, Division B should be high priority. Divisions C and D may not be performing up to par, and remedial action may be needed in these segments of the company. Management should at least seek information on why the sales of these divisions are low.

The firm may need further sales analysis to place management in a position for sound decision making. The analysis can reveal what products and customer types are contributing the most sales. For example, it may show that only a few large customers are contributing most of the sales for Division A and that the firm should treat these customers with considerable care.

D. Cost analysis

Cost analysis goes beyond sales analysis by breaking down costs according to important segments of the company. When combined with sales analysis, cost analysis can reveal which segments are the most profitable. There are two approaches to cost analysis.

(1) **Contribution margin approach**. Some firms allocate only *direct costs* to each segment. **Direct costs** are expenses that can be traced to a particular segment and are assigned to it. Direct costs for Division A, for example, would include advertising to customers of that division and transportation to these customers.

(2) **Full cost approach**. Other firms allocate both direct and indirect costs to each segment; this is called the *full cost* approach. **Indirect costs** are those which cannot be traced specifically to a segment. For example, the president's salary is an indirect cost, as are expenses for advertising that benefits the whole firm rather than particular divisions.

Those who favor the contribution margin approach believe that it is not sound to allocate indirect costs to segments, since there is no specific way of deciding which segment should be assigned particular costs. Those who follow the full cost approach believe that since all costs must be covered by the company, they must be allocated.

EXAMPLE 17-15: Referring again to Example 17-14, cost analysis may reveal that costs are $22,800,000 for Division A and $4,600,000 for Division B. This means that B is actually the most profitable division. This may lead management to reduce various budgets for Division A and to shift the funds to Division B.

E. The marketing audit

The **marketing audit** is a systematic and critical review of the total marketing operation. Auditors consider goals, policies, procedures, personnel, and the type of organization that a firm uses in reviewing the entire marketing operation. Audits are infrequent and costly, but they can reveal important strengths and weaknesses. Firms that conduct audits are in a position to discover where their overall strengths and weaknesses lie.

RAISE YOUR GRADES

Can you explain . . . ?

☑ what marketing management consists of in a large company
☑ the difference between goals, policies, and procedures in a marketing department
☑ why marketers have both short-run and long-run marketing plans
☑ why many marketing departments are organized by function
☑ how financial compensation can motivate marketing employees
☑ what most marketers need to do to set up controls
☑ what major control techniques are useful to marketers

SUMMARY

1. Marketing management is the development and implementation of marketing plans.
2. Marketing management is oriented toward the future.
3. Marketing planners develop goals, policies, and procedures:

   • Goals are the objectives or targets of the planning unit.

   • Policies are guidelines for company personnel to follow in carrying out their activities.

   • Procedures are specific means used to carry out goals and policies

4. Marketing managers establish goals, policies, and procedures for both the long run (more than a year) and the short run (one year or less).
5. Organization involves deciding who will be responsible for various activities needed to achieve company goals. Typically, this is broken down by function.
6. The departments within a company may be organized in various ways, such as geographically, by product, or by type of customer.
7. Motivation involves influencing employee attitudes toward their work, the company, and their superiors so that they will work diligently toward company goals.
8. Motivation can be effected through both financial and nonfinancial means.
9. One of the more important means of implementing marketing plans is through the use of a control process.
10. Criteria of desirable performance are standards against which marketing managers can compare performance.
11. Measuring actual performance against criteria involves making provisions for flows of information about performance.
12. If the measures indicate that actual performance is below the criteria, management may decide that remedial action is necessary.

13. Marketers use a number of techniques for control purposes:

- Budgets are financial plans for a specific future time period, such as a year.
- Market share analysis involves computing company sales as a percentage of total industry sales.
- Sales analysis involves breaking down sales by important segments of the business, such as by division, product or product group, type of customer, or geographic area.
- Cost analysis goes beyond sales analysis by breaking down costs according to important segments of the company.
- The marketing audit is a systematic and critical review of the total marketing operation.

RAPID REVIEW   Answers

Multiple Choice

1. Marketing management involves the development and carrying out of marketing (**a**) goals, (**b**) organizations, (**c**) plans, (**d**) policies. [See Section 17-1.]   *c*

2. The process of carrying out plans is called (**a**) coordination, (**b**) implementation, (**c**) processing, (**d**) expediting. [See Section 17-1.]   *b*

3. All marketing goals should contribute to (**a**) company policies, (**b**) overall company goals, (**c**) long-run goals, (**d**) long-run plans. [See Section 17-2.]   *b*

4. Policies in a marketing department generally consist of (**a**) rules, (**b**) procedures, (**c**) detailed plans, (**d**) guidelines. [See Section 17-2.]   *d*

5. Marketing procedures are (**a**) detailed guides, (**b**) overall targets, (**c**) overall guidelines to marketing personnel, (**d**) budgets to control expenses. [See Section 17-2.]   *a*

6. Long-run marketing plans (**a**) are for periods of one year or less, (**b**) tend to be very specific, (**c**) are not changed often, (**d**) are subject to abrupt change. [See Section 17-2.]   *c*

7. Short-run marketing plans should support (**a**) organization, (**b**) financial motivation techniques, (**c**) remedial actions, (**d**) long-run plans. [See Section 17-2.]   *d*

8. Deciding who will be responsible for various activities needed to achieve company goals is known as (**a**) organization, (**b**) planning, (**c**) controlling, (**d**) long-run planning. [See Section 17-3.]   *a*

9. In a one-person company, there is no need for (**a**) marketing, (**b**) long-run plans, (**c**) organization, (**d**) short-run plans. [See Section 17-3.]   *c*

10. A typical marketing department is organized by (**a**) type of customer, (**b**) type of product, (**c**) function, (**d**) budget levels. [See Section 17-3.]   *c*

11. Which of the following managers would *not* be expected in the marketing department of a large firm: (**a**) physical distribution (**b**) sales, (**c**) production, (**d**) advertising. [See Section 17-3.]   *c*

12. If a firm has a sales manager for the New England area, it is organized (**a**) by product, (**b**) geographically, (**c**) by type of customer, (**d**) by product groups. [See Section 17-3.]   *b*

13. Marketing managers mainly carry out their plans through (**a**) organization, (**b**) the control process, (**c**) motivation, (**d**) subordinates. [See Section 17-4.]   *d*

14. In order to be effective motivators, pay scales need *not* be reasonably high relative to (**a**) others in the company, (**b**) others in the community, (**c**) employees of other companies, (**d**) the marketing budget. [See Section 17-4.]   *d*

15. Financial incentives fulfill all of the following functions *except* (**a**) serving as status symbols, (**b**) supporting standards of living, (**c**) exceeding budget levels, (**d**) telling employees how much the company values their services. [See Section 17-4.]   *c*

16. Marketing executives will be motivated if they feel that contributing to company goals will help them (a) gain status, (b) receive a higher salary, (c) avoid being fired, (d) fulfill individual goals. [See Section 17-4.]   *d*

17. Marketing control criteria should be based on (a) financial motivators, (b) company goals, (c) nonfinancial motivators, (d) company procedures. [See Section 17-5.]   *b*

18. Which of the following is *not* a variable that marketing control systems provide flows of information on: (a) company stock prices, (b) sales, (c) share of market, (d) profits. [See Section 17-5.]   *a*

19. Marketing budgets are (a) adhered to strictly, (b) developed for each department, (c) not rigid, (d) financial plans for a future time period. [See Section 17-6.]   *d*

20. Which of the following is *not* a segment that sales are broken down into when a firm conducts a sales analysis: (a) division, (b) budget, (c) product, (d) type of customer. [See Section 17-6.]   *b*

SOLVED PROBLEMS

PROBLEM 17-1 Assume that you have been placed in a marketing management job at a large company. Why would you find it necessary to develop plans?

Answer: Plans are necessary if your department is to anticipate and prepare for the future. Without plans, the department may be forced to take emergency actions that are not well thought out. This being the case, it is necessary to decide what will be done in the future, by whom, with what, and when, to attain company goals. If your department does not plan, its efforts are not likely to be coordinated with other company departments, and your performance will suffer as a result. [See Section 17-1.]

PROBLEM 17-2 A marketing manager for a company that produces flooring has related to you that her major responsibility is to implement plans. What does she mean by implementation?

Answer: By implementation, she means the carrying out of plans. The company must organize its operations so that they work together in helping to attain company goals. The marketing manager should motivate the personnel who are assigned to her unit so that they will carry out their work diligently and in a creative manner. Also, she should have a control system in place that will detect operations that are not running according to expected levels. [See Section 17-1.]

PROBLEM 17-3 An executive with a fast-food company is in charge of setting goals for the chain. How should the executive go about this process?

Answer: Goals are the objectives or targets of the fast-food chain. The overall marketing goals should be set so that they contribute to the company goals. In turn, the firm should have broad overall marketing goals and narrower goals that support the overall ones for individual marketing functions and departments. The fast-food industry is a very competitive one and profit margins are slim. A company without well thought-out goals is likely to be rapidly overtaken by rivals. This executive has a very important function in the company. [See Section 17-2.]

PROBLEM 17-4 A friend has taken a marketing position with a company that provides telephone service to ten states. Part of the job is to examine various company policies to see if they need changing. Your friend is confused as to exactly why the firm should have policies, however, and needs this information in order to complete the assignment effectively. How would you answer your friend?

Answer: Policies are guidelines for the company's personnel to follow in carrying out their activities. They furnish answers to questions as to what course of action is appropriate when various conditions arise. Well developed policies contribute to the attainment of goals. As with goals, there are broad policies for the whole firm and more specific ones for individual departments and marketing functions. For example, the company might have a policy of having the advertising manager check individual ads to make sure that the media have prepared them according to company plans. Your friend should carefully study this and other policies to determine if they sufficiently contribute to company goals. Perhaps someone else should check the ads. They may have to be checked more frequently or more thoroughly. Your friend's actions should be guided by such inquiries. [See Section 17-2.]

PROBLEM 17-5 If you were setting up marketing procedures for an airline company, how would the procedures differ from goals?

Answer: The procedures for an airline company are specific means of carrying out goals and policies. They are detailed guides to company personnel and are often set up as rules. Goals, on the other hand, are much more general. They are the targets or objectives of the marketing unit. An example of an airline procedure might be that requests for a fare change go from a sales representative to a sales manager, where each request is reviewed and passed on to top management. If this procedure is ineffective, you might suggest that it be modified or replaced with an entirely different one. [See Section 17-2.]

PROBLEM 17-6 What characteristics should the long-run marketing plans have for a large producer and distributor of crop protection chemicals?

Answer: This company's long-run plans are for time periods longer than one year. They should be general, rather than detailed, and should reflect top management's ideas on what the company should be doing over a broad span of years. They should not be changed often, as they are intended to set a consistent course of action that is not subject to abrupt change. A hasty and not fully researched decision to abandon agricultural products and move into cosmetics products, for example, could be very harmful to a company whose expertise lies in manufacturing and marketing farm, not cosmetic, products. [See Section 17-2.]

PROBLEM 17-7 Why is it necessary to organize marketing operations in very large firms?

Answer: In one-person companies, there is no need for organization, since one person does everything. As a firm gets larger, however, certain people tend to specialize in certain ways. As a company continues to grow, it reaches the stage where a structure, such as the functional one illustrated in Figure 17-2, is required. A very large firm may have thousands of employees, hundreds of whom are in marketing. Each of these employees specializes in certain functions, such as sales or physical distribution. The need for efficiency and coordination requires that such organization take place. [See Section 17-3.]

PROBLEM 17-8 Assume that you have been asked to recommend an overall marketing organization structure for a medium-sized (500 employees) manufacturer of consumer dishware and pottery. What functional managers would you have reporting to the vice president of marketing?

Answer: This company could probably use a fairly standardized structure, with managers in charge of physical distribution, sales, advertising, and product planning reporting to the vice president of marketing. This would ensure that all of the major marketing activities required for consumer dishware and pottery are headed by appropriate managers. If the firm is heavily involved in exporting, it might place an individual in charge of a department that is responsible for this function. [See Section 17-3.]

PROBLEM 17-9 What are the major ways that departments under the vice president of marketing might be organized in a company that sells beauty and health care products to consumers?

Answer: The departments may be organized geographically. This would be logical since the demand for beauty and health care products varies from one geographical area to another. Or, if the products differed substantially, there may be managers organized by product or product line. If the types of customers served are quite different (e.g., if supermarkets, drug stores, department stores, and variety stores all sell the products), the managers may be organized by type of customer. [See Section 17-3.]

PROBLEM 17-10 Assume that you are in charge of setting salaries for employees in the advertising department of a company. What guidelines would you use in determining the amounts of the salaries?

Answer: The advertising employees are most likely to be highly motivated if they feel their salaries are reasonably high, relative to others in the company. The advertising personnel also should have salaries that compare favorably to others in the communities where they live and in the industry. The salaries should support a desirable standard of living and communicate how much the company values their services. This will allow the company to attract and retain highly qualified advertising employees. [See Section 17-4.]

PROBLEM 17-11 How can participation and variety in work affect the motivation of marketing employees at a company?

Answer: A company is likely to find that a useful means of motivation is to allow marketing employees to participate in making decisions that affect them. This can be much more effective than treating them as robots who receive and carry out orders. Also, variety in their work can be a useful motivator. Variety reduces boredom and brings about creativity and a genuine interest in facing new challenges. [See Section 17-4.]

PROBLEM 17-12 How can communication by marketing managers to employees improve employee motivation?

Answer: Marketing employees are more likely to be motivated if they know what their goals are and how well management believes they are accomplishing these goals. This means that downward communication by company sales, promotion, distribution, and other managers is highly important. Those who do not know where they stand in the firm are not likely to be highly motivated. In very large companies, communications to employees are especially important, since rumors and misinformation can badly damage morale. [See Section 17-4.]

PROBLEM 17-13 How can knowledge of employee goals help a marketing manager to motivate the work force in the department?

Answer: To a large extent, marketing employees will be motivated to high performance if they feel that they can attain important individual goals (such as salary and recognition) by contributing to company goals (such as profit and cash flow). If marketing managers know the individual goals, they are in a position to set up operations so that employees can accomplish their goals as they work toward company goals. [See Section 17-4.]

PROBLEM 17-14 Assume that the management of a company discovers that sales are substantially below expected levels. What should management do?

Answer: If the measures indicate that actual performance is below the criteria, management may decide that remedial action, such as changing supervision methods, is necessary. Ordinarily, further fact finding is undertaken before remedial action is followed, however. This fact finding may consist of examining company reports, conducting marketing research, or accessing the company's marketing information system. The nature of the remedial action depends on the nature and size of the differences between actual and expected levels of sales. If the difference is very substantial, management may take drastic action, such as eliminating a brand or dropping prices to a level just above cost. [See Section 17-5.]

PROBLEM 17-15 What are some of the major variables that marketers might measure for control purposes?

Answer: One of the major variables is sales. Marketers should also carefully monitor costs, especially during periods of inflation. Share of market is another significant variable, particularly if the company is in a very competitive industry. Also, profit is an important variable—it largely determines the fortunes of the company. These variables can be broken down by geographic area, territory, product, type of customer, and other categories. Such breakdowns are particularly useful for a company that sells many different products in numerous geographical areas to a variety of customers. [See Section 17-6.]

PROBLEM 17-16 Assume that you are employed in the physical distribution department of a corporation and are required to use budgets for control purposes. How would you go about employing budgets for this purpose?

Answer: For the corporation, budgets are financial plans for a future time period. Control through budgets involves comparing the financial plans with actual performance and determining if the difference between the two is important enough to merit further factor remedial action. For effective control, the company needs budgets for sales, major expense categories broken down by activities and decisions, and cash. [See Section 17-6.]

PROBLEM 17-17 Assume that you have been asked to recommend a set of marketing budgets to be used by a company that sells over-the-counter drugs to combat motion sickness. What major budgets would you recommend?

Answer: Among the major budgets for the drug producer would be sales, selling expenses, advertising expenses, research expenses, and administrative expenses. The company should consider breaking these down for segments such as sales territories and sales representatives. The sales budget would be the most important one for the drug producer, since all other budgets are based upon it. [See Section 17-6.]

PROBLEM 17-18 In 1986, Balanchine Industries discovered that the share of the toy market which its Super Sudsy Doll accounted for had declined since 1985. What does market share mean?

Answer: In market share analysis, Balanchine Industries' management computes company sales as a percentage of total industry sales. Ordinarily, this is done for the firm at large and for its major segments, such as particular divisions, product lines, products, and geographic areas. Then management compares market share with target levels, past levels, and the market share of rivals, to decide if remedial action may be needed. Essentially, market share measures the success of the firm relative to the industry. The decline in Super Sudsy Dolls sales may signal the need for a change in promotion or pricing. [See Section 17-6.]

PROBLEM 17-19 Assume that you have been asked to do a sales analysis for a large supermarket chain. How would you go about this task?

Answer: Sales analysis requires breaking down the supermarket's sales by important segments of the business, such as by division, product, product group, or geographic area. The segments with low sales are flagged for possible remedial action, while segments with high sales may be given larger budgets. In order to do the sales analysis, you would have to assemble a considerable amount of past store sales data and subdivide the data according to the segments you want to examine. If the company has a well developed marketing information system, this task is greatly facilitated. [See Section 17-6.]

PROBLEM 17-20 What is the difference between cost analysis and a marketing audit?

Answer: Cost analysis is an important control device where costs are broken down by important segments of the business. When combined with sales analysis, it can reveal which segments are the most profitable. It also can indicate which, if any, costs are excessively high. The marketing audit is broader in scope. It is a systematic and critical review of the entire marketing operation. Auditors examine goals, policies, procedures, personnel, and the organization the marketing unit uses. It is especially useful in identifying marketing strengths and weaknesses that are not readily apparent. [See Section 17-6.]

18 SERVICES MARKETING AND NONPROFIT MARKETING

THIS CHAPTER IS ABOUT

☑ **Differences Between Goods and Services**
☑ **Characteristics of Services Marketing**
☑ **The Use of Marketing by Nonprofit Organizations**
☑ **Characteristics of Nonprofit Marketing**

18-1. Differences Between Goods and Services

A. The nature of services

Many of the offerings that consumers and industrial buyers purchase are services, rather than tangible goods. **Services** consist of *actions* that consumers and buyers purchase in order to obtain direct satisfaction. In contrast, *goods* are physical entities purchased by consumers and buyers in order to obtain satisfaction from the items purchased, rather than directly from the seller. Figure 18-1 illustrates these differences.

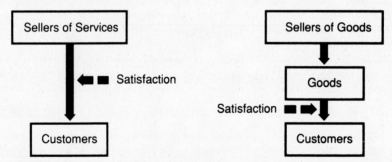

FIGURE 18-1: Buyer satisfaction obtained from the purchase of goods and services.

EXAMPLE 18-1: When a consumer rents a Chrysler New Yorker from Avis, he or she has purchased a service. If, however, the consumer purchases a New Yorker from a Chrysler dealer, he or she has acquired a good.

The range of services that consumers and industrial buyers purchase is considerable. Table 18-1 sets forth some examples of services. It is evident that services are very extensive and account for a large portion of buyers' expenditures. Slightly less than one-half of consumer expenditures is for services. Further, the proportion of service buying is growing rapidly and will probably continue to do so in the foreseeable future as the prices of services advance, consumers earn higher incomes, and individuals seek increased convenience and leisure.

B. Attributes of services

There are several attributes of services that are important to marketers. Specifically, services are intangible, heterogeneous, inseparable from the marketer, and perishable.

TABLE 18-1: Examples of Services That Buyers Purchase

· Legal advice	· Child care
· Medical assistance	· Investment counseling
· Tax preparation assistance	· Banking services
· Hotel and motel accommodations	· Hospital services
· Airline tickets	· Dental services
· Insurance policies	· Automobile repair
· Haircuts	· Landscaping
· Physical fitness advice	· Education
· Housecleaning	· Pet grooming and boarding
· Janitorial services	· Mortuary services
· Auto rentals	· Consulting service
· Education	· Telephone service
· Marriage counseling	· Dry cleaning
· Stock brokerage services	· Realtors' service

1. Intangibility

Services are intangible—i.e., they do not have physical substance. Consumers cannot touch, see, smell, or taste services before purchasing them. This poses difficulties for the services marketer because target customers may be reluctant to buy what they cannot physically examine. Unlike some goods, services cannot help sell themselves, so a marketer may be forced to sell a service aggressively through advertising, personal selling, and/or sales promotion. One of the best stimulants to sales is word-of-mouth promotion, where one target customer tells others about the quality of the services. Most individuals are impressed by favorable recommendations from a friend or acquaintance, rather than from a commercial source such as advertising.

EXAMPLE 18-2: Consumers cannot physically examine H & R Block tax preparation services to see if they want to purchase them. The company attempts to counteract the intangibility of their offering by extensive advertising on television and in magazines and by locating many of its tax preparation booths in malls where many consumers pass by. In addition, Mr. Block seeks out guest appearances on television talk shows before and during tax season; by doing this he provides advice to taxpayers and thereby helps build a positive image of the company.

2. Heterogeneity

Services are heterogeneous—i.e., they are not standardized. The nature of the offering of any one seller may differ from one time period to another. Further, two or more employees of one firm may provide services that are quite different from each other. It is therefore difficult for target customers to evaluate the offerings of a company, as they may vary over time and place. Marketers experience difficulty in producing a standardized offering and must take care that their "products" are not of inferior quality from time to time. In other words, they must practice quality control in much the same way as do marketers of goods.

EXAMPLE 18-3: The management of Hilton Hotels realizes that the services that are provided by desk clerks, cleaning personnel, restaurant staff, and others must be of a consistently high quality to satisfy the expectations of guests. The hotel chain selects employees with great care, provides them with detailed training, and supervises them closely, in order to ensure that they provide consumer satisfaction and work efficiently.

Part of the reason why services are heterogeneous is that the customer often participates in the service act. This means that the behavior of the buyer has an effect on the quality of the services.

Since buyers differ from one another, they may receive different services. Further, the same buyer may receive different services at two or more times because he or she behaves differently in each instance.

EXAMPLE 18-4: Some patients of a physician are very cooperative in explaining all of the symptoms they have. This makes it easier for the doctor to make a correct diagnosis and recommend treatment that will result in healing. Other patients are reluctant to reveal some symptoms and, as a result, may receive ineffective treatment.

---

3. *Inseparability*

Marketers and the services they provide are always inseparable—i.e., they are continually at the same place at the same time. Services cannot exist unless the marketer is present. One lawyer, for instance, can handle only a limited number of cases. Obviously, this can limit the growth of a service company, unless the number of service providers, is increased, as when a lawyer forms a legal firm with one or more partners. Further, inseparability usually necessitates direct distribution—intermediaries are not feasible in most cases.

EXAMPLE 18-5: A hair stylist cannot be separated from the services which he or she provides. Unless more employees or partners are brought in, a hair stylist will probably never be able to serve more than about seven customers in a given day.

---

4. *Perishability*

Services tend to have very short life spans. Tangible goods can be produced and then placed in inventory, so that they are available when and where customers want them. Services, however, cannot be stored. Services companies therefore can suffer unnecessary costs unless demand can be accurately forecast, because employees and facilities will be idle when customers do not demand services.

EXAMPLE 18-6: If club members do not come to a Nautilus physical fitness center while an instructor is on duty, the instructor's services are wasted. The center must still pay the instructor's wages and thus forgoes profits.

18-2. Characteristics of Services Marketing

In many ways, the marketing of services is very similar to the marketing of tangible goods. In both cases, companies select target customers and design a marketing mix made up of some combination of product, price, promotion, and place. Further, managers adjust their marketing strategies and tactics to the environment surrounding the firm. In some ways, however, the marketing task for services differs from that of goods. These differences relate to the marketing concept and the four P's.

A. The marketing concept

The marketing concept is as important for service as it is for product marketers, as a means of providing for stability and growth. Many service marketers, however, have not pursued the marketing concept, following instead a sales or a production orientation. Some have survived, often simply because of good fortune or very hard work, but many others have not been successful.

EXAMPLE 18-7: Some of the industries in the United States that have suffered the highest business failure rates are laundromats, restaurants, motels, barbershops, videotape rental units, and tanning salons.

Many service marketers are not trained in marketing. Their major expertise is in production. For example, a truck driver who is employed by a carrier, such as the Preston Trucking Company, may decide, after years of serving as an employee, to quit the firm and start a trucking company. This is common in the industry. This individual knows the operations end of truck transportation very well, but may be very naive with respect to marketing. Thus, it is probable that a sales or production orientation will be adopted, rather than the marketing concept.

Not all service firms, of course, have ignored the marketing concept. You are probably familiar with neighborhood barbershops, hair salons, and other firms that are closely attuned to consumer satisfaction. Some large organizations, including the Texas Air Corporation, Merrill Lynch & Co., Visa International, and Southwestern Bell telephone company, have demonstrated a strong commitment in this direction. Nevertheless, many companies have a long way to go.

B. Selection of target customers

Service marketers should select a set of particular target customers, rather than attempting to satisfy everyone. This requires looking at various possible groupings of potential customers, their purchasing power and desires, and deciding if they would be good target markets. Service marketers must also look for trends in the environmental variables that can signal opportunities for success.

EXAMPLE 18-8: E.F. Hutton once oriented its services primarily toward males, since men were the primary decision makers on the purchase of securities. Today, there is a large group of working women with purchasing power, so the company attempts to make a major appeal to women. Some of its ads appear in magazines read primarily by women and feature women investment counselors and investors.

C. Service planning

Service planning consists of determining the nature of the services that will be offered to target customers. A firm may add, delete, or change its service mix over time. The ability to react to changes in the environment through alterations in services can be one of the keys to success. Changes in demand, technology, social forces, and the law can open up significant new opportunities. A marketer should be on the alert for opportunities in market segmentation and product differentiation, in much the same way as are the marketers of goods.

EXAMPLE 18-9: During the 1980's, the Prudential Insurance Company expanded the scope of the services its agents offered. Once confined mainly to insurance, they moved into selling stocks, bonds, and mutual funds. This change was a very profitable one for the firm.

D. Pricing

Pricing is a very important activity for service providers. Because the offerings are perishable, service prices must be low enough to attract a steady flow of customers. On the other hand, prices must be high enough to cover costs and leave a margin for profit. If prices are too high, some target customers will perform the services for themselves or will switch to competitors.

Many services marketers base their prices primarily on costs—they fail to consider demand and competition. This can be a serious error because well-formulated prices must be based on all three factors.

EXAMPLE 18-10: Most dentists base their fees on how much time they devote to a patient and the cost of materials (such as fillings and crowns). Some dentists have lost business to practitioners at clinics who, recognizing the importance of demand elasticity, discount their services.

E. Promotion

Marketers of services are frequently extensive users of advertising, personal selling, sales promotion, and publicity. Many smaller service firms depend heavily on personal selling. They develop close interpersonal relationships with customers and make a major effort to satisfy customer needs. In turn, customers are very loyal to many such firms, especially if they know the managers or the employees personally.

Some service marketers rely heavily on advertising. Since their offerings are intangible and cannot be displayed, they will not sell themselves. Advertising, however, can describe the benefits that can result from using the services. This form of promotion is used extensively by airlines, insurance companies, banks and other financial institutions, hotels and motels, and others. It is even being increasingly used by professionals, such as doctors and lawyers, as competition in these fields becomes increasingly intense.

EXAMPLE 18-11: The McPherson Medical Clinic in Dallas advertises on television and radio and in newspapers. The ads stress reasonable prices, a highly qualified staff, and no need for appointments. They make a strong appeal to those who need medical services on an emergency basis but find hospital emergency rooms to be unappealing.

F. Physical distribution

The major physical distribution decision that most service marketers face is where to locate the facilities that serve customers. This decision should be based primarily on the overall marketing strategy. Lawyers who appeal to corporate and high-income clients often locate in prestigious office buildings and suites. Mortuaries are often situated in quiet, neat-appearing neighborhoods. Travel agents tend to locate in sites that are convenient for their customers. All of these types of firms base their location on the nature of the target market and the desires of target customers.

G. Channels of distribution

Generally, services are marketed directly, so there is only one possible channel of distribution. This is the case because those who furnish services and the services themselves are essentially inseparable. Intermediaries are used in a few cases, however; for example, independent insurance agents sell policies issued by several different insurance companies and travel agents sell airline tickets for most airlines.

18-3. The Use of Marketing by Nonprofit Organizations

Traditionally, marketing has been used by businesses for which profit is an important objective. However, recent years have witnessed the utilization of marketing philosophies and techniques by nonprofit organizations as well. These organizations have come to realize that they cannot achieve their objectives without some means of effectively dealing with their "consumers." Nonprofit organizations compete with one another for funds and for donations of time and goods from members of the public. As financing from the federal government has dropped over the years, they have turned to the use of marketing tools to solicit funds. Some have attempted to raise money from the general public in much the same way that a consumer marketer does. Others have aimed their efforts at businesses, foundations, and other associations.

EXAMPLE 18-12: The United Fund solicits funds from businesses and the public through annual fund-raising drives. This organization chooses leading members of the community to head up its drives. Considerable publicity is generated through public relations efforts, resulting in news coverage by the media. Solicitors ("sales" representatives) call on individuals and seek donations. This charity even suggests "fair share" donation levels, which is a form of pricing. The money that is collected is divided up among participating charitable organizations.

Recent years have seen an explosion of marketing activities by nonprofit organizations. Political candidates use television, radio, newspaper, and billboard advertising extensively. Churches, through evangelical activities, seek members and pledges of funds in what amounts to personal-selling methods.

Museums sell books and other items to the public to support their financial needs. The armed services market their organizations to potential recruits, both for enlisted personnel and officer candidates.

18-4. Characteristics of Nonprofit Marketing

Many of the marketing activities undertaken by nonprofit organizations are similar to those undertaken by profit-seeking businesses. There are, however, some fundamental differences.

A. Goals

By their very nature, nonprofit organizations do not seek to make a profit, but to provide services to the public at large or to some special group. The lack of profit motivation does not mean that nonprofit organizations do not need money, however. They must obtain funds from some source in order to cover their expenses and to perform the service they are established to perform. Without revenues they will cease to exist, regardless of the value of the services that they perform.

EXAMPLE 18-13: The American Cancer Society sponsors advertisements in magazines and on television asking for financial contributions. In addition, collection boxes are placed in retail outlets, where consumers can insert coins and bills as donations. These donations support the ongoing research and related activities of this organization.

B. Consumers

Nonprofit organizations must direct their marketing mix to different groups of consumers, often called *publics*. One group consists of those who *receive* the services that the organization offers. For instance, the Salvation Army must reach individuals who are in need of its facilities for food and shelter. Another public consists of those who *donate* funds, services (such as volunteer help), and commodities (such as clothing for the poor). Still another public consists of those who attempt to generate support for the organization (such as Sally Struthers for the Christian Children's Fund and Jerry Lewis for Muscular Dystrophy). To be successful, the organization must direct a marketing mix to each of these publics. It can be difficult to succeed, because many other organizations are competing for these publics also.

C. The marketing mix

1. Product

The "products" offered by many nonprofit organizations are in fact services. This being the case, the materials relating to the marketing of services that were presented in the early part of this chapter are applicable. Many of the services that can be offered are limited by the organization's charter, objectives, or legal standing. Thus, a church cannot sell new automobiles and the U.S. Postal Service cannot engage in the manufacturing and marketing of canned goods.

EXAMPLE 18-14: The Heart Fund is chartered as a charitable organization with the objective of raising funds for research and the dissemination of information to prevent heart disease. It cannot engage in other services, according to its charter.

---

2. Price

Pricing by nonprofit organizations differs in some ways from pricing by businesses. Some do not assess a price to their clients, but provide free services. On the other hand, they may charge a fee to those who desire to become members of the organization.

EXAMPLE 18-15: The National Association for the Advancement of Colored People (NAACP) assesses various fees for memberships. Affiliate memberships are available for $5 per year. Various other memberships are also available, ranging all the way up to $500 for a lifetime membership. Members are entitled to attend branch and regional meetings, wear organization pins, vote in elections, and receive NAACP publications.

Some nonprofit organizations charge a fee for their services, but the fees are less than the cost of the service. Many municipal transportation systems, for example, price in this way and make up the remainder of their expenses through subsidies granted by the federal, state, or local governments. Finally, some nonprofit organizations charge prices that are based on analyses of demand, cost, and competition, in much the same way as do businesses. An example is the U.S. Postal Service.

3. Place

The physical distribution and channel of distribution decisions that nonprofit organizations must make are usually quite similar to those of business marketers of goods and services. Many are not allowed to employ intermediaries, however, and must carry out all of the necessary marketing activities without assistance. For marketers of nonprofit organizations, as for marketers of services, the major physical distribution problem frequently is site selection (location of offices and other facilities). However, some nonprofit organizations, such as the commissary system for the U.S. Army, are involved in all of the physical distribution functions. Goods sold in commissaries must be transported and stored in much the same way as they are in private businesses.

4. Promotion

Nonprofit organizations, like businesses, make extensive use of promotion. They utilize advertising, personal selling, sales promotion, public relations, and publicity for this purpose. Some, such as the U.S. Army, spend large amounts on advertising. For those which are charities, free publicity is often made available by the media.

RAISE YOUR GRADES

Can you explain . . . ?

☑ why the fact that services are intangible poses problems for marketers who sell the services
☑ why the fact that services are perishable poses a problem for the firm
☑ why the manager of a service company might not follow the marketing concept
☑ why service planning is important to service marketers
☑ why advertising can be significant to marketing managers in service firms
☑ why candidates for public office use marketing techniques to help win elections
☑ who the major classes of consumers are for service firms

SUMMARY

1. Services are actions that buyers purchase in order to obtain satisfaction directly from the seller.
2. The range of services that consumers and industrial buyers purchase is considerable.
3. Services are intangible, meaning they do not have physical substance.
4. Services are heterogeneous, meaning they are not standardized.
5. Services are inseparable from the marketers who provide them.
6. Services are perishable, meaning they have a short life span.
7. In many ways, the marketing of services is very similar to the marketing of tangible goods.
8. The marketing concept is as important for service as it is for product marketers, as a means of providing for stability and growth.

9. Service marketers should select a set of particular target customers, rather than attempting to satisfy everyone.
10. Service planning involves determining the nature of the services that will be offered to target customers.
11. Because the offerings are perishable, service prices must be low enough to attract a steady flow of customers.
12. The major physical distribution decision that most service marketers face is where to locate the facilities that serve customers.
13. Services are generally marketed directly, so there is only one possible channel of distribution.
14. Service marketers are frequently extensive users of advertising, personal selling, sales promotion, and publicity.
15. Recent years have witnessed the utilization of marketing philosophies and techniques by nonprofit organizations.
16. By their very nature, nonprofit organizations do not seek to make a profit, but to provide services to the public at large or to some special group.
17. Nonprofit organizations must direct their marketing mix to different groups of consumers, often called publics.
18. Nonprofit organizations must tailor the marketing mix to their particular offerings.

RAPID REVIEW   Answers

Short Answer

1. Services are _____ that buyers purchase in order to obtain satisfaction. [See Section 18-1.] — *actions*

2. Consumers allocate slightly less than _____ of their expenditures for services. [See Section 18-1.] — *one-half*

3. Since its services are intangible, Dale Carnegie motivation classes may not _____ themselves. [See Section 18-1.] — *sell*

4. Heterogeneity of services means that Mr. Goodwrench auto repairs may be difficult for consumers to _____. [See Section 18-1.] — *evaluate*

5. Since the services of a plumber are inseparable from the marketer, it may be difficult to achieve company _____. [See Section 18-1.] — *growth*

6. The perishable nature of services means that they cannot be _____. [See Section 18-1.] — *stored*

7. Some furnace repair companies are not pursuing the marketing concept but are following the _____ concept in doing business. [See Section 18-2.] — *production or sales*

8. Health maintenance organizations should select a set of particular _____ _____, rather than attempting to satisfy everyone. [See Section 18-2.] — *target consumers*

9. Many service marketers base their prices mainly on their _____. [See Section 18-2.] — *costs*

10. Numerous small service firms, such as neighborhood grocers, depend heavily on _____ _____ as a promotion tool. [See Section 18-2.] — *personal selling*

11. The major physical distribution decision that most marketers of services make is _____. [See Section 18-2.] — *location*

12. Businesses such as E.F. Hutton differ from charitable organizations in that one of their more important goals is _____. [See Section 18-3.] — *profit*

13. Nonprofit organizations have increasingly looked for financing from the public as funding from the _____ _____ has dropped. [See Section 18-3.] — *federal government*

14. Recent years have seen increases in marketing activities by _____ organizations. [See Section 18-3.] — *nonprofit*

15. Many nonprofit organizations, such as a municipal water system, have as a goal the provision of services to _____ _____. [See Section 18-4.]   *the public*

16. The offerings of many nonprofit organizations are in fact _____. [See Section 18-4.]   *services*

17. Important "publics" for many nonprofit organizations are those who donate funds, those who help generate support, and those who _____ the services that the organization offers. [See Section 18-4.]   *use*

18. The services that the Episcopal church can provide are limited by its _____. [See Section 18-4.]   *charter*

19. A nonprofit organization may raise funds by _____ for membership. [See Section 18-4.]   *charging*

20. For charitable nonprofit organizations, free _____ is often made available by the media. [See Section 18-4.]   *publicity*

SOLVED PROBLEMS

PROBLEM 18-1   A fellow student has read that consumers are spending more and more of their incomes on services and wonders how these are distinguished from tangible goods. How would you answer?

Answer: Services consist of actions that buyers purchase in order to obtain satisfaction. They are intangible. Examples are banking, hairstyling, and tax preparation services. This is in contrast to goods, which are physical entities purchased by buyers. For example, a homeowner could purchase a storage shed (a good) or have goods stored in a commercial storage unit (a service). [See Section 18-1.]

PROBLEM 18-2   The services of a hospital are intangible. How does this pose a problem for its marketing staff?

Answer: Intangibility means that the hospital services do not have physical substance. Patients cannot touch, see, smell, or taste them before purchase. This poses difficulty for the marketer in differentiating them from competitors' offerings, since patients have trouble comparing that which they cannot physically perceive. Unlike some goods, services cannot sell themselves, so the marketer may be forced to aggresively sell them through advertising, personal selling (involving medical doctors), and sales promotion. Since hospital services are "unsought goods" for many patients, the problems relating to intangibility are especially great. [See Section 18-1.]

PROBLEM 18-3   The services of a management consulting firm are heterogeneous. What are the implications of this to management?

Answer: Heterogeneity refers to the fact that the consulting services are not standardized. The nature of the offerings of the firm differs from one time period to another. Further, two or more employees of the firm may provide services that are quite different. This makes it difficult for target customers to evaluate the offerings of the company, as they may differ over time and place. Marketers experience difficulty in producing a standardized offering and must take care that their "products" are not of inferior quality from time to time. [See Section 18-1.]

PROBLEM 18-4   Buyers participate in the services of tax preparation firms. How does this affect the nature of the services?

Answer: Part of the reason why tax preparation services are heterogeneous is that the client participates in the service act. He or she provides information and documents to the tax preparer. This means that the behavior of the client has an effect on the quality of the services. Since clients differ from one another, they receive different services. For example, an uncooperative client who refuses to provide the tax preparer with enough information needed to take advantage of various provisions of the tax code may receive much lower quality services from the tax preparer than a cooperative client. [See Section 18-1.]

PROBLEM 18-5 Interior decorators and the services they provide are inseparable. How does this affect such companies?

Answer: Services of interior decorators cannot exist unless the marketer is present. This may prevent the company from growing beyond a certain point and achieving economies of scale. One interior decorator can only handle a limited number of customers. Growth is possible by increasing the number of interior decorators in a firm. Further, inseparability usually necessitates direct distribution. Intermediaries are not feasible in most cases. [See Section 18.1.]

PROBLEM 18-6 The services of a symphony orchestra are perishable. How does this affect marketing?

Answer: Perishability refers to the very short life of the symphony services. Tangible goods can be produced and then placed in inventory, so that they are available when and where customers want them. This is not possible for the orchestra. Its services are depleted immediately after a performance so the channel of distribution must be direct. It also restricts price markdowns made when the services do not sell—symphony prices cannot be reduced during a performance. [See Section 18-1.]

PROBLEM 18-7 The owners of some automobile repair garages have prospered even though they follow the production concept. How can you explain this?

Answer: Some auto repair garages have done well, even though they embrace the production concept. Some have survived because of good fortune or hard work. They may have been located in an area where competition was weak or demand particularly strong. If the owners or employees were particularly talented in repairs, and received good word-of-mouth promotion, this could account for their success. Many, however, have not been successful and have gone out of business. [See Section 18-2.]

PROBLEM 18-8 Why do many small service marketers, such as locksmiths, not practice the marketing concept?

Answer: Many service marketers are not trained in marketing. Locksmiths, for example, have their major expertise in production. They think of themselves as specialists in working with keys and locks rather than with marketing tools, such as promotion and price. The production concept is common among such individuals. [See Section 18-2.]

PROBLEM 18-9 "Virtually all service firms have ignored the marketing concept." Do you agree with this statement?

Answer: Not all service firms have ignored the marketing concept. Many small service organizations, such as insurance agencies and appliance repair shops, are dedicated to customer satisfaction. Further, some large organizations, such as banks, stock brokerage houses, and airlines, have demonstrated a strong commitment in this direction. With the passage of time, it can be expected that more will adopt the marketing concept. [See Section 18-2.]

PROBLEM 18-10 Assume that you are a marketing executive for a car rental company. How would you go about selecting target consumers?

Answer: You should examine various possible groupings of potential customers, their purchasing power and desires, and decide if they would be good target markets. Some promising groupings are demographic (especially age and income), benefit, and psychographic. Car rental companies target heavily on business travelers and tourists in above-average income categories. You should be on the alert for trends in automobile renting patterns among various possible target customer groups, as these patterns can change over time. [See Section 18-2.]

PROBLEM 18-11 How should a motel and restaurant chain go about the service planning process?

Answer: Service planning consists of determining the nature of the motel and restaurant services that will be offered to target customers. The firm may add, delete, or change the service mix over time. The ability to react to changes in the environment through alterations in services can be one of the keys to success. The company should keep track of customer desires through marketing research and analysis of complaints. It should monitor what competing motels and restaurants are doing, in order to keep pace with the market. Management should attempt to stimulate a flow of creative new ideas on the service mix from all employees, both high- and low-level. [See Section 18-2.]

PROBLEM 18-12 What are some of the major factors that a hospital should consider in pricing its services?

Answer: A hospital should consider the demand for its services. For inelastic-demand services, such as physical therapy, prices can be higher than for elastic-demand services, such as outpatient services. Cost is another important pricing consideration. Generally, an attempt should be made to at least cover the variable cost of providing a service, through charges to patients. Also, competition must be analyzed in setting prices. Hospitals and clinics that are rivals may force the hospital to keep charges for some services low in relation to costs. Also, the actions of the government, through Medicare and other programs, should be evaluated. [See Section 18-2.]

PROBLEM 18-13 A dentist has informed you that she does not use advertising because the excellence of her services will sell themselves through favorable publicity. Do you agree?

Answer: Advertising may be a useful technique for the dentist. Since her services are intangible, they cannot be displayed and will not sell themselves. Advertising, however, can describe the benefits that result from using the services. Publicity and word-of-mouth communication are unreliable and can even carry negative messages, so they should not be relied upon exclusively for the promotion effort. Many dentists have found the cost of advertising to be very small, in relation to the revenues that the advertising created. [See Section 18-2.]

PROBLEM 18-14 According to the manager of an appliance repair shop, "Physical distribution is of no interest to us. After all, we sell services, not goods." How would you react to this statement?

Answer: The appliance repair shop manager is not right, and *should* be concerned with the location of the facility. This decision should be based primarily on the overall marketing strategy. The shop should be located at a site that is convenient for target customers, perhaps near their homes, places of work, shopping areas, or a busy street. It should provide convenient access. Rental or lease payments should be reasonable. The manager should avoid any location with a reputation that might cast a bad image on the shop. [See Section 18-2.]

PROBLEM 18-15 A newly hired employee for the U.S. Postal Service has informed you that this organization has no need for marketing because it does not seek profits. Do you agree?

Answer: The employee is incorrect. The fact that the organization does not seek profits does not mean that it does not need marketing. This organization cannot achieve its goals without some means of effectively dealing with postal service users. The U.S. Postal Service competes with private firms, such as Federal Express, and a failure to recognize this could result in substantial setbacks for the postal service. [See Section 18-3.]

PROBLEM 18-16 "Few nonprofit organizations are involved in marketing." Do you agree with this statement?

Answer: The statement is incorrect. Recent years have seen an explosion of marketing activities by nonprofit organizations. These include political candidates, churches, museums, the armed services, other branches of government, and charities. These organizations are involved in marketing research, choosing target customers, product or service planning, promotion campaigns, setting prices, channels of distribution, and physical distribution decisions. Some, such as the U.S. Army, have very well organized marketing organizations. [See Section 18-3.]

PROBLEM 18-17 How do the goals of the American Heart Association differ from those of a company such as General Mills?

Answer: By its very nature, a nonprofit organization such as the American Heart Association does not exist to earn profits. Rather, the goal is to provide health-related services to those with heart problems. This does not mean that the organization has no need for money, however. It, like General Mills, must obtain funds from some source in order to cover expenses. Management is charged with the responsibility of installing marketing programs that will bring in donations from individuals, foundations, and companies, and permit the AHA to continue furnishing services to its beneficiaries. [See Section 18-3.]

PROBLEM 18-18   Assume that you are a manager for a charity that solicits funds for the support of poor children in foreign countries. What publics would you direct your marketing mix toward?

Answer: One group of publics consists of those who receive the services that the organization offers; namely, poor children. Another public consists of those who donate funds, services, and goods. Many of these are in the upper middle- and upper-income classes. Still another public consists of those who attempt to build support for the organization. Celebrities often make up a large proportion of this group. [See Section 18-4.]

PROBLEM 18-19   How does the U.S. Postal Service go about pricing its services?

Answer: The U.S. Postal Service must consider the same elements as any firm when setting prices—demand, cost, and competition. Demand for its services can be measured by tabulating revenue figures and by consulting with the public. Also, postal costs are given very strong consideration. If costs go up, postage charges are likely to rise. Finally, competition is an element. The postal service competes with United Parcel Service, Federal Express, the telephone companies, and other firms. Its services should be reasonably priced in relation to these. [See Section 18-4.]

PROBLEM 18-20   The director of a city museum does not engage in advertising, feeling that this will not benefit an organization that does not seek profits. Do you agree?

Answer: Advertising could be of substantial value to the museum. It can provide information on what is available to see in the museum and other factors, such as the location and hours of operation. It also can be effective in convincing individuals and families to visit the facility. Even small advertisements in newspapers and radio can have a strong positive impact on museum attendance. This promotion method can be especially useful in attracting tourists, many of whom may not be aware of the facility and its holdings, hours of operation, or admittance charge. [See Section 18-4.]

19 THE LAW AND MARKETING

19-1. The Impact of Law on Marketing

Most newspapers and magazines that you pick up today have stories about government regulation of business. Much of this news is about marketing, which is heavily regulated by federal, state, and local agencies. In fact, few marketing activities are exempt from some kind of law or ordinance, whether it be federal, state, county, metro, or city, and whether it focus on the consumer, the product, price, place, or promotion.

As shown in Figure 19-1, failure to obey the law can result in very undesirable consequences. A firm that is found guilty of disobeying a law may receive fines and it's possible that its officers may go to prison. The courts may require that a company take actions that result in a substantial loss of funds. Negative comments in the news media can easily damage the reputation of a company and result in loss of business. Marketers should be familiar with the law as it pertains to their actions and should strive to follow the directions the law prescribes.

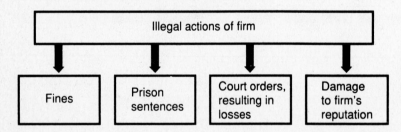

FIGURE 19-1: Failure to obey the law can have very undesirable consequences.

This does not mean that marketers need to be lawyers. But it does mean that they should be generally familiar with their legal responsibilities. When legal issues arise, marketers should consult attorneys, either those employed by their own firms or independent lawyers. The law is a very complex field and much of it requires the expert interpretation of legal counsel.

There are a number of major legal fields that pertain to marketers. Each of the elements of the marketing mix—product, price, place, and promotion—is the target of government regulation. One of the fields that is of major significance is antitrust legislation.

19-2. Antitrust Laws

During the 19th century, many big business "barons" such as Andrew Carnegie and Cornelius Vanderbilt acquired near-exclusive, monopoly control over industries such as steel, railroads, sugar, and alcohol. To combat these monopolies (called **trusts**), the U.S. Congress began to pass antitrust laws, starting with the Sherman Antitrust Act of 1890. Because the Sherman Act and other antitrust acts are *federal* laws, only those companies engaged in *interstate commerce* are regulated by those acts. **Interstate commerce**, which comes under federal jurisdiction, means business involving more than one state. If a company sells or buys in more than one state or engages in business practices that affect business in other states, it is involved in interstate commerce. In practice, all but the very smallest of businesses are considered to be participating in interstate commerce under the law.

Companies that violate antitrust laws are subject to very strong penalties. Under the Sherman Act, for instance, companies in violation can be fined up to one million dollars plus damages. Individuals can be fined as much as $100,000 plus damages and can be sent to prison for up to three years.

There are three major antitrust acts which curtail monopolistic behavior on the part of business: the Sherman Act, the Clayton Act, and the Robinson Patman Act. The major actions prohibited by these laws are discussed below and summarized in Figure 19-2.

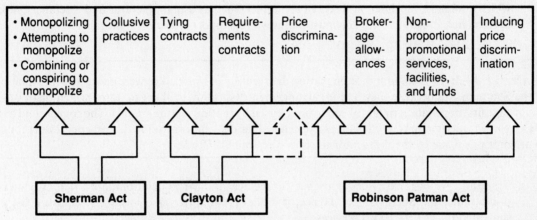

FIGURE 19-2: Major actions prohibited by antitrust laws.

A. The Sherman Antitrust Act

This law outlaws two types of practices. The first of these is *monopolizing*, including attempting to monopolize and combining or conspiring to monopolize. The second is *collusive practices* in restraint of trade.

1. Monopolizing

The courts view **monopolizing** to exist when a company has a large enough market share in an industry to permit it to dictate prices and other elements of competition. To be guilty of monopolizing, a firm must be engaging in activities that give it monopoly power.

EXAMPLE 19-1: In 1985, the Supreme Court ruled that the Aspen Skiing Co., which owned three of the four ski slopes in Aspen, Colorado, had engaged in practices designed to drive another ski company, Aspen Highlands Skiing Co., out of business. Aspen had refused to continue a joint ticketing arrangement with Highlands which had been profitable for both parties. The court ruled that Aspen's intent in refusing to work with Highlands was to drive the latter out of business.

A firm need not be monopolizing the entire U.S. market for it to be in violation of the Sherman Act. If a firm is ruled to be monopolizing in a smaller market, such as a state or region, it may be in violation of the law. Also, monopolizing exists in the context of a particular **line of commerce**, which is a group of companies that compete for the same customers.

EXAMPLE 19-2: Courts have ruled that a producer of aluminum foil must be monopolizing in the whole "flexible packaging" market, not just the aluminum foil market, to be in violation of the law. The flexible packaging market includes cellophane and other plastic food wrappings.

Predatory pricing is a practice that has often been found to be in violation of the Sherman Act. A company is said to be engaging in predatory pricing when it lowers its price to a very low level, perhaps below costs, in order to drive competitors out of business. Often, the motive of the predatory pricer is to raise prices to a very high level once competitors have been driven out.

2. Collusive practices

The Sherman Act also outlaws *collusuive practices* that *restrain trade* and result in monopoly power. **Collusive practices** are illegal agreements between two or more companies to restrain trade and to gain monopoly power. **Restraint of trade** means an injury to particular competitors or injury to the extent of competition in a line of commerce. While one company can monopolize, it takes two or more to collude in restraint of trade.

A type of collusion that the Sherman Act is quite strict about is price agreements. Agreements on price between competitors, called **horizontal collusion**, are always illegal, regardless of whether or not an agreement restrains trade. In the case of **vertical collusion**, in which companies at different levels in a channel (such as a manufacturer and a retailer) make agreements, a restraint of trade must be shown to support a charge of illegality.

EXAMPLE 19-3: In 1985, four motion picture distributors in Milwaukee were charged with violation of the Sherman Act because they had an arrangement that allowed them to agree which distributor would have first negotiation rights for each film released by motion picture studios. The court found that this agreement was horizontal collusion and instructed the distributors to stop this practice, even though no attempt was made by the prosecutor to show a restraint of trade.

Trade and professional associations, such as medical and bar associations, are not allowed to fix prices under the Sherman Act. Hence, it is illegal for a bar association to publish a list of suggested prices for various services.

B. The Clayton Act

The Clayton Act prohibits several actions relating to antitrust. Those provisions most applicable to marketing are discussed below.

1. Tying contracts

Tying contracts occur when a supplier indicates that it will not sell one brand or product to a customer unless the customer buys another brand or product from that supplier. These contracts are illegal if it appears that they might restrain trade or create a monopoly.

EXAMPLE 19-4: Data General produced an illegal tying contract when it required that purchasers of its copyrighted and highly demanded RDOD computer operating system must also buy its Nova hardware.

---

2. Requirements contracts

In the case of *requirements contracts* (sometimes called *exclusive dealing arrangements*), buyers must fill ALL of their needs for a specific product from a supplier if they are to acquire ANY of this product. These contracts are illegal if it can be shown that they might restrain trade or create a monopoly.

EXAMPLE 19-5: Suppose a producer of sailboats wants to fill its resin needs by buying half from Supplier A and half from Supplier B, thereby avoiding becoming dependent on either one. If Supplier A has a requirements contract, it would not furnish any resin to the sailboat manufacturer unless it bought all of its resin from Supplier A. This contract would probably be considered illegal under the Clayton Act.

---

3. Price discrimination

The Clayton Act also prohibits *price discrimination*. The provisions of this law have been amended by the Robinson Patman act, to the extent that the latter is the major regulator of marketers.

C. The Robinson Patman Act

The Robinson Patman Act prohibits price discrimination; brokerage allowances; nonproportional promotional services, facilities, or funds; and inducing price discrimination.

1. Price discrimination

The Robinson Patman Act outlaws price discrimination to purchasers of like goods who are similarly situated, if the effect of that discrimination may be to lessen competition or create a monopoly. Discrimination exists when two or more competing buyers who are at the same level of competition (such as two wholesalers) are charged different prices. The goods must be "of like grade and quality," rather than different items. The Robinson Patman Act does *not* outlaw price discrimination to consumers. Furthermore, it applies only to tangible goods and not to services.

EXAMPLE 19-6: Procter and Gamble discriminated in price when it sold Folgers coffee to retailers in the Pittsburg area at significantly lower prices than it did elsewhere. However, a used-car dealer who quoted a price of $2,600 for a 1984 Mercury Cougar to one customer and a price of $2,000 to another would not be guilty of price discrimination under the Robinson Patman Act.

If prohibited price discrimination has been revealed, a defendant can defend its actions in certain ways. If it can be shown that the discrimination is based on lower costs of manufacturing, selling, or delivery to some customers but not to others, the action may be ruled as legal. Or if the discrimination was made to meet the equally low price of a competitor, it may be justified. Finally, discrimination because of a damaged goods sale or a going out of business sale is allowed.

2. Brokerage allowances

The Robinson Patman Act outlaws brokerage allowances , which are payments to a customer who buys directly from the supplier, rather than through a broker.

EXAMPLE 19-7: Retailer A (a small grocery store) buys household cleaning products from a manufacturer through a broker. Retailer B (a large supermarket chain) buys directly from the manufacturer. Retailer B asks the manufacturer to pass on to it the margin that normally would be paid to the broker. Paying (or receiving) this margin would be illegal under the Robinson Patman Act.

---

3. Nonproportional promotional services, facilities, and funds

The Robinson Patman Act requires that promotional services, facilities, and funds that are provided to customers must be provided on proportionally equal terms to all competing customers. Proportionally equal terms refers to the amount of merchandise that customers purchase from the supplier, relative to the purchases of other customers.

EXAMPLE 19-8: The Salem Spring Distilled Water Company provided end-of-aisle displays for its products to a liquor store chain that bought over $10 million per year from Salem Spring. But Salem Spring did not provide any displays or other promotional aids to a competing liquor dealer that purchased approximately $3 million per year from the firm. The court ruled that this disproportional provision of promotional aids was in violation of the Robinson Patman Act, and ordered that Salem Spring would have to furnish 30% of the promotional support to the second firm that it did to the first.

---

4. Induced price discrimination

The Robinson Patman Act makes it illegal for a buyer to *induce* price discrimination, that is, to convince or coerce a seller to discriminate. Thus, both buyers and sellers can violate the Act. This provision of the law makes it difficult for large buyers to exert pressure on suppliers for special price discounts that may not be available to smaller buyers.

19-3. Product Laws

There are a number of important federal laws that have an impact on the product planning activities of marketers. These laws help to protect the consumer.

A. General law

The law requires that offerings be suitable for their intended use. If a product is not suitable for its intended use, the manufacturer can be sued for negligence, breach of contract, or fraud. Warranties are an additional element of general law.

(1) **Negligence**. Negligence exists when a marketer has acted with less care than a reasonable person would take under the circumstances.

EXAMPLE 19-9: An automobile producer manufactures a car that does not have adequate brake seals. The brake fluid leaks out, causing an accident for the owner. The owner could sue the manufacturer for negligence.

---

(2) **Breach of contract**. Breach of contract occurs when one of the parties to a contract fails to fulfill an obligation that the contract requires.

EXAMPLE 19-10: A prospective groom buys a diamond ring for his bride, having been assured by the jeweler that the diamond is one karat. A later appraisal shows that it is only three-fourths of a karat. The groom could sue the jeweler for breach of contract.

---

(3) **Fraud**. Fraud consists of making untrue statements that cause another party to enter into a contract.

EXAMPLE 19-11: A husband and wife who purchase a time-share condominium unit are assured by a sales representative that the project is free of debt. The project goes bankrupt because the developer had placed it under a burden of excessive indebtedness. The husband and wife could sue the sales company for fraud.

---

(4) **Warranties**. Some manufacturers specify warranties with their products. These set forth the conditions under which the manufacturer agrees to stand by its products; for example, an electric clock producer may stipulate "guaranteed against defects in materials and worksmanship for 90 days." The law does not require warranties, but it does require that producers who have them must abide by them. The law states that warranties should not deceive (trick) consumers. Further, producers cannot eliminate their obligation to provide products that are fit for their intended use by providing warranties that are not favorable to consumers.

B. Specific legislation

A number of specific federal laws regulate product quality and safety.

(1) **Food and Drug Administration Act**. Among the more significant federal laws is the Food and Drug Administration Act, which pertains to foods, drugs, cosmetics, and therapeutic

products. The Food and Drug Administration (FDA), a federal agency, conducts tests to determine if products perform as intended, are properly labeled, and if their promotion claims are true. The FDA can ban products that are found to be unsafe or unhealthful. It can also prohibit packages that are misleading; for example, it may prohibit packages that appear to contain more than they really do. Often, rather than conducting the tests itself, the FDA instructs marketers to do the testing that proves that their products, packages, or promotions are within the limits of the law.

(2) **Consumer Product Safety Commission Act.** This Act provides for a commission that oversees product safety. The Consumer Product Safety Commission conducts research, develops standards, and provides information to consumers about product safety. It can ban the sale of unsafe products, such as dangerous toys.

(3) **Motor Vehicle Air Pollution Control Act.** This Act establishes limits for the exhaust emissions of automobiles. It provides standards that require producers to bring their cars up to legal levels by certain dates.

(4) **Fur Products Labeling Act** and the **Textile Fiber Products Identification Act.** These Acts regulate what constitutes the definitions of various fur and textile products. They are designed to prevent such practices as labeling artificial fur as "mink."

(5) **Flammable Fabrics Act.** This Act forbids selling clothing made of materials that are highly flammable.

19-4. Promotion Laws

Federal law regulates the promotion activities of firms. The most important prohibitions are on deception of consumers and unfair methods of competition.

A. Consumer deception

The **Federal Trade Commission Act** is administered by the **Federal Trade Commission (FTC)** and prohibits consumer deception. Consumer deception refers to deliberate attempts to trick consumers into doing something that they would not do otherwise, such as buying a faulty product. This law does not identify what acts are deceptive, but leaves this decision up to the Federal Trade Commission.

EXAMPLE 19-12: In 1985, the FTC found that Southwest Sunsites, a land sales company, had violated the Act. Southwest stated to purchasers that land they bought would realize profits within a short time, that they could expect to double or triple their money, and that the land was suitable for homesites, farming, ranching, and related uses. It also implied that oil exploration in the area was under way. Southwest did *not* disclose the substantial risks associated with buying the land and the difficulties that might take place in trying to sell it.

EXAMPLE 19-13: The FTC found that the Kimberly Gem Company, a gem investment company, misrepresented the types, characteristics, quality, and retail value of gemstones and other investments. The company employees stated that its stones were sold at wholesale prices, but they really were priced many times higher than the prices retailers charge.

- The FTC can apply to a federal district court for a **cease and desist order**, and can order a company to substantiate claims or even run corrective ads.

A cease and desist order requires that a company stop doing what the order prohibits; for example, a company may be ordered to stop running a particular advertising campaign. The cease and desist order is binding 60 days after it has been issued. Also, the FTC can require that firms *substantiate*, or prove, claims that they have made in advertisements. Sometimes, if it appears that consumers have been misinformed or deceived, the FTC will order *corrective advertisements*, which present the other side of the story and try to clear up confusion on the part of consumers who have been misinformed by deceptive ads.

EXAMPLE 19-14: The FTC ruled that Listerine Mouthwash ads that claimed that the product prevented and cured common colds were deceptive. The agency ordered the producer to run corrective ads, stating clearly that Listerine was *not* effective in preventing and curing colds.

- The FTC has been active in regulating advertisements directed toward vulnerable consumers, such as children and older people.

Advertisements which suggest that youngsters use products in a dangerous manner (such as racing bicycles on sidewalks) have been banned. The FTC has also been critical of toy company offerings that seem to advocate violence, as in the case of war toys. Similarly, the FTC is alert to promotions that appear to be taking advantage of older consumers whose faculties may be impaired. Some older people, like children, may be unable to effectively evaluate certain promotion offers and products.

- The FTC has found that **bait-and-switch advertising** is illegal.

Bait-and-switch advertising takes place when a brand is advertised at a low price but is not readily available when consumers arrive at the retail store. The store may be out of stock, or sales personnel may make an overly strong attempt to convince the consumer not to buy the advertised brand but to purchase a more expensive brand instead.

EXAMPLE 19-15: In several cases, the FTC has found that Sears, Roebuck, and Company has practiced bait-and-switch tactics. Consumers who arrived at company stores to buy advertised low-priced models were put under very strong pressure by sales personnel to buy more expensive models.

- The FTC regulates personal selling practices.

The FTC has found companies that use misleading personal selling practices to be in violation of the law. For example, a company that informed consumers that it would inspect their furnaces for a nominal sum was found to be in violation of the Act when it charged excessive prices to repair the furnaces or to put the furnaces back together once they had been torn down.

B. Unfair methods of competition

The **Whealer Lea amendment** to the FTC Act prohibits *unfair methods of competition*. These actions, like deceptive acts, are not listed in the law. Rather, it is up to the FTC to decide what is unfair. One action which has been found to be unfair is to obtain the trade secrets of competitors. For instance, if a rival soup company broke into the safe of Campbell's and stole its recipes, the rival would probably be found guilty of an unfair method of competition.

Disparaging the products of rivals dishonestly is also an unfair method of competition. For example, if a restaurant owner spreads a rumor that a competitor serves tainted meat, and this rumor is untrue, this owner could be held to be guilty of unfair practices. Similarly, if an ad pointed out that one brand of bread contained more vitamin C than another brand, when in fact it did not, the company that ran the ad could be in violation of the law.

19-5. Other Major Federal Regulations

A. Trademarks and trade names

Trademarks and trade names are legally protected ways of identifying goods and services. Federal law stipulates that legal protection can be granted to a company which is the first to use a trademark and trade name and then continues to use them. Protection is given by registration with the United States Patent Office. Trademarks and trade names that are protected cannot be too descriptive, nor can they apply to the product *class* as a whole. If, for example, consumers extensively use a trade name to refer to a type of product and not to a specific brand, that name may become a *generic name*, which is not legally protected.

EXAMPLE 19-16: Some manufacturers have lost the legal protection for their brand names, which have become generic. Among those which have been found to be generic are *formica*, *nylon*, *dry ice*, and *aspirin*.

Producers cannot use brand or company names that are deceptively similar to those of competitors. It would probably be illegal, for example, to introduce "Bampers" disposable diapers or "IBN" computers to the consumer market.

B. Franchising

Sometimes franchisees and franchisors disagree as to the obligations and the rights that each party possesses. Franchisors, for example, may insist that franchisees should sell and advertise their products in certain ways and decorate their stores in a specified manner.

In some cases, franchisors have attempted to require that franchisees purchase equipment and supplies from them. Such a practice, of course, could increase the profits of the franchisor considerably. The courts have found this to be unreasonable in a number of cases.

Franchisors are allowed to require that their franchisees follow certain rules and regulations that are necessary to maintain the value of the franchise system. However, they are not allowed to coerce franchisees into unreasonable practices that are not specified in the franchise agreement.

C. Utilities

Certain utilities, such as telephone and railroad companies, are highly regulated by the federal government. These organizations have near-monopolies and their services are very important to the public at large, so the federal government feels justified in regulating such things as rates, return on investment, and employment practices.

19-6. State and Local Regulations

State, city, county, and other government bodies have imposed numerous regulations on businesses that operate within their territorial limits. Some of these laws are similar to the federal laws that have already been covered in this section, particularly the antitrust, product safety, unfair competition, and consumer deception laws. Many states, for instance, have laws closely resembling the Federal Trade Commission Act.

Some state and local regulations are quite different from any federal laws. The insurance industry is regulated by the states, not the federal government. Some states have **unfair trade practice acts**, which prohibit retailers from selling goods at a level below cost plus a normal profit margin. Some states have laws regulating water, air, and noise pollution. Others have **usury legislation**, which sets a maximum on the interest charges that firms can assess. Also, there are **Green River ordinances** passed by various municipalities. These ordinances may prohibit door-to-door selling, or they may require that such salespersons post bond before selling, obtain permission from householders to make a sales call before asking to be let in, or otherwise comply with regulations that restrict their activites. Firms that are new to a state, city, county, or other government subdivisions should carefully check the local laws that may pertain to them.

RAISE YOUR GRADES

Can you explain . . . ?

☑ why marketing managers should be aware of government regulation of marketing
☑ why companies should avoid making agreements with competitors as to the price of their products
☑ how marketers can legally defend charging different prices for the same good to different retailers
☑ why a firm probably should avoid advertising messages that make untrue claims

☑ why sales representatives should not spread false rumors that their competitors' products are dangerous
☑ how a company might go about getting legal protection for a new trademark
☑ why government bodies place heavy regulations on utility companies

SUMMARY

1. Marketing is heavily regulated by federal, state, and local agencies.
2. Marketers should be generally familiar with the regulations that most directly affect them as failure to obey the law can result in very undesirable consequences.
3. Federal antitrust laws govern companies engaged in interstate commerce:

   • the Sherman Antitrust Act outlaws monopolizing and collusive practices;
   • the Clayton Act prohibits tying contracts, requirements contracts, and price discrimination;
   • the Robinson Patman Act prohibits price discrimination; brokerage allowances; nonproportional promotional services, facilities, or funds; and inducing price discrimination.

4. General law requires that offerings be suitable for their intended use.
5. A number of specific federal laws regulate product quality and safety; these laws include the Food and Drug Administration Act, the Consumer Product Safety Commission Act, and the Motor Vehicle Air Pollution Control Act.
6. The Federal Trade Commission Act, which is administered by the Federal Trade Commission (FTC), prohibits consumer deception and unfair methods of competition:

   • the FTC can apply to a federal district court for a cease and desist order, and can order a company to substantiate claims or even run corrective ads;
   • the FTC has been active in regulating advertisements directed toward vulnerable consumers;
   • the FTC has ruled that bait-and-switch advertising is illegal;
   • the FTC regulates some personal selling practices;
   • the Whealer–Lea amendment to the Federal Trade Commission Act prohibits unfair methods of competition.

7. Trademarks and trade names are legally protected ways of identifying goods and services.
8. Franchising is regulated by the federal government.
9. Certain utilities, such as telephone and railroad companies, are highly regulated by the federal government.
10. Many state and local regulations are similar to existing federal regulations, while some state and local regulations are quite different from any federal ones.

RAPID REVIEW   Answers

Multiple Choice

1. _____ marketing activities are exempt from government regu-   c
   lation. (a) All, (b) Most, (c) Few, (d) No. [See Section 19-1.]
2. Failure to obey the law can result in all of the following *except* (a) fines,   c
   (b) imprisonment, (c) positive word-of-mouth, (d) loss of funds. [See Section 19-1.]
3. When legal issues arise, marketing executives should (a) stop doing what   d
   caused the issue, (b) ignore the issue, (c) revise marketing strategy, (d) consult
   attorneys. [See Section 19-1.]

4. A firm that is monopolizing has the power to dictate (**a**) prices, (**b**) demand, (**c**) laws, (**d**) supply. [See Section 19-2.]   *a*

5. Under the Sherman Act, the market that a company may be ruled as monopolizing is called the (**a**) line of commerce, (**b**) market area, (**c**) market region, (**d**) market designation. [See Section 19-2.]   *a*

6. If two car manufacturers make price agreements, this is called _____ collusion, under the Sherman Act. (**a**) vertical, (**b**) horizontal, (**c**) unfair, (**d**) monopolizing. [See Section 19-2.]   *b*

7. If an electronics firm tells buyers for retail outlets that it will not sell them its videotape recorders unless they also buy its videotape cassettes, this is a (**a**) tying contract, (**b**) requirements contract, (**c**) monopoly, (**d**) price discrimination. [See Section 19-2.]   *a*

8. If the Bi-Tuminous Coal Company tells an electric utility that it will not sell it coal unless the utility buys all of its coal from Bi-Tuminous, this is a (**a**) tying contract, (**b**) requirements contract, (**c**) monopoly, (**d**) price discrimination. [See Section 19-2.]   *b*

9. A company might be guilty of price discrimination if it charged retailers different prices for _____ offerings. (**a**) like, (**b**) unlike, (**c**) consumer-purchased, (**d**) service. [See Section 19-2.]   *a*

10. A pharmaceutical company could be found in violation of the Robinson Patman Act if it discriminated in price when it sold analgesic capsules to retailers *and* it was found that the effect of this discrimination might be to (**a**) lower prices, (**b**) raise prices, (**c**) lessen competition, (**d**) increase advertising expenditures. [See Section 19-2.]   *c*

11. If a company grants _____ to some wholesalers, it may be in violation of the Robinson Patman Act. (**a**) collusion, (**b**) brokerage allowances, (**c**) monopolies, (**d**) deceptions. [See Section 19-2.]   *b*

12. The Robinson Patman Act prohibits buyers from _____ discriminatory prices from suppliers. (**a**) agreeing to, (**b**) not reporting, (**c**) signing contracts for, (**d**) inducing. [See Section 19-2.]   *d*

13. General law in the United States stipulates that the offerings of a company must be _____ for their intended use. (**a**) guaranteed, (**b**) warranted, (**c**) suitable, (**d**) extensively tested. [See Section 19-3.]   *c*

14. When a manufacturer fails to fulfill an obligation that a contract requires, this is called (**a**) negligence, (**b**) fraud, (**c**) collusion, (**d**) breach of contract. [See Section 19-3.]   *d*

15. The Food and Drug Administration Act does *not* cover (**a**) therapeutic devices, (**b**) drugs, (**c**) foods, (**d**) automobiles. [See Section 19-3.]   *d*

16. The Federal Trade Commission Act prohibits _____ consumers. (**a**) overcharging, (**b**) deception of, (**c**) negligence toward, (**d**) unequal shipping charges for. [See Section 19-3.]   *b*

17. _____ advertising takes place when a low-priced, advertised good is not available in retail stores. (**a**) Discriminatory, (**b**) Bait-and-switch, (**c**) Collusive, (**d**) Monopolizing. [See Section 19-3.]   *b*

18. If a fast-food retailer steals secret recipes from competitors, this may be found to be a(n) (**a**) unfair method of competition, (**b**) fraud, (**c**) negligent act, (**d**) breach of contract. [See Section 19-4.]   *a*

19. Legal protection is given to trade names by the U.S. (**a**) Customs Service, (**b**) Patent Office, (**c**) Attorney General, (**d**) Congress. [See Section 19-5.]   *b*

20. Many states have laws closely resembling the _____ Act. (**a**) Food and Drug Administration, (**b**) Robinson Patman, (**c**) Federal Trade Commission, (**d**) Sherman. [See Section 19-6.]   *c*

SOLVED PROBLEMS

PROBLEM 19-1   An owner of a drug store has informed you that "The United States is a free country, so few marketing activities are regulated by the government." Do you agree?

Answer: The drug store owner is incorrect. Marketing is heavily regulated by federal, state, and local agencies. In fact, few marketing activities are exempt from some kind of law. For example, if the drug store lowers its prices very much in order to drive a competitor out of business, it may be committing an illegal act. Similarly, the store may be violating the law if its sales clerks or advertisements present arguments that mislead consumers. It cannot sell certain drugs, except by prescription. These are just a few examples of government regulations that affect drug stores. [See Section 19-1.]

PROBLEM 19-2   What are some of the possible consequences to the executives of a manufacturing company that violates the laws pertaining to marketing?

Answer: Failure to obey the law may result in fines for the firm, some of which can amount to millions of dollars. The firm's officers may be prosecuted and go to prison or receive suspended sentences. The courts may require that the company take actions that result in substantial losses of funds; it may, for example, be ordered to drop a product. Negative comments in the news media can damage the reputation of the company on a regional or even a national basis. [See Section 19-1.]

PROBLEM 19-3   An executive for a company wonders how the federal government decides what constitutes monopolizing a market. What is your answer?

Answer: According to the courts, monopolizing would exist if the company has a large enough market share in an industry to permit it to dictate prices and other elements of competition. To be guilty of monopolizing, the firm must be engaging in activities that give it monopoly power. The company need not monopolize the entire U.S. market to be in violation of the Sherman Antitrust Act. If it is ruled to be monopolizing in a smaller market, such as a state or city, it may be in violation of the law. Also, monopolizing exists in the context of a particular line of commerce, which is a group of companies that compete for the same customers. [See Section 19-2.]

PROBLEM 19-4   A hardware dealer in a small town wants to strike an agreement on lumber prices with a major competitor, feeling that this would be legal because both companies are small and a price agreement "surely would not restrain trade." Do you agree?

Answer: The proposed price agreement by the hardware dealer and its competitor would constitute horizontal collusion, which is illegal under the Sherman Antitrust Act. Such agreements are always illegal, regardless of whether or not they restrain trade. The fact that the two competitors operate only in a small town, and not in the national market, makes no difference in the legality of the agreement. The hardware dealer should avoid making this agreement. [See Section 19-2.]

PROBLEM 19-5   All of the medical doctors in a community charge the same amount for an office call. Is it possible that the doctors may be in violation of the law?

Answer: It is possible that the doctors are in violation of the federal antitrust laws. Professional associations are not allowed to fix prices under the law. It may be that the doctors have made agreements on office call prices through their medical association or in some informal way. If they have, they are guilty of violating the law, regardless of whether or not competition has been damaged. [See Section 19-2.]

PROBLEM 19-6   A manufacturer of copiers and copying paper is considering the use of a tying contract. Under the stipulations of this contract, buyers who purchase a company copier would have to agree to buy all of their copying paper from the company. Is this necessarily illegal?

Answer: The copier producer's contract is not necessarily illegal, but could be so. It violates the Clayton Act only if it is shown that it might restrain trade or create a monopoly. If it appears that the contract could severely damage the profits of certain competitors or give the copier producer a large market share in the future, a judge might rule it to be illegal. The company should study the contract and its expected results very closely before putting it into effect. [See Section 19-2.]

PROBLEM 19-7   Assume that a toy company charges a department store $19.00 for one of its new action toys, and it charges a wholesaler $11.50. Does this price discrepancy constitute illegal price discrimination under the Robinson Patman Act?

Answer: The toy company's actions do not constitute illegal price discrimination under the Robinson Patman Act. The law prohibits discrimination to purchasers of goods who are similarly situated. In this case, the firms are not on the same level in the channel of distribution—one is a retailer and the other a wholesaler—so they are not similarly situated. [See Section 19-2.]

PROBLEM 19-8   Jones, a consumer, goes to a retail store and purchases a cedar chest for $299 as a gift for his daughter. Later that week, he becomes infuriated when he discovers that Smith bought an identical cedar chest at the same retail store for $229. Has the retail store violated the Robinson Patman Act?

Answer: No, the retail store has not violated the Robinson Patman Act. This law does not outlaw price discrimination to consumers. Illegal discrimination takes place when different business or nonbusiness organizations pay different prices for the same goods. [See Section 19-2.]

PROBLEM 19-9   If a dog food company sells its dog food to a large supermarket chain at a price that is 10% lower than it charges a small grocery store, does this mean that it has violated the Robinson Patman Act?

Answer: The dog food company has not necessarily violated the Robinson Patman Act. The company may be able to defend the discrimination by showing lower costs of manufacturing, selling, or delivery to the supermarket chain. If, for example, the chain makes orders that are large enough to receive truckload transportation rates, but the small grocery store does not, these savings can legally be passed to the chain. Also, the company may be able to show that the discrimination was made to meet the equally low price of a competitor who was trying to obtain business from the chain. [See Section 19-2.]

PROBLEM 19-10   Assume that a computer company promised to grant advertising allowances of up to $200,000 to a retail store chain that sells its computers. This chain bought $25,000,000 worth of the computers during the last year. The company also agreed to pay advertising allowances of $100,000 to another chain that purchased $20,000,000 worth of the computers during the last year. Is this illegal?

Answer: It is illegal under the Robinson Patman Act. This law requires that promotional services, facilities, and funds that are provided to customers must be provided on proportionally equal terms to competing customers. Proportionally equal terms refers to the amount of merchandise that customers purchase from the supplier. In the case above, the second chain should have received 80% of the amount that the first chain obtained (80% of $200,000 is $160,000). [See Section 19-2.]

PROBLEM 19-11   On a car assembly line, an employee fails to tighten the lug bolts on an automobile tire. A consumer buys the car, but when he drives it away from the dealership, the wheel comes off and causes the consumer to demolish the car. Is the car company liable?

Answer: In this case, the company is guilty of negligence. A firm is considered to be negligent when it has acted with less care than a reasonable person would take under the circumstances. The guilty party was an employee of the company, which makes the company liable for the damages. [See Section 19-3.]

PROBLEM 19-12   The Browns read an advertisement in the New York Times that solicits sales for the "Pleasant Valley Ranch Sites" in California. The ad describes the sites as beautiful, near major roads, containing bountiful streams and ponds, and suitable for working ranches. The Browns buy the land without inspecting it for $35,000. Later, they discover that what they have bought is six acres of near-worthless desert land. Is this a violation of general law?

Answer: Yes. The ranch site promoter is in violation of the law. When a party makes untrue statements that cause another party to enter into a contract, the first party is guilty of fraud. In this case, the advertisement contained statements that were clearly false, and the Browns purchased the land site because of the advertisement and its promises. [See Section 19-3.]

PROBLEM 19-13   An executive for a pharmaceutical company has been informed by several scientists in the company's research laboratory that they have developed a new drug which may be very useful in treating arthritis sufferers. What actions will the Food and Drug Administration take regarding the product?

Answer: The Food and Drug Administration will see to it that the pharmaceutical company has undertaken a series of tests to determine that the drug performs as intended (in treating arthritis sufferers), that it is properly labeled, and that its promotion claims are true and not misleading. If the drug is found to be ineffective, unsafe, or unhealthful, the Food and Drug Administration may prevent its introduction into the market. [See Section 19-3.]

PROBLEM 19-14   What federal agency has jurisdiction over the safety features of bicycles?

Answer: The Consumer Product Safety Commission has jurisdiction over the safety features of bicycles. It is charged with overseeing product safety for all goods that are produced and distributed in the United States. The commission conducts research, develops standards, and provides information to consumers about safety. It can ban the sale of unsafe products. This agency has focused a great deal of effort on the bicycle industry, because bicycles account for numerous consumer accidents each year. [See Section 19-3.]

PROBLEM 19-15   Assume that you have been asked to evaluate an advertisement that an oil company would like to run in magazines. Management wants you to judge whether the Federal Trade Commission might find the ad to be deceptive. How would you judge the advertisement?

Answer: The Federal Trade Commission Act prohibits the deception of consumers, which means deliberate attempts to trick consumers into doing something they would not do otherwise. The law does not mention which acts are deceptive, but leaves this up to the Federal Trade Commission. Therefore, it would be useful for you to study past cases, especially those that are recent, to determine what kinds of things the commission had found to be unlawful. You might logically look for FTC rulings on oil companies to determine the views of the commissioners on how this industry should communicate with consumers. [See Section 19-4.]

PROBLEM 19-16   Ads directed to certain classes of consumers are more likely to be illegal under the Federal Trade Commission Act than are ads directed to the public at large. What classes of consumers are in this first category?

Answer: Vulnerable consumers are those who may be unable to effectively evaluate certain promotion offers and products and, as a result, are susceptible to deception. Older consumers are in this category. Some have difficulty in understanding the nature of the promotion offer and tend to trust advertising sponsors, even when trust is not merited. A second grouping is children, who are more gullible than are older consumers. [See Section 19-4.]

PROBLEM 19-17   How should a retailer run a sale and still avoid charges of bait and switch by the Federal Trade Commission?

Answer: When the retailer runs a sale, it should have a large enough stock of the goods that are advertised at low prices to satisfy the expected number of consumers who will come into the store to buy the advertised product. This may require higher than normal inventory levels. Management should instruct sales clerks not to try too zealously to convince consumers who seek the low-priced brand to buy a higher-priced model. If these programs are well planned and implemented, charges of bait and switch are unlikely. [See Section 19-4.]

PROBLEM 19-18   What is the danger that a clothing store owner runs if the owner and employees tell customers that a competitor's merchandise has been illegally smuggled into the United States from Mexico?

Answer: If the statements by the clothing store manager and employees are false, they may be ruled as unfair methods of competition by the Federal Trade Commission. Disparaging the products of rivals is an unfair method of competition if the statements are untrue. The store owner should be certain that the products were illegally smuggled into the United States or remain silent on the issue. [See Section 19-4.]

PROBLEM 19-19   Coca Cola Company executives have expressed fear in the past that the trade name "coke" might become a generic term. What does this mean?

Answer: If a trade name becomes generic, it applies to the product class as a whole, so that consumers use the name to refer to the product and not to the brand. If the name is ruled to be generic, it can no longer belong to just one company. Pepsico, Dr. Pepper, Shasta, and other producers could use the name "coke" to refer to their offerings. The result would be the loss of a very valuable property on the part of Coca Cola. [See Section 19-5.]

PROBLEM 19-20   A book company sells religious, educational, and other books on a door-to-door basis. How can Green River ordinances affect this firm?

Answer: Green River ordinances exist in various municipalities. They might prohibit door-to-door selling; or they might require that such sales persons post bond before selling, obtain permission from householders to make a sales call before asking to be let in, and otherwise limit their activities. Since the book company sells door-to-door, it is heavily affected by such ordinances. Its representatives should avoid selling in cities where very strong Green River ordinances are in effect. Where weak ordinances exist, the representatives can often comply with the law by phoning consumers before calling at their homes, or by making appointments. [See Section 19.6.]

20 ETHICS AND SOCIAL RESPONSIBILITY IN MARKETING

THIS CHAPTER IS ABOUT

☑ **Ethical Perspectives**
☑ **Ethical Systems**
☑ **Implications of Ethics for Marketing Managers**
☑ **The Meaning of Social Responsibility**
☑ **Specific Social Responsibility Issues**
☑ **Means of Resolving Social Responsibility Issues**

20-1. Ethical Perspectives

Ethical issues often arise in marketing. For example, is it ethical *not* to place gas tank explosion shields in automobiles in order to keep prices down? Should a sales representative who has loyally served a company for twenty years be fired because his recent fits of temper have resulted in the loss of several important customers? Should advertisements be created in such a way that they make rival products appear to be inferior, even if they are not? What if a customer asks a sales representative for an item the company does not stock? Should the sales representative refer the customer to a competitor who does stock the item? Different marketing executives will have different answers to these and related questions.

EXAMPLE 20-1: The advertising director of a women's fashion clothing store knows that ads featuring slim models sell the most clothing. Yet these ads may induce some young women to become obsessive about slimness and develop anorexia (self-starvation) or bulimia (vomiting to control weight). Should the advertising director continue to feature slim models and thus risk her job if the clothing does not sell in high volume?

- **Ethics** refers to what is morally good, *right* or *wrong*, according to accepted standards of behavior.

A retailer, for instance, might avoid trying to sell a very expensive vacuum cleaner to a low-income consumer because he believes that the ethical, or *right*, thing to do is to demonstrate an inexpensive model.

Generally, the field of ethics is related to the codes of personal conduct that one recognizes as a guide to day-to-day behavior. This field furnishes insights as to how to deal with others in a moral sense. In marketing, ethical conduct is based upon dealings with other parties, and is guided by codes of personal conduct and various ethical principles.

Ethical conduct in marketing is sometimes problematic because different people have different ideas of what is ethical. There are no fixed answers to most ethical questions, and marketers must choose a standard of conduct that suits their environment, as well as their personal codes. To some extent, marketers learn ethical values from the culture of which they are members. They also learn these values from the specific company for which they work. Still, individual differences remain.

EXAMPLE 20-2: Some marketing executives feel that it is not dishonest to take small items, such as pens, envelopes, and writing paper from their employers for personal use. Others believe that thefts of even small items are unacceptable.

The marketing concept can provide some ethical guidelines. This concept suggests that marketing executives conduct themselves in a manner that leads to customer satisfaction and company profits. Many marketers believe that by providing customer satisfaction, they are meeting the needs of others as well as their own. Many followers of the marketing concept also believe in providing satisfaction to numerous publics, including employees, low-income groups, and the public at large, as well as target customers.

20-2. Ethical Systems

There are a number of ethical systems which are based on different ethical principles. These principles range from the utilitarian "[doing] the greatest good [to] the greatest number," to the religious "do unto others what you would have them do unto you." Marketing managers find some of these principles to be useful guidelines (not necessarily specific rules) in determining morally correct behavior. They usually find, however, that ethics is an art, not a science. A principle that may seem very appropriate to one marketer may appear to be without redeeming value to another. In some cases, a combination of ethical principles from several ethical systems is useful to a particular manager.

A. Idealism

Idealists believe that there are certain universal and abstract moral rules that should be followed at all times. One rule, for instance, is not to behave in a way that would be harmful if all people behaved in that way.

EXAMPLE 20-3: A product manager might avoid the production of inferior-quality products because he believes that consumer standards of living would deteriorate considerably if all companies produced inferior products.

Stoics are a particular group of idealists who believe that individuals should endure hardship and adversity and should avoid overly emotional behavior. Stoics set their sights on goals they believe to be important and do not allow personal desires, such as a desire for status or leisure, to prevent goal achievement. To them, correct ethical decisions are those that allow the attainment of proper goals.

EXAMPLE 20-4: A stoic store manager might work diligently for long hours in order to increase the profitability of her store. She would make decisions designed to promote the financial well-being of the store and would expect her employees to do likewise.

Libertarians are idealists who are strong believers in the freedoms of others. They think that it is unethical to interfere with these freedoms.

EXAMPLE 20-5: Various marketers require applicants for jobs to take polygraph (lie detector) tests to assess their honesty. A libertarian manager, however, would be inclined to believe that this infringes on the right to privacy (a freedom) and would avoid such tests.

B. Hedonism

Hedonists follow the notion that happiness or pleasure is the greatest good, and think that what a person truly desires is by definition moral. However, they believe that careful thought on the part of most people will reveal that the real desires of most are unselfish goals, such as world peace and the elimination of suffering, rather than selfish goals, such as relaxation and overeating. Marketers who follow the hedonist philosophy carefully decide what their most important personal objectives are. Then they behave in a way that furthers these objectives.

EXAMPLE 20-6: A hedonist marketing manager might decide that a very important personal goal is to help preserve the dignity of other people. This manager would probably make a special effort to avoid hurting the feelings of others and might be very sensitive to problems that lowered the self-respect of employees or customers.

Utilitarians are a special kind of hedonist. They believe in the "greatest good for the greatest number" and believe that "good" means utility or satisfaction.

EXAMPLE 20-7: A utilitarian who has product-planning responsibilities for a drug company might believe that it is better to manufacture low-priced vitamins to be sold to large numbers of low-income consumers than it is to sell a smaller number of high-priced vitamins to wealthy individuals.

Hedonists think that the greatest happiness is obtained when people are engaged in activities that they are especially able to perform and that permit the full development of their lives. This being the case, a hedonist marketing manager would probably recruit employees for jobs in which they might be able to attain feelings of accomplishment and satisfaction.

C. Judeo-Christianity

Followers of the **Judeo-Christian ethic** believe that authority over correct behavior arises from God. The Judeo-Christian system sets forth a number of rules for proper behavior that are commanded by God, such as "do not judge others," "do unto others as you would have them do unto you," "do not steal," and "do not covet the property of others." This ethic stresses an attitude of caring for others and providing for their needs. This being the case, it can be in harmony with the marketing concept.

EXAMPLE 20-8: A sales representative who follows the Judeo-Christian system of ethics might make a dedicated attempt to determine the needs of each individual prospect and then work diligently to satisfy these needs. The representative's intention would be to fulfill the objectives of the prospect, even if this might not maximize the objectives of the marketer. The representative might pass up an opportunity to sell a higher-priced product if it appeared that a less expensive product would be adequate for the prospect.

D. Instrumentalism

Instrumentalists do not place any stock in abstract moral principles, but believe that individuals should adjust their conduct to the situation that exists at the time an ethical decision is made. Instrumentalists simply do what they believe to be "right," based on their intuition, judgment, attitudes, and perceptions in each specific instance.

EXAMPLE 20-9: A marketing manager is faced with the decision as to whether or not to terminate an employee who seems to be past his prime and is not as productive as he once was. The manager decides to retain the employee on the payroll because he does not "feel right" about terminating him.

E. Hegelianism

Hegelians believe that moral behavior is that which agrees with the customs and laws of the society in which the decision maker is operating. These individuals are likely to say "obey the law," or "do not go against the group," in determining what is proper.

EXAMPLE 20-10: When confronted with an ethical problem, a variety chain store manager consults the company's written code of ethics for guidance. This provides a ready-made frame of reference for moral decisions. If the code of ethics states that "no employee should be dismissed without a fair hearing," for instance, the manager who follows procedure is making a proper decision in Hegelian terms.

20-3. Implications of Ethics for Marketing Managers

The implications of ethics for marketing managers depend to a large extent on the ethical problem faced.

A. Examples of ethical problems

Ethical problems arise in conjunction with virtually all marketing decisions. There are some that are of special importance, however.

1. Product planning

Every marketing manager has to determine the quality of the products and services offered. It might appear that the most ethical action would be to produce products of the highest quality possible. However, this might result in high prices, making the product unattainable to many consumers. Further, consumers do not insist on high quality for all items.

EXAMPLE 20-11: Tonka marketing managers could have its wooden toys engineered to very fine specifications. However, many parents and children are content with loose specifications, especially since this makes the toys affordable to most. On the other hand, some critics accuse toy companies of producing inferior products that break too easily.

Planned obsolescence is another product-planning issue. Should marketers continually bring out new models that make last year's offering obsolete? This can be costly to consumers, many of whom strive to have the "latest thing." On the other hand, improved products can upgrade consumer living standards.

2. Pricing

Some manufacturers and retailers quote prices that appear to be bargains, but really are not. These include some going-out-of-business, damaged-goods, and two-for-one sales. In striving for ethical behavior, marketers should try to predict how consumers will interpret such sales—will they pay higher prices than are justified?

Various marketers are tempted to make price agreements with rivals in order to reduce price competition. Of course, this is against the law and may bring on legal complications. But some marketers may decide to risk getting caught and make agreements anyway.

Should marketers offer gifts and bribes to companies and government officials in order to get their business? In certain countries, bribes are expected—and often necessary—in order to compete. On the other hand, bribes are illegal in many instances, and numerous marketing managers consider them to be improper.

Should marketers charge high prices for drugs (such as insulin) that are expensive to produce and are needed by some individuals to survive? It can be argued that demand elasticity is low for such items and high prices are justified. On the other hand, high drug prices contribute to high medical costs for those who are ill.

3. Promotion

Advertising, personal selling, and sales promotion can be used to deceive consumers. Some believe that companies should be able to say whatever they want in promotions, as long as they tell the truth. (Then these marketers have to figure out what "truth" is, and how much of it to tell.) Others think that marketers should look carefully at the impressions that promotions make, especially on such groups as children and teenagers. Perhaps marketers should not feature excessively thin models in ads directed toward teenagers, since such ads may lead to an unhealthy desire to live up to this model.

When advertising campaigns are not successful, some marketers dismiss their advertising agencies, often treating them as scapegoats. Others believe that this practice is unethical and that other possible causes of the failure should be sought out.

Sometimes sales representatives are guilty of unethical behavior. They may promise customers more than the company can deliver, oversell customers in order to win a sales contest, or cheat on expense accounts. While these practices are viewed by many people as unethical, some sales representatives may feel that they are justified.

4. Place

Some manufacturers are quick to eliminate a wholesaler or a retailer from the channel of distribution because its sales are not adequate or it is not performing up to expectations in some other capacity. Others feel that this is not proper because small intermediaries should not be forced out and their existence terminated without giving them a second chance.

Various large manufacturers use their bargaining strength to win concessions from wholesalers and retailers. They may, for instance, be capable of coercing the latter into carrying larger inventories or advertising more. Other producers consider this to be unethical behavior.

B. Solving ethical problems

1. The law

One way of solving ethical problems is simply to obey the law. Firms that do this are following the fundamental rules of society. However, firms can obey the law and still be guilty of treating others unethically.

EXAMPLE 20-12: A supermarket chain closes down its markets in low-income areas because these stores are not earning a return on investment as high as that in affluent neighborhoods. This causes many low-income residents to become dependent on inefficient and high-cost smaller stores for their grocery items.

---

2. Industry self-regulation

Some industry groups help to prevent unethical conduct through self-regulation. Various industries, such as the packing industry, have written codes of ethics to guide managers. Better Business Bureaus investigate charges of illegal and unethical business behavior and attempt to change these when they are discovered. The American Association of Broadcasters will not accept some ads that are judged to be in bad taste. However, none of these groups has any legal power to enforce their decisions. Essentially, they must rely on their ability to persuade executives to put a stop to unethical behavior.

3. Informed self-interest

Numerous marketers realize that they are very dependent on outside parties, such as consumers and government officials. If marketers create hostility with these groups through unethical behavior, many unwanted results may follow. These can include loss of esteem and goodwill, loss of customers, increased legal costs, and loss of valued suppliers. Many marketers, then, realize that ethical behavior is in their own self-interest.

20-4. The Meaning of Social Responsibility

• **Social responsibility** means that marketers have an obligation to numerous groups in society.

These groups include consumers, stockholders, employees, suppliers, government officials, labor unions, the public at large, and particular components of the public, such as minorities. (See Fig-

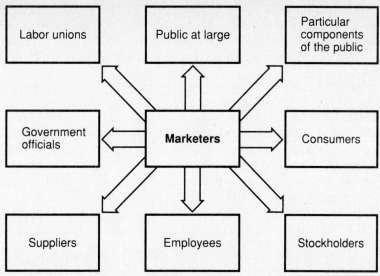

FIGURE 20-1: Social responsibility means marketers have obligations to many groups in society.

ure 20-1.) Marketers who are socially responsible take steps to improve the status of these and other groups.

Traditionally, it has been felt that marketers are responsible primarily to the owners of business to make a profit. Many marketing managers, however, are now coming to realize that they have certain responsibilities to their customers and that the business probably would not be profitable if they ignored these responsibilities. Finally, marketers are beginning to come to the conclusion that they are responsible to a number of other groups in addition to target customers.

EXAMPLE 20-13: McDonald's Corporation makes a strong effort to assist parents of children who are in hospitals for extended care. Through Ronald McDonald houses, it provides housing for such parents who need to stay close to their sick children.

• Socially responsible managers realize that they are dependent upon society for their existence.

Marketing will deteriorate if society does. High levels of unemployment, polluted air, overpopulation, energy shortages, and poverty, for example, do not contribute to a smooth-operating marketing system. Countries that have major social problems, such as Iran, Nicaragua, and Nigeria, have very poorly developed marketing systems.

20-5. Specific Social Responsibility Issues

A. Consumerism

Consumerism is a belief that consumers are entitled to safe and effective products at reasonable prices, as well as full information about the products and their uses. This belief is very widespread in the United States and other developed countries today. In fact, it has assumed the proportions of a movement, with such leaders as Ralph Nader who have numerous followers.

Today's consumers have high expectations regarding the goods and services that they purchase. If these goods and services are not up to expectations, consumers believe that they are entitled to refunds, exchanges, repairs, or other means of redress. This attitude is unlike that of the consumer of the past, who felt that little could be done when he or she was stuck with a "lemon."

Many marketers today realize that it is in their own self-interest not to fight, but to cooperate with the consumer movement. The attitude fostered by this movement is, after all, compatible with the modern marketing concept. Satisfied consumers serve the interests of business. Little is gained by arguing with or fighting consumers in court cases.

EXAMPLE 20-14: K-Mart has a very liberal returns policy. If a consumer is dissatisfied with a purchase, he or she can return it, along with the sales slip, within a reasonable time after the purchase. The customer need not explain the reason for the dissatisfaction in order to obtain a refund or replacement product.

B. Ecological issues

A second major area of social responsibility relates to the physical environment. Marketers have come to realize that they should be concerned with such problems as air and water pollution, depletion of scarce resources, and spoiling the beauty of the natural landscape. While marketers, standing alone, cannot overcome these problems, they can assist in preventing new ones and overcoming long-standing ones.

EXAMPLE 20-15: The advertising community has been active in attempting to prevent littering. The Advertising Council (an industry association that devotes its efforts to social responsibility issues) features billboards and television ads that attempt to convince consumers not to litter.

EXAMPLE 20-16: When petroleum products were scarce during the 1970's, many retailers set their thermostats at low temperatures during cool months and at high temperatures during warm months. They ran the risk of alienating customers who would be uncomfortable in the stores, but were able to achieve some substantial fuel savings.

C. Minority groups

Numerous marketers have attempted to aid minorities by providing members of these groups with job opportunities. Many companies have developed affirmative action programs, whereby they seek, attract, hire, and promote minority-group members.

Another way in which marketers have attempted to fulfill social responsibilities relating to minority groups is to develop products specifically for individuals in these groups. Products as diverse as hair conditioners, dolls, and magazines, for example, have been designed specifically for Blacks. Also, television programs are available for non-English–speaking minorities.

20-6. Means of Resolving Social Responsibility Issues

There are various means that may be effective in promoting social responsibility on the part of marketers. On one hand, federal and state governments can pass restrictive legislation, which compels marketers to act in certain ways by law. On the other hand, the courts may require businesses to pay for social costs.

A. Restrictive legislation

One means of encouraging marketers to undertake socially responsible behavior is through legislation that restricts their freedom to act. Laws can require businesses to do some things a certain way and to stop doing other things. For example, hire minorities, stop polluting the air and water, and provide safe products to consumers. This approach can be effective in some cases. But such laws often require costly inspection and enforcement personnel, and are sometimes difficult to pass through legislatures. In addition, they are *negative*—they are capable of punishing bad conduct but cannot reward good conduct. Many businesses resist such laws and lobby against them. Restrictive legislation can be useful, then, but it does not provide a complete answer to social responsibility questions.

EXAMPLE 20-17: Anti-pollution laws exist at both the federal and state level. However, inspection personnel are very limited, so some water and air pollution must go undetected. Further, although most companies attempt to comply with the regulations, a minority actively attempt to circumvent the law by hiding or disguising their pollution. Some companies have been known, for example, to make secret dumps of hazardous chemicals at night.

B. Requiring businesses to pay for social costs

Social costs are those costs a business passes on to society or to particular groups, rather than paying them itself. Examples of social costs are expenses that cities and counties incur for picking up litter, expenses that municipal waste-treatment plants incur for cleaning water polluted by business, hospital bills that consumers pay when they are injured by dangerous products, and earning power lost by minority group members when they are not hired.

- A means of encouraging socially responsible behavior is to require that every company must pay for the social costs that it creates.

If each company were required to pay for the social costs it creates, more companies would be motivated to act in a socially responsible manner. Companies might be less reluctant to act responsibly if each knew that its rivals had to pay for their social costs as well. (If just one company acts in a responsible manner, its expenses may be higher than those of competitors.) If, for example, a firm polluted the water, it would be made to pay any sewage fees required to transform the water back to its original condition. Or, if a party suffered damages from the polluted water, the firm would be required to pay these.

Legislation may be passed that prescribes what companies must do about social costs. Also, civil court cases, where consumers and other parties are awarded damages to be paid by business concerns, are providing precedents that may compel businesses to engage in socially responsible behavior.

RAISE YOUR GRADES
Can you explain . . . ?

☑ how a product manager might use idealist principles to guide everyday behavior
☑ how a small business manager might practice a stoic principle of ethical behavior
☑ how ethical principles can affect a company's product planning
☑ how informed self-interest might lead a corporate marketing executive to adopt ethical behavior
☑ why marketing executives should have an interest in social responsibility
☑ why consumerism is important to marketers
☑ how requiring businesses to pay for social costs might affect marketers

SUMMARY

1. Ethical issues arise in most marketing decisions.
2. Ethics refers to what is morally good, "right" or "wrong," according to accepted standards of behavior.
3. Some of the major ethical systems are based on idealist, hedonist, Judeo-Christian, instrumentalist, and Hegelian principles.
4. There are important ethical implications for managers in the areas of product planning, pricing, promotion, and place.
5. There are three major ways that marketers can use to solve ethical problems: obeying the law, industry self-regulation, and informed self-interest.
6. Social responsibility means that marketers have obligations to various groups in society.
7. Socially responsible managers realize that they are dependent upon society for their existence.

8. Among the major social responsibility issues are consumerism, ecological issues, and the treatment of minority groups.
9. Two potentially useful means of resolving social responsibility issues are restrictive legislation and requiring businesses to pay for social costs.

RAPID REVIEW   Answers

Short Answer

1. Ethics refers to what is _____ good, according to accepted standards of behavior. [See Section 20-1.]   *morally*

2. A physical distribution manager who believes that individuals should endure hardship is following a _____ principle of ethical behavior. [See Section 20-2.]   *stoic*

3. A hedonist store manager believes that what a person _____ is moral. [See Section 20-2.]   *desires*

4. A utilitarian sales manager believes that "good" means _____ or _____. [See Section 20-2.]   *utility, satisfaction*

5. An advertising manager who is a follower of the Judeo-Christian ethic believes that correct behavior arises from _____. [See Section 20-2.]   *God*

6. An instrumentalist product manager believes that individuals should adjust their conduct to the _____ that exists at the time an ethical decision is made. [See Section 20-2.]   *situation*

7. A _____ store manager is likely to advise obeying the law as a guide to moral behavior. [See Section 20-2.]   *Hegelian*

8. Ethical problems can arise during all phases of the development of the _____ _____. [See Section 20-3.]   *marketing mix*

9. Better Business Bureaus, which investigate charges of illegal and unethical business behavior, rely on _____ to change these when they are discovered. [See Section 20-3.]   *persuasion*

10. The American Association of Broadcasters is involved in industry _____. [See Section 20-3.]   *self-regulation*

11. If a company fails to practice informed _____, it may suffer loss of esteem and goodwill, loss of customers, increased legal prosecution, and loss of valued suppliers. [See Section 20-3.]   *self-interest*

12. Social responsibility means that a company has an _____ to numerous groups in society. [See Section 20-4.]   *obligation*

13. Socially responsible managers realize that they are dependent upon _____ for their existence. [See Section 20-4.]   *society*

14. The traditional view is that businesses are responsible primarily to the _____ of a business. [See Section 20-4.]   *owners*

15. After the traditional view, companies came to realize that they were responsible to _____. [See Section 20-4.]   *customers*

16. According to the consumerism belief, marketers should provide _____ and _____ products at reasonable prices. [See Section 20-5.]   *safe, effective*

17. The attitude fostered by the consumer movement is _____ with the marketing concept. [See Section 20-5.]   *compatible*

18. The _____ issues that businesses face relate to the physical environment. [See Section 20-5.]   *ecological*

19. Many companies have established _____ _____ plans to assist minorities in gaining employment. [See Section 20-5.]   *affirmative action*

20. Social costs are those costs which a business passes on to _____ or to particular groups, rather than paying them itself. [See Section 20-6.] *society*

SOLVED PROBLEMS

PROBLEM 20-1 A friend who is the manager of a women's clothing store has told you that ethical problems are uncommon in marketing. Do you agree or disagree?

Answer: The friend is incorrect. Ethical issues often arise in marketing. In fact, ethical questions are implicit in virtually every marketing decision in one way or another, because these questions have to do with what is right or wrong for all parties concerned. For instance, if prices are too high, essential products may be unavailable to low-income consumers; if prices are too low, the company may suffer losses and some employees may have to be dismissed. What, then, is the "right" price? Advertisements may be drawn up in such a way that they encourage consumers to dwell on selfish needs and to be materialistic. Is such advertising "right"? Or, when one sales representative is promoted to sales manager, more "deserving" representatives may be passed up. By what criteria are "deserving" sales reps judged, and are the criteria "right"? [See Section 20-1.]

PROBLEM 20-2 A classmate has read about an investigation into the ethics of the marketing managers at a large book publishing company. She is not sure just what the investigation entails but has asked you for a definition of ethics. How would you respond?

Answer: Ethics refers to what is morally good, "right or wrong," according to accepted standards of behavior; that is, ethical conduct means moral or proper conduct. The marketing managers for the publishing company may have made decisions that unfairly promoted their own well-being or profits of the company at the expense of the public, consumers, employees, competitors, or others. Or they may have made questionable charitable donations that might be construed as "bribes" to customers (such as school boards or library associations). Although these actions might be strictly legal, they might be considered unethical or improper if they resulted in undue harm to affected parties. [See Section 20-1.]

PROBLEM 20-3 According to a local Chamber of Commerce official, "Most marketing executives agree on what kinds of behavior are ethical and what are unethical." Comment on this statement.

Answer: The official is not correct. Different people in general, and different marketing personnel in particular, have different ideas as to what is ethical. There are no fixed answers to most ethical problems. This is because people do not always agree on what is desirable for society and what constitutes proper behavior in the business world. Most marketing executives believe that they conduct themselves ethically, even though others may disagree. [See Section 20-1.]

PROBLEM 20-4 How might a stoic sales manager for a cinema chain go about making ethical decisions in evaluating members of the sales force?

Answer: Stoics believe that individuals should endure hardship and adversity and avoid overly emotional behavior. They attempt to achieve goals that are believed to be important and do not allow personal wants, such as a desire for status or leisure, to prevent goal achievement. A stoic sales manager would give high evaluations to representatives who contributed high volumes of sales and profits. He or she would tend to evaluate in an objective manner, according to how hard members of the sales force worked. Such a manager would probably be impatient with representatives who offered excuses for less than expected performance. Also, stoic sales managers could be expected to negatively view any employees who attempted to rise in the organization by "politicking." [See Section 20-2.]

PROBLEM 20-5 How might a hedonist marketing manager for an oil company go about arriving at ethical decisions?

Answer: Hedonists believe that happiness or pleasure is the greatest good and that what a person desires is by definition moral. However, hedonists also hold the opinion that most people truly desire unselfish goals. A hedonist marketing manager would decide what his or her most important personal objectives were, and then behave in a way that furthered these objectives. A hedonist might choose public service as a primary goal. In that case, the manager might decide that the company should hold prices in line, in order to satisfy the objective of inexpensive transportation for the public. Or a hedonist might decide that preserving scarce resources is an important goal, so a typical action could be to feature ads which appeal for energy conservation. [See Section 20-2.]

PROBLEM 20-6   A paper company marketing executive is a believer in the Judeo-Christian ethic as it relates to marketing decisions. In what respects is this ethic compatible with the marketing concept?

Answer: The Judeo-Christian ethic can be quite compatible with the marketing concept. Followers of this ethic believe that authority over correct behavior arises from God, and that the rules for proper behavior are based on an attitude of caring for others commanded by God. The paper company executive should find that this ethic fits in well with the idea of providing satisfaction to consumers and profits to owners of company stock; that is, the executive could view the company as a means of serving the needs of others. A belief in the Golden Rule, for instance, might lead him to insist that the firm produce only very high-quality paper products and charge reasonable prices. [See Section 20-2.]

PROBLEM 20-7   Assume that you are an instrumentalist employed by a supermarket chain. If you had to decide whether or not to close supermarkets in several low-income areas, what ethical principles would guide your thinking?

Answer: Instrumentalists do not place any stock in abstract moral principles, but believe that individuals should adjust their conduct to the situation that exists at the time an ethical decision is made. In the supermarket case, your decision would have to be based on what seems right to you at the time. You would have to use your own intuition, judgment, attitudes, and perceptions. You might, for example, study the situation carefully and find out that closing stores in low-income areas would deprive residents of quality food at reasonable prices. If your own intuition and judgment tell you that such closings would be wrong, you might decide against the closings. [See Section 20-2.]

PROBLEM 20-8   How might a Hegelian marketing manager decide what is morally right in promoting junior marketing executives into higher level positions?

Answer: Hegelians believe that moral behavior is that which agrees with the customs and laws of the society in which the decision maker is operating. They are likely to go along with the law and with groups that have influence in their culture. It could be expected that a Hegelian marketing manager would carefully consult written company guidelines on the criteria for promoting personnel and would not depart from these. In addition, a Hegelian manager would probably confer with other junior and senior marketing executives—particularly those who are informal group leaders. If informal, unwritten guidelines existed in the company (such as a precedent of promoting the most senior executive), this manager could be expected to follow these guidelines. [See Section 20-2.]

PROBLEM 20-9   Executives at a clothing manufacturer frequently bring out new versions of the company's most popular brand of slacks in order to increase company sales. Are there ethical issues involved here?

Answer: This clothing manufacturer is practicing planned obsolescence, which is a product-planning issue that has ethical aspects. The question here is, "*Should* manufacturers continually bring out new stock versions that make last year's offerings obsolete?" Such a practice can be costly for consumers, especially for teenagers (and their parents), who are very fashion-conscious. It can lead to waste, as consumers discard perfectly good, but old styles and replace them with new styles. On the other hand, new products can upgrade consumer living standards, provided that they really offer more benefits to consumers. If the new slacks are more durable or more comfortable than the old ones, or if they make consumers feel better about their appearance, new versions may be justified on ethical grounds. [See Section 20-3.]

PROBLEM 20-10   What is the ethical dilemma regarding gifts and bribes that marketers may face in certain foreign countries?

Answer: Some marketers feel that they must offer gifts or bribes to company employees and government officials in order to do business in a foreign country—or to get permission to do business there. In certain countries, these are expected, and often necessary, in order to compete. Failure to provide a bribe may simply mean that a competitor gets the business, even though its marketing mix may be inferior. On the other hand, most gifts and bribes are considered illegal under United States law, and numerous managers consider them to be improper. This situation poses a difficult dilemma for many marketers in this country. [See Section 20-3.]

PROBLEM 20-11 A classmate believes that, as long as marketing executives obey the law, they are acting ethically. Do you agree?

Answer: One way of being ethical is simply to obey the law, as your classmate suggests. Managers who do this are following the most fundamental rules of society. They are avoiding behavior that elected representatives and the courts have found to be undesirable. However, managers can obey the law and still be guilty of treating others unethically. It may, for instance, be *legal* to fire an advertising executive with 20 years' tenure with the company just before he or she is entitled to company lifetime health benefits, but the ethics of such an action are very questionable. [See Section 20-3.]

PROBLEM 20-12 A well known business leader has commented, "Industry self-regulation is all that is needed to ensure ethical behavior in marketing." Do you agree?

Answer: The business leader has a point. Industry self-regulation can be of considerable value in promoting ethical behavior in marketing. For example, television networks have agreed not to accept commercials that show the consumption of hard liquor. However, self-regulation groups (many are trade associations) do not have legal power to enforce their decisions. Essentially, they must rely on their ability to persuade marketers to stop unethical behavior. Even Better Business Bureaus are dependent upon persuasion—they have no enforcement authority. [See Section 20-3.]

PROBLEM 20-13 A marketing executive has been quoted as saying that, "Ethical behavior is in the informed self-interest of our company." Why would the executive feel this way?

Answer: The marketing executive may realize that the firm is dependent on outside parties, such as consumers and government officials. If marketers create hostility with these groups through unethical behavior, many unwanted results may follow. This can include heavy taxation, loss of esteem and goodwill, loss of customers, increased legal prosecution, and loss of valuable suppliers. If, on the other hand, a company is regarded as a good citizen, outside parties are likely to treat the company fairly and in a positive manner. [See Section 20-3.]

PROBLEM 20-14 An owner of a liquor store has been asked if he conducts his business in a socially desirable manner. He does not know how to respond because he is unsure of the exact meaning of social responsibility. Can you help clarify his understanding?

Answer: Social responsibility means that the liquor store owner has an obligation to numerous groups in society. These include consumers, employees, suppliers, government officials, labor unions, the public at large, and particular components of the public, such as minorities. If the liquor store owner is socially responsible, he will take steps to improve the status of these and other groups. These steps might include charging reasonable prices and stocking quality products, paying reasonable wages, treating suppliers fairly, and not selling liquor to those who are intoxicated or are minors. [See Section 20-4.]

PROBLEM 20-15 A marketing manager has stated that, "Socially responsible managers realize that they are dependent on society for their existence." What is meant by this statement?

Answer: The executive means that marketing companies will deteriorate if society does. High levels of unemployment, polluted air, overpopulation, energy shortages, poverty, and other problems are not conducive to a smoothly operating marketing system. If marketing at a company is to remain healthy, such problems must be avoided. Foreign countries with major societal problems do not have efficient and effective marketing systems. [See Section 20-4.]

PROBLEM 20-16 The owner of an auto supplies store has asked you what consumerism means. How would you respond?

Answer: You could state that consumerism is a belief that consumers are entitled to safe and effective products at reasonable prices and to full information about the products and their uses. In light of this philosophy, the auto supplies store management should stock products that have been carefully screened to determine if they are high in quality and reasonably priced. Management should therefore use advertising, personal selling, and sales promotion to inform consumers, so that they can make intelligent choices for auto supplies. [See Section 20-5.]

PROBLEM 20-17   Should marketing executives at most firms resist the consumerism movement?

Answer: It is not a good idea to resist the consumerism movement. Many marketers realize that it is in their own self-interest not to fight but to cooperate with the consumerism movement. It is, after all, compatible with the marketing concept. Little is gained by arguing with or fighting consumers in court cases. In accord with the consumerism movement, a retailer may offer a very liberal return policy. If a customer is not satisfied with an item, it can be returned for a refund or an exchange, with little red tape and waste of time. The company may also label items carefully, so that consumers can make an informed choice. Getting along with the consumer brings the consumer back, and that is good for business. [See Section 20-5.]

PROBLEM 20-18   Assume that marketing executives of an airplane manufacturer have decided to make an effort to preserve the physical environment. What major physical environmental problems might they address?

Answer: There are many environmental problems that an airplane manufacturer could address. Air pollution is one. The company could design engines that do not emit heavy concentrations of toxic pollutants. Another is developing fuel-efficient engines, which would not use up undue amounts of this country's petroleum reserves. Noise pollution is also a major problem for the airline industry. The company could insist on product design that results in quiet engines. Finally, the company's manufacturing plants can be fitted with machinery and equipment that does not pollute the air and water. [See Section 20-5.]

PROBLEM 20-19   What are some of the major programs that toy companies can use to assist minorities through marketing?

Answer: Toy companies can aid Blacks, Hispanics, Native Americans, and other minorities by providing members of these groups with job opportunities. They can construct affirmative action programs, whereby the company actively seeks, hires, and promotes minority group members. Another possibility is to develop products specifically designed for these groups. Dolls, for example, can be depicted as members of minority races. Also, advertisements can be used that feature minority models. [See Section 20-5.]

PROBLEM 20-20   How can restrictive legislation help bring about socially responsible behavior by marketers?

Answer: Laws can require that business engage in activities in certain ways, such as hiring minorities, furnishing safe products to consumers, cleaning up air and water that has been polluted, initiating programs to clean up the natural landscape, and promoting safe consumption through advertising programs. This approach can be effective in some cases, although there are some major drawbacks to it, especially when business and society at large are not committed to a particular issue. For example, promotion programs to keep truck driving speeds down, thereby saving lives and fuel, have been somewhat ineffective for this reason. [See Section 20-6.]

PROBLEM 20-21   How can requiring all businesses to pay for social costs encourage socially responsible behavior by marketers?

Answer: If companies are made to pay the social costs of their activities, they are motivated to take socially responsible action. They are not as reluctant to take responsible action as they would be if they knew that their rivals did not have to pay for their own social costs. Businesses could, for example, be required to return the environment to its original state if they had caused an undesirable change in its condition. Or businesses could be required to pay damages which, in turn, could be used to correct the condition. Many authorities believe that this remedy for social problems is superior to passing and enforcing new laws. Experience in other countries, such as Japan, supports this idea. [See Section 20-6.]

FINAL EXAM
(Chapters 11–20)

Part 1: Multiple Choice (50 points)

1. Channels of distribution carry _____ _____ goods.
   - (a) title to
   - (b) delivery of
   - (c) promotion of
   - (d) discounts for

2. _____ is *not* a major activity of middlemen.
   - (a) Selling
   - (b) Product planning
   - (c) Financing
   - (d) Producing goods

3. Direct distribution is likely to be desirable for a producer when _____.
   - (a) products are light in weight
   - (b) order sizes are small
   - (c) target customers are few in number
   - (d) products are perishable

4. Intensive distribution is most likely to be used for _____ goods.
   - (a) specialty
   - (b) convenience
   - (c) shopping
   - (d) unsought

5. _____ wholesalers carry out all or most of the marketing functions that wholesalers can perform.
   - (a) Service
   - (b) Voluntary chain
   - (c) Agent
   - (d) Brokerage

6. Retailers serve as contacts between _____ and other members of the channel of distribution.
   - (a) shippers
   - (b) carriers
   - (c) agents
   - (d) consumers

7. Many sellers of _____ operate in a manner that is very similar to retailing.
   - (a) services
   - (b) installations
   - (c) accessories
   - (d) components

8. Retail _____ are members of companies that have multiple outlets.
   - (a) chains
   - (b) independents
   - (c) department stores
   - (d) wholesale stores

9. _____ shoppers want stores that offer products that are seen as a good buy for the price.
   - (a) Personalizing
   - (b) Apathetic
   - (c) Economic
   - (d) Ethical

10. Retailers who use the _____ approach have packages and displays that do most of the selling, and sales people are few in number.
    - (a) personalizing
    - (b) self-service
    - (c) soft-sell
    - (d) hard-sell

11. Push promotion strategies are directed toward _____.
    - (a) intermediaries
    - (b) consumers
    - (c) advertising agencies
    - (d) freight forwarders

12. Which of the following is *not* a major use of promotion? _____
    - (a) to inform
    - (b) to persuade
    - (c) to remind
    - (d) to renounce

13. _____ is a major source of interference with communications.
    - (a) Fallout
    - (b) Noise
    - (c) Feedback
    - (d) Refraction

14. The receivers of personal selling are _____.
    (a) interviewees
    (b) channels
    (c) prospects
    (d) audiences

15. Which of the following is *not* a general goal of promotion? _____
    (a) understanding
    (b) attention
    (c) changing roles
    (d) changing attitudes

16. Institutional advertising would *not* state that _____.
    (a) the company cares about society
    (b) consumers should buy a company brand
    (c) the company provides many jobs
    (d) the company is a good citizen

17. Included in the major advertising goals is _____.
    (a) reach
    (b) intention
    (c) inaction
    (d) decrease in value

18. Closing periods are very short for _____.
    (a) magazines
    (b) newspapers
    (c) television
    (d) radio

19. The motives of target customers to which advertisements should be directed are _____.
    (a) illustrations
    (b) headlines
    (c) appeals
    (d) layouts

20. Which of the following do advertising agencies typically *not* perform? _____
    (a) set the advertising budget
    (b) design advertising campaigns
    (c) assist in developing advertising goals
    (d) make contacts with media

21. Personal selling involves _____ communication.
    (a) mass
    (b) interpersonal
    (c) impersonal
    (d) advertising

22. _____ means convincing others to change their thoughts and actions.
    (a) Understanding
    (b) Rapport
    (c) Post-purchase behavior
    (d) Persuasion

23. Which of the following is *not* a major source of recruits for sales positions? _____
    (a) newspaper advertisements
    (b) interviews on college campuses
    (c) advertising agencies
    (d) employment agencies

24. A major means of motivating sales representatives is through a(n) _____ system.
    (a) compensation
    (b) achievement
    (c) carryover
    (d) response

25. Which of the following provides considerable incentive for sales representatives to produce? _____
    (a) straight salary
    (b) straight commission
    (c) expense accounts
    (d) stock purchase plans

26. The highest percentage of U.S. exports arises from sales of _____.
    (a) chemicals
    (b) crude materials (inedible)
    (c) machinery and transportation equipment
    (d) mining, fuels, and related materials

27. The largest purchaser of U.S. exports is _____.
    (a) Asia
    (b) North America
    (c) Europe
    (d) Oceania

28. International marketers usually seek out markets with _____ competition.
    (a) considerable
    (b) limited
    (c) regulated
    (d) extensive

29. Which of the following is *not* a major factor that international marketers should consider when setting prices? _____
    (a) regulation by government
    (b) competition
    (c) cost
    (d) company stock prices

30. If a U.S. firm produces goods in a foreign country, the firm is called a(n) _____.
    (a) foreign producer
    (b) exporter
    (c) licensor
    (d) joint venture

31. _____ consists of carrying out marketing plans.
    (a) Development
    (b) Implementation
    (c) Forecasting
    (d) Setting objectives

32. Which of the following are specific means of carrying out goals and policies? _____
    (a) procedures
    (b) objectives
    (c) forecasts
    (d) targets

33. Common ways of organizing marketing do *not* include organization by _____.
    (a) method of production
    (b) product
    (c) geographic area
    (d) function

34. The effectiveness of marketing managers is largely based on their ability to _____ their personnel.
    (a) control
    (b) motivate
    (c) supervise
    (d) monitor

35. The control process in marketing does *not* include _____.
    (a) taking remedial action when necessary
    (b) checking forecasts to see if they are precise
    (c) measuring performance against criteria
    (d) setting up criteria of desirable performance

36. Services consist of _____ that buyers purchase in order to obtain satisfaction.
    (a) commodities
    (b) goods
    (c) actions
    (d) articles

37. Some consumers are reluctant to buy services because they are _____.
    (a) profitable
    (b) low in price
    (c) tangible
    (d) intangible

38. Because of their _____, services cannot be stored.
    (a) tangibility
    (b) perishability
    (c) high cost
    (d) long life

39. For effective promotion, many smaller marketers depend heavily on _____ to develop close interpersonal relationships with customers.
    (a) personal selling
    (b) advertising
    (c) sales promotion
    (d) publicity

40. In the channels of distribution for nonprofit organizations, _____ are often not included.
    (a) marketers
    (b) consumers
    (c) intermediaries
    (d) customers

41. Laws that deal with the field of monopoly are called _____ laws.
    (a) antitrust
    (b) monopolizing
    (c) antibusiness
    (d) takeover

42. According to the Sherman Act, _____ collusion is always illegal.
    (a) vertical
    (b) horizontal
    (c) parallel
    (d) perpendicular

43. _____ consists of making untrue statements that cause another party to enter into a contract.
    (a) Negligence
    (b) Breach of contract
    (c) Embezzlement
    (d) Fraud

44. The Federal Trade Commission Act prohibits _____.
    (a) monopoly and conspiracy to monopolize
    (b) tying contracts in interstate commerce
    (c) deception of consumers
    (d) price discrimination to business

45. _____ names refer to the product and not to the brand and cannot be protected by copyright law.
   (a) Generic
   (b) Brand
   (c) Trade
   (d) Complex

46. _____ are convinced that there are certain universal and abstract moral rules that should be followed at all times.
   (a) Idealists
   (b) Hedonists
   (c) Utilitarians
   (d) Instrumentalists

47. _____ believe that moral behavior is that which agrees with the customs and laws of the society in which the decision maker is operating.
   (a) Hegelians
   (b) Hedonists
   (c) Instrumentalists
   (d) Idealists

48. Codes of ethics, such as those adopted by the American Association of Broadcasters, are a means of solving ethical problems through _____.
   (a) legal means
   (b) informed self-interest
   (c) industry self-regulation
   (d) the courts

49. Socially responsible marketers realize that they have an obligation to _____.
   (a) numerous groups in society
   (b) a few groups in society
   (c) no one
   (d) the government only

50. Which of the following is *not* a severe ecological problem that marketers and others face?
   _____
   (a) air pollution
   (b) changing values of consumers
   (c) depletion of scarce resources
   (d) spoiling the beauty of the landscape

Part 2: Short Answer (50 points)

1. Channels of distribution extend from producers to _____.

2. Middlemen are often called _____.

3. When producers sell to consumers or industrial buyers without using intermediaries, this is called _____ _____.

4. Marketers who employ _____ distributors use only one wholesaler or retailer for each geographic area served.

5. The channel _____ is the leader of the channel of distribution.

6. Retailing consists of the activities involved in selling goods and services to _____.

7. _____ retailers are owned separately—they are not members of a chain.

8. _____ retailers offer a wide product line, in comparison to other retailers.

9. Discounters operate on a _____ inventory turnover and low margin basis.

10. _____ are groups of stores that are clustered together along streets and roads but do not work together in a cooperative fashion.

11. Promotion consists of marketing _____ with target customers.

12. In a communications system, the party that desires to do the communicating is called the _____.

13. _____ consists of interpersonal communication that is paid for by an identified sponsor and directed to groups.

14. The general promotion goal that is designed to result in consumer purchase is called _____.

15. A widely recommended method for developing the promotion budget which is based on determining the amount needed to reach intended goals is the _____ method.

16. When a company uses advertising to build demand for a product rather than for a company brand, the company is building _____ demand.

17. _____ _____ ads attempt to convince targets to respond immediately.

18. _____ _____ are the major determinant of which media are best.

19. A(n) _____ consists of a coordinated program including a number of advertisements that have a common goal or goals and are scheduled to be completed within a specified time.

20. _____ _____ are useful means of measuring attitudes changes.

21. Sales representatives who attempt to win new customers and get old customers to buy more are called _____ _____ .

22. _____ consists of developing a list of prospects who have the ability and the need to purchase company offerings.

23. _____ _____ are those individuals who direct and guide the sales force.

24. In the sales training method of _____ _____ , trainees practice on others who act as prospects.

25. Many standards for sales representatives are specified as _____ or targets.

26. When companies manufacture products in this country to sell abroad, this is called _____ .

27. When a firm markets in many countries, the company is engaging in _____ _____ .

28. The U.S. Corrupt Foreign Practices Act forbids major _____ .

29. When a U.S. marketer sells the same products overseas as it does in this country, this is called a(n) _____ _____ strategy.

30. When a U.S. firm establishes independent companies abroad, these companies are called _____ .

31. _____ _____ is the development and implementation of marketing plans.

32. _____ are the objectives or targets of marketing planners.

33. _____ consists of deciding who will be responsible for various activities needed to achieve company goals.

34. Marketing employees are likely to be highly motivated if they feel that they can attain important _____ goals by contributing to company goals.

35. Criteria of desirable performance are _____ against which marketers can compare performance.

36. _____ means that services do not have physical substance.

37. _____ refers to the fact that services are not standardized.

38. Because of _____ , services cannot exist unless the marketer is present.

39. Many service marketers have not pursued the _____ concept.

40. Nonprofit organizations serve different groups of consumers, which are often called _____ .

41. Business involving more than one state is called _____ _____ .

42. The Robinson Patman Act prohibits _____ _____ to purchasers of like goods.

43. _____ exists when a marketer has acted with less care than a reasonable person would under the circumstances.

44. The Whealer Lea Amendment to the Federal Trade Commission Act prohibits unfair methods of
_____.

45. _____ _____ ordinances impose restrictions on door-to-door selling.

46. Ethics refers to what is _____ good.

47. _____ believe that individuals should endure hardship and adversity and avoid overly
emotional behavior.

48. When marketers realize that they are dependent on outside parties, they may attempt to solve
ethical problems by informed _____ _____.

49. Social responsibility means that marketers have a(n) _____ to numerous groups in
society.

50. _____ is a belief that consumers are entitled to safe and effective products at reasonable
prices and to full information about products and their use.

ANSWERS

Part 1: Multiple Choice (50 points)

1. (a)	[Section 11-1]	18. (d)	[Section 14-3]	35. (b)	[Section 17-6]
2. (d)	[Section 11-2]	19. (c)	[Section 14-6]	36. (c)	[Section 18-1]
3. (c)	[Section 11-3]	20. (a)	[Section 14-7]	37. (d)	[Section 18-1]
4. (b)	[Section 11-3]	21. (b)	[Section 15-1]	38. (b)	[Section 18-1]
5. (a)	[Section 11-5]	22. (d)	[Section 15-1]	39. (a)	[Section 18-2]
6. (d)	[Section 12-1]	23. (c)	[Section 15-4]	40. (c)	[Section 18-4]
7. (a)	[Section 12-1]	24. (a)	[Section 15-5]	41. (a)	[Section 19-2]
8. (a)	[Section 12-2]	25. (b)	[Section 15-6]	42. (b)	[Section 19-2]
9. (c)	[Section 12-2]	26. (c)	[Section 16-1]	43. (d)	[Section 19-3]
10. (b)	[Section 12-4]	27. (a)	[Section 16-1]	44. (c)	[Section 19-4]
11. (a)	[Section 13-1]	28. (b)	[Section 16-2]	45. (a)	[Section 19-5]
12. (d)	[Section 13-2]	29. (d)	[Section 16-3]	46. (a)	[Section 20-2]
13. (b)	[Section 13-3]	30. (a)	[Section 16-4]	47. (a)	[Section 20-2]
14. (c)	[Section 13-3]	31. (b)	[Section 17-1]	48. (c)	[Section 20-3]
15. (c)	[Section 13-5]	32. (a)	[Section 17-2]	49. (a)	[Section 20-4]
16. (b)	[Section 14-1]	33. (a)	[Section 17-3]	50. (b)	[Section 20-5]
17. (a)	[Section 14-2]	34. (b)	[Section 17-4]		

Part 2: Short Answer (50 points)

1. consumers [Section 11-1]
2. intermediaries [Section 11-2]
3. direct distribution [Section 11-3]
4. exclusive [Section 11-3]
5. captain [Section 11-4]
6. consumers [Section 12-1]
7. Independent [Section 12-2]
8. General merchandise [Section 12-2]
9. high [Section 12-2]
10. Strips [Section 12-4]
11. communication [Section 13-1]
12. source [Section 13-3]
13. Advertising [Section 13-4]
14. action [Section 13-5]
15. objective [Section 13-6]
16. primary [Section 14-1]

17. Direct action [Section 14-1]
18. Advertising goals [Section 14-4]
19. campaign [Section 14-5]
20. Attitude scales [Section 14-8]
21. order getters [Section 15-1]
22. Prospecting [Section 15-2]
23. Sales managers [Section 15-3]
24. role playing [Section 15-4]
25. quotas [Section 15-7]
26. exporting [Section 16-1]
27. multinational marketing [Section 16-1]
28. bribes [Section 16-2]
29. identical product [Section 16-3]
30. subsidiaries [Section 16-4]
31. Marketing management [Section 17-1]
32. Goals [Section 17-2]

33. Organization [Section 17-3]
34. individual [Section 17-4]
35. standards [Section 17-5]
36. Intangibility [Section 18-1]
37. Heterogeneity [Section 18-1]
38. inseparability [Section 18-1]
39. marketing [Section 18-2]
40. publics [Section 18-4]
41. interstate commerce [Section 19-2]

42. price discrimination [Section 19-2]
43. Negligence [Section 19-3]
44. competition [Section 19-4]
45. Green River [Section 19-6]
46. morally [Section 20-1]
47. Stoics [Section 20-2]
48. self-interest [Section 20-3]
49. obligation [Section 20-4]
50. Consumerism [Section 20-5]

GLOSSARY

ability to purchase Customer possession of sufficient incomes, savings, or capability to borrow in order to finance purchasing.

accessories Industrial goods that organizations must have, in addition to installations, to produce goods and services.

advertising Impersonal communication that is paid for by an identified sponsor and directed to groups.

advertising agency A specialist in preparing advertisements and arranging for their placement in advertising media.

advertising campaign A coordinated program including a number of advertisements that have a common goal or goals and are scheduled to be completed within a specified time.

advertising media Promotion channels that advertisers can use.

agents Wholesalers that do not take title to the goods they carry and receive commissions.

anthropologists Scholars who study the behavior of large groups.

antitrust laws Laws that prohibit various kinds of monopoly.

apathetic shoppers Consumers who want to minimize the time and effort spent in shopping.

appeals Motives of target customers to which advertisements are directed.

approach The first sixty seconds or so in a sales presentation.

associations of independents Retail ownership groupings that attempt to gain some of the advantages of chains and still be independent.

attention Getting members of a target audience to focus their minds on a message.

attitudes Positive or negative stages of readiness to respond in a particular way.

baby boomers Consumers born in the years immediately following World War II.

bait and switch advertising An illegal practice wherein a product is advertised at a low price but consumers cannot readily buy it or are put under heavy pressure to buy a more expensive item.

basing point prices The practice of charging customers for freight from some location, called a basing point, to their site.

benefit segmentation Aiming a marketing mix at subgroups of target customers who seek particular benefits from the product or service.

brands Words, marks, or symbols that identify company products and services.

brand names Parts of brands that can be communicated orally.

breach of contract Failure of one of the parties to a contract to fulfill an obligation that the contract requires.

breaking bulk Moving large shipments to warehouses located near markets and breaking down shipments at the warehouse for individual orders to customers.

broadcast media Radio and television.

brokerage allowances Payments in lieu of brokerage services that are not needed.

brokers Limited-function wholesalers who are specialists in buying and selling, and bringing buyers and sellers together.

budgets Financial plans for a specific future time period.

business activities Activities that organizations carry out in order to earn profits.

buyers Buying-center members with formal authority for contracting with suppliers.

buying center A group made up of persons who are involved in a buying decision.

carloads Large shipments that receive low railroad rates.

carriers Companies that furnish transportation services.

cash discounts Price reductions to customers who pay their bills within a specified time period.

cease and desist order Order by a court for a company to stop a particular practice.

chains Members of companies that own multiple retail outlets.

channel Method of transmitting information.

channel captain The leader of a channel of distribution.

channels of distribution Networks of companies that carry out marketing activities as goods and services move from producers to customers.

Clayton Act A federal antitrust law prohibiting tying and requirements contracts and price discrimination.

closing The selling step during which sales representatives ask for orders.

closing periods Lapsed time between an ad's submission to media and its first appearance to the audience.

cognitive dissonance Post-purchase regret that leaves a consumer in a dissatisfied state.

collusive practices   Illegal agreements among companies to restrain trade and gain monopoly power.

commercialization   Making a full-scale introduction of products that have passed test marketing.

commissions   Percentages of sales that wholesalers and retailers receive from producers.

communication   Transmitting symbols that carry meaning to other parties.

community shopping centers   Medium-sized shopping centers in which convenience goods, services, and some shopping goods are sold.

consumer behavior   Activities wherein individuals decide whether, what, when, how, and from whom to buy goods and services.

consumer goods   Company offerings that persons buy to satisfy personal needs.

consumerism   A belief that consumers are entitled to safe and effective products at reasonable prices and to full information about products and their use.

consumer markets   Markets made up of those who buy goods and services for personal use and the satisfaction of personal desires.

Consumer Product Safety Commission Act   A federal law that regulates product safety.

consumers   Those who buy and or use goods and services for personal satisfaction.

containers   Large holders of bulk goods for shipment by one or more transportation carriers.

controlling   Setting up standards of desirable performance, comparing actual performance with the standards, and taking remedial action when necessary.

control group   A group of subjects in an experiment who are not exposed to a treatment.

convenience goods   Goods that consumers are not willing to go to much trouble to buy.

convenience samples   Samples taken when researchers contact individuals who are easy to reach.

convenience stores   Stores that customers shop in because they are conveniently located and furnish easy shopping.

cooperative advertising   Type of advertising in which producers pay for part of an intermediary's advertising of the producers' products.

cooperative chains   Independent retailers who arrange to do their own wholesaling.

corrective advertisement   Court-ordered advertisement to clear up consumer confusion or misinformation.

Corrupt Foreign Practices Act   A United States law that prohibits major bribes to foreign customers and officials.

cost analysis   Breaking down costs according to important segments of the company.

cost-per-contact   Total cost of advertising divided by the number of readers, listeners, or viewers.

cost-plus pricing   Determining prices by adding a margin to unit costs.

cues   Stimuli that produce responses intended to satisfy drives.

culture   A large group of persons who share similar values and lifestyles.

cumulative quantity discounts   Price reductions given to customers who purchase certain minimum quantities during a time period.

cycles   Recurring patterns of advances and declines in sales.

data collection forms   Questionnaires and other guides that tell interviewers and observers what to say and do.

deception of the consumer   Misleading or tricking consumers, as through promotion methods.

deciders   Buying-center members with authority to choose particular goods and services.

decline   Stage in the product life cycle during which sales and profits fall from previous levels.

demand curve   Curve showing how much customers will purchase at various prices.

demographics   Statistical facts about target customers.

department stores   Large stores with many product lines, low-turnover, high margins, and many customer services.

dependent variable   A variable whose behavior is based on the performance of independent variables.

depth   The variety of offerings within product lines.

derived demand   Demand for industrial goods based on demand for consumer goods.

development   Deciding exactly what kind of new product to produce.

differential advantage   Creating a marketing mix that target customers find to be superior to those of competitors.

diffusion of innovation   The spread of new products, brands, and services through a group.

direct action advertisements   Advertisements that attempt to convince target customers to respond immediately.

direct costs   Costs that can be traced to a segment of the company.

direct distribution   Type of distribution in which producers sell directly to consumers and industrial buyers, thereby avoiding intermediaries.

direct mail   Type of promotion in which companies forward letters, fliers, brochures, catalogs, and other promotion pieces to target customers.

direct marketing   Serving customers through a producer firm's own personnel, rather than through intermediaries.

direct-selling retailers Retailers that sell by mail, telephone, or vending machine, and by calling at customers' homes.

discounters Stores that operate on a high inventory turnover and low margin basis.

discounts and allowances Price reductions to customers who are willing to give up benefits or perform specified activities.

discrimination Response of consumers who react differently to different cues.

draw A loan against future commissions that sales representatives can acquire when commissions are low.

drives Individual desires that require satisfaction.

early adopters Members of a society who accept new products already accepted by innovators.

early majority Members of a society who follow early adopters in accepting new products.

economic evaluation Estimating expected sales and costs of a proposed new product.

economic shoppers Consumers who want stores with products that are seen as a good buy for the price.

economy The combined behavior of production, income, employment, and prices.

editing Checking data for interviewer or interviewee error or dishonesty.

ego Freudian term applied to the thinking or rational dimension of the human mind.

elastic demand Relationship of demand to price in which the percentage change in quantity of goods sold exceeds the percentage change in price.

equilibrium State of balance; specifically, balance between what consumers pay and what they obtain.

ethical shoppers Shoppers who select retailers because they want to support small business or businesses that are locally owned and operated.

ethics That which is morally good, "right" or "wrong", according to accepted standards of behavior.

exclusive distribution Type of distribution in which producers use only one wholesaler or retailer for each geographic area served.

expense accounts Payments made to cover job-related expenses of company employees, such as sales personnel.

experiment A study conducted to provide evidence that one action caused a particular outcome.

experimental group A group of subjects in an experiment who are exposed to a treatment.

exploratory research Research whereby analysts attempt to identify problems.

exporting Producing products in one country to sell in other countries.

family brands Brands placed on numerous products sold by one firm.

family life cycle A series of stages families pass through over time, based on age, marital status, and number of children.

Federal Trade Commission Act A federal law prohibiting deception of consumers and unfair methods of competition.

fishyback Moving loaded truck trailers or railroad cars by ship.

fixed costs Costs that do not change as a firm increases or decreases its output.

Flammable Products Act A federal law that forbids producing clothing that is highly flammable.

FOB A pricing policy indicating what party pays freight and who owns the goods.

Food and Drug Administration Act A federal law mandating that foods and drugs perform as intended and are properly labeled.

foreign producers Firms that produce products abroad.

form utility Satisfaction arising from the manufacture of goods and services.

franchise Agreements between franchisors and franchisees whereby the latter obtain a company name, advice, and other advantages, in exchange for royalties and other payments.

fraud Making untrue statements that cause another party to enter into a contract.

freight absorption Type of freight payment in which marketers pay some of the freight to customers who are located at a distance.

freight forwarders Firms that consolidate many small shipments from various shippers into carload and truckload movements.

functional discounts Price reductions given to intermediaries to compensate them for the marketing activities that they perform.

Fur Products Labeling Act A federal law requiring that fur products be properly labeled.

gatekeepers Buying-center members who control the flow of information into the buying center.

generalizing Response of consumers whose reactions to two or more separate cues are the same.

general merchandise retailers Retailers that offer a wide product line.

generic brands Form of product identification in which the product itself is labeled but no specific brand name is offered.

generic trademarks Names or symbols that apply to a product class as a whole and not to a brand and cannot be given legal protection.

geographic segmentation Aiming the marketing mix at certain regions where target customers are located.

gestalt psychology A theory that looks at how consumers perceive their environments.

goals Objectives or targets of a planning unit.

Green River ordinances Local laws prohibiting door-to-door selling or requiring that companies fulfill certain conditions before selling.

growth Stage in the product life cycle during which sales grow rapidly and profits appear.

habitual behavior Type of behavior in which a buyer routinely places an order from a supplier, probably one that has been used successfully in the past.

hedonists Believers in the ethical theory that happiness or pleasure is the greatest good.

Hegelians Followers of the theory that ethical behavior agrees with the customs and laws of the society in which the decision maker is operating.

heterogeneity An attribute of services, meaning that they are not standardized.

horizontal collusion Agreements among competitors to restrain trade.

id Freudian term for the part of the mind that seeks pleasure and avoids pain.

idealism An ethical theory holding that there are certain universal and abstract moral rules that should be followed at all times.

identical-product strategy Selling the same product overseas as in the home country.

illustrations Drawings, photographs, graphs, paintings, charts, and other visual devices in an advertisement.

implementation Carrying out marketing plans.

independents Retailers that are owned separately and are not part of a chain.

independent variable A variable that influences the behavior of another variable.

indirect action advertisements Advertisements in which an attempt is made to establish favorable attitudes toward the offerings of a sponsor.

indirect costs Costs that cannot be traced to a segment of the company.

individual brands Brand names for specific products sold by a firm.

industrial buyers Those who buy goods for business, rather than for personal use.

industrial goods Products or services that individuals purchase for use in a business or a nonprofit organization.

industrial markets Markets consisting of those who buy to satisfy the requirements of the organization for which they work.

inelastic demand Relationship of demand to price in which changes in prices do not bring about significant changes in revenue.

influencers Buying-center members who influence decisions by providing information and criteria for evaluating goods and services.

innovators The first group in a society to try out an innovation.

inseparability An attribute of services, meaning that services and their producers are always together.

installations Expensive industrial goods that organizations must have to produce goods and services.

institutional advertising Advertising in which an attempt is made to build the image of a company.

institutional markets A term sometimes used to refer to nonbusiness organization buyers.

instrumentalists Followers of the theory that ethical behavior is based on particular situations.

intangibility An attribute of services, meaning that they do not have physical substance.

intensive distribution Type of distribution in which a producer sells through a large number of retail or wholesale units.

intermediaries Wholesalers and retailers used in channels of distribution.

international marketing Marketing efforts that extend across national boundaries.

interpreting Examining data and deciding what they mean, in terms of the research problems that a study is examining.

interstate commerce Business involving more than one state.

introduction Stage in the product life cycle when the product is new and sales grow slowly.

job descriptions Documents that highlight the major duties and responsibilities required of persons filling various positions in an organization.

joint venture A partnership involving a U.S. firm and one or more foreign firms.

Judeo-Christian ethic An ethic that is based on the idea that authority over correct behavior arises from God.

judgment sample A sample taken wherein researchers use their judgment in choosing individuals who seem to be representative of the population.

laggards Members of a society who are the last to accept an innovation.

late majority Members of a society who do not accept an innovation until it becomes popular.

layout The way in which the various parts of an advertisement are positioned with respect to one another.

leaders Lower-than-normal prices to entice customers into stores.

licensor A firm that licenses other firms to produce or market its goods.

lifestyle segmentation Aiming the marketing mix at target customers with certain psychological characteristics, such as attitudes, interests, opinions, and activities.

limited-line stores Stores that have only one product line or similar product lines.

line of commerce A group of companies that compete for the same customers.

location The determination of where stores and warehouses should be situated.

long-run forecasts Forecasts for over one year.

macro-marketing The study of marketing as a participant in the overall society.

manufacturers' agent Limited-function wholesalers that carry numerous brands and sell part of the output of each producer.

manufacturers' brands Brands that producers own.

margin An amount added to unit costs to produce a profit.

market Individuals or organization that have the money and the desire to buy a product or service.

market segmentation Developing and carrying out marketing programs that are aimed at subgroups of the total market.

market share analysis Calculating company sales as a percentage of total industry sales.

marketing The process of planning and executing the conception, pricing, promotion, and distribution of ideas, goods, and services to create exchanges that satisfy individual and organizational objectives.

marketing attribute segmentation Aiming a marketing mix at subgroups made up of target customers that are attracted to the same elements of the marketing mix.

marketing audit A systematic and critical review of the total marketing operation.

marketing concept A philosophy that a company's major goal is to serve customer needs at a profit.

marketing environment Those forces outside the company that have an important effect on the success of the marketing strategy.

marketing information systems Groups used for continuous collection and analysis of data and provision of information to marketing decision makers.

marketing management The development and carrying out of marketing plans.

marketing mix The major marketing activities that an organization performs, relating to product, price, promotion, and place.

marketing planning Developing goals, policies, and procedures for marketing operations.

marketing research Projects designed to gather and analyze information to improve marketing decisions.

marketing strategy An overall marketing plan to achieve company goals; it specifies the target customer, customer needs, and the marketing mix.

marketing tactics Specific and detailed activities that companies use to carry out strategies.

mass communication Directing promotion efforts to large groups of receivers.

maturity A stage in the product life cycle where sales grow slowly and then fall as profits decrease.

merchandising Product planning by retailers.

micro-marketing The study of marketing in fulfilling the objectives of an organization.

middlemen Wholesalers and retailers used in channels of distribution.

missionary sales representatives Sales representatives who do not take orders but attempt to build goodwill with customers.

modified rebuy Activity of a buying center that decides to re-evaluate a supplier and its products to see if it should still be used.

motivation The reasons why individuals behave as they do.

multinational marketing Marketing in many countries.

negligence Acting with less care than a reasonable person would take under the circumstances.

neighborhood shopping centers Small, local shopping centers that feature mainly convenience goods and services.

new-task buying Activity of a buying center that has no experience in buying a particular kind of product and is not aware of which supplier or product to choose.

noise Forces that interfere with the communication process.

noncumulative quantity discounts Price reductions provided to customers who buy minimum quantities in a single order.

nonprobability samples Samples for which researchers do not know the probability that various members of the population will be included in the sample.

objections Indicators of what prospects are thinking.

observation Activity of researchers who take note of an individual's behavior, either in person or by mechanical means.

odd-even pricing Assessing prices that end in odd numbers.

on-the-job training Training programs in which new hires learn a job by doing it.

operating supplies Industrial goods that buyers use in carrying out their business activities.

opinion leaders   Individuals to whom others look for advice.

order getters   Sales representatives who attempt to win new customers and convince old customers to buy more.

order takers   Sales representatives who serve existing customers.

organization   Deciding who will be responsible for various activities needed to achieve company goals.

outdoor advertising   Signs and billboards.

parts and processed materials   Industrial goods that become parts of products and are charged as expenses.

penetration pricing   Charging prices for a new product that are low relative to costs.

personalizing shoppers   Consumers who look for retail outlets that are hospitable and friendly.

personal selling   Person-to-person communication between sales representatives and their prospects.

persuasion   Convincing others to change their thoughts and actions.

physical distribution   The efficient movement of finished goods from producers to customers.

piggyback   Moving loaded truck trailers by railroad.

place utility   Satisfaction that arises when buyers are able to acquire legal title and physical control of items they desire.

policies   General rules or guidelines that indicate what kinds of decisions company employees should make in order to fulfill company objectives.

political environment   The environment that is made up of various special interest groups.

population   The number of individuals who live in a particular place at a given time.

post-purchase activities   Activities that take place after a good or service has been acquired.

posttests   Tests of effectiveness made after advertising has been exposed to an audience.

preapproach   Gathering information about the characteristics and needs of sales representatives' prospects.

presentation   Selling step in which sales representatives attempt to convince prospects to purchase goods or services.

pretest   Tests of effectiveness made before advertising is exposed to an audience.

price   The amount of money that is exchanged to obtain a good or a service.

price discrimination   Charging two or more buyers who are at the same level of competition different prices for identical goods.

price lining   Having a few established prices for a line and fitting items into the prices.

primary data   Data collected by a researcher.

primary demand   Demand for the product rather than for a company brand.

print media   Advertising channels that convey messages visually.

private brands   Brands owned by wholesalers or retailers.

private carriers   Shippers who own their own transportation equipment.

probability sampling   Samples for which researchers know the probability that a member of the population may be in the sample.

problem recognition   Recognizing a difference between a desired condition and an actual condition that can be solved through buying.

procedures   Specific measures used to carry out goals and policies.

producers   Organizations that create goods and services.

product advertising   Advertising that is used to promote specific company products.

product life cycle   Stages in the life of a product from introduction to decline.

production concept   A philosophy that an organization should emphasize efficiency in producing and distributing goods and services.

product lines   Combinations of similar items in a product mix.

product mix   The total of all goods and services that a company offers.

product positioning   The alignment of finished products and services in relation to one another and to those of competitors, in the minds of consumers.

promotion   Communications an organization uses to convince potential customers to buy the product or take other actions that the organization believes to be desirable.

promotional allowances   Price reductions given to intermediaries to compensate them for promotion activities that they have undertaken.

prospecting   Developing a list of prospects who have the ability and the need to purchase company products.

prototype   Actual model of a new product to be introduced later.

psychology   The study of individual behavior.

publicity   Mass communication that is free and pertains to newsworthy events.

public relations   Communication activities directed to the public at large and other groups.

pull promotion strategies   Directing most of the promotion effort to selling consumers, rather than intermediaries.

purchase requisition   A document requesting that a purchasing agent acquire an item.

purchasing agent   An employee of an industrial buying company with formal authority to buy.

push money Money paid by producers to retail sales people for selling producers' offerings.

push promotion strategy Directing most promotion efforts to intermediaries.

quotas Standards specified as targets for sales personnel.

random sampling Type of sampling in which every member of the population has an equal chance of being included in a sample.

raw materials Commodities sold in their natural state.

reach To expose an adequate number of target customers to a message.

reciprocity Characteristic of transactions in which one firm purchases from another only if the second buys from the first.

recruiting Promoting job openings to possible applicants.

reference groups Groups from whom consumers seek guidance for proper behavior.

regional shopping centers Large shopping centers that include convenience, shopping, and specialty-goods stores.

regression Using the relationship of sales to some other variable to predict future sales.

reinforcement Encouragement that occurs when an individual's responses to cues are rewarded.

requirements contracts Contracts specifying that buyers must fill all of their needs for a product from one supplier.

restraint of trade Injury to particular competitors or to the competition within a line of commerce.

retailers Firms that earn most of their revenues from sales to consumers.

retailing The activities involved in selling goods and services to consumers.

return on investment A pricing policy designed to produce a desired profit as a percentage of invested capital.

revenue delays Unrealized revenues that a company passes up because a decision is being postponed while information is being sought.

Robinson Patman Act A federal antitrust law that forbids certain kinds of price discrimination and discrimination in promotion to industrial buyers.

role playing Training wherein sales representatives practice on others who act as prospects.

roles Patterns of behavior assumed by group members who specialize in certain activities.

sales analysis Breaking down sales by important segments of the business.

sales concept A business philosophy that the major objective of management is to persuade potential buyers to make purchases.

sales managers Individuals who direct and guide a sales force.

sales promotion Company-sponsored promotion activities that supplement advertising and personal selling.

sampling Collecting information from a portion of the population under study.

scanning Carefully monitoring the behavior of environmental elements.

scrambled merchandising Type of merchandising in which retailers have added new lines to traditional ones and have become general merchandise retailers.

screening Evaluating product ideas and eliminating those with little chance of earning a profit.

seasonal sales patterns Recurring advances and declines in sales that take place during a typical year.

secondary data Data that have been collected by someone other than a researcher.

secondary demand Demand for a particular brand.

selecting Deciding which job applicants to hire.

selective distribution Distribution in which marketers limit the number of middlemen to those they believe have the most potential.

self-concept Perceptions by consumers as to the kinds of persons they think they are and that they believe others think they are.

selling agents Limited-function wholesalers who sell all of a producer's output of one or more items.

services Actions that customers purchase in order to obtain satisfaction.

service planning Determining the nature of the services that will be offered to target customers.

service wholesalers Organizations that carry out all or most of the wholesaling functions.

Sherman Antitrust Act A federal law prohibiting monopolizing and conspiracies among companies.

shippers Marketers who are the customers of carriers.

shopping centers Combinations of retail units that coordinate their activities in order to attract consumers.

shopping goods Offerings on which consumers spend considerable effort in order to compare and make the best buy.

shopping stores Outlets that consumers compare to other stores in deciding which one to patronize.

short-run forecasts Forecasts for a year or less.

skimming Charging new product prices that are high relative to costs.

social classes Groupings of people with similar occupations, sources of income, types of homes, and locations of homes.

social classes   Groupings of people with similar occupations, sources of income, types of homes, and locations of homes.

social costs   Costs that businesses pass on to society or to particular groups.

social factors   Customs, practices, and expectations that arise from the actions of groups.

social responsibility   A belief that marketers have an obligation to certain groups in society.

societal orientation   A philosophy that an organization should attempt to provide satisfaction to all of the important parties with which it has exchanges.

source   A party who desires to communicate with others.

specialty advertising   Messages on novelty or useful articles.

specialty goods   Items for which the consumer is willing to expend considerable effort to acquire the preferred brand.

specialty stores   Stores that target consumers have a strong positive attitude toward and expend effort to shop in.

standard industrial classification   A system of classifying industrial firms by their industry.

stockout   Situation in which a firm is out of inventory when orders come in.

storage   Keeping items in inventory.

straight commission   A percentage of sales paid to sales representatives.

stoics   Believers in the ethical theory that individuals should endure hardship and adversity and avoid overly emotional behavior.

straight rebuy   Continuing to purchase a product bought previously.

straight salary   A fixed amount of compensation per year.

subcultures   Groups within a culture that share certain values and ways of life.

subjects   Individuals whose behavior is studied in experiments.

subsidiaries   Independent companies that are owned by a parent company.

superego   Freudian term applied to the "conscience" of the individual—that part that holds the ego in check.

supermarkets   Stores that sell both foods and nonfoods and operate with high inventory turnovers and low margins.

suppliers   Companies that provide marketers with goods and services.

surveys   Asking individuals for information through the mail, over the telephone, or in person.

system   A grouping of parts that are interrelated and that work together toward one or more common goals.

tabulating   Forming data into statistics, such as means, averages, medians, and percentages.

target customers   Particular potential customers to which an organization aims its marketing mix.

tariffs   Taxes on imports and exports.

testing   Finding out how well a proposed new product will sell in the marketplace.

test markets   Markets in which products are sold to gain sales forecasting data.

text   Written or spoken part of an advertisement—the part that follows the headline.

Textile Products Labeling Act   A federal law requiring that textiles be properly labeled.

time series forecasts   Estimates in which analysts project past sales into the future.

time utility   Satisfaction that arises when customers receive goods when they desire them.

total revenue   Price times output of a good or service.

trademarks   Brands that have legal protection so that other firms cannot use them.

tradeoffs   Increasing costs in one part of a physical distribution system to reduce other costs or improve customer service.

transactions   The exchange of things of value.

transit advertising   Advertising that is posted on the outsides of taxis, buses, streetcars, and railroad cars.

transportation   Moving products from plants or warehouses of sellers to receiving facilities of buyers.

treatment   Administration of independent variables in experiments.

trend analysis   Forecasts in which analysts extend past general patterns of sales to future periods.

truckloads   Large shipments that receive low truck carrier rates.

tying contracts   Illegal contracts in which a supplier indicates that it will not sell one brand or product to a customer unless the customer buys another brand or product from that supplier.

understanding   Part of the communication process in which receivers interpret messages in the manner that the source intended.

unfair methods of competition   Marketing practices in which competitors are unjustly treated; made illegal under the Federal Trade Commission Act.

unfair trade practice laws   State laws prohibiting retailers from selling below cost plus a normal profit margin.

uniform delivered prices   Situation in which all customers, regardless of their location, pay the same price.

unsought goods   Items that most consumers are not eager to purchase.

users Buying-center members who use the goods and services that are purchased.

utilitarians Believers in the ethical theory that one should try to achieve the greatest good for the greatest number.

utility Satisfaction that buyers receive.

variable costs Costs that increase or decrease as the output of a company changes.

variety stores Retail establishments that are much like department stores except they typically are smaller and have fewer services and lower prices.

vertical collusion Illegal agreements to restrain trade made between companies at different levels in a channel.

volume segmentation Aiming a marketing mix at target customers in subgroups according to the extent to which they use the product or service.

voluntary chains Independent retailers that bond together into organizations that do wholesaling for themselves.

warehousing and storage Holding and housing goods for the time between manufacture and sale.

warranties Statements setting forth the conditions under which a marketer agrees to stand by its products.

waste circulation Exposure of individuals who are not target customers to an advertising medium.

Whealer Lea Amendment A part of the Federal Trade Commission Act that forbids unfair methods of competition.

wheel of retailing A theory that predicts that low margin, low cost, and limited service retailing types continually enter the market and replace established retailers.

wholesalers Companies that earn most of their revenues from sales to retailers, other wholesalers, manufacturers, and nonprofit organizations.

width the number of product lines in a product mix.

zone pricing Situation in which all buyers in a particular geographic area pay the same price.

INDEX